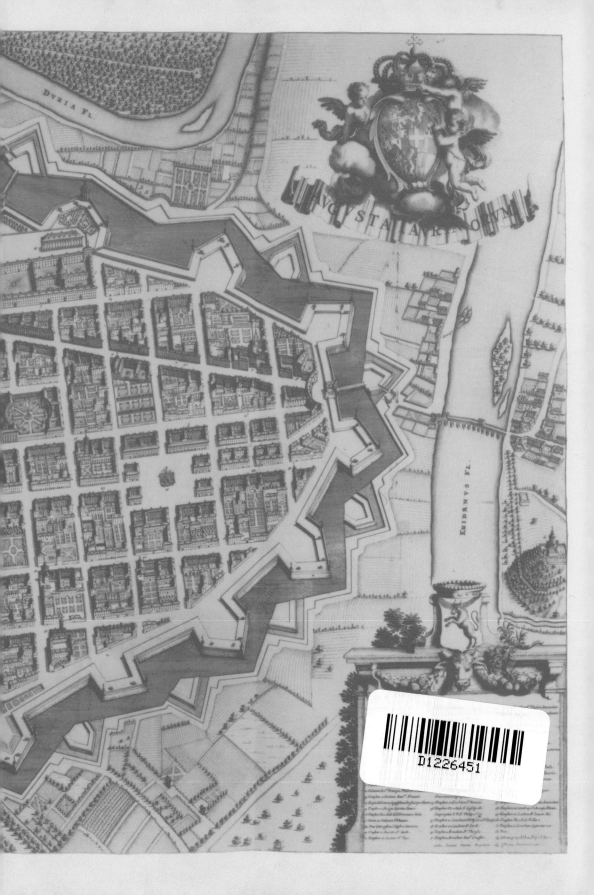

DVRIA FL.

AVGVSTA TAVRINORVM

ERIDANVS FL.

TURIN

1 5 6 4 - 1 6 8 0

TURIN

1564-1680

*Urban Design, Military Culture,
and the Creation of the
Absolutist Capital*

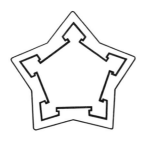

MARTHA D. POLLAK

THE UNIVERSITY OF CHICAGO PRESS

Chicago and London

M A R T H A   D.   P O L L A K is assistant professor of the history
of architecture at the University of Illinois, Chicago.

The University of Chicago Press, Chicago 60637
The University of Chicago Press, Ltd., London
©1991 by The University of Chicago
All rights reserved. Published 1991
Printed in the United States of America

00 99 98 97 96 95 94 93 92 91 5 4 3 2 1

Library of Congress Cataloging in Publication Data

Pollak, Martha D.
    Turin, 1564–1680: urban design, military culture, and the
creation of the absolutist capital / Martha D. Pollak.
        p.   cm.
    Includes index
    ISBN 0–226–67342–1 — ISBN 0–226–67344–8 (pbk.)
        1. City planning—Italy—Turin.   2. Architecture—Italy—Turin.
3. Military architecture—Italy—Turin.   4. Turin (Italy)—
Buildings, structures, etc.   I. Title.
NA9204.T78P66   1991
720'.945'1209032—dc20   90–44409
                                                                    CIP

This book is printed on acid-free paper.

Publication of this book has been aided by a grant from the
Millard Meiss Publication Fund of the College Art Association.

To My Parents

Contents

Illustrations

44. Carlo di Castellamonte, Porta Nova or Victoria, 1682. From *Theatrum,* vol. 1.

45. Antonio Tempesta, joust in Piazza Castello, Turin, 1620, oil painting. Galleria Sabauda.

46. View of Turin from east with ceremonial procession, c. 1620, ink and wash. ASCT, Coll. Simeon, D141.

47. Giacomo de Fornazeris, equestrian portrait of Carlo Emanuele I, with the plan of Turin and procession behind him, c. 1612, engraving. BN, Paris, Estampes (Phot. Bibl. Nat. Paris).

48. View of Turin from southeast [misnamed "la ville de Bude"], c. 1628, ink. BN, Paris, Estampes, Vb.132v, fol. 2 (Phot. Bibl. Nat. Paris).

49. Antoine de Ville, design for the fortification of a town divided by a river with view of Turin in the background. From A. de Ville, *Les Fortifications* (Lyons, 1629), pl. 42.

50. Frontispiece, with claim to royal title. From Pierre Monod, *Coelum Allobrogicum* (Lyons, 1634).

51. Montafilans, design for the fortification of Turin's expansion, 1632, brown ink and wash. AST, Sez. Ia, Carte topografiche per A e B, Torino.

52. Carlo di Castellamonte, study of existing and proposed fortifications of Turin, 1632, ink and black chalk. AST, Sez. Ia, Carte topografiche per A e B, Torino.

53. Carlo di Castellamonte, presentation plan of Turin's expanded fortifications, 1632, ink and watercolor. AST, Sez. Ia, Carte topografiche per A e B, Torino.

54. Giovenale Boetto, view of Turin, c. 1632, engraving. ASCT, Coll. Simeom, D 142.

55. Giovenale Boetto, view of the new expansion of Turin, 1634, detail from frontispiece to the theses of Carlo Francesco di Robilant, engraving. BN, Paris, Estampes (Phot. Bibl. Nat. Paris).

56. Giovenale Boetto, frontispiece to the theses of Robilant, 1634, engraving. From Nino Carboneri and Andreina Griseri, *Giovenale Boetto, architetto e incisore* (Fossano, 1966), fig. 136.

57. Michele Antonio Raynero, siege of Turin in 1640, engraved by Giovenale Boetto, 1643. ASCT, Coll. Simeom, D11.

58. Giovenale Boetto, frontispiece, engraving. From Luigi Giuglaris, *Funerale fatto nel duomo di Torino alla gloriosa memoria* [di] *Vittorio Amedeo Duca di Savoia, Prencipe di Piemonte, Re di Cipro* (Turin, 1638).

59. Giovenale Boetto, cathedral facade ornamented for the funeral of Vittorio Amedeo, engraving. From Giuglaris, *Funerale fatto nel duomo di Torino* (1638).

60. Giovenale Boetto, nave ornament inside cathedral of Turin, engraving. From Giuglaris, *Funerale fatto nel duomo di Torino* (1638).

61. Giovenale Boetto, catafalque of Vittorio Amedeo under cathedral dome, engraving. From Giuglaris, *Funerale fatto nel duomo di Torino* (1638).

62. Siege of Turin, c. 1642, engraving. BN, Paris, Estampes, Id. 24, fol. 36 (Phot. Bibl. Nat. Paris).

63. Plan of the siege of Turin, c. 1640, ink. Biblioteca Ambrosiana, Milan, MS F213, inf. 13.

64. Plan of Turin with fortified Città Nuova and citadel pitted against the city, c. 1645, ink and watercolor. BN, Paris, Estampes, Id.24, fol. 34 (Phot. Bibl. Nat. Paris).

65. Bartolomeo Fenis, the ceremony of changing the citadel's guard, with Turin in the background, c. 1657–59, engraving. BN, Paris, Estampes, QC 1, vol. 7, fol. 8 (Phot. Bibl. Nat. Paris).

66. Carlo di Castellamonte, design study for the Borgo di Po expansion area, Turin, c. 1637, ink. AST, Sez. Ia, Carte topografiche per A e B, Torino.

67. Michele Antonio Raynero and Giovenale Boetto, siege of Turin in 1640, detail of figure 57.

68. Carlo di Castellamonte, design study of Città Nuova, Turin, c. 1637–38, ink and watercolor. BN, Paris, Estampes, Vb.6, fol. 36 (Phot. Bibl. Nat. Paris).

69. Design for the facade of Piazza Reale, Turin, second half of seventeenth century, ink. BN, Paris, Estampes, Vb.7, fol. 37 (Phot. Bibl. Nat. Paris).

70. Plan of unified Turin, c. 1656, ink and watercolor. Biblioteca Ambrosiana, Milan, Cod. T 189, sup. fol. 119.

71. Carlo Morello, design for the expansion of Turin to the north, east, and south, 1656, ink and watercolor. BRT, MS Militari 178, fol. 16.

118. Guarino Guarini, Palazzo Carignano, Turin, begun 1679, engraving. From *Disegni d'architettura civile e ecclesiastica* (1686).

119. Gianlorenzo Bernini, Louvre, designs for the east facade, ink and wash: (a) first project, 1665 (Louvre, Paris; phot. © R.M.N.); (b) second project, 1665 (National Museum, Stockholm).

120. Guarino Guarini, Palazzo Carignano, facade detail, Turin, 1679. Photo: Marco F. Diani.

121. Guarino Guarini, Collegio dei Nobili, southeast corner, Turin, 1679. Photo: Marco F. Diani.

122. Guarino Guarini, Collegio dei Nobili, detail of facade, Turin, 1679. Photo: Marco F. Diani.

123. Amedeo di Castellamonte, Ospedale Maggiore di San Giovanni, floor plan, Turin, 1680. Adapted from Giuseppe Luigi Marini, *Architettura in Piemonte* (Turin, 1963), 78.

124. Amedeo di Castellamonte, Ospedale Maggiore di San Giovanni, north facade, Turin, 1680. Photo: Marco F. Diani.

125. Piazza Carlina, detail from figure 98, square designed by Amedeo di Castellamonte in 1674, illustration drawn by Tommaso Borgonio, c. 1674. From *Theatrum,* vol. 1.

126. Amedeo di Castellamonte, design for Piazza Carlina, Turin, 1673–78, ink. ASCT, Coll. Simeom, D246.

127. Michelangelo Garove, plan of Turin with study for Piazza Carlina, 1678, ink. Biblioteca Ambrosiana, Milan, Cod. T. 189, sup. 116.

128. Pietro Cataneo, plan of ideal city. From *I quattro primi libri di architettura* (Venice, 1554).

129. Bellino, layout of Piazza Carlina with four market pavilions, 1693, ink. ASCT, cart. 39-1.4.

130. Piazza Castello, Turin, section through the Galleria, 1682, engraving. From *Theatrum,* vol. 1.

131. Giovanni Battista Borra, Piazza Castello, Turin, 1749, engraving. ASCT, Coll. Simeom, D371.

132. Domenico Piola, King Eridanus holding a map of Turin, engraving by Giorgio Tasniere. From Emanuele Tesauro, *Historia della augusta città di Torino* (Turin, 1679), 32.

Acknowledgments

I AM GLAD TO acknowledge the grants and fellowships from the Fulbright-Hays Commission in Italy, the Accademia dei Lincei in Rome, the Center for Advanced Study in the Visual Arts of the National Gallery of Art in Washington, the American Philosophical Society, and the Campus Research Board of the University of Illinois in Chicago which supported this research.

In Turin, Dr. Chiara Passanti gave intellectual support and much practical aid. Dr. Isabella Ricci, Director of the Archivio di Stato, provided encouragement as she generously introduced me to the extensive collections under her control, while her assistants, especially Dr. Federica Paglieri and Dr. Barbara Bertini helped in searching out important documents. The staffs at the Archivio Storico Comunale, the Manuscript Collection of the Biblioteca Nazionale, and especially at the Biblioteca Reale were quick and punctilious. Professor Augusto Cavallari Murat offered precious hints drawn from his life-long study of Turin and Piedmont; his published work and that of Dr. Vera Comoli Mandracci provided firm foundations for subsequent research on the development of Baroque Turin. Toni Cordero, Jeannot Cerutti and Prof. Carlo Olmo involved me in the current architectural life of Turin, while Anna and Emilio Accusani di Porta Nuova provided a home away from home inside the very buildings I was studying.

In Rome, I benefited from the Tricentennial seminar on Bernini organized by Prof. Marcello Fagiolo dell'Arco which gathered together a great number of scholars of the Italian Baroque, and the committed aid of Monsignor Ruysschaert, then Prefect of the Biblioteca Apostolica Vaticana, who permitted me to delve deeply in the collections. Profs. Giorgio Ciucci, Marta Calzolaretti and Giuseppe Rebecchini gave hospitality and much good advice; the intellectual community of American scholars in Rome, especially Profs. Laurie Nussdorfer, Steven Ostrow and Sharon Cather, enhanced the already stimulating setting for thinking about Baroque urbanism.

In Paris my best discoveries were made at the Cabinet des Estampes of the Bibliothéque Nationale where Madame Françoise Jestaz greatly facilitated the study and reproduction of autograph drawings and rare engravings. My work at the Bibliothéque du Génie and the Archives du Génie was rendered fruitful by Mme. Lecoq. Prof. Michèle Fogel shared her insights on seventeenth-century militarism; Prof. Maurice Aymard provided generous encouragement and an institutional affiliation at the Maison de Science de l'Homme.

The completion of the book was aided by the prompt assistance of the staffs at the Newberry Library Special Collections, especially by its Director Robert Karrow, at the Houghton Library, and at the Rare Book Rooms of the University of Chicago and the University of Michigan.

For valuable criticism, perceptive comments, photographs and documents generously offered I wish to thank Prof. Nicholas Adams, Dr. Walter Barberis, Dr. David Buisseret, Dr. Simona Cerutti, Dr. Marco Diani, Profs. Sheila ffolliott, David Friedman, Carlo Ginzburg, Hellmut Hager, Giovanni Levi, Elisabeth MacDougall, Dr. Susan Munshower, Profs. John Pinto, Richard Pommer, Cesare de' Seta, and Geoffrey Symcox. My most enduring debts are to Professor Henry A. Millon, who introduced me to Piedmontese studies and whose architectural research and standards of excellence have been a great challenge and inspiration for me, and to Professor James G. Turner—assiduous reader of successive drafts—whose publications and invaluably expert editorial criticism guided me through every stage of the writing.

Abbreviations

ASCT	Archivio Storico Comunale Torino
AST	Archivio di Stato Torino
BAV	Biblioteca Apostolica Vaticana
BN, Florence	Biblioteca Nazionale, Florence
BN, Paris	Bibliothèque Nationale, Paris
BN, Turin	Biblioteca Nazionale Universitaria, Turin
BRT	Biblioteca Reale Torino
BORELLI	Giovanni Battista Borelli, *Editi antichi e nuovi di sovrani prencipi della Real Casa di Savoia, delle loro tutrici e de' magistrati di qua da' monti, raccolti d'ordine di Madama Reale Maria Giovanna Battista* (Turin, 1681).
DUBOIN	Felice Amato Duboin, *Raccolta per ordine di materie delle leggi, editti, manifesti, ecc. pubblicati dal principio dell'anno 1681 sino agli 8 dicembre 1798 sotto il felicissimo dominio della Real Casa di Savoia in continuazione a quella del Senatore Borelli* (Turin, 1818–69), 31 vols.
FESTE REALI	Mercedes Viale Ferrero, *Feste delle Madame Reali di Savoia* (Turin, 1965).

MEMORIALE

Gaudenzio Claretta, *Memoriale autografo di Carlo Emanuele II, duca di Savoia* (Genoa, 1878).

MONARCHIA PIEMONTESE

Ercole Ricotti, *Storia della monarchia piemontese* (Florence, 1861–69), 6 vols.

SCHEDE VESME

Augusto Baudi di Vesme, *L'arte in Piemonte dal XVI al XVIII secolo* (Turin, 1968), 3 vols.

TAMBURINI

Luciano Tamburini, *Le chiese di Torino dal rinascimento al barocco* (Turin, 1968).

THEATRUM

Theatrum Statuum Regiae Celsitudinis Sabaudiae Ducis Pedemontii Principis Cypri Regis (Amsterdam, 1682), 2 vols.

THEATRUM, ed. Firpo

Theatrum Sabaudiae, ed. Luigi Firpo (Turin, 1984), 2 vols.

TURIN

1564-1680

Introduction

"TURIN SEEMS to me the prettiest town in all of Italy, and, I believe, in all of Europe," wrote the enlightened French traveler Charles de Brosses in 1739; he found in "the alignment of its streets, the regularity of its buildings, and the beauty of its squares surrounded by porticoes" a vivid sign of central power and authority.[1] Emphatically praised by numerous authors of eighteenth-century travel books, Turin emerged as the most rational, uniform, and regular city of western Europe, "its streets all beautiful and broad, intersecting at right angles, its buildings of the same height and of a striking richness."[2] Architectural historians now give the highest praise to the innovative buildings of Guarini and Juvarra, Turin's most talented architects in the seventeenth and eighteenth centuries, paying less attention to the streets and facades, and almost none to the military gates and walls—only demolished in 1801. At the time, however, these Baroque masterpieces were judged eccentric and even bizarre; connoisseurs valued instead the straight and wide streets, large squares, regular buildings, and awe-inspiring fortifications. Thomas Nugent records a comprehensive impression:

1. *Lettres historiques et critiques sur l'Italie* (Paris, 1739), 3:382–83: "Turin me paroit la plus jolie ville de l'Italie, et, à ce que je crois, de l'Europe, par l'alignement de ses rues, la régularité de ses batiments et la beauté de ses places dont la plus neuve est entourée de portiques." De Brosses goes on, "Il est vrai que l'on n'y trouve plus, ou du moins rarement, ce grand goût d'architecture qui regne dans quelques endroits des autres villes; mais aussi on n'y a pas le désagrément d'y voir des chaumières a côté des palais."

2. Abbé Jérôme Richard, *Description historique et critique d'Italie* (Dijon, 1766), 1:42: "Les rues de cette partie de la ville [the expansions studied in this book] sont toutes belles et larges, tirés a ligne droite, les batiments du même hauteur et d'une richesse frappante."

I

It is one of the finest cities in Italy for the magnificence of its buildings, the beauty of its streets and squares, the number and sociable temper of its inhabitants, and for all the conveniences of life. The town is of a square figure, about three miles in circumference, and fortified as well as the nature of the ground would permit. . . . The streets are broad and straight, the houses large, high and almost all uniform, they appear to be of stone but are most of them only of plastered brick. The street that reaches from the castle to the new gate is very beautiful, it crosses two open fine piazza's of regular figure one of which called Piazza Reale is surrounded with houses exactly uniform, with a large portico all around it like that of Covent Garden.[3]

For many visitors, this monumental uniformity suggested the deliberate display of a stage set: Charles-Nicholas Cochin praised the "theatrical taste" of the ornate courtyards, visible from and contrasting with the austere street facades, and Joseph-Jérôme de La Lande proclaimed that the regularity and orthogonal alignment of the squares and streets "make the most beautiful spectacle that can possibly be seen."[4] Bernini himself, according to another travel writer, declared that the centrally planned streets and squares of Turin "had not their equal anywhere in Italy."[5]

Only a hundred years before Bernini's visit, however, the hereditary ruler of the territory—Emanuele Filiberto, duke of Savoy—had bemoaned the fact that his duchy lacked a city adequate for the ambitious role that he destined for his capital and his nation. At the time Turin was a small and provincial town emerging from three decades of foreign, if benign, French military occupation. Emanuele Filiberto perceived the strategic importance of the city, located in the foothills of the Alps at the entry-point of Italy for visitors and invading armies from the northwest. In 1566 he spoke to the Venetian ambas-

3. *The grand tour: or a journey through the Netherlands, Germany, Italy and France* (London, 1778), 3:170, 174.

4. Cochin, *Voyage d'Italie* (Paris, 1758), 1:30: "L'entrée des maisons est un atrio ou vestibule sous la porte cochère, décoré de colonnes et de pilastres et enrichi de quantité d'ornemens. Sous ce vestibule est le grand escalier. Le fond de la cour, qui se voit de la rue, est toujours décoré d'architecture, le plus souvent dans un goût théâtral. Cet atrio donne la commodité de descendre de carosse à couvert, et dans un lieu orné. Il en résulte un autre avantage. Toute la décoration est sur la rue, au contraire de ce qui est en usage à Paris, où presque tous les beaux hôtels sont au fond d'une cour, et ne contribuent point, ou très peu, a l'embellissement de la ville." De La Lande, *Voyage en Italie fait dans les années 1765 et 1766* (Paris, 1769), 1:50: "Les dix places qu'il y a à Turin et toutes les rues de la ville sont d'une régularité et d'un alignement qui fait le plus beau spectacle qu'on puisse voir."

5. Johann Georg Keyssler, *Neueste Reisen* (Hanover, 1751), 1:220.

sador of his desire for a vast and symmetrical urban expansion, and "motivated by this wish he found the strength to enlarge Turin." In the event, however, "since the expense of the expansion and the fortification was too great, he resolved to build only the citadel."[6] At the end of his reign the city of Turin, newly fortified and established as the official capital of Piedmont and Savoy, remained a medieval city enclosed within the rectangular walls of the Roman castrum.

In this book I examine the transformation of this garrison town into the capital of an absolutist dynastic state, a transformation that took place in the remarkably short period of 120 years, between 1560 and 1680. My analysis is focused upon the fortifications, streets, squares, and residential buildings realized during this crucial period because they have influenced profoundly the subsequent history of the city, and their singular forms survive to this day. My goal is to combine all the available evidence into a coherent narrative history, to synthesize the history of military architecture and urban design, and to place the expansion of Turin within the context of dynastic royal ideology—propagated in treatises, inscriptions, *imprese,* verse panegyrics, theatrical *feste,* and urban rituals. I trace connections between the royal decrees and the political theories of the intellectuals in charge of educating successive dukes of Savoy, and I reconstruct, from unpublished manuscript sources as well as printed materials, the organization and administration of the royal building projects. I show that the expansion program had already been initiated in the sixteenth century, and that the plan of expansion actually realized in 1680 had been conceived in the 1610s, much earlier than previously thought; in tracing the execution of this plan, I establish the crucial role played in the construction of the city by the Regent Cristina, a female ruler in this male-dominated society.

6. Giovanni Correr, "Relazione della corte di Savoja 1566," in *Le relazioni degli Ambasciatori Veneti al Senato durante il secolo decimosesto,* Eugenio Albèri, ed. (Florence, 1858), ser. 2, 5: "Dimostra ancora l'altezza del suo animo collo sdegnarsi che in tutto il suo stato non vi sia una sola città, la quale per grandezza di circuito, e per ogni altra qualità convenevole, sia degna d'esser chiamata metropoli di tutte le altre. . . . Piu d'una volta si è rammaricato con me che i suoi maggiori mai applicassero l'animo ad alcuna di queste due cose. . . . Portato da questo desiderio ebbe animo di aggrandir Torino, e fu per darvi principio; poi spaventato della spesa, perchè voleva fortificarlo, si risolse di far la cittadella, la quale a giudicio di ognuno riesce una bella e ben considerata fortezza. Ora è di nuovo entrato in questo pensiero, e vuol tirar due ale che uniscono insieme la città con la cittadella, e cosi aggrandir il circuito." For a lucid summary of the geographical and political situation of Piedmont, see Geoffrey Symcox, *Victor Amadeus II: Absolutism in the Savoyard state 1675–1730* (Los Angeles and London, 1983), 13–67.

Each of these investigations contributes to two larger questions: How was the city planned and built? How were its forms endowed with meaning?

MY PRINCIPAL THEMES, then, are the conception and creation of Turin as a new capital city, the high status of military architecture and its role in the design of the city, the role of dynastic ideology in conceiving and carrying out the enlargement, the representational and formal aspects of the architecture of the capital city, the establishment of a state-run building industry, and—not to be forgotten in this collective royal enterprise—the contribution of individual architects.

Turin became the capital of Savoy upon the transfer to it of the ducal residence and administrative institutions from Chambéry; at the same time, Italian was declared the official language.[7] Drawing upon the pragmatic philosophy of state popularized by Machiavelli, Emanuele Filiberto (known popularly as "Testa di Ferro") reinforced the city's institutional status in military terms, by sponsoring the construction of an indestructible citadel. In addition, by transferring to Turin the Holy Shroud—the Savoy rulers' most precious Christian relic—Emanuele Filiberto strengthened the city's religious identity. His heir Carlo Emanuele I borrowed from contemporary philosophy of government and political science—and specifically from his protégé Giovanni Botero, who wrote one of the first treatises on cities—in order to refine the ideological and political identity of Turin as the capital of an absolutist state. Subsequent rulers reinforced the position of Turin as capital city by claiming royal rank (Vittorio Amedeo I and the Regent Cristina) and by propagating the image of the newly expanded city in a magnificent atlas (Carlo Emanuele II). Thus the legitimization of Turin as the capital of the dynastic state was pursued through institutional, military, and ideological means, all of which required buildings of increasing cost and splendor.

My second theme—the high status of military architecture—is in many ways the most important, having been largely neglected in the study of architecture and of cities. Military architecture and strategy exercised a great influence upon the form of the city in the sixteenth and seventeenth centuries, ranging from immediate empirical effects (demolishing houses, erecting the fortification girdle, disciplining the citizens) to the creation of mental attitudes

7. Helmut Georg Koenigsberger, "The Parliament of Piedmont During the Renaissance," in his *Estates and Revolutions: Essays in Early Modern European history* (Ithaca, 1971), 19–80.

that in turn greatly altered the appearance of the cities' streets, squares, and buildings.

The following chapters explore the significance of the architect's contribution as military engineer, as writer, and as city planner; the influence of military architecture upon squares, streets, and residential architecture; and the importance of cartographic and surveying methods that, improved through military research, served a crucial role in the evolution of the representation and visual image of the city. My thesis is that the abstraction and regulation of urban form that so impressed eighteenth-century visitors, the economy and the expressive power of the buildings, and the new advances in surveying, cartography, and topographical draftsmanship that made the expansions possible are all products of the military culture that had dominated the Piedmontese court since the late Renaissance. The architects who transformed Turin—including Guarini himself—combined secular, religious, and military architecture; designed interiors; drew up city plans; and wrote treatises on fortification. In demonstrating their achievement, and showing how closely they were attuned to the prevailing military culture, I implicitly criticize the modernist tendency to separate the architect from the engineer—the latter a term itself derived from military architecture.[8]

The citadel became the microcosm of the city in the fifteenth century. It was the physical realization of a clearly structured political organization, and the model for the ideal city because it could be conceived, designed, and built as a complete work of art. In the seventeenth century the ideal city, whose principles had been developed by Alberti, Filarete, and Francesco di Giorgio Martini, became wholly associated with the ideal fortress. Since many civil architects practiced as military architects until the middle of the eighteenth century, there was a continual exchange of influence between military and civic design. This manifested itself through the adoption of the hallmarks of military design—regularity, uniformity, austerity—for the planning of parts of cities, or even of entire cities. The straight street, for example, defined by repetitive uniform buildings (borrowed from barracks) was a response to military needs; Palladio actually called it the "military street" (in a section of his *Four Books of Architecture* dedicated to Emanuele Filiberto). It permitted unob-

8. The writings of John Hale, Stanislaus von Moos, Paolo Marconi, Angela Marino, Nicholas Adams, and Simon Pepper, among others, have begun to sway the opinion of architectural historians, who now realize that architects fulfilled the functions of military planner, as well as designer of buildings, decorative objects, and furniture. For further discussion see my "La storia delle città: testi, piante, palinsesto," *Quaderni Storici,* n.s. 67, 23 (1988): 223–56; my introduction to *VRBI,* 11 (1989): III–V, and chap. 1 below.

structed movement through town for soldiers, horses, and equipment, and connected the gates to the main square, allowing surveillance of the entries to the city and the approaches to its center. The central square, no longer only a marketplace or cathedral square, became a place of refuge during attack, a parade and drill ground. It was flanked by the residence of the town's military commander, who thus could enjoy an authoritative, almost totalitarian perspective. Military architecture influenced the physical aspect of the preindustrial city also through the restrictive quality of the fortified walls, which increased the density of the population, sharpened the differentiation between town and country, enforced the hierarchy imposed by the gates, and determined the placement of secondary squares. Its effects were aesthetic as well as pragmatic, however: fortifications were intended to awe through their beauty as well as their strength, and the city gates, in particular, were to be as ornate as possible. The post-cannon fortification thus renewed the vocabulary of urban design and endowed it with fresh meaning.

As the seventeenth century developed, military architecture was increasingly influenced by the intellectual and political dominance of France. This was particularly relevant to the dukes of Savoy, who were closely related to the French royal family (Carlo Emanuele II and Louis XIV were cousins) and yet had to maintain their national independence against the threat of French expansionism. Military engineering was associated with developments in mathematics, geometry, and cartography—it was the only branch of warfare that had achieved scientific status—and it also came to be linked ideologically with royal absolutism. Military architects aspired to the high social and political status of statesmen, and to ensure the acceptance of military architecture as one of the political arts. Through this association with science, military architecture and strategy established the equation between the power of method (or reason) and political power, thus embodying Descartes' notion that the universe is a network of mathematical relations. The deep affinity of military architecture, urban design, absolutist government, and the philosophy of method is illustrated, in fact, by a famous passage in Descartes' *Discours de la méthode* (part 2). He draws an extensive analogy between the individual building, the city plan, the political constitution, and the intellectual system, arguing in each case that the rational plan "originated by a single individual and all tending to a single end" is better than a random accretion; thus the city that has grown from a medieval village, with its uneven buildings and crooked irregular streets, is greatly inferior to "regularly constructed towns that have been freely planned and laid out in open countryside by an *ingénieur*" (a military architect). Descartes' expert analogy even allows us to see the difficulties faced in the expansion of Turin according to rational and centralist principles: much as they would like to, the philosopher and the architect "cannot pull down all the houses of a town with the single design of rebuilding them differently and thereby rendering the streets more handsome," but must transform existing materials to activate their vision.

Cartographical innovations and advances bequeathed by military engineering improved the quality of the main forms of representing the city—the plan and the view—and this in turn influenced the emerging design of the expansion. Much of my evidence consists of plans and views, some autograph and some engraved. This poses certain problems of interpretation. These artifacts are records of urban form, whether projected or achieved, but they are also representations of the mental structure of their makers. Plans and views thus serve a double function: they are assumed to provide reliable facts about the city—after careful checking against independent documents and against the surviving streets and buildings—but they are also interpreted as a key to understanding the way in which the city was seen in the past. Their distortions may be just as significant as their accuracies.

I recognize, too, that the view and the plan involve different political ends. The view is narrower, more old-fashioned, and more concrete and is used mainly to influence the perception of the city by others; the plan is more comprehensive and uniform and became a powerful tool for the sovereign and his architects to control and transform their own urban environment. It could be argued that the view is an *expression* of power, its single-point perspective appropriate for the personal tyranny of the Renaissance prince, while the plan is an *instrument* of power, suiting the needs of the seventeenth-century absolutist state. But both were fully exploited in the *Theatrum Statuum Sabaudiae,* the great atlas that proclaimed the completion of the capital in 1682. Conscious distortions were made in order to emphasize the beauty of the "city as a work of art," and thus to garner the respect and the fear of enemies. In one plate (fig. 100), a principal square is shown framed by two symmetrical church facades, even though this design was not actually completed until 1834. On the other hand, figure 99 shows the city as it was in the early 1660s, before the second expansion celebrated in the atlas as a whole; the power of this perspective view evidently conveyed the right dynastic message, even though it shows features that had already been superseded by new building.

THE STRUCTURE of this book—a chronological history organized according to the reigns of successive monarchs—emphasizes the distinctive contribution of the ruling dukes and regents; in the new absolutist system the ruling family *is* the state. The expansion of Turin would have been impossible without the continuity of interest within the House of Savoy, sustained by a dynastic ideology passed on from generation to generation. Concurrently, the dukes' attempt to be recognized as kings played a great role in determining the form of the city and its architecture because these had to be in keeping with the rulers' "royal" rank. Turin was the principal theater for the legitimization process of the Savoy dynasty; the situation was very different in Rome, where each pontiff had to establish his own distinctive enclave and artistic contribution in a single lifetime, or in France, where Louis XIV asserted his authority by abandoning his capital and beginning anew at Versailles. All Piedmontese rulers were personally involved in making projects, keeping abreast of discoveries in military architecture and of commissions sponsored by other rulers. Thus Carlo Emanuele I may well have drawn plans as well as commissioning planning studies and composing tracts on political philosophy; Carlo Emanuele II sponsored the ultimate representation of his duchy, the *Theatrum*, in which the names of the contributing local artists are conveniently omitted. Eclipsing their architects, the rulers present themselves as the "edificators" of the state—they build and also educate the population through the medium of state-supported architecture.

This political condition entails a more complex methodology, a synthesis of cultural and architectural history. I analyze the architecture of Turin both in its formal development and as part of a larger system of representation and display of the dynastic ideology. I discuss the iconography and epigraphy of gates and foundation stones, for example, and examine the royal rituals and festivities in some detail. These ceremonies and *feste*—wedding and funeral processions, exhibitions of the Shroud, official receptions, public entries, open-air ballets, and allegorical dramas—illustrate the intimate relationship between the political and the architectural. The *feste* of Savoy were vividly recorded by Tommaso Borgonio, who would later provide many plates for the appropriately named *Theatrum*. Roy Strong begins his study of "art and power" by describing one of them; in the Regent Cristina's synthesis of politics, spectacle, and allegory, as in the French *ballets de cour* and the masques of Inigo Jones, Strong discovers "a manipulation of visual art and aural experience perfectly attuned to the ideological demands of the courts of Baroque Europe."[9] I go further, to demonstrate that these public ceremonials provided the templates for the monumental architecture of Turin. The theme of display

9. *Art and Power: Renaissance Festivals 1450–1650* (Berkeley, 1984), 5.

leads me to study the interrelation between the royal buildings and the royal *feste,* which shows that structures like the ceremonial gate were erected in wood and canvas for dynastic celebrations, only then to be recreated in stone as a permanent feature of the new city. The theatricality perceived by eighteenth-century visitors to Turin was not the arbitrary association of the travelers, but the deliberate intention of the designer.

How then was the city actually built? To understand how this continuity of vision was maintained, and how a large-scale conception was actually translated into stones, bricks, and mortar, it has been necessary to reconstruct the workings of Fabriche e Fortificationi, the ducal building agency whose mandate was refined over time. It was through this agency that the edicts of the crown—published and partly studied before by Augusto Cavallari Murat—were put into effect.[10] The edicts provided the general principles of Fabriche e Fortificationi; in reality the agency dealt not only with the planning of the expansion but with such important details as the price and quality of building materials. While the acquisition of meaning for the city's forms can be followed through the cultural and political interests of the patrons—recorded in their edicts, diaries, correspondence, and library catalogues—and through the rituals and festivities they sponsored, the activity of the building industry can be traced through the extensive manuscript archives of Fabriche e Fortificationi, admirably preserved in Turin.

This supervisory agency contained and employed an army of architects and artists ready to deal with all aspects of the expansion. They drew up the plans and were responsible for carrying them out in harmony with the intentions of the ruling family. But their extensive contributions have never been properly recognized. In particular the achievements of the Castellamonte, father and son, run as a thread throughout my book; the detailed analysis of Amedeo's designs for Contrada di Po, which culminates in chapter 7, completes a history of family involvement that begins with the early examination of plans by Amedeo's father Carlo, discussed in chapter 2. Many of the architects at court, including the Castellamonte, were from an aristocratic background, as Henry Millon has shown.[11] Their profile is similar to that of other courtiers surrounding the dukes. In their aristocratic origins, which seem to have increased their

10. *Forma urbana ed architettura nella Torino barocca: Dalle premesse classiche alle conclusioni neoclassiche* (Turin, 1968), 2:451–87. Cavallari Murat's typological approach and focus upon the development of the local residential building do not permit him to integrate the ducal edicts within the history of the realized expansion stages.

11. "Native Origins of Architects in Turin and the Piedmont," in *Scritti di storia dell'arte in onore di Eduardo Arslan* (Milan, 1966), 675–78.

authority and secured the respect of the ruling dukes, the architects at the Savoy court may well have differed from architects elsewhere.

This book, then, studies the interplay of various emblematic, ideological, and architectural problems inherent in the application of military culture to urban design. My intentions have been to uncover a "genealogy" of artistic interests, political goals, and intellectual methods, and to describe the public life shared by patrons and designers. This court culture—in which the architect Guarini was both a main protagonist and an outsider—formed the basis of a consistent and rigorous architecture, appreciated and imitated over the following centuries. The seventeenth-century design of Turin established an expressive form so resonant of power that it continued to inspire architectural and urban form long after the demise of the absolutist military state.

PART ONE
1564–1630

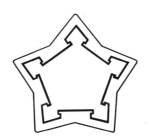

I

Arte et Marte

Military Culture and the Capital
as Theater of War

Il Sig[nor] Duca suol dire che non ha cosa più cara dopo il Prencipe di quella cittadella et che e la più pretiosa gioia del suo tesoro.
   —Venetian *Relatione*, 1576

Chi è padrone di Torino, è padrone del Piemonte.
   —Emanuele Filiberto

WHEN HE RETRIEVED Piedmont from the French in 1560 as the result of the treaty of Cateau-Cambrésis (April 1559), Emanuele Filiberto, duke of Savoy, the victorious general of the Spanish forces in the battle of Saint-Quentin, decided to move his capital from Chambéry to Turin.[1] Simultaneously, he restructured the government of the duchy, establishing its legislative and juridical agencies in Turin. He decreed that the official language of the duchy would be Italian.[2] The transfer of the capital and the switch to Italian were part of Emanuele Filiberto's program to align his duchy ideologically and politically with the Italian states. He achieved this by abandoning his French capital. His pro-Italian policy established the Savoy as the gatekeepers of the

1. For a discussion of the battle of Saint-Quentin, the events leading up to it, and the outcome, see Corrado Vivanti, "La storia politica e sociale," in *Dalla caduta dell'Impero romano al secolo XVIII*, ed. Corrado Vivanti and Ruggiero Romano, Storia d'Italia 2 (Turin, 1974), 385–97; and Ruggiero Romano, "La pace di Cateau-Cambrésis e l'equilibrio europeo a metà del secolo XVI," *Rivista storica italiana*, 61 (1949): 526–50.

2. For a discussion of Emanuele Filiberto, his character, and his contributions, see Giovanni Botero, *Saggio dell'opera de' prencipi e capitani illustri* (Turin, 1607), 217–23; Elvira Brunelli, ed., *I diari delle campagne di Fiandra* (Turin, 1928); Cesare Patrucco, ed., *Lo stato sabaudo al tempo di Emanuele Filiberto* (Turin, 1928); Arturo Segre, *Emanuele Filiberto* (Turin, 1928), 2:281–84; and *Emanuele Filiberto*, ed. Costanzo Rinaudo (Turin, 1928).

Alps and the crusaders for a united Italy, a project that remained unrealized until the nineteenth century. In the intervening centuries, however and especially in the seventeenth century, the dukes of Savoy were kept busy by the task of preserving their inheritance from French and Spanish encroachments.

To create a new capital, Emanuele Filiberto had to muster all his political, military, and cultural resources, including those of religion. In order to raise the spiritual level of the city, in 1578 he transferred the family's most precious pious possession, the Holy Shroud, from Chambéry to Turin.[3] Emanuele Filiberto believed in the coercive power of religion, maintaining that it enhanced the power of the prince because the pious are more orderly and consequently more obedient.[4] The transferral of the Holy Shroud to Turin made the city the focus of important pilgrimages, which naturally translated into significant income for the ducal and communal treasuries. But it also made new architectural and urbanistic demands. The appropriate sheltering and exhibition of the Shroud was not satisfactorily resolved until the end of the seventeenth century, when the chapel in which it was placed, built especially for it above the choir of the cathedral and connected to the *piano nobile* of the ducal palace, was finished and decorated.[5]

The town to which Emanuele Filiberto transferred his capital was a modest settlement that had preserved its castrum form (fig. 1). Founded c. 30 B.C. under Augustus as a colony for military veterans, it had been continuously, if not prosperously, inhabited.[6] The neighboring Piedmontese towns of Asti and Chieri were much more developed, commercially and culturally, than Turin in the Middle Ages. The castrum plan of Turin—with an orthogonal grid of streets, the forum at the crossing of the two major streets (the *cardo* and the *decumanus*), and the towered brick walls with one gate cut through each—had

3. The immediate excuse for moving the Holy Shroud to Turin was to shorten the penance of Cardinal Carlo Borromeo, who had made an ex-voto to walk barefoot to the relic from Milan. For a brief history of the Holy Shroud (Santissima Sindone) see Michele Ruggiero, *Storia del Piemonte* (Turin, 1979), 341–44; for a more detailed examination, see Joe Nickell, *Inquest on the Shroud of Turin* (Prometheus, 1983).

4. "La gente, infervorata di devozione è molto più regolata; e per consequenza più ubidiente al Suo Prencipe, che la dissoluta" (Giovanni Botero, *Detti memorabili di personaggi illustri* [Turin, 1608], 241).

5. For the history of the Holy Shroud chapel, see Nino Carboneri, "Vicende delle cappelle per la Santa Sindone," *Bolletino della Società piemontese di archeologia e belle arti,* 18 (1964): 95–109.

6. For the history of ancient Turin, see Carlo Promis, *Storia della antica Torino* (1869; rpt., Turin, 1969), especially chaps. 7, 8, and 9.

survived to the sixteenth century. There were only a few significant additions. The Roman gate in the east wall, originally composed of two towers connected by a curtain wall, had been turned into a castle c. 1260 by Guglielmo of Monferrato, who used it as a *cassaforte*. Around 1415 it was enlarged with the addition of two towers connected by wings, and became the residence of Lodovico, count of Acaja (fig. 2). This Castello was the headquarters of the French garrison when the dukes of Savoy lost their hegemony over Turin and Piedmont, for three decades, in the mid-sixteenth century. It was reinforced with a bastion by the French occupying force. Four additional bastions were built at this time, one at each corner of the castrum, and the ancient walls were buttressed by a curtain of earth.[7]

The only other large building was the cathedral. It was erected in 1499 to the design of the Tuscan architect Meo da Caprino, commissioned by the archbishop, Domenico della Rovere (fig. 3). Located in the northeast corner of the castrum, on what has subsequently been shown to be the site of the ancient Roman theater, it faced west towards the city hall and public market to which it was connected by a narrow passageway that crossed diagonally the ancient orthogonal grid of streets.[8] Its east end was surrounded with parts of the archbishop's residence. Upon the transfer of the capital of the duchy from Chambéry to Turin in 1563 Duke Emanuele Filiberto went to live in this palace near the cathedral, rather than in the traditional residence in the Castello. This was done in an attempt to dissociate the duke from the preceding French presence and to coopt the religious dominion of the bishop for the ruling family.

There were thus two areas in which ducal intervention was fundamentally required: the fortification of the city, and the appropriate housing of the court and administrative agencies of the duchy. While the reconstruction and transformation of the archbishop's palace proceeded slowly, Emanuele Filiberto

7. A critical overview of Turin's military defense after the French had fortified it is found in Nicolo Tartaglia, *De' quesiti et inventioni diversi* (1554), cited in Luigi Cibrario, *Storia di Torino* (Turin, 1846), 2:17: "Che le quattro fazze di questa città con li detti baluardi ovver bastioni sono state fatte modernamente de muraglia nova grossisima, et hanno lasciato dentro di sè tutta la muraglia vecchia. . . . Nel mezzo di ciascuna muraglia, due forme piatte, ovver cavaglieri che guardano li baluardi; e fosse che circondano la città." For the history of the Castello, see Marziano Bernardi, *Torino, guida storica e artistica della città e dintorni* (Turin, 1965), 60–69; and "Le sedi," in *Mostra del barocco piemontese*, ed. Vittorio Viale (Turin, 1963), 1:1–8.

8. Concerning the cathedral see Silvio Solero, *Il Duomo di Torino* (Pinerolo, 1956); and Günter Urban, "Der Dom von Turin und seine Stellung zur römischen Architektur des Quattrocento," *Römisches Jahrbuch für Kunstgeschichte*, 9/10 (1961/1962): 245–62.

concentrated his energies and means upon turning Turin into an unbreachable fortress. His first act was to commission a citadel for the southwest corner of the city. It was designed by Francesco Paciotto, and built by Francesco Horologgi between 1564 and 1566. Paciotto proposed a five-sided fortress, with three bastions oriented towards the countryside, defending the approach to the city from the west, and two bastions facing the city, ready to bring it under control in case of riotous uprisings against the duke (fig. 4).[9] Although the regular pentagon was considered the perfect form for the urban fortress, and one that fascinated military architects in the sixteenth century, none had been realized before the construction of the citadel in Turin. Paciotto's design, informed perhaps by the five-pointed irregular pentagon plan of the Fortezza da Basso in Florence (fig. 5) and by the geometrically perfect Palazzo Farnese in Caprarola (fig. 6), was the first of a number of pentagonal citadels, such as those of Antwerp (1567), also by Paciotto, and Parma (1591) (figs. 7, 8).[10]

Emanuele Filiberto had met Paciotto in Flanders, where they fought in the employ of Philip II of Spain. Paciotto built the fortress of Antwerp for the king of Spain, for whom he fortified several smaller towns. He was employed also by the Farnese family, who were among the foremost patrons of art, architecture, and urban design in the sixteenth century. Paciotto built a gallery for Ottavio Farnese in Parma in the 1580s, while Alessandro Farnese commissioned the pentagonal fortress there in 1591. But Paciotto's connection with the Farnese family began much earlier. He was consulted on the design of the pentagonal palace at Caprarola in the late 1550s, when Vignola was about to continue the construction begun by Antonio da Sangallo.[11] Paciotto thus had the chance to examine closely the problems inherent in the design of pentagonal buildings—particularly the relation between interior and exterior. He suggested the design for the round *cortile* at the center of the pentagon, which was replicated in the Turin citadel with an intricate circular fountain and cistern.

During the same period, Vignola's design for the Farnese palace in Piacenza

9. For the sixteenth-century discussion of the meaning and role of the citadel, see John Hale, "To Fortify or Not to Fortify? Machiavelli's Contribution to a Renaissance Debate," in *Essays in Honor of J. H. Whitfield*, ed. H. C. Davis et al. (London, 1975), 99–129.

10. For Paciotto's military milieu and architectural background, see Angela Marino Guidoni, "L'architetto e la fortezza," in *Momenti di architettura*, ed. Federico Zeri, Storia dell'arte italiana 12 (Turin, 1983), 87–89; and George Kubler, "Francesco Paciotto, Architect," in *Essays in Memory of Karl Lehmann*, ed. Lucy Freeman Sandler (New York, 1964), 176–89.

11. See Loren Partridge, "Vignola and the Villa Farnese at Caprarola," *Art Bulletin*, 52 (1970): 81–87.

was submitted for criticism to Paciotto (fig. 9).[12] Although Paciotto accused Vignola of megalomania, it is likely that through analyzing the project in Piacenza he became acquainted with the effect of unplastered brick in large-scale construction. In Vignola's designs for the palaces at Caprarola and Piacenza, the military aspect of the structures was emphasized by the undressed brick cladding, which replaced the customary stucco finish. The immense size of both buildings was augmented by contrast with the small dimensions of the brick. This interest in the effect of brick construction was underlined at the Roman residence of the Farnese family (fig. 10). This imposing palace, the building that established the standard for Roman papal family palaces, was built of rubble masonry, which was covered with brick-hued plaster. In turn, this plaster was drawn over so that the building seems to be faced in brick. Paciotto's design for the citadel of Turin may thus have been inspired by the form of the palace at Caprarola, and by the building materials of all three Farnese palaces.

The fortification of Turin had become a military necessity when the duke of Savoy moved the capital there from Chambéry; it was now the occasion for the duke to display his formal and ideological alliance with the imperial powers. Emanuele Filiberto had close cultural and diplomatic contact with the king of Spain, whom he had so successfully served in the battle of Saint-Quentin. By choosing Paciotto to design his citadel, an architect who had practiced both in Italy and in the Spanish empire, he forged links simultaneously with the Farnese family and with the Spanish crown.

The innovative pentagonal citadel that resulted from this partnership became the most important element in the defense of Turin (figs. 4, 11). It introduced an object that was geometrically and formally pure and incorporated the latest military innovations. It became the standard and reference point for all future fortification projects for Turin. According to a Venetian *Relatione* of 1576, the duke used to say that—after his heir—he loved the citadel best, and that it was his most precious jewel.[13] The strength and visual appeal of the military structure was such that it reinforced Emanuele Filiberto's fame as one of the best-known strategists of the period and established Turin's reputation as a famous *piazzaforte*.[14]

12. See Bruno Adorni, *L'architettura farnesiana a Piacenza 1545–1600* (Parma, 1982), 2: chap. 3.

13. *Relatione dello Stato del Signor Duca di Savoia*, 1576, BN, Paris, MS Ital. 418, fol. 479v (cited as epigraph to this chapter).

14. For a discussion of the Italian context, see Enrico and Angela Marino Guidoni, *Storia dell'urbanistica: Il cinquecento* (Bari, 1982), 394–405.

Contrary to his immediate predecessors, Emanuele Filiberto maintained a certain distance from his subjects and visitors, pretending to the titles of *Altezza* and *Serenissimo* granted him by Emperor Charles V, and thus practicing the aristocratic hauteur worthy of a Renaissance prince, as counseled by Castiglione.[15] Nonetheless, he spent many hours in the company of Paciotto, designing fortresses and war engines; in the workshops of his watchmakers, jewelers, and alchemists, making things with his own hands; and in his gardens, planting trees—even though such activities could be considered incongruous with princely demeanor. His avidity for learning and intellectual company was often remarked upon by those who examined his character.[16] His research seems to have been above all focused upon artillery, war engines, fortification models, and the strategy of siege attack and defense.

Emanuele Filiberto's interest in military science was particularly urgent because of the precarious position of Savoy. He had regained his duchy by diplomatic rather than military means, and indeed the dukes of Savoy had to navigate through numerous and contradictory treaties, throughout the later sixteenth and seventeenth centuries, in order to maintain the independence of the duchy.[17] But military consolidation was essential if he was to maintain his territory and succeed in a difficult balancing policy between Spain and France. Both used Piedmont as a last resort against one another, as a cushioning device. Piedmont was considered the bastion of Italy by the popes as well; it thus enjoyed a condition both marginal and indispensable, rather like that of Venice earlier in the sixteenth century, when that city served as a bastion against the Turks. These strategic considerations established in Turin a condition of watchfulness, and a prevailing military culture.

THE MILITARY INTERESTS of the crown were evident not only in the building of the citadel, but also in every aspect of daily life and in all the cultural activities sponsored by the ducal court. Emanuele Filiberto, like other Italian princes of his time, commissioned scholarly treatises; employed archi-

15. Baldassare Castiglione, *Il cortegiano, con una scelta delle opere minori,* ed. Bruno Maier, Classici italiani 32 (Turin, 1955), *passim.*

16. *Monarchia piemontese,* 2:409–35; also Ercole Ricotti, "Degli scritti di Emanuele Filiberto Duca di Savoia," *Memorie dell'Accademia delle scienze di Torino,* 17 (1858): 69–164. For the idea that princes should not involve themselves in the practical business of warfare, see Castiglione, *Il cortegiano,* 109; and Botero, chap. 2, note 43.

17. *Monarchia piemontese,* 2 and 3: *passim.*

tects, painters and decorators; and established a collection of art, antiquities, maps, manuscripts, and printed books.[18] But the outstanding aspect of his intellectual patronage and of his collections is their strong military inclination. While superior and controlled architecture and urban design were a matter of pride and social dominance for all rulers, the Piedmontese state had a more particularly pressing need to develop military architecture. To this end, Emanuele Filiberto encouraged the professional development of the military architect, enriched the ducal library with an important collection of sixteenth-century architectural and military treatises, and stimulated the production of new works. Both Paciotto and Horologgi, the designer and the builder of the citadel, wrote treatises under his patronage, and Palladio dedicated to Emanuele Filiberto the entire second half of his *Quattro libri dell'architettura* (Venice, 1570), remarking that Emanuele Filiberto, alone among modern princes, displayed the heroic spirit of the ancient Roman builders.[19] The books the duke acquired, which are known to us from an inventory of 1659, show his thorough acquaintance with contemporary theory of war.[20]

The renewal of the ancient Roman literary form, the military treatise, can be dated to 1534, the year in which Pope Paul III convened a meeting of military specialists to advise him on the fortification of Rome. This meeting defined the military architect as a professional man and outlined the responsibilities of the discipline.[21] During the next eighty years, Italian military engineers were employed throughout Europe, and Italian military treatises—often composed from the actual experiences of the writers, who were proud of their practice in the battlefield—were read and collected at every court. This literature forms the theoretical foundation of the new post-cannon military sci-

18. The patronage of Emanuele Filiberto has been studied by Alessandro Manno, "I principi di Savoia amatori d'arte," *Atti della Società di archeologia e belle arti per la provincia di Torino*, 2 (1879): 197–226.

19. See Francesco Horologgi, "Breve ragione del fortificare," BN, Florence, col. Magliabecchiana, MS 127, classe xix (still unpublished); Palladio, *I quattro libri*, 3:3.

20. AST, Sez. Ia, Real Casa, mazzo 5 d'addizione, mazzo 30, fols. 54–74. Many of the books in the inventory are listed in M. J. D. Cockle, *A Bibliography of English Military Books up to 1642, and of Contemporary Foreign Works* (1900; rpt., London, 1957), and in Pietro Ricardi, *Bibliografia matematica italiana* (Modena, 1870); they are discussed in Horst de la Croix, "The Literature on Fortification in Renaissance Italy," *Technology and Culture*, 1 (1963): 30–50.

21. The convention of engineers is discussed by Horst de la Croix, "Military Architecture and the Radial City Plan in Sixteenth-Century Italy," *Art Bulletin*, 42 (1960): 263–90.

ence.[22] Its concerns included discussion of the education and practice of the military architect, the design of fortresses, and the attack and defense of fortified cities.

Military treatises were crucial in teaching applied geometry, survey methods, and stereotomy, and useful in calculating materials needed in masonry construction. Like the architectural treatises they parallel, they range from pragmatic technical discussions to the aesthetic and theoretical aspects of design. As in architectural design, interest in the aesthetic aspects of fortification was manifested through emphasis on perfect geometrical form and proportions.[23] These treatises on warfare and fortification sought to raise the status of the military architect, to render him indispensable, and to establish *militaria* as a political and scientific discipline.[24] Writings and publications increased in time of peace, while engineers looked for the next patron to whom they might dedicate their works, and for whom they might fight in the next war; the military architect aspired to be a strategist in his own right. The treatises themselves legitimize the subject by displaying an erudite awareness of the writings of the ancients and a concern with aesthetic theory; above all, they establish a connection between fortress design and contemporary architectural and ideal-city planning.

A brief discussion of a few of the most significant and popular military treatises of the sixteenth century—all recorded in the inventory of the ducal library—will illuminate their main topics and areas of repeated concern, and will help to define the issues that faced Emanuele Filiberto and his successors as they attempted to transform Turin into a national capital. It was by no means universally accepted that fortifications were necessary for a city. Popular sentiment raged against them—in Bologna, for example, the walls were repeatedly torn down in riots—and Palladio, in the commentary dedicated to Emanuele Filiberto himself, revived the Spartan notion that the only fortification a city needs is the strength and devotion of its citizens.[25] The ruler would have to resolve a potential dichotomy between civic virtue and military

22. See John Hale, "Printing and Military Culture of Renaissance Venice," *Medievalia et Humanistica: Studies in Medieval and Renaissance Culture*, n.s. 8 (1977): 21–62.

23. See John Hale, *Renaissance Fortification: Art or Engineering?* (London, 1977), *passim*.

24. See John Hale, "The Argument of Some Military Title Pages of the Renaissance," *The Newberry Library Bulletin*, 6 (1964): 91–102.

25. Richard J. Tuttle, "Against Fortification: The Defense of Renaissance Bologna," *Journal of the Society of Architectural Historians*, 41 (1982): 189–201; see also Leon Battista Alberti, *De re aedificatoria*, trans. Giovanni Orlandi (Milan, 1966), 1:292–302, for the fortification of free cities.

readiness. Military treatises, naturally, stress the paramount importance of fortification. Civic design plays a subordinate part in these treatises, and it may
be omitted entirely in the more technical handbooks; but they show us, either
directly or by implication, the great significance of military strategy for urban
development. The position of gates and bastions determined the internal arrangement and form of the city's components; Palladio even defined the
straight street as a "military street." [26] The broad perimeter cleared for cannon-
fire isolated the city from the surrounding country and defined it more sharply
as a conceptual and spatial unit. This abstract self-awareness is reinforced, as
we shall see, by other developments brought about by military engineers, in
surveying and cartography. In general terms, the strategic requirements of
military culture imposed on urban planning an aesthetic of regularity, austerity, and grandeur of scale.

The treatise *I quattro primi libri di architettura* by Pietro Cataneo (Venice,
1554) is a remarkable work in that it expertly deals with both civic and military
architecture. It is a fifty-four-page volume, typographically undistinguished,
divided into four parts. Three of these parts concern building materials, eccle-
siastical design, and residential design; one is devoted to town planning and
defense, significantly combined into a single topic. The military prescriptions
are contained in this part, which is the first of the book. The classic requirements for a good site are discussed (good air, pure water, and the advantages
inherent in the topography), followed by a description of the hierarchical layout of the town (large central square with the most important buildings, secondary market squares with the neighborhood buildings). The orthogonal
grid pattern of the streets results in regimented blocks and squares. The form
of the peripheral blocks follows the *poemerium* or ring-road that separates the
residential areas from the enclosing fortification and runs parallel to the fortification. The *poemerium* was one of the innovations of sixteenth-century military design and marked the beginning of the separation between military and
civilian domains within town. It divided the urban street grid from the fortification belt while connecting the bastions to one another. Although Cataneo
avoids the technicalities of the fully developed fortification treatise (the construction of the bastion, and the range and pattern of cannon-fire), his discussions and his illustrated town plans make an important contribution by drawing on the parallel of military and civic architecture (fig. 12).

26. *I quattro libri*, 3:8: "le vie principali, che militari havemmo nomate, si devono nelle
città compartire che camminino dritte, e vadino dalle porte della città per retta linea a riferire
alla piazza maggiore e principale, e alcuna volta anco conduchino cosi dritte fino alla parte
opposta." See also Alberti, *De re aedificatoria*, 1:304–8, on military streets in cities.

Not all authors of military treatises adopt a comprehensive approach to urban design. Giovambattista de' Zanchi, for example, initiated a series of concise and specialized handbooks, and defined what were to become the standard topics of the art of fortification: ideal location of the fortress (whether on a mountain or in the plain), artillery and the history of offensive war instruments, the plan of the fortification, and the design and construction of the individual elements of the fortification system. But his *Del modo di fortificar le città* (Venice, 1554) does not consider the city as a whole, in its own right. Giacomo Lanteri's work on planning and design of fortifications, *Due dialoghi* (Venice, 1557), was even more circumscribed than Zanchi's. His illustration for the ideal fortification did not include reference to the layout of the fortified city. Only the bastions and walls with their appendages were discussed and drawn, while the interior of the town remained blank (fig. 13).

Girolamo Maggi, in contrast, attempts an encyclopedic range in his *Fortificatione della città* (Venice, 1564), which contains a more pragmatic and technical chapter on fortification by Jacopo Castriotto. Not only does Maggi expand upon all the topics broached by Zanchi, but also he publishes several comprehensive designs for ideal city fortresses. Maggi had a good ballistic reason for the flower-like elaborations of his bastions: Castriotto's proposal for angled walls allowed for more cannon locations while reducing the area of the settlement, and Maggi designed multiple projecting bastions, suitable for small maneuverable cannon, which would prevent the use of the countryside by the enemy rather than simply raking the adjoining curtain wall. Yet it is clear that he is also driven by aesthetic enthusiasm, delight in his own inventiveness and skill. The resulting idealized eight-sided fortress comes to resemble a geometrical ideal city, with deeply angled walls made by the overlap of two squares and an octagonal central piazza from which issued eight radial streets leading to eight bastions (fig. 14). Nevertheless, the needs of the urban population are somewhat neglected in these designs, since habitable space is eroded with each increase in the complexity of the bastions. Maggi did suggest, however, that the citizens could plant vegetables between them in peacetime.

The growing aesthetic and conceptual sophistication of treatises on fortification may be gathered from Girolamo Cataneo's *Opera nuova di fortificatione* (Brescia, 1564)—which proposes a totally abstract settlement pattern for a military camp, a centralized but nonhierarchical arrangement of uniform piazze—and from Galasso Alghisi's *Delle fortificationi libri tre* (Venice, 1570). Alghisi's work is beautifully printed, self-consciously erudite, and professionally confident. By Alghisi's time the conviction that the plan of the fortress was as important as the courage of the defending captain had made military architects rather bold in using self-praise in their quest for acceptance of the profession. Alghisi conceives the engineer's work as an art form of great strategic importance, adapting Alberti's precept that the defense of the fortress requires first of all the genius of a good designer, and only secondarily the valor of the captain.[27] He addresses his treatise to fellow professionals, and explicitly attacks the Spartan idea that a town needed only worthy men to preserve its independence. He defines his own achievement by detailed comparison with other treatises, and he insists that construction must only be undertaken by experts in draftsmanship, geometry, algebra, and perspective. (Evidently, Alghisi felt that the educational level of his fellow practitioners needed improving.) His own fortification designs had become highly sophisticated, and were supported by detailed discussion of other systems. But Alghisi gives scant attention to the street pattern and the interior organization of a fortified system. Indeed, since the curtain walls of Alghisi's fortresses were angled deeply inward, the ratio of habitable area to fortification was greatly reduced. Paradoxically, urban interests are subordinated to the fortification that is supposed to defend them (fig. 15).

Francesco de' Marchi of Bologna was perhaps the most influential of all the writers of military treatises of the sixteenth century, and his *Architettura militare* was an avowed influence on Pagan and Vauban, the greatest fortifiers of the seventeenth century.[28] The work was not published until 1599, after de' Marchi's death, but manuscript versions circulated from c. 1545 onwards. De' Marchi worked for Pope Paul III and for the imperial army in Brussels, during the time that Paciotto and Emanuele Filiberto himself were there; the duke almost certainly knew his work. One of de' Marchi's manuscripts contains a study for a four-bastioned fortress just west of Turin, which demonstrates his familiarity with the military enterprises of the duke of Savoy (fig. 16).[29]

De' Marchi's ideas were lavishly illustrated with town plans and views,

27. Alberti, *De re aedificatoria*, 1:10: "E anzi mia opinione [echoing Vitruvius, Book 10:12:2] che se si indaga da chi siano state sconfitte e costrette alla resa, fin dai tempi più antichi, tutte le città che in seguito ad assedio pervennero in mano del nemico, si vedrà che ciò si dovette all'opera dell'architetto. . . . Se poi si richiamano alla memoria le campagne di guerra condotte in passato, risulterà probabilmente che le vittorie vanno attribuite in maggior numero alle arti e alla valentia dell'architetto che alla guida e agli auspici del comandante; e il nemico più frequentemente fu sconfitto dall'acume dell'uno senza le armi dell'altro, che dal ferro di questo senza l'intelligenza di quello."

28. See Daniela Lamberini, "Francesco de' Marchi," *VRBI*, 11 (1989): XXIV–XXV.

29. "Atlante di Piante Militari" (c. 1565), BN, Florence, MS II, I 280.

which gave to the work the character of a pattern-book, easier to copy than to interpret (fig. 17). But he does address theoretical issues, and—though national and strategic considerations are always uppermost—he does clearly define the relation between the town and its fortifications. The requirements of the former are entirely subservient to the needs of the latter. Urban design is characterized by the customary placement of the principal elements. The public buildings are at the center of town framing the major square; radial streets connect the square to the bastions and bisect the secondary squares. The widened *poemerium* separates the residential areas from the military fortified belt. This belt begins to widen, jutting into the countryside, as de' Marchi explores the design and use of foreworks; these are placed in front of the walls and bastions, forming a protective screen for the bastions whose function they replicate (raking fire and shooting into the countryside). Thus the enemy would be kept farther away from the walls of the town, and the town itself would become more sharply differentiated from its surroundings.

De' Marchi's abstract illustrations of fortified settlements reveal two contrasting impulses in sixteenth-century military architecture: the desire to codify a lifetime's experience of siege warfare, and the impulse to produce idealized, geometrically perfect fortresses. Though urban and military requirements sometimes conflicted, the development of the fortified city and the theories that ruled its implementation overlapped with, and grew out of, the interest in idealized urban design that was part of the revived study of antiquity. The proposals for "ideal cities" written from the end of the fifteenth century were a call for urbanistic and architectural control of the environment, for an order that was to state and reinforce the hierarchy inherent in society.[30] The ideal fortress expresses the same desire for order and the display of power, but in a form more appropriate for the militarized and absolutist societies that emerged in the sixteenth century.[31]

Among the town plans proposed by Filarete, Francesco di Giorgio, and Dürer, the earliest and most important writers on urban design, two types can be considered fundamental, and both are intimately connected to military architecture. One called for a circular fortification enclosure and a central square

30. See Georg Münter, "Die Geschichte der Idealstadt," *Städtebau*, 9 (1929): 249–56, 12 (1929): 317–40; Susan Lang, "The Ideal City," *Architectural Review*, 112 (1952): 91–101; Gerhard Eimer, *Die Stadtplannung in Schwedischen Ostseereich 1600–1715, mit Beitragen zur Geschichte der Idealstadt* (Stockholm, 1961), 43–148.

31. See Pierre Francastel, "Paris et la création urbaine en Europe au XVIIe siècle," in *L'Urbanisme de Paris et l'Europe 1600–1680*, ed. Pierre Francastel (Paris, 1969), 9–37.

from which emanated radial streets; the other had a square enclosure and an orthogonal street system. Sforzinda, the ideal city designed by Filarete for the duke of Milan in 1470, had a centralized plan where the location of buildings with governmental and social functions was predetermined (fig. 18). The prince's palace and the church occupied the center of the city, the perimeter walls were equidistant from the center, and the social importance of the inhabitants could be measured by the distance of their houses from the center. The character of the urban environment was to be clarified through the imposition of geometrical order in the plan of the streets and squares, and of uniformity in the size and materials of buildings. Together with the centralized church, the radial city plan represented the highest goals of a period that placed human beings at the center of the universe.[32] The centrally planned city with radial concentric street pattern, suggested by Filarete, was later developed by Francesco di Giorgio (fig. 19). The former intended it as the symbol of the prince's power represented in architectural and urbanistic form. The latter's circular city plan was intended for both civilian and military settlements.[33]

The city with rectangular perimeter was endowed with straight streets with right-angled blocks. Suggested by Dürer, it was a direct descendant of the Roman military camp, the castrum still visible in the street layout of Turin. In it, two main streets crossed at right angles near the center of the settlement. This crossing, around which originally the military command was encamped, became the central forum. The four quarters of the settlement were occupied by the rest of the army and by service buildings (fig. 20). In Dürer's ideal city the military hierarchy was to be replaced by a civilian hierarchy with a centralized power structure.

Suggestions for ideal cities, or rather idealized urban designs, were made in most of the Italian and French architectural treatises published between 1500 and 1570. While research on the typology of urban structures continued, interest in how the pieces would fit together grew. The ordered urban environment became the physical realization of the well-organized political structure. Of the two ideal plan types, with orthogonal and radial streets, neither could be literally realized in the existing dense urban settlements. However, the Roman military plan was used extensively in the planning of colonial towns in

32. See Robert Klein, "L'Urbanisme utopique de Filarete à Valentin Andreae," in his *Le Forme et l'intelligible* (Paris, 1970), 310–67; also Eugenio Garin, "La città ideale," in *Scienza e vita civile nel rinascimento italiano* (Bari, 1935), 33–56.

33. Francesco di Giorgio Martini, *Trattato di architettura civile e militare,* ed. Corrado Maltese (Milan, 1967), 1:fols. 7–7v; 2:fols. 29–29v.

Central America, after its adoption as the principal model for the Spanish planning code known as the *Laws of the Indies*.[34] Contrary to the gridiron plan implemented in American colonial cities, the radial city plan was not widely adopted as a valid urban solution, with the notable later exception of Washington, D.C. Its elaboration took place in the treatises of the military architects discussed above. The radial plan was actually used in the fortress town of Palmanova, built at the end of the sixteenth century, and in Granmichele, built in 1693.[35] New fortified settlements, developing the circular form of ideal-city planning into the regular polygon of the ideal fortress, continued to be built throughout the seventeenth century, particularly to define the military boundaries of France.[36]

THE TRANSFORMATION of Turin in the sixteenth and seventeenth centuries should thus be understood in the context of the new forces that raised the status of military architecture and shifted the focus of urban planning from the ideal city to the ideal fortress. The descent of Charles VIII into Italy at the end of the fifteenth century with an army outfitted with heavy cannon was a decisive event in the history of military strategy. In the wake of his conquests in the Italian peninsula, the vanquished princes and communities had to reconsider the defensive systems of their cities. The use of cannon required major changes in the defensive fortification of towns, and thereafter new developments in artillery would always bring about changes in military defense.[37] Fortification had also become imperative as the free cities lost their independence to absolute rulers. The citadels dominating most cities ensured the cooperation of the citizens, as well as defending the city from outside attack. Existing cities were difficult to change, and thus the elements of the ideal city could be inserted only in a fragmentary manner. All interventions required authoritative

34. Enrico Guidoni and Angela Marino Guidoni, *Storia dell'urbanistica: Il cinquecento* (Bari, 1982), 349–89.

35. See Horst de la Croix, "Palmanova, a Study in Sixteenth-Century Urbanism," *Saggi e Memorie*, 5 (1962): 23–41; and Angela Marino Guidoni, "Granmichele," in *Inchieste su centri minori*, ed. Federico Zeri, Storia dell'arte italiana 8 (Turin, 1980), 407–41.

36. On French military architecture in the seventeenth century, see Annie Blanchard, *Les Ingénieurs du roy de Louis XIV à Louis XVI* (Montpellier, 1979), 51–68.

37. For the relationship between artillery and defense, see Simon Pepper and Nicholas Adams, *Firearms and Fortifications: Military Architecture and Siege Warfare in Sixteenth-Century Siena* (Chicago, 1986), 3–31.

support, which imparted to them a strongly political quality. Since demolition was required for most new construction, it was a way for the ruler to undermine the established power of certain family groups and restructure the town's social and political hierarchy. The new walls required increased territory and a wider field of vision for defense. Thus, when the fortifications were updated without expansion of the city, the suburbs were razed, as was done with Turin's suburbs and extramural monasteries in the 1530s.[38] Even the few urban projects that can be considered *ex novo* required the restructuring of an existing rural settlement.

The new capital at Turin was produced by a new kind of rule, that of the absolutist dynasty, and a new class of designer, the military architect. Traditional architectural training had included large-scale projects, such as hydraulics, draining of marshes, and bridge construction, and among these large-scale construction enterprises was the design and fortification of towns. As the need for defense grew, these military skills were given greater emphasis: already in the late fifteenth century Leonardo deemed it advantageous to present his ability as military and hydraulic engineer as equal to his better-known artistic talents, and the importance of military architecture had been recognized in the writings of architects such as Leonardo himself and Francesco di Giorgio.[39] By the 1540s, after the introduction of the portable cannon had revolutionized every aspect of warfare, there had developed a group within the architectural profession almost exclusively occupied with fortification design. These men were called engineers, from the term *engine,* which was used to describe war machines.[40] The knowledge and experience required of the military architect

38. See Tamburini, 3–11.

39. The text of Leonardo's letter to Ludovico Moro, duke of Milan, is in Pietro C. Marani, *L'architettura fortificata negli studi di Leonardo da Vinci* (Florence, 1984), 280 (and see 11–48 for Leonardo's military studies in Milan); Francesco Paolo Fiore, *Città e macchine nel '400 nei disegni di Francesco di Giorgio Martini* (Florence, 1978), 17–21, 40–56, 120–40.

40. Pierre Lazard, *Vauban 1633–1707* (Paris, 1934), 3: the siege "nécessitait des machines spéciales qu'on appelait *engins* au Moyen-Age. D'où le nom d'*Ingénieur* appliqué à ceux qui faisaient construire les engins et qui en dirigeaient la mise en oeuvre dans l'attaque, et la défense, des places"; see also Carlo Pedretti, "Leonardo da Vinci," in *Macmillan Encyclopedia of Architects,* ed. Adolf Placzek (New York, 1982), 2:684: "The Renaissance term 'ingegno' for machine explains etymologically the designation of 'engineer' in a classical sense, which it retained somewhat in the English language, of one who is dealing with the technological aspects of architecture in general and of military architecture in particular. The invention of war machines . . . pertains to the architect in his capacity of engineer, that is, the engine maker."

became increasingly differentiated from those of the civil architect. Whereas the civil architect would often be trained in interior decoration, painting, and sculpture, the military specialist received his training through apprenticeship in war and through study of treatises that, as we have seen, tried to raise his social status, his educational level, and his theoretical awareness. In addition to design and construction methods, the military architect had to master surveying, ballistics, and attack strategy. Since the new fortifications were rendered necessary by improvement in cannon, the use of mines, and the renewal of strategies practiced in antiquity, acquaintance with the latest discoveries and interpretations was essential. Most engineers had little formal education, however, and their knowledge of architecture was largely pragmatic, concerned with the use of materials and their strength in resisting the impact of cannonballs, the ventilation of the shooting chamber, and the defense of the bastion.

In the second half of the sixteenth century, Italian military engineers dominated in European construction of fortification. As the design of fortifications improved because of more sensitive measuring instruments, better building materials, and more opportunities for experimentation, various local schools developed. Their methods, although derived from Italian military architecture, began to acquire national characteristics, responding to local conditions and materials. Towards the end of the century when the major military conflicts had moved from the Italian peninsula to the borders shared by France with Spain, the Netherlands, and the German principalities, the influence of the Italian engineers waned. This loss of hegemony may well have been an outcome of the growing nationalistic sentiments in the west European countries, most clearly seen in France. Once parity had been achieved, native military engineers were given preference over foreign mercenaries, and their research was encouraged. In France, the formation of an institutional corps of engineers (Sully's Corps du Génie) by 1600 rendered the services of Italian engineers redundant.[41] The encouragement of Piedmontese military architects by Emanuele Filiberto and his successors reflects precisely this emergent nationalism and dynastic ambition in the House of Savoy.

The concerns of the military planners focused on the fortified perimeter of the city, but they also exercised a great influence on urban design within the city itself. The fortification belt widened with the increased sophistication of the defensive measures, and towns were increasingly separated from the surrounding countryside. The girdle of walls and bastions usually influenced the

41. See David Buisseret, "Les ingénieurs du roi au temps de Henri IV," *Bulletin de la Section de Géographie*, 77 (1964): 80.

street pattern of the enclosed town, the layout of the major square and the monumental buildings, and the connections between them. After the mid-sixteenth century, then, fortifications altered the hierarchy and composition of the city and its relation to the countryside.

The circular circumference of the ideal city was replaced by the many-sided polygonal defense enclosure of the military settlement. In sixteenth-century settlements like Palmanova, the enclosing wall and the bastions became more important than the central square with its monumental buildings inhabited by the leading citizens (fig. 21), while the square reasserted itself at Granmichele (fig. 22). But the relation between the center and the fortification then changed. The direct connection between the gate and the central square, realized in Palmanova, was replaced in the designs of influential theoreticians such as Maggi and de' Marchi by a direct link between the bastion and the central open space. In their designs for fortified cities, the central square was used as a parade and shooting ground and the place from which the streets leading to the fortifications could be kept under surveillance. The streets opening in front of the gates often led to secondary squares, or to the ring-street connecting the radial streets. The secondary streets, not connected to the center, were also necessary to reduce the size of the larger blocks at the periphery of the circular enclosure.

The city with regular polygonal walls and radial streets became the ideal form of the active defense fortification. However, the circular enclosure was often juxtaposed, in treatises and in actual settlements, with an orthogonal street pattern. An attempt was made in the fortification and urban designs proposed by Cataneo, de' Marchi, and others to connect both bastions and gates to the main square, thus unifying the two conflicting requirements of the urban design, military and civilian. Then with the introduction of the *poeme-rium,* the ring-street that connects the bastions and separates the fortification belt from the urban street grid, a schism between military and civilian domains was introduced. The fortification belt, interconnected and self-supplied, was functionally divorced from the town. The wide streets of the ideal military city were no longer necessary, as cannon carriages passed along the *poemerium* from one bastion to another. In Turin, the streets connecting the gates to the central square became important organizing elements in the urban structure, as the civilian use of the city reasserted itself.

Militarily conceived settlements had difficulty in attracting commercial activity, however. Treatise writers had insisted on the importance of the site for the settlement, but they had obviously emphasized strategic rather than social and economic criteria. Fortified towns such as Palmanova were built where they were needed for national defense and expansion. This often meant that the site was not suited for manufacture or commercial exchange; once the military problem had been solved their sole function expired and their development languished. In building a capital that would function both as an ideal city and as an ideal fortress, the dukes of Savoy had to avoid such catastrophes and to resolve, by an assertion of power, the potential conflict between civic and military requirements. Emanuele Filiberto's own contribution—the pentagonal citadel juxtaposed to the orthogonal city, with two of its five bastions trained upon the citizens themselves—expressed this dichotomy all too clearly.

THE COLLECTION and study of military treatises provided a theoretical strategy for the use of the new weapons and for the design and defense of modern fortifications. But Emanuele Filiberto and his architects also needed to know how some of these precepts had been put into practice elsewhere. This concern was manifested through another well-endowed part of the ducal library, the collection of maps, town views, and plans. Of these, a five-volume atlas collection has survived.[42] Each volume consists of about 120 sheets, which include large-scale maps of entire continents or regions; sieges, fortifications, and fortresses of foreign cities; Piedmontese towns; fortification proposals; and drawings explicative of ballistics. The number of these prints and drawings was enlarged by each succeeding sovereign; they are an index of the immediate concerns of the ducal government. The collection was augmented by the court engineers, who returned from visits to enemy towns with sketch views and autograph plans. These drawings could be used for inspiration in fortification and urban design, and for the formulation of attack strategy.

The survival of the earliest city views and plans is perhaps due to this new practice of binding them into atlases.[43] The collections of plans and views, in atlases or as loose sheets, became the norm for princely libraries in the sixteenth century, part of the princes' thirst for knowledge and military dominion. Thus the form of the city could be grasped through study in which firsthand experience was replaced by a reading equally rich in overt and implicit messages.[44] The great number of extant historical views and plans, their aston-

42. Now in AST, Sez. Ia, Disegni di Architettura Militare e Fortificationi.

43. Edmund Pognon, "Les plus anciens plans de villes et les événements militaires," *Imago Mundi,* 22 (1968): 13–19.

44. Stanislaus von Moos, *Turm und Bollwerk* (Zürich, 1974), 198–200; see also R. V. Tooley, "Maps in Italian Atlases in the Sixteenth Century," *Imago Mundi,* 12 (1939): 12–47.

ishing artistic appeal and apparent scientific precision, demonstrate that from the sixteenth century there was a growing awareness that representation could bear an objective relation to the measured world, and this introduced a process of visualizing human thought, actual physical conditions, and the reciprocal play of transformation between these realms.[45]

This renaissance of topographical draftsmanship can also be attributed to the rise of the military architect, whose functions often overlapped with those of the artillery officer and the spy. He would travel a great deal, at a time when movement between towns was difficult, to maintain fortresses and to plan sieges. His talent in drafting was called upon for the description of towns that were to be fortified or besieged.[46] He provided sketches of the layout and views of the town, which helped to formulate the strategy of attack. Out of the need for precise information regarding the urban layout, and with the help of the new, more sophisticated survey instruments, grew the new science of cartography. Mapmaking became an important tool in waging war. In turn, the new maps intended for military use were able to be adapted to peaceful purposes. The advance in surveying methods and mapmaking was one of the major contributions of military architecture to city planning.

By the middle of the sixteenth century there were views of most Italian cities, but few precise plans.[47] Despite the great advances in the understanding of perspective, these profile views were not thoroughly accurate, and were rather a symbolical representation of the most important aspects of the city, using the panoramic form already familiar in painting and fresco. Even de' Barbari's bird's-eye view of Venice (1500), which seems to combine the visual realism of the view with the cartographic precision of the plan, has been shown to contain serious distortions.[48] From mid-century onwards, however, attempts were made to represent cities systematically. One of the first such enterprises was sponsored by Philip II of Spain, who commissioned the topo-

---

According to Tooley, sheet maps were first compiled into atlases in Italy around 1570— inspired by Ortelius' *Theatrum*—and this permitted Italian maps to survive in better condition than those in other European countries.

45. The importance of views in determining the image of the city is examined in Jürgen Schulz, "Jacopo de' Barbari's View of Venice: Mapmaking, City Views and Moralised Geography Before the Year 1500," *Art Bulletin*, 60 (1978): 425–72.

46. See Pepper and Adams, *Firearms and Fortifications*, 178–81.

47. For a full collection of topographical views and plans, see the twenty-five volumes on individual Italian cities in the series *Le città nella storia d'Italia,* ed. Cesare De Seta (Bari, 1979–).

48. Schulz, "De' Barbari's View of Venice," 425.

graphical artist Anton van den Wyngaerde to illustrate the principal cities of Spain.[49] Another artist, Jacob van Deventer, had been commissioned to engrave the plans of cities in the Low Countries.[50] Since the cities were in a part of the Spanish domain which Philip II held with uncertainty, there was an obvious military intention and political usefulness in his ordering precise plans. Military planning, in fact, brought about important developments in cartography and surveying: as early as 1443, Alberti had adopted new military technology—a range-finding device used by gunners—for the "more delightful work of surveying land and portraying the great city."[51] Improvements in surveying, in turn, were crucial for the geometric precision of cannon fortification layout. These improvements resulted in more accurate plans of cities, and this brought new precision to the view (fig. 23). Initially drawn as aids for the development of strategic defense or attack, or as spy drawings, these new plans and views became of overriding importance for the visual image of the city.

The relation between the bastioned wall, built to resist the siege with cannon and introduced at the end of the fifteenth century, and contemporary mapmaking has been traced by a number of historians of architecture and cartography.[52] The fortification was conceived as a whole and mapped out in its entirety, thus prompting improvements in cartography. Ichnographic plans eliminated the profusion of views typical of medieval and early Renaissance representations of the city, and replaced them with an abstracted, dominant, and thus controllable point of view.[53] Throughout the seventeenth century cartography developed simultaneously with innovations in the increasingly complex fortification of cities. By providing a scaled and measurable representation of the city, plans—surveyed and drawn by military architects—acquired a crucial role in the understanding of the city as an entity. The accurate, abstract plan of the city became a powerful instrument in the manipulation and transformation of urban form by the architect and the town planner.

49. See Richard Kagan, ed., *Spanish Cities of the Golden Age* (Berkeley, 1989).

50. See Guidoni and Marino Guidoni, *Il cinquecento,* 450.

51. *Ludi matematici* (1443), cited in Joan Gadol, *Leon Battista Alberti: Universal Man of the Early Renaissance* (Chicago and London, 1969), 171: "Ma io lo adopero a cose molto dilettevole come a commensurare il sito d'un paese, o la pittura d'una terra, come feci quando ritrassi Roma."

52. See, for example, Myra Nan Rosenfeld, review of *Turm und Bollwerk* by Moos, *Journal of the Society of Architectural Historians,* 36 (1977): 275–77.

53. See John A. Pinto, "Origins and Development of the Ichnographic City Plan," *Journal of the Society of Architectural Historians,* 35 (1976): 35–50.

The plans of towns could also serve peaceful purposes, of course. They could manifest pride of place, and they were an essential ingredient—more so than the views, which were not as abstract—in the conceptualization of the town's image. In urban design the availability of the accurate plan was an important step that led to the articulation of large-scale projects by clarifying the relation between different parts of town. The ability to visualize the entire town and to conceive of it as a whole enabled planners to have a comprehensive vision, rather than continuing in the fragmentary manner common until then. Throughout the sixteenth and seventeenth centuries, however, military purposes were inseparable from these civic and civilian uses of the plan and the view. The military heritage manifested itself in the political tendency to commission official representations of the city: the commissioner acquired power over the city whose secrets were thus exposed. He controlled the diffusion of the plan or view, which became an instrument of secret strategy or dynastic showmanship. Autograph plans were jealously guarded, while engraved representations—diffused throughout Europe and collected in atlases of rival princes—were designed and distributed under close supervision for the maximum impact. The supreme example of this controlled display, as we shall see, is the *Theatrum Statuum Sabaudiae* (1682), the atlas of plans and views commissioned by Duke Carlo Emanuele II to celebrate (and anticipate) the transformation of Turin into an absolutist capital. Cartography provided the technical means for the design of new towns, while the civil and military architectural treatises provided the theoretical foundation.

In the late Renaissance mind, this conjunction of military planning and urban representation could be placed among the highest works of art. The strategic content in the representation of the city was hinted at by Castiglione, who informed the courtier that from painting, in itself a worthy and noble art, many useful skills can be derived and *not the least for military purposes*: "knowledge of the art gives one the facility to sketch towns . . . and citadels, fortresses and similar things which otherwise cannot be shown even if, with a great deal of effort, the details are mentioned." [54] A more militant and bellicose

54. Castiglione, *Il cortegiano*, 172–73: "della qual [painting], oltra che in sé nobilissima e degna sia, si traggono molte utilità, e massimamente nella guerra, per disegnar paesi, siti, fiumi, ponti, ròcche, fortezze e tali cose; le quali, se ben nella memoria si servassero, il che però è assai difficile, altrui mostrar non si possono"; the example of painting confirms Castiglione's central thesis that the principal calling of the courtier is military, and that all the arts should be considered subordinate to the *ars militaria* (109, 164–65). See also Kim Veltmann, "Military Surveying and Topography, the Practical Dimension of Renaissance Perspective," *Revista da Universidade de Coimbra*, 27 (1979): 263–79.

ideology of painting, suggested by the seventeenth-century military scientist Nikolaus Goldmann, asserted that "one could not find a more magnificent picture than the perspective of places won from the enemy especially in the court of a victorious and triumphant prince." Sir Philip Sidney, drawing on Italian platonic treatises, gives as an example of the highest form of creative imagination a "fine picture, fit for building or fortification." [55] This is probably the impulse behind the establishment of geographic galleries of cities, such as the one at the Vatican (which included a view of Turin, fig. 24); and, as we shall see, the first major intervention of Emanuele Filiberto's successor, Carlo Emanuele I, was the decoration of such a gallery. The novelty of portraying cities in the Renaissance, a loving "description" with a latent tendency to idealization, lay in the accuracy of the image, which now—under the discipline of military requirements—was no longer purely symbolic.

In the shift in military strategy in the sixteenth century, then, innovations in perspectival drawing, firearms, and ideal city planning were assimilated and transformed into a new military urban philosophy. The earliest true plans coincide with the reconstruction of the cities' fortifications after the beginning of cannon warfare (fig. 25). We shall see that, in the case of Turin, the construction of the extended walls was simultaneous with the first accurate plans and views of the city. Both enterprises, cartographic and military, are evidently part of the attempt—prolonged over several generations—to gain royal status for the city and to establish it as the capital of a nation-state. As we shall see in later chapters, all the efforts of the dukes of Savoy and the Regent Cristina— the reconstruction of the ducal palace, the attempt to change ducal symbols into royal ones, the diplomatic efforts to gain recognition as a kingdom from the principal European monarchies, the publication of the *Theatrum,* as well as the expansion of the city itself—can be interpreted as manipulations of a single military-dynastic program.

55. Goldman quoted in Veltmann, "Military Surveying," 270; Sidney, *A Defence of Poetry,* ed. Jan van Dorsten (Oxford, 1966), 54–55. I owe the latter reference to James G. Turner.

2

"Ragion di Stato" and "Grandezza della Città"
Carlo Emanuele I's Expansion Plan for Turin

Opportune.
> —Motto of Carlo Emanuele I

Augustam Taurinorum . . . ad pristinam augusti nominis amplitudinem
restituere Carolus primus voluit.
> —Inscription on foundation stone, Borgo di Po expansion, 1673

CARLO EMANUELE I's reign of fifty years (1580–1630) is unparalleled
in the history of the House of Savoy for its bellicosity and sudden reverses, its
expansionism and cruel defeats. He inherited from his father Emanuele Filiberto a newly fortified capital city in Turin, which had quickly acquired the
fame of a powerful *piazzaforte;* an insecurely placed state (between the two
largest European competitors, Spain and France) whose survival depended on
preservation and expansion; and a pro-Spanish foreign policy.[1] This turbulence
and insecurity created many obstacles to the completion of official building
projects. Nevertheless, it is to Carlo Emanuele I, whose prodigious energy
and aggressive military and political philosophy were spurred by precisely
these difficulties, that we owe the first conception of an expanded, unified, and
"beautified" Turin.

A formidably ambitious military leader, Carlo Emanuele nurtured a number of grandiose projects (such as acquiring the crown of France, and the dominion of Provence) that involved him in almost numberless military cam-
paigns, wars of both offense and defense during which he continuously

---

1. For a detailed analysis of Carlo Emanuele I's political enterprises, see *Monarchia piemontese*, 3 and 4: *passim;* also Roberto Bergadani, *Carlo Emanuele I, 1562–1630* (Turin, 1932);
and for the sixteenth-century part of his reign, Italo Raulich, *Storia di Carlo Emanuele I, Duca
di Savoia*, 2 vols. (Milan, 1896–1902).

changed allies. Thus in his panegyric of 1609 Giambattista Marino could write about him "Hor quì più che temuto, amato alberga / Signor congiunto a la corona Ibera" (Here, loved more than feared, lives the lord tied to the Iberian crown), referring to the alliance through marriage with Caterina, infanta of Spain, who, however, was dead by then. Later in the same poem he elaborates the theme of martial strength and royal alliance still further:

> E'nsieme formidabile si rende
> Et amabile al Franco, et a l'Hispano,
> Si che l'un gli è congiunto, e l'altro amico
> Il gran FILIPPO, e'l valoroso HENRICO.

To the Spanish and the French he is both formidable and amiable, so that the great Philip is his relative, the other, the valorous Henry, his friend.[2]

Thus Carlo Emanuele's attempt to find a secure, if costly, niche between the two great enemies could also be found praiseworthy by his contemporaries. His widely known activities were acknowledged and followed by a large public. The Roman diarist Giacinto Gigli provides another telling epitaph for the Piedmontese ruler. In his entry for August 1630, having heard of the duke's death, he notes that alive Carlo Emanuele had been very restless, and dead, he was the primary cause for the wars and great tensions in Italy.[3] He thus lays at Carlo Emanuele's grave the charge of reckless and capricious war-mongering.

But Carlo Emanuele's activities were not random, and he can be said to have been keenly aware of, and in some instances to have closely followed, the political thinking current in his lifetime. His mode of action was based upon the concept of *ragione di stato,* the philosophical approach to politics explored and propagated by several writers who were the inheritors and critics of Machiavelli's earlier treatises on the conduct of the ruling prince in his relations with his subjects, cities, and territory. Among these the closest and the best known to Carlo Emanuele was Giovanni Botero, a Jesuit of Piedmontese origin, who was employed as the preceptor of the ducal heirs from 1599 and had his literary and political tracts published in Turin.[4] In charge of the moral and com-

---

2. *Il Ritratto del Serenissimo Don Carlo Emanuello Duca di Savoia* (Venice, 1609), stanzas 31 and 100.

3. *Diario romano (1608–1670),* ed. Giuseppe Ricciotti (Rome, 1958), 116: "in vita era stato huomo inquietissimo, et al presente bona causa delle guere, et romori, che si sentono grandissimi nell'Italia." I owe this reference to Laurie Nussdorfer.

4. Federico Chabod, *Giovanni Botero* (Rome, 1934), reprinted in his *Scritti sul Rinascimento* (Turin, 1967), 271–446, is the principal reference work on the philosopher, but for a com-

intellectual education of Carlo Emanuele's three older sons, Filippo Emanuele, Vittorio Amedeo, and Emanuele Filiberto (who were guest-hostages in Madrid between 1603 and 1606), Botero subsequently educated the two younger princes, Maurizio and Tommaso. Except for the oldest who died while still in Madrid, the princes all played significant, if secondary, roles in the political and cultural life of the first half of the seventeenth century.[5]

Botero's own education was based upon Jesuit teaching, and upon the Counter-Reformation rhetoric of the cardinals Federico Borromeo (whose councilor he was from 1585) and Carlo Borromeo, whom he served as secretary.[6] In Turin his closeness to the duke, whom he served as collaborator and as literary critic, is commemorated by Marino, who wrote of Carlo Emanuele that he

> Prende in privata, e solitaria parte
> Col gran BOTERO à divisar talvolta,
> E del'antiche, e ben vergate carte
> Le chiare historie attentamente ascolta.
>
> (*Il Ritratto,* stanza 165)

Takes private and solitary part in conversation with the great Botero, and listens carefully to the limpid stories drawn from ancient and well-laid papers.

Botero's literary reputation was established before his arrival at the Savoy court by two seminal works, *Della ragione di stato* (Venice, 1589) and *Delle cause della grandezza delle città* (Rome, 1588).

In *Della ragione di stato* Botero deals with the assumption that the state is built on the union of power and morality, a confluence of the two principal definitions of the state proposed by Machiavelli (the state founded on power)

---

plete biographical account see Luigi Firpo, "Giovanni Botero," in *Dizionario biografico degli italiani.*

5. Emanuele Filiberto (1588–1624) became a grandee of Spain and viceroy of Sicily, where he died of the plague, but not before having his portrait painted by Anton van Dyck, as did his brother Tommaso; both Tommaso and Maurizio remained closer to the Savoy court in Turin, and became major figures in the dynastic war discussed in chapter 5. Botero dedicated a number of publications to his charges; for instance, his collection *I Prencipi* (Turin, 1600) contains an essay on Alexander the Great dedicated to Filippo Emanuele, an essay on Julius Caesar dedicated to Vittorio Amedeo, and one on Scipio Africanus dedicated to Emanuele Filiberto. Later, his *Saggio dell'opera de' prencipi e capitani illustri* (Turin, 1607), was addressed to Vittorio Amedeo, prince of Piedmont.

6. See Chabod, *Scritti,* 284–300.

and Bodin (the state founded on right).[7] Twentieth-century criticism has considered Botero as the most conservative of the Italian political thinkers at the end of the sixteenth century, and mediocre in comparison with Machiavelli. Meinecke, for example, shows his dislike of Botero through an architectural metaphor: the edifice of his doctrine evokes a Jesuit church, developed from the Renaissance style and rich with decoration.[8] However unpopular it later became, Botero's political treatise was nevertheless widely read and emulated in its own time.

Botero's success was probably due not to the originality of his political philosophy, but to his vast and systematic exposition of the new problematic that the modern state implied: taxing, military organization, commerce, industry, and urbanism. The *Ragione di stato* documents the transition from the feudal and tyrannical state to the "politic" state based on centralized administration and bureaucratic hierarchy; Botero seeks to reconcile the conflicting interests that Machiavelli had analyzed so acutely, organizing their cooperation in smoothly operating institutions. Thus he proposes a concord between political power and the Church, forging an alliance between Machiavelli's three pillars of power (state, law, and army) and religion. In foreign relations, likewise, he proposes a typical Counter-Reformation, and Jesuitical, policy: always conform to the interests of the Church, and always preserve peaceful relations with its great allies. Though his *ragione di stato* covers the foundation, the preservation, and the expansion of a state, Botero himself obviously values preservation rather than expansion, a middle-sized state rather than one too small or too large. But despite his moderate and diplomatic approach, Botero could not finally avoid seeing that the immovable essence of all political activity was the self-centered interest of the prince or of the state. He thus comes to confirm the Machiavellian analysis of the princely city-state: what the prince does in his own interest is almost always harmful for the city, and when he acts for the good of the city it is to his own detriment.[9]

Botero's earlier treatise, on the causes for the grandeur of cities, hesitates likewise between cooperative idealism and hard-headed pragmatism. This lucid and penetrating essay is perhaps Botero's best work.[10] It elaborates, for the

7. For the intellectual relationship among Machiavelli, Bodin, and Botero, see Friedrich Meinecke, *Die Idee der Staatsräson in der neueren Geschichte,* ed. Walter Hofer, vol. 1 of *Werke* (Munich, 1957), 77–82. I owe this reference to Simona Cerutti.

8. *Die Idee der Staatsräson,* 78.

9. Niccolò Machiavelli, *Discorsi,* 2:47, cited in *Die Idee der Staatsräson,* 38.

10. Written and first published in Rome, the original edition was dedicated to Cornelia d'Altemps Orsini, a relative of the Borromeo family; it was followed by several others

first time, a scientific theory about population movement and the increase of urban agglomerations that identifies precise relations among the natural environment, economic resources, and demographic development. In this theory, the size and the importance of the city are ultimately determined, not by its site and its wall enclosure, but by the number of its citizens. The Greek city-state had failed because it limited its population strictly, whereas Rome could found a great military empire because it drew in and deployed vast multitudes.[11] But Botero recognizes that numbers alone do not make a city great and magnificent, suitable to be the capital of a nation run on the principles of *ragione di stato*. He identifies several other motive forces, which the ruler must manipulate with care: populations are moved together by authority, by force, by utility, or by pleasure. Botero's prescriptions for the ideal city include a powerful appeal to aesthetic pleasure, to "everything that feeds the eye and delights the sense, and which gives an impulse to curiosity; everything that is innovative, and strange, extraordinary, marvelous, grand or artistic."[12] This seems to be precisely the list of characteristics elaborated subsequently in Baroque art and architecture.

Carlo Emanuele's entire plan for Turin may be understood as an attempt to tackle the issues raised by Botero—in particular, the conundrum of reconciling the interests of the prince with the interests of the city. Carlo Emanuele's literary remains, such as his manuscript entitled "I paradossi della ragion di stato," are witness to his fascination with the theory of *ragione di stato* and *grandezza delle città*.[13] In some respects he refused to follow Botero's suggestions; he broke with Spain and assumed an aggressively expansionist foreign policy.[14] In urbanism, however, Botero's influence is profound, and Carlo

---

around the turn of the century: Spanish edition 1593, Latin 1602, English 1606. Subsequent quotations are from the Turin 1596 edition.

11. *Grandezza delle città*, 70: "Gli antichi fondatori delle città, considerando, che le leggi, e la disciplina civile non si può facilmente conservare, dove sia gran moltitudine d'huomini, perche la moltitudine partorisce confusione; limitarono il numero de' cittadini. . . . Tali furono Licurgo, Solone, Aristotele. Ma i Romani, stimando che la potenza (senza la quale una città non si può lungamente mantenere) consiste in gran parte nella moltitudine della gente, fecero ogni cosa, per aggrandire, e per popolare la patria loro."

12. Ibid., 11–12. "Tutto ciò . . . che pasce l'occhio, e che diletta il senzo, e che dà trattenimento alla curiosità; tutto ciò che ha del nuovo, e del insolito, del straordinario, e del mirabile, del grande ò del artificioso."

13. Carlo Emanuele's list of literary projects, and his extant literary (manuscript) remains, have been published in *Monarchia piemontese*, 3:413–40.

14. *Monarchia piemontese*, 3:81–124.

Emanuele frequently draws upon his precepts in edicts, designs, and proposals for the enlargement of Turin in the 1610s and 1620s. Echoes of Botero's teaching, reiterated and extravagantly elaborated in the maxims of Emanuele Tesauro, the historiographer and epigraphist of the Savoy dynasty, will be subsequently found as fresh inspiration for the ideals of Carlo Emanuele II, Carlo Emanuele I's grandchild and successor in the later seventeenth century.[15] Botero, in his turn, pays tribute to the urban ambitions of Carlo Emanuele. In 1588 he had written, while discussing the provisioning of the city, that "it is not enough, for the grandeur of the city, to have a rich hinterland, because we see many very well-provisioned regions without a great city—such as Piedmont, the richest area of Italy that had fed for many years the armies of Spain and France."[16] This must have sorely rubbed Carlo Emanuele's vanity. By 1607, Botero would adroitly redress his earlier description; in the "Relatione di Piemonte" the entire region is described, proudly, as "a city with a three-hundred-mile perimeter."[17]

EVEN BEFORE Botero had formulated his theories of the state and the city, and had conveyed them to the ducal family, Carlo Emanuele and his architects had begun the process of transforming the garrison town into a capital that would express the political ambitions of the House of Savoy. The task was to reconcile various urban, rural, and national interests, and to translate this ideological program into the built environment. These interventions had to assert the duke's authority over alternative centers of power, such as the mercantile, and provide an example of orderly and beautiful architecture—constraining, molding, and delighting the population according to the principles that Botero

15. See chapter 6 below. For Tesauro see Franco Croce, "Critica e trattatistica del barocco," in *Storia della letteratura italiana*, vol. 5, ed. Emilio Cecchi and Natalino Sapegno (Milan, 1967), 473–520.

16. *Grandezza delle città*, 16: "Ma non è bastante, per constituir grandezza di città, la fecondità della terra: perche veggiamo provincie abbondantissime non havere nessuna grossa città; come per esempio è il Piemonte, del quale non è paese in Italia, dove sia maggior abbondantia di formenti, di carne, e di vini, e di frutti eccellenti di ogni sorte, il che vi ha mantenuto tanti anni gli esserciti, e le forze di Spagna, e di Francia."

17. *I Capitani* (Turin, 1607), 194: "E finalmente paese tanto habitato, che non fu impertinente la risposta, che un cavallier Piemontese diede ad un gentil'huomo Venetiano, che gli domandava, che cosa fosse Piemonte, dicendogli, esser *una città di trecento miglia di giro*" (emphasis mine).

was discovering during the same decade, the 1580s. Above all, the entire project had to develop within the pressing requirements of military strength.

The first of these attempts was to reconstruct the ducal residence and to expand its influence upon its immediate urban surroundings. It began with construction of the gallery wing in c. 1570 to house the various ducal collections. The library, whose earliest inventory dates from 1435, had grown copiously under the reign of Emanuele Filiberto, who spent important sums on it, particularly in 1579.[18] As discussed in chapter 1, the most striking feature of Emanuele Filiberto's valuable library was its collection of manuscript and printed military treatises. Carlo Emanuele I had a keen appreciation of painting, sculpture, and architecture, as well as *militaria,* and he was an avid collector, accumulating many excellent Roman marbles.[19] Since his successors in the first half of the seventeenth century had less opportunity to collect, because of short reigns, civil wars, and political intrigues, it can be assumed that most of the objects listed in mid-seventeenth-century inventories of the ducal villas and library had been acquired by Carlo Emanuele. One of his first architectural commissions as ruler was thus designed to contain these growing collections.

The Galleria, first shown in Giovanni Caracha's wood-block view of Turin (1572), but also present in contemporary Savoy dynastic portraits and representations, had thirty-two arcaded bays at the ground level and an equal number of windows on the floor above (figs. 23, 26, 27). The roof served as a rampart. The gallery itself, known as *il teatro,* housed the extensive art collection, the archive of Carlo Emanuele I, and the library.[20] The literary collection was enlarged under Carlo Emanuele I to such an extent that Marino could, without too great a fear of ridicule, write about it in his *Primavera* as the "Libreria della qual non fu più piena / L'Alessandrina, nè la Pergamena" (library no less well stocked than those of Alexandria and Pergamon).[21] The Galleria also played an important role in the family life and education of the children of Carlo Emanuele I; the ten-year-old Vittorio Amedeo tells of meals taken in the gallery, from which views of the Po and the countryside could be en-

18. For Emanuele Filiberto's library, and the fate of the Savoy dynasty's literary collection, see Gianfrancesco Galeani Napione di Coconato, "Notizia delle antiche biblioteche della Real Casa di Savoia," *Memorie della real accademia delle scienze di Torino,* 36 (1833): 41–62.

19. For Carlo Emanuele as collector see Gaudenzio Claretta, "Inclinazioni artistiche di Carlo Emanuele I di Savoia e de' suoi figli," *Atti della Società di archeologia e belle arti di provincia di Torino,* 5 (1894): 4–10.

20. For a detailed history of the gallery, see Gaudenzio Claretta, *Il pittore Federigo Zuccaro nel suo soggiorno in Piemonte e alla corte di Savoia (1605–1607)* (Turin, 1895), 52–62.

21. Cited by Napione di Cocconato, "Notizia," 50.

joyed.[22] It contained the most precious and sophisticated possessions of the court, while at the same time being a part of the city's fortification enclosure. Just as it contained the military and the aesthetic, so this Galleria combined urban and rural characteristics. On the side facing Turin it defined the open square flanked also by the ducal palaces, and connected two important residences. The side facing into the country was open, however, allowing contemplation of the hills and the Po River (fig. 27).

While precedents for such structures existed at least as far back as the building of the Belvedere court by Bramante at the Vatican, the enclosed gallery at the edge of town, using the countryside beside the town as though it were a controlled landscape, was a relatively recent building type. One such gallery was built by Scamozzi in Sabbioneta, the town planned *ex novo* for the dukes of Gonzaga, and Carlo Emanuele no doubt knew of it because of his relationship with the dukes of Mantua, and because Scamozzi dedicated to him the chapter on military architecture in his *L'idea della architettura universale* (1615). Carlo Emanuele's Galleria elicited warm praise from travelers in the late sixteenth and early seventeenth centuries. Giovanni Paolo Lomazzo, author of one of the two most important texts on art theory from this period, published at the end of the sixteenth century and dedicated to Carlo Emanuele, hailed him as "the most liberal protector of all the arts" and ranked the gallery as the fourth most beautiful of its kind, after those of the king of Spain, of the emperor, and of the grand duke of Tuscany.[23] Thomas Coryat, who visited Turin in 1611, thought it "a work of notable magnificence . . . of stately height and built all with white stone." According to him, it was "incomparably the fairest that ever I saw saving the king of France's at the Louvre."[24] Carlo Emanuele would have been pleased with these judgments, since not only was his gallery appreciated, but also it was compared to those built by the very monarchs that he was trying to emulate. Thus the dynastic ideological program through

22. AST, Sez. Ia, Lettere Principi Savoia, Serie Duchi e Sovrani, Vittorio Amedeo I, mazzo 46, number 6, 1597.

23. *Tempio della pittura* (Milan, 1585). The other important contemporary text on art theory, also dedicated to Carlo Emanuele, is Federico Zuccaro's *L'idea de' pittori, scultori et architetti* (Turin, 1607); for Carlo Emanuele's relationship to both of these authors see *Schede Vesme,* 3:1111–29; for his relationship to Marino, see Gerald Ackerman, "Gian Battista Marino's Contribution to Seicento Art Theory," *Art Bulletin,* 43 (1961): 326–36. For the Gonzaga gallery see Kurt Forster, "From Rocca to Civitas: Urban Planning at Sabbioneta," *L'Arte,* 2, 5 (1969): 25; David Coffin, *The Villa in the Life of Renaissance Rome* (Princeton, 1979), 69–87, also discusses galleries.

24. *Coryat's Crudities* (1611; rpt., Glasgow, 1905), 1:229–32.

which he attempted to place himself on the same level with the kings of France and Spain, and which had been challenged and spurred by the more important title of grand duke granted to the Medici, had worked its desired effect through his patronage of artistic, architectural, and urbanistic commissions.

The decorative program of the interior of the Galleria reinforced the ducal program. Thirty-two princes of the House of Savoy were shown on horseback along the walls of the gallery, while the niches between them sheltered representations of spouses, protector saints, monuments, and coats of arms belonging to individual members of the family. The two ends of the gallery were decorated with portraits of the five emperors and four popes descended from the House of Savoy. The cosmography of the world and the constellations were painted on the vault. It was this decorative program that impressed the prince of Condé when he visited Turin in 1622; he thought the gallery was the duke's greatest asset, describing its vault, walls, books, and marbles.[25] The fame of this gallery was also diffused by Federico Zuccaro (partly in self-interest, since he had himself painted large parts of the ceiling decoration),[26] and by Marino:

> Portico altier frà gli edifici primi
> Pur dianzi eretto, opra pomposa, e ricca
> Con pareti magnifiche, e sublimi
> Quì da pianta eminente al ciel si spicca;
> E quì rapite al predator de'lustri
> Mille splendon d'honor memorie illustri.
>
> (*Il Ritratto,* stanza 56)

Haughty portico, foremost among buildings, eloquent and rich work with sublime and magnificent walls that rise skyward from an outstanding design. Here, stolen from the predator of lights, the thousand illustrious memories of honor brilliantly shine.

Thus the Galleria went beyond the *sala degli antenati* that was its model, joining to it the educational function of the *Kunstkammer* and the library. It succeeded

25. Henri II de Bourbon, prince de Condé, *Voyage de Monsieur le Prince de Condé* (Bourges, 1624), 6: "ce qui est le plus beau c'est la galérie de son altesse: en plancher sont les signes et autres choses celestes: la généalogie des Ducs de Savoye y est en des grands tableaux tout au long: où il y a plus de trente mil volumes de livres tant manuscripts qu'imprimées, disposez par ordre selon les matières: dessus ladites armoires sont des antiques de marbre très excellentes: il y a aussi les testes de plusieurs Empereurs."

26. *Il passagio per l'Italia* (Bologna, 1608), 45–47.

in the glorification of the House of Savoy by the vivid evocation of the dynastic ideals of its members, their consistency, and their interest in and patronage of the fine arts.

THE PALACE COMPOUND of Turin, of which the Galleria was only one wing, was not yet a cohesive group of buildings in the 1580s. Even in 1622, when the prince of Condé visited Turin, it was still an assemblage of various structures renovated to house the ducal family, and it probably deserved Condé's hard-boiled estimate that "the palace of His Highness contiguous with the residence of the Duchess, and those of the Princes and Princesses, are very extensive but without consistency or rule of construction or architecture."[27] The reconstruction of the Palazzo Reale (the principal ducal residence), with the redesign of the public spaces surrounding it, was one of the principal objectives of Carlo Emanuele I's building campaign. This thoroughly transformed the northeast corner of the city, placing emphasis on it as the command center of Turin and of the duchy. Diagonally across the city from the fortress, Emanuele Filiberto's principal contribution to the form of Turin, the ducal residence was to form a civilian pendant to the military stronghold of the city (fig. 27).

The plans to transform the northeast corner into the monumental command center coincide with the arrival in Piedmont of Ascanio Vitozzi. A descendant of the aristocratic Braschi family from Orvieto, Ascanio Vitozzi (1539–1615) was an architect, engineer, spy, and military strategist. He participated in the battle of Lepanto and in the conquest of Portugal with the army of Philip II. He probably studied architecture with Giacomo Barozzi da Vignola, and in 1569 and 1570 he carried out the damming of the Tiber in Rome. It was at that time that he became acquainted with the work of Antonio da Sangallo and Michelangelo in Rome. He is one of the three "foreign" architects (the other two being Guarini and Juvarra) who changed fundamentally the architecture and urban layout of Turin. Habitually referred to as captain, Vitozzi was nominated first court architect and engineer by Carlo Emanuele I in 1584. As offi-

27. Condé, *Voyage*, 6: "Le palais de son altesse qui si tient avec le logis de Madame, et ceux des Princes et Infantes, sont d'une très grande estendue sans règle de bastiment ny d'architecture."

cer, spy, and fortifications engineer, he often in the course of his work visited other towns of the duchy and towns that the duke of Savoy was besieging.[28]

The task that confronted Vitozzi had already been defined as an urban intervention, a contribution to *la grandezza della città:* the building of the new ducal palace in 1584 also entailed the redesigning of the Piazza Castello. The old ducal residence, next to the cathedral, occupied the rooms of what had been formerly the bishop's palace. A plan to open an axial street leading from the rebuilt palace to Mirafiori, the ducal villa south of the city, was contemplated from 1587.[29] In addition, there were strong intentions to unify this area of the Castello. The major testimony is provided in a drawing of 1605 signed "Monsa" (fig. 28). Monsa's view, despite its amateurish quality, gives a largely accurate representation of developments that would transform the area of Piazza Castello during the following decade. Although not an official project, this drawing contains the major design ideas that were being discussed and studied by ducal architects.[30] The two urban areas transformed in this design— using what were to become the essential elements of Baroque city planning, the monumental square and the uniform street—were the Piazza Castello itself and the new street to the south.

The redesign of the Piazza Castello consisted of the definition of its perimeter through uniform porticoed facades, the rebuilding of the ducal palace, and the demolition of the structures that had stood in the middle of the square, diminishing its monumentality. Carlo Emanuele pushed forward the execution of these designs by a combination of civic legislation and *ragione di stato.* Typically, it was a dynastic and strategic alliance that gave the impetus for their completion. The arcades around the square were built after Vitozzi's design for the wedding celebration in 1608 of the two daughters of Carlo Emanuele. Having cast around for royal husbands for his daughters Isabella and Maria, Carlo Emanuele finally gave them away in a double wedding ceremony to the

28. For Vitozzi see Carlo Promis, "Gli ingegneri militari che operarono o scrissero in Piemonte dall'anno MCCC all'anno MDCL," *Miscellanea di storia italiana,* 12 (1871): 584–90; *Schede Vesme,* 3:1098–99; see also Nino Carboneri, *Ascanio Vitozzi, un architetto tra Manierismo e Barocco* (Rome, 1966), and Aurora Scotti, *Ascanio Vitozzi, ingegnere ducale a Torino* (Florence, 1969).

29. Carboneri quotes the letter patent of 1587 where it is proposed to "far una nuova strada per la quale si vada dritto da questo nostro palazzo a Miraflores" (*Vitozzi,* 137).

30. Monsa's drawing was first published and analyzed by Vittorio Viale, "Un antico progetto per la sistemazione di Piazza Castello e del centro di Torino," *Bollettino storico-bibliografico subalpino,* 44 (1942): 52–62.

dukes of Modena and Mantua, respectively. The alliances could have proven profitable, since Carlo Emanuele was disputing with both the Este and the Gonzaga over contested territories.[31] The wedding ceremony provided an occasion for the construction of the porticoes that his letter patent of 1606 had imposed unsuccessfully upon the owners of buildings bordering on the square.[32]

Through this letter patent property owners along Piazza Castello were specifically invited to render their houses "more useful and comfortable for their own benefit" because the duke desired the "embellishment of the city." Beauty and utility combine into a single program directed by authority, as Botero had suggested. This beautification was to be achieved through the construction of porticoes in front of existing buildings on land provided by the crown. Each owner would thus increase his property by 2½ *trabucchi* in Piazza Castello (1 *trabucco* equaled approximately 3 meters). Public passage was demanded at ground level, however, and the construction was to be completed within eighteen months. Owners unable or unwilling to comply were to inform the architect Vitozzi and be ready to sell their building at its current value (without consideration of the enlarged parcel) to a buyer willing to obey the ducal order.[33]

Placed in front of the existing irregular houses, the porticoes—built at the duke's expense in 1607—provided uniformity and an impressive background

31. For a description of the wedding festivities, see BAV, MS Urbinati Latini 1076, fols. 216–17, which includes the seating arrangement at the banquet, the order of the joust, and this odd spectacle: "Il sabato si fecero entrar in uno steccato due leoni maschio e femina, due tigri, un cinghiale, due tori, una mula, una simia, e molti cani con pensiero che dovessero azzuffarsi insieme, ma se ne stettero tutti taciti sino a sera lasciando tutti gli spettatori mal sodisfatti."

32. See Carboneri, *Vitozzi,* 138–39, for the construction sequence of porticoes, built in marble and wood during 1607 for the double wedding held in February 1608.

33. Duboin, 910–11: "Desiderando noi per abellimento di questa città, che quelli che hanno case sopra la piazza del castello se le rendano più utili e commode a benefitio loro facciano portighi tirando la facciata di esse case a retta linea, conforme al dissegno che dall'ingegnere Ascanio Vitozzi gli sarà dato, la qual cosa non potendosi fare senza l'aiuto nostro in ampliargli il sito, . . . diamo licenza . . . a quelli che hanno case sopra detta piazza . . . di avanzarsi verso suddetta piazza secondo le facciate delle sue case, e avanti di essi sopra la strada per lo spatio di due trabuchi e mezzo . . . obbligandosi pero essi patroni delle sudette case di compire le fazzate, e fabriche d'essi portighi, ogniuno secondo suo tenimento, et sito fra un anno e mezzo. . . . Et in caso che alcuni d'essi non potessero . . . o di non volere saranno tenuti di vender esse case a chi vorrà comprarle al valor presente."

for the elaborately mounted nuptial festivities. But by 1612 the porticoes, built at least partly as ephemeral architecture, were probably decaying and a source of discomfort for the inhabitants of houses around the square whose view and light they blocked. In his letter patent of March 1612 Carlo Emanuele donated the porticoes built for the wedding of 1608 to house owners with the stipulation that they must build two floors above them; "this reasonable expedient," he explains in Boterian terms, will leave "the owners satisfied, the Castello and Piazza more ornamented and amplified, and ourselves, finally, singularly contented."[34] The design of the upper levels of the facades was once again provided by Ascanio Vitozzi. His composition, visible at the center of a view of Piazza Castello of 1613, draws upon local Piedmontese models, but alters them significantly (fig. 29). The dominant urban characteristic of Piedmontese towns, such as Carignano, Carmagnola, and Chivasso, was the arcade with the low, flat vaults that defined the major streets and squares (figs. 30, 31, 32). They seem to have been constructed together with the buildings behind them, which extend above the arcade; the vaulted bays are not uniform, but the arcades, usually whitewashed and springing from thick piers, provide a continuity that transcends the lack of rigorous architectural uniformity. Vitozzi's design for the Piazza Castello echoes this Piedmontese tradition of porticoed streets, but its application at the urban scale of Turin established a new monumental architectural language that became the fundamental model and point of departure for subsequent urban design in seventeenth-century Turin. Vernacular tradition was transformed by the ideological program of the ruling dynasty.

The street connecting Piazza Castello to the new southern gate, next to the

34. Ibid., 912: "Vedendo noi che il lasciar tuttavia nel stato nel qual oggidi si ritrovano li portici et galleria aperta sopra, che nel tempo de' matrimonii delle due infanti maggiori nostre amatissime figliole fecimo fare alla circonferenza di questa piazza detta del Castello, apportarebbe eccesivo danno, et pregiudicio alle case che loro sono dietro et contigue, levandogli et la vista, et la luce ancora, vi habbiamo preso per espediente ragionevole l'infrascritta donatione nostra, della quale ci persuadiamo che li patroni delle medesime case ne rimarranno sodisfatti, il castello et piazza stessa con più ornamento, la città abellita et ampliata d'honorate stanze, et a noi finalmente con singolar contento; . . . rimettiamo a tutti li posidenti . . . la parte di essa galleria per quanto s'estende, e sta avanti di caduna di esse case a dirittura verso la piazza con carico però ad essi possidenti, et patroni di far fabbricar essa parte ogn'uno sì et come gli tocca per la detta dirittura, cioè sopra li portici due stanze, o siano piani l'uno sopra l'altro . . . con le finestre, poggioli et ornamenti che saranno designati et ordinati dall'ingegniere nostro capitan Ascanio Vitozzi."

bastion of Santa Margherita in the southeast corner of the city, was opened in 1615, cutting through existing buildings.[35] This straight north-south street, the Contrada Nuova (now Via Roma), followed the sixteenth-century model of the *stradone,* linking the urban and suburban residences of the ruler at the expense of a densely inhabited quarter of the city. Once again, a local model may have influenced the design: Saluzzo, desired and then wrested from France by the duke in 1588, had been the subject of civic improvement in the last quarter of the sixteenth century; the resulting two-block-long street, straight and with uniform facades, may have provided the idea of the Contrada Nuova (fig. 33). Unlike the Piazza Castello itself, it was not porticoed; Vitozzi, still the chief architect of the duke, designed the uniform facades to be built in front of the disemboweled structures of the crowded neighborhood (fig. 34). The opening of the Contrada Nuova had the effect of reorganizing the hierarchy of streets within the Roman castrum plan and reinforcing ducal control over urban form. In the following decade, in fact, Palazzo Reale was partially rebuilt—again to Vitozzi's design—so that its main portal was aligned with the newly opened south street (fig. 35). Since the new street was aligned axially with the gate of the ducal palace, it connected the latter directly to the new south gate. The medieval Castello was itself connected to a gate, but in this new scheme the mode of connection changed significantly: proximity was replaced by axiality. The new formal relation among gate, street, and palace portal heightened the importance of the new artery and demoted the existing streets around it. The importance of the old forum, on which the municipal Palazzo di Città was located, was also diminished by the opening of the new south gate with a direct connection to Piazza Castello, since entering traffic no longer passed by it (fig. 36).

The embellished Piazza Castello was connected in 1619 to the marketplace west of it in front of the Palazzo di Città. The duke himself announced the cutting of this street to the city council in July 1619.[36] Once again, reactions to this intervention confirm the Machiavellian thesis of conflict between municipal interests and state authority. The councilors did not rejoice at the news, ostensibly because the new street cut through municipal property and dimin-

---

35. Carboneri, *Vitozzi,* 140. For the history of urban developments in Turin in the early seventeenth century, see also Mario Passanti, "Le trasformazioni barocche entro l'area della Torino antica," in *Atti del X congresso di storia dell'architettura* (Rome, 1959), 69–100.

36. ASCT, Ordinati, 13 July 1619: "aver inteso per relazione del Signor Paulo Domenico Lodi soprastante alle fabriche di S[ua] A[ltezza] che essa ha fatto far disegno di fare una strada nova per drittura dalla galleria del Castello verso la piazza et palazzo della questa Città."

ished its value.[37] But more important, the new street asserted once again the ducal dominion of Turin. It did this not only by damaging municipal property, but also by humiliating municipal pride, since the duke was acting without the opinion of the council. In addition, by bringing the market within the orbit of Piazza Castello, the new street put city hall under ducal surveillance.

Thus the three streets that radiated from the Piazza Castello were each anchored to a major ducal structure. The oldest of these connections, the Roman *decumanus maximus* or Doragrossa aligned with the Castello, provided the model for Carlo Emanuele's early seventeenth-century additions. The Contrada Nuova, which connected to Palazzo Reale and enhanced its importance by alignment, and the new street connecting the Galleria to the municipal market both reiterate the statement of power established in ancient Roman city planning. The multiplication of this urban form announces the absolutist rule, the historical continuity, and the dynastic single-mindedness of the House of Savoy. Thus rebuilt and clarified, the ducal command center in the northeast corner could function as the counterpart of the military citadel in the southwest corner. These two ducal settlements, diagonally across the city from one another, held Turin prisoner.

THE ESTABLISHMENT of the ducal command center in the northeast corner of Turin was only one aspect of the embellishment of Turin, which had been Carlo Emanuele I's principal local concern ever since he inherited the title and the duchy of Piedmont. As we have seen, his main interest was the enlargement of his realm at the expense of his neighbors—an attitude that departed from the preservationist policy recommended by Botero and involved him in nearly continuous wars during his long reign. We may identify a division in his political ambitions between the unification and improvement of his existing realm, and the improvement of his dynasty through aggressive expansion. His plans for the capital city have likewise a double focus. Though the interventions so far studied in this chapter all lie within the old Roman walls, Carlo Emanuele had probably discussed expansion projects for Turin as early as 1584, at the arrival of Ascanio Vitozzi. Wars and intrigues continued to impede these ambitions, however.

37. Ibid.: "havendo la città alcune case e botteghe quali restano nel sito dove ha da esser detta strada quali converra demolir et indi redifficar la qual demolitione portarà diminutione di reddito a detta città piu di ducatoni tricento annui oltre la spesa della redifficatione."

The duke's ideas regarding urban improvement were made manifest as early as 1584, when he promulgated an edict ordering all those who owned property adjacent to an owner who wanted to enlarge his building to sell upon request, thus encouraging and rewarding the initiatives of wealthier citizens.[38] Despite all his distractions, he was able over the next thirty-five years to evolve a coherent policy of urban improvement and expansion, synthesizing the various agencies that Botero had identified as the shaping forces of the great city. The stated intentions, officially declared only in 1621, were these: to enlarge the capital and to stimulate still further the population growth that began with the return of the dukes of Savoy, to embellish the existing city, and to attract religious orders that would help in the spiritual control of a population with strong Protestant tendencies.[39]

The design projects for the expansion of Turin involved a number of military, aesthetic, and ideological requirements. They were based on two sets of models for city planning, outlined in chapter 1: the sixteenth-century notions of ideal city planning known to practicing Italian architects and their patrons, and the highly developed requirements of strategic military defense. In addition, the expansion plan for Turin had to take into account existing topographical conditions.

As we have seen in chapter 1, the pentagonal fortress was attached to the southwest corner of Turin, whose walled perimeter was an almost perfect square. Since the two regular polygons formed a unified whole, when the moment came to expand Turin it may have been difficult to conceive of the appropriate form for the new city. The earliest expansion plans—those suggested by Vitozzi in the 1580s and 1590s, and those proposed by the court architects Ercole Negro di Sanfront and Carlo di Castellamonte around 1600 and 1612—continued to depend in part on perfect geometrical forms borrowed from Renaissance ideal-city planning. The architects suggested circular or semicircular additions to the existing square and pentagon: the square wall perimeter of Turin was to become curved and the orthogonal grid of streets to be transformed into a radial street system. Together with the practical difficulties it posed, this approach to urban design ran counter to Carlo Emanuele's spirit of dynastic expansion, since its fixed and closed geometric forms did not allow for dynamic growth. By contrast, military requirements called for the enclosure of as much territory as possible with the least number of bastions, since the cost of fortification in construction and maintenance was calculated

38. Borelli, 892.

39. Borelli, 917–19; for the history of Turin's religious institutions, see Tamburini, *passim*.

by the number of bastions needed. The expansion ought not to diminish the ability of the citadel to defend Turin, and it should place the palaces of the ducal family in a centralized location within the street grid. The design of the expansion and the implementation of its parts were to be carried out by military architects and engineers at court. Most of them (Vitozzi, Castella-monte, Negro di Sanfront, Gabrio Busca, Jacopo Soldati) were commissioned officers of the artillery or cavalry in the duke's army. Some, such as Busca, were involved in the theoretical aspects of fortification and engineering.[40] Their assignments and contributions are documented usually in the form of reports on the condition and proposed improvement of existing fortresses in Piedmont, while their interests were made manifest in published or manu-script treatises on military architecture.

Ascanio Vitozzi was aided from 1595 by his nephew Vitozzo, who died before Ascanio, but not before drawing two proposals for the expansion of Turin. In the first, continuing the planning vocabulary of the square castrum and the pentagonal fortress, he proposed a regular polygon with a radiocentric layout of streets (fig. 37). Only marginally adapted to the conditions of the site, it aligned itself well, however, with ideal city planning conceptions. The second solution would have reorganized the perimeter as well as the internal structure of the city by adding a nearly almond-shaped, thirteen-sided fortifi-cation enclosure that would have engulfed the existing walls and citadel (fig. 38). This "engulfing" proposal is unlike the fortification girdle proposed in the third planning study (fig. 39) and in the theoretical works of other military engineers, although de' Marchi, for example, proposed fortifications for poly-gons with four to twenty-two sides (fig. 40).

These early proposals of the 1580s and 1590s were largely abandoned, even though the two Vitozzi predicted accurately—as we shall see in the following chapters—the areas for the future expansion of Turin.[41] This continuity should not be surprising, since Carlo Emanuele I remained close to the design projects throughout the planning process. The earliest seventeenth-century evidence demonstrating that work on Turin's expansion was an ongoing project is a

40. See Scotti, *Vitozzi,* chaps. 5 and 6, and Busca, *Della espugnatione et difesa delle fortezze* (Turin, 1585), dedicated to Carlo Emanuele. See also Soldati, "Discorso intorno al fortificare la città di Torino," AST, Sez. Ia, Materie Militari, mazzo 1, number 3, published in Bruno Signorelli, "Note di architettura militare," *Bollettino della Società piemontese di archeologia e belle arti,* 21 (1969–70): 130–36.

41. For Vitozzo Vitozzi, see Carlo Brayda, "Vitozzo Vitozzi ingegnere militare e alcuni disegni di Torino antica," *Torino,* 19 (1939): 15–19.

payment order of 1612 for a study model and drawing.[42] Neither is extant, but the measurements for them were made by Giorgio Chianale, who, although not an architect or draftsman at court, is mentioned in this payment order, which turns up in the registers of the ducal treasury.

The earliest version of the development plans that led to the actual realization is also the most important, since it appears to be an autograph drawing by Carlo Emanuele himself (fig. 41). A handwritten inscription attributes it to the duke or to his heir, depending on the interpretation accepted for the title "Serenissimo Prencipe." Officially this title was meant for the prince of Piedmont, but Carlo Emanuele—like his successors, including Carlo Emanuele II—was often addressed thus in correspondence and in dedications. Carlo Emanuele's authorship of this drawing is supported by his close personal involvement with artists, architects, and writers, and by the family tradition of direct participation in design. Whether it is from the hand of the duke or Prince Vittorio Amedeo (who had shown himself responsive to urban design and landscape at an early age), this drawing must derive from the innermost circle of the court; it is based upon an earlier ink drawing, probably by Ascanio Vitozzi, showing the fortifications of the existing city and the citadel (fig. 36), which has clearly been used as a template, as the transfer holes and its similarity to subsequent study plans convincingly indicate. The "Serenissimo Prencipe" drawing, crucial evidence for the early conception of the Turin expansions, can be dated with some precision. The commission from Chianale of a study model serves as the *terminus ante quem;* since his work is done directly in the service of the duke it refers to a design not commissioned from or made by any of the court engineers. The *terminus post quem* is 1619, because by that time the site and extent of the expansion were known, even though the official laying of the foundation stone did not take place until the end of 1620, as we shall see in the following chapter. Although very important for the information it provides about the form and direction of the expansion, the fortification shown in this drawing is faulty at least in the connection between the citadel and the south wall: thus it cannot have been drawn by any of the sophisticated military architects at the court.

Carlo Emanuele's plan, as we may safely term it, proposes that Turin be

---

42. AST, Sez. Riunite, art. 207, mazzo 1, R 9, 8 December 1612: "Fabriche diverse devono pagare 156 di D[ucato]ni 22 . . . 13 pagati d'ordine del T[esoriere] Antiochia . . . Giorgio Chianale a bon conto della misura et theppi [drawings] che deve fare dell'agrandimento che vole fare S[ua] A[ltezza] alla questa città come per mand[amen]to di questo giorno con una quitt[anz]a." Also in AST, Sez. Riunite, art. 202, mazzo 1, 1609 in 1612, 26.

expanded in two directions, to the south and eastward to the Po. His drawing clearly outlines the bastioned fortification trace, with two alternative defenses proposed for meeting the river. Also sketched in are two radial streets, one connecting the future Po gate to the Castello, the other linking the same gate to the fortress. This Po-citadel connection occurs only in this drawing, but the other diagonal street, from the river to the Castello, would later become the principal thoroughfare of the expansion completed by Carlo Emanuele's grandson. Through the convergence of two main streets upon it, the Po gate would have become the main node for internal circulation; since this was not in keeping with the desired hierarchy, the connection between the citadel and the Po gate was abandoned. Emphasis was placed on the Piazza Castello as the center from which all the gates could be reached, and which had to be traversed in order to go from one part of the city to another. The fortifications in Carlo Emanuele's plan are likewise not definitive; two alternatives were suggested for the river shore, while the bastions at the southwest corner near the citadel and at the east corner are not well designed and were subsequently changed. In the event, the ten full and the two half-bastions proposed in this plan were realized in two stages, as four for the expansion south and six for the expansion to the east.

This autograph plan for the expansion demonstrates Carlo Emanuele I's vivid interest in the design of Turin; the ascription of an actual expansion study to him does not seem peculiar when one remembers that his father Emanuele Filiberto had also designed fortresses, as we have seen in chapter 1. Despite the convention that such dabbling in the mechanical or fine arts was not worthy of a prince—"since the prince's business was not to design and build fortresses, but to use judiciously those who can provide these services"[43]—Carlo Emanuele personally took part in the embellishment and fortification of his capital city, and was praised by Marino for it since his involvement had a demonstrably classical background:

> Hor con Euclide, hor con Vitruvio tratta
> Di Forte, ò di città la pianta, e'l sito.
> Hor come il muro hostil s'assaglia, e batta
> Con Vegetio, e Frontin prende partito.

43. Giovanni Botero, *Della reputazione del Prencipe* (Rome, 1598), and *Ragione di stato,* 53: "Perche l'ufficio suo non è di fabricar ponti, e macchine di guerra, . . . non di disegnare, o edificar fortezze; ma di servirsi giudiciosamente di quei, che fanno professione di tutte queste cose." See also chap. 1, note 16.

E'n varie corna, e'n varie fronti apprende
Partir le schiere, e trincerar le tende.
(*Il Ritratto*, stanza 166)

Now he discusses in turn with Euclid and with Vitruvius the plan and site of
fortress and city, now engages Vegetius and Frontinus in siege strategy; he
thus learns on various fronts how to lay siege and defend the camp.

He maintained the tradition of employing numerous military architects, established by Emanuele Filiberto. But his military architects were employed on a
wide range of projects; architects such as Vitozzi and Castellamonte could design festival and stage sets, interiors of buildings, and ideal-city plans, as well
as fortification. Through his patronage of prolific writers, Carlo Emanuele
ensured that widespread publicity would be provided for his building efforts.
Thus even before the great project for Turin got under way, Marino could
already associate Carlo Emanuele's munificence with his gifts of fine buildings
made to his city:

TORO felice, e fortunato, hor questa
E del bennato Heroe la patria sede.
Città, ch'oltra le belle erge la testa,
Ma se bene in beltà cotanto eccede,
Pur di tempi, e palagi altera in vista
Nove dal suo Signor bellezze acquista.
(*Il Ritratto*, stanza 55)

Happy and fortunate bull [Turin], you are now the homeland of the blessed
hero, city that already exceeds others in beauty, continuously receives new
palaces and churches as adornments from its lord.

Simultaneously, the graphic documents regarding the construction of Turin
that date from the beginning of Carlo Emanuele I's reign show the elaborate
and original thinking of the ruler and his architects. The transformation of the
center of power, the fusion of the ideals of sixteenth-century city planning
with military concerns, and the establishment of the directions for Turin's enlargement in the seventeenth century were achieved between 1585 and 1619. It
is during this relatively brief period that the characteristics of Turin as we
know it today were successfully outlined.

3

The Making of a Baroque Capital

Fortification and Urban Design as Instruments of Dynastic Representation

Non abbracci molte imprese d'importanza in un tempo:
perche, chi molto abbraccia, poco stringe.
　　　—Botero, *Ragione di stato*

WHILE THE RECONSTRUCTION of the ducal palace, the conceptualization of the Piazza Castello as ducal forecourt, and the opening of the Contrada Nuova as ducal *stradone* were taking place within the Roman walls, the duke and his group of military architects and engineers were planning the outward expansion of the city. As we have seen, the intentions of the expansionary interest were most clearly expressed in the duke's own drawing of c. 1612–19 (fig. 41). According to this planning study, Turin was to be extended not only to the south, but also east towards the Po. This autograph plan determined the growth of the city for the rest of the century. Despite interruptions, retrenchments, and conflicts, by the end of the seventeenth century Turin had been enlarged as Carlo Emanuele I had intended. The adhesion of successive ruling members of the House of Savoy to this early expansion plan suggests that the embellishment and enlargement of the capital was a continuous objective of the ducal and royal ideological programs. The extension of the city south and east fulfilled symbolic and strategic requirements. The expansion area to the south could be defended by the citadel, while proximity to the Po was to assure the city's provisioning and rescue during siege. The expansion in both directions brought formerly rural ducal villas, like Valentino, Moncalieri, Mirafiori, and Villa della Regina, closer within the orbit of the city. The proximity to the Po River was to reestablish an ancient link between Turin and the largest of the rivers that surround it.

Carlo Emanuele's conception, illustrated in his autograph plan, established the royal vision for Turin. It represents a striking advance beyond the geometrically regular but impractical ideal-city plans proposed by Ascanio and Vitozzo Vitozzi. His intention, synthesizing Botero's theories of the city with his own dynastic and political requirements, was to reconcile civic magnificence with military strategy and display, and to create a monumental capital. The key elements of this urbanistic ideal were the citadel, the command center, and the two new gates—at the southern edge of the city and at the Po. The importance of these key elements is underlined by the diagonal streets that connect them in the duke's plan. Linking these key sites and buildings strategically to one another, they superimposed a radial street system over an orthogonal street plan.[1]

The specific form of the new enlargement is known to us from a drawing attributed to Carlo di Castellamonte, made c. 1615–19 and probably intended as the "official" plan (fig. 42). An entire block had been set aside for the church and monastery of San Carlo, and since this institution was founded in 1619 it provides a *terminus ante quem* for the official plan.[2] The parceling of the blocks indicates that along the principal street of the expansion area residential construction had begun, as confirmed in the *Ordinati* of 1620, in contrast with the blocks near the citadel, which were used as gardens or remained unoccupied.[3] The grid of orthogonal streets east and south of the existing city—now the Città Vecchia—was derived from the checkerboard street layout of the Roman castrum. This official plan differed from the drawing attributed to Carlo Emanuele I in three particulars: in the larger area enclosed, in the more continuous curved outline of the perimeter of the fortification, and in the better designed connection between the south wall and the citadel (not unlike figure 39). A semicircular expansion to the north, enclosing little territory considering the large expense of three bastions, was not practical and may well be the remnant of ideal-city planning ideas, proposed in the 1590s by the Vitozzi, which had lost their prescriptive force by the time the expansion commenced.

The design for fortifications indicated near the Po bridge shows two alternatives: a large enclosure with a trident of diagonal streets emanating from the

1. Similar linkages were implemented by Sixtus V in Rome in the 1580s. For the most recent study of Sixtus' planning for Rome, see Stefano Borsi, *Roma di Sisto V, la pianta di Antonio Tempesta, 1593* (Rome, 1986).

2. Tamburini, 121–27.

3. ASCT, Ordinati, 7 December 1620: "havendo il Ser[enissimo] Carlo Emanuele per gra[tia] di Dio Duca di Savoia nostro Sig[no]re sin dall'anno mille sei cento diece nove fatto dar principio et designato il sito nel qual si ha da fabricar la città nova fuori et apresso la p[rese]nte città vecchia verso mezo giorno et levante nel qual sito molti particolari hanno fatto fabriche et tuttavia se ne vano cominciando et fabricando."

Po gate towards the Castello and the southern expansion area, and a more restricted version. Each plan had its advocates among the ducal architects. The latter was championed by Ercole Negro di Sanfront and his assistant Carlo Morello, who also provided architectural designs for small ducal projects in Turin.[4] Ercole Negro di Sanfront (1541–1622) is the least well documented of the numerous planners of Turin. Of Piedmontese origin, he served in the French army of Henri III before entering the service of Carlo Emanuele I, who ennobled him in 1589. An architect, engineer, and officer, he became general of artillery in 1604, and then superintendent of artillery. Promis' observation that he was an excellent draftsman is borne out by his carefully delineated views and perspectives of cities and fortresses (fig. 43), of which several have survived in the bound albums of military drawings first collected by Emanuele Filiberto and augmented by his successors.[5] But between 1600 and 1604, and again between 1619 and 1622, he was governor of Savigliano. Thus, even if he participated in the early discussions regarding the expansion, he was absent from Turin in the crucial years of the laying of the foundation stone for the expansion.

The larger version of the expansion was advocated by Carlo di Castella-monte, the probable draftsman of the "official" plan who had been Ascanio Vitozzi's assistant and the supervisor of his work after Vitozzi's death. Belong-ing to the Cognengo branch of the counts of Castellamonte, Carlo di Castel-lamonte was ducal engineer (1615), member of the Magistrato delle Fabriche (1621), superintendent of fortresses, councilor of state, and lieutenant of artil-lery (1637). Neither Castellamonte nor Sanfront seems to have had a signifi-cant professional training, but, though Castellamonte's theoretical training was sketchy, he did have a master in Vitozzi. He visited Rome briefly in 1605, perhaps to supervise the construction of the church commissioned by the con-fraternity of the Santissimo Sudario.[6] He also made a fundamental contribu-tion to the urbanism of Turin, to the military landscape of Piedmont, and to the development of the local palace type. His role as liaison between the duke

4. For Sanfront and Morello see Carlo Promis in *Miscellanea di Storia Italiana*, 12 (1871): 591–602, 477–79. Morello's drawings are in his "Avvertimenti sopra le fortezze di S[ua] A[ltezza] R[eale]," BRT, MS Coll. Saluzzo, Militari 177. For both architects see also Carlo Brayda et al., *Ingegneri et architetti del sei e settecento in Piemonte* (Turin, 1963), 51–52.

5. AST, Sez. Ia, Architettura militare, 3:fols. 20, 56–57, 59–60, 113.

6. See Camillo Boggio, *Gli architetti Carlo ed Amedeo di Castellamonte e lo sviluppo edilizio di Torino nel secolo XVII* (Turin, 1895); L. Collobi, "Carlo di Castellamonte primo ingegnere del Duca di Savoia," *Bollettino storico-bibliografico subalpino*, 39 (1937): 232–63; and *Schede Vesme*, 1: 291–94.

and the city council in matters of construction was greatly appreciated by both sides, and he received numerous ducal commissions and honors.

Since Vitozzi died before 1619, his contribution to the actual expansion was not direct. However, the urban projects designed by him for the Piazza Castello and completed by Carlo di Castellamonte established a precedent that provided cues for the design of the larger expansion. The dry and static Vitozzian architectural vocabulary served well in large-scale projects, and Castellamonte was able to enliven it through the admixture of Palladian ideas. Castellamonte's achievement in urban design is his seamless blending of the seemingly mutually exclusive objectives of city planning and fortification. His city planning was orderly, economical, and disciplined, the hallmarks of military architecture. His work of fortification had a strong aesthetic component and exceeded his architectural concerns in the amount of time that he dedicated to it, and in its importance for the duchy.[7]

ALTHOUGH THE foundation stone was officially placed only in December 1620, the fact that the duke intended to begin the expansion of Turin was public knowledge by the beginning of 1619, the year when—as we have seen—construction of houses commenced in the area south and east of the Roman walls. The immediate choice of 1619 as commencement date was due to the wedding ceremony of Carlo Emanuele's heir Vittorio Amedeo, the prince of Piedmont, to Henri IV's second daughter Cristina. As with the double wedding of 1608, this family event exteriorized the dynastic ideology of the ruling house by incorporating the temporary festive architecture of the wedding into the urban composition of the capital. This alliance, negotiated in January 1619 by Cardinal Maurizio, the bridegroom's younger brother, was part of Carlo Emanuele's complicated relations with the French crown. The construction of celebrative temporary structures in preparation for the triumphal reception of the newlyweds served as a catalyst for the commencement of the expansion.

After their arrival from France in December 1619 the couple waited in

7. Versed in hydraulics—as seen from his extant manuscript "Parere sopra la fabrica dell'imbocatura da farsi al naviglio che scorre da Ivrea a Vercelli" (1616), BRT, MS Coll. Saluzzo, Militari—he was also responsible for the rebuilding of Verrua, Momigliano, and Savigliano. Although these three major fortresses have been destroyed, they are portrayed in seventeenth-century engravings. For Palladian elements in Castellamonte's design of Piazza Reale, see chap. 5.

Chieri for the staging of their official entry into Turin, which took place only on 15 March 1620. While the court was in a flurry of preparations, the royal couple had already had a taste of Savoy hospitality in Moncenisio. There a staged naval battle on the subject of Amedeo IV of Savoy rescuing Rhodes—the event alluded to in the motto "FERT" ("Fortitudo Eius Rhodum Tenuit"), which is the House of Savoy's battle cry and the literary part of the *impresa* of the Order of the Annunziata—was fought on the mountain lake for their delight.[8] With this first welcome, Cristina thus received her initial lesson in the dynastic history of the House of Savoy. The forced residence in Chieri was enlivened by incognito visits into Turin, and then amply rewarded by the definitive wedding reception.[9] Following an established Italian tradition for solemn entries, a majestic avenue was prepared for their welcome. In Turin the need for ceremonial gates and triumphal arches provided an incentive to build the gate outside the existing walls and thus commence the expansion. This outer gate, Porta Nova, was placed at the south end of the extended Contrada Nuova, the street on axis with the portal of the ducal palace that had been opened by Vitozzi in 1615. This extended Contrada Nuova became eventually the principal north-south artery of the southern expansion area. The importance of the triumphal entry sequence lay in its duplication of gateways: the inner gate—an opening in the southern Roman wall of Turin—stood at the

8. "Tutti i propositi che si sentono alla Corte sono di feste et altri trattenimenti, et pare che poco si curi gli altri andamenti del mondo," cited in *Feste Reali*, 9–10; for the mock naval battle, see *Feste Reali*, 24, and Claude-François Menestrier, *Traité des tournois, ioustes, carousels et autres spectacles publics* (Lyon, 1669), 58–59: "Au passage de Madame Chrestienne de France, épouse de Victor Amedée Prince de Piémont Charles Emanuel Duc de Savoye, père de ce Prince, luy fit donner sur le Montcénis un divertissement agréable, sur le lac qui est au dessus de cette montagne, où il fait representer le secours de Rhodes, donné autrefois par Amedée IV surnomée le Grand. Il y a presque au milieu de ce lac une petite isle, dont on se servit pour représenter la ville de Rhodes, et la Princesse ayant disné dans la sale d'un grand bâtiment fait exprès sur cette montagne pour la recevoir, elle vit de l'une des fenetres quatre armées rangées au bataille, deux sur mer, et deux sur terre, deux des Turcs et deux des Chrestiens, où l'on voyoit briller les aigles de Savoye, avec les croix blanches des chevaliers de Rhodes [and the arms of Savoy]. On fit les attaques sur l'eau, et sur terre avec des defys particuliers, et des décharges agréables." The Annunziata is the higher of the two orders awarded by the dukes of Savoy.

9. BAV, MS Barberini Latini 1088, fol. 18, 8 January 1620: "et di Turino avvisano che volendo pure la Ser[enissi]ma Prencipessa sposa veder Turino si era andata incognita col Prencipe suo marito, e tornatasene poi l'estesso giorno a Chieri per aspettare che siano all'ordine gli appartam[en]ti nuovi, li param[en]ti delle stanze, e le livree destinate per la sua solenne entrata in quella città."

end of the realized segment of Contrada Nuova, while the new gate, Porta Nova, was built on axis with this inner portal to mark the southern edge of the future expansion. For the reception of Cristina the outer gate was built of wood and canvas, as was customary for state entries, theaters, and other temporary structures.

An accurate description of this ephemeral gate, to be built of solid materials within the year, can be found in figure 44, while the constitutive parts of the permanent gate are listed in the contract that the city council made with the stone-carvers who undertook to build it.[10] In contrast with the city walls, which were the property and the concern of the ruling duke, the gates were under the jurisdiction of the city council. The council's minutes show the conflict between the builders and the civic representatives over the cost of the gate. Since the payments did not come from the ducal treasury, the duke had proposed a sumptuous marble gate, which was not to cost more than 2,000 *ducatoni*.[11] The council successfully challenged the enormously enlarged bill presented eventually by the builders, reducing it by one-third—from 6,300 *ducatoni* to 4,395 *ducatoni*—with the aid of Carlo di Castellamonte, who helped in making an estimate of construction costs.[12] The gate was finished in 1621, built of marble and decorated with the arms desired by the duke. The design for the gate had been prepared by Carlo di Castellamonte, who monitored the

10. ASCT, Ordinati, 15 January 1621. There are two lists of elements, one presented by the contractor Nicola Ramello, the other by the hired estimator Giacomo Fontana. The latter is closer to the engraved version of the gate, listing three inscriptions rather than two, and it provides the value of each part in greater detail.

11. The wording of the final contract between the city and the gate's contractors is: "Havendo S[ua] A[ltezza] ordinato et comandato che si face una porta nova fuori della città verso mezzogiorno ove detta S[ua] A[ltezza] intende agrandir la città et habbi comandato che la città faci la spesa di d[ett]a porta et paghi la fattura di essa si dalle pietre di marmore che ogn'altra cosa" (ASCT, Ordinati, 15 January 1621); while initially Carlo Emanuele had personally instructed the councilors that "dovendosi far la porta nova desideravo che la città facesse le spese et quanto prima se non poteva di marmore almeno di pietra negra et se non poteva di pietra negra almeno di mattoni et in cio non dovesse metter difficoltà . . . esser anco necessario la città faci li archi trionfanti per detta venuta di Madama Ser[enissi]ma," while the entire "spesa non eccedeva ducatoni due mille" (ASCT, Ordinati, 7 April 1619).

12. ASCT, Ordinati, 15 January 1621: "havendo rimostrato con raggioni aparenti detta dimanda esser essorbitante et che la città intendeva far venir esperti da Venetia e Roma per far l'estimo sudetto credendo aver pagato forse piu di quello sara detta opera estimata manco come la città pretende sara vergogna habbino chiamato somma cosi eccessiva et habbino voluto ingannar la città o haver poco cognitione dell'opera et finalmente detti capitani si sono risolti finirla per non perdervi piu tempo et si sono contentati."

construction. The effort was noted almost immediately by the prince of Condé who wrote, after visiting Turin in 1622, that "at the entry to the city there is a very beautiful gate with a Latin inscription about the marriage of the Prince with Madame, daughter of the King of France."[13] Traditionally gates were the only part of a town's fortification to receive extensive architectural ornament, as though to compensate for their inherent weakness through lavish decoration; the walls of the fortification, in contrast, had at best a decorative cornice or parapet. The gate was a support for the temporary inscriptions and statues placed upon it, which illustrated the dynastic and religious claims of the House of Savoy. There were stone statues of the city's protector saints, and the arms of France and Savoy. The definitive inscription on the Porta Nova, also known as Vittoria, praised Carlo Emanuele, whose magnificence as ruler and heroism as military leader had been extended in order to welcome the newlywed prince of Piedmont and his French bride: "The council and the people of Turin dedicate the gate to Carlo Emanuele, duke of Savoy, who, after defending the freedom of the nation with arms—paying for peace with war—consolidated the security of the state with the matrimony of his son with the most Christian Cristina of France, and built for their arrival a new city, while restoring the magnificence of the old one."[14] This inscription officially marks the southern part of the expansion as the *nova urbs*, and it came to be known as Città Nuova. A third, but temporary, gateway—in the form of a triumphal arch—was built for the ceremonial entry south of Porta Nova and thus outside the limits of the expansion area. The road between this triumphal arch and the new southern gate was flanked by statues representing the principal regions and towns of the duchy.[15] Most important, the Porta Nova served as a symbolic foundation

13. Condé, *Voyage*, 6: "A l'entré y a un portail très beau, où est ensuite une inscription latine concernant le mariage du Prince avec Madame fille de France."

14. Carolo Emanueli Sab[audiae] Duci
    Quod libertate armis vindicata
    Pace bello parta securitate pub[lica]
    Victoris Ameddei F[ilii] et Christianae
    Christianiss[imae] coniugio firmata
    in eorum adventu
    Novam urbem instituerit et
    antiquam illustrarit.
    S.P.Q.T. An[no]M.DC.XX. (*Theatrum*, 1:fol. 30)

15. ASCT, Ordinati, 15 March 1620: "esservi fatto un arco trionfante poco discosto da d[ett]a porta della Città Nova con molte statue e altri pomposi ornamenti et inscrittioni et dal d[ett]o arco sino alla porta di detta Città Nova da ambi li latti della strada messe molte

stone for the entire southern expansion project, giving it the impetus and cred-
ibility necessary for the actual start.

According to the description of the event in the documents of the city council, the inner gate was flanked by gigantic effigies of Beroldo and Emanuele
Filiberto, respectively the most ancient and the most recent ancestor of the
ruling family. The elevations of the Contrada Nuova and of the Piazza Castello, already complete by the time of the royal wedding with rows of uniform
buildings, were decorated with tapestries and the windows filed with throngs
of people. The facade of the old ducal palace had also been restored, and its
numerous niches were filled for the occasion with statues. The palace gate was
flanked by eight statues of emperors; the Castello's entry portal was guarded
by four statues, two representing the Emperor Charles V and Emanuele Filiberto of Savoy.[16] Many other sculptures were placed above the Castello. Although not reliable for an appraisal of the quality of the objects displayed, the
minutes of the city council may represent accurately the number of statues
employed. This display of sculpture gives a hint of the extensive collection
owned by Carlo Emanuele, as well as the rich, stage-like effect intended for
the outdoor festivities.

The sequence of enclosures that the princely couple passed through had
become the traditional monuments of a *possesso* procession: a triumphal arch
upholding the family claims, a road flanked by the representation of the family
properties, a first outer gate surrounded by patron saints, and a second inner
gate displaying the images of famed family ancestors. The city councilors, and
the entire Piedmont militia, welcomed the prince of Piedmont and his bride
under a baldachin at the inner gate, while the military governor of Turin con-
ferred upon them the keys to the city.[17] Passing through the uniform and viv-

---

statue significanti et rapresentanti li statti, provincie et principali città del dominio di S[ua]
A[ltezza]."

16. Ibid.: "Poco discoste dal ponte di d[ett] a porta messevi l'effigie di Beroldo gigante da
quale dicesa la Ser[enissi]ma Casa di Savoia et l'invitissimo Em[anuele] Filliberto ambi a
cavallo in forma di giganti . . . si entrava nella Contrada nova fabricata tutta uniforme et le
finestre delle case di d[ett]a strada nova tutte erano ornate di richi tapeti et occupate da
gentilhuomini e gentildonne e giungendo alla piazza castello fatta di novo quadra circondata
di fabriche anco uniforme et di molte statue diverse. . . . il palazzo di S[ua] A[ltezza] vechio
ristaurato con la faciata tutta fatta a nichie et ogni nichia una statua di marmore et dalli canti
della porta del detto palazzo otto statue d'Imperatori. . . . et alla porta del castello inanti
quattro statue due di Carlo Quinto Imperatore et Emanuel Filliberto di Savoia et altri due
Imperatori."

17. Ibid.: "D[ett]a città fece far a sue spese un baldachino . . . di sei bastoni per recevergli

idly decorated Contrada Nuova the procession arrived at the well-defined Piazza Castello, which, with its decorations, statues and tapestries, resembled an outdoor stage. According to Emanuele Tesauro, this enclosure symbolized the union of urban, rural, and national concerns; the city was transformed into a garden by means of theatrical decoration, but that garden in turn represented the Piedmontese state.[18]

The tournament with which the wedding was celebrated in Piazza Castello has been portrayed in a painting by Antonio Tempesta (fig. 45). Looking at the piazza from the south, we are presented with the uniform residential buildings designed by Vitozzi at the western edge of the square, and at the east with the decorated facade of the Castello—designed and rebuilt for the occasion by the court architect Carlo Morello—whose center was occupied by the royal box. The facade of Palazzo Reale is largely masked by a pavilion raised upon an arcade to the level of the surrounding palaces' *piani nobili*. The arcade separates the square immediately in front of the ducal palace—still occupied by a motley group of houses and the ducal foundry—from Piazza Castello proper, and is in turn partly masked from it by a series of hills that rise to the pavilion's center, while below an arched passage has been kept open. The square is filled with spectators and horsemen in ceremonial parade attire, some jousting and some watching. In the foreground, his splayed legs arched to form an entry into the square, stands the immense figure of a giant—an allusion to the Colossus of Rhodes (who became part of Vittorio Amedeo's iconography) as well as to the ancestor Beroldo; armed and palpably ready for combat, it presided over the tilt. Its scale was commensurate with the hill and pavilion at the other end of Piazza Castello, thus making a connection between the two ends of the square.

Antonio Tempesta (1555–1630) was a Florentine view painter, trained by Stradano, who had been part of the Farnese entourage, working on the fresco cycle at Caprarola and the Horti Farnesiani, and then among the painters em-

---

sotto luoro Altezze Ser[enissi]me . . . fuori della porta della città nova ove erano tutte le militie di Piemonte circa vinti cinque milla fanti . . . tutta la cavalleria in numero circa di tre milla cavalli . . . l'Ill[ustrissi]mo Sig[no]r Gaspar Purpurato cavaglier Gran Croce et Governator della città in compagnia di detti Sig[no]ri Sindici . . . presento le chiavi della città alla Ser[enissi]ma Madama."

18. *Il cannocchiale aristotelico* (1654), 2d. ed. (1670; rpt. Berlin, 1968), 56–57: "Tutta la Piazza era un Giardino, dove col Febraio scherzava Aprile; e negli horrori del verno rideva Flora. Le barriere dello steccato, erano siepi; che tirate in quadri e diagonali; frondavano di fresche verdure instelate di fiori . . . peroche il Giardino metaforicamente rappresentava il Piemonte; chiamato apunto dagli antiqui Storiografi Giardin dell'Italia."

ployed by Gregory XIII in decorating the Vatican palace. Excluded from papal patronage by Sixtus V, he retreated into private commissions and became a practitioner of the "pittura dell'utile," as remarked by Giovanni Paleotti in 1582. His oeuvre—for patrician families such the Massimo, Colonna, and Giustiniani—included hunting, battle, and siege scenes, and descriptions of cities and the countryside.[19] He developed an interest in engraving in the last decade of the sixteenth century, and executed a view of Piazza Castello in Turin during the exhibition of the Holy Shroud on 4 May 1613 (fig. 29). Showing the piazza thronged with visitors, it illustrates the elaborate events of an intensely religious life that paralleled the worldly and brilliant parties of the court. This work shows familiarity with Turin's main public space, and its tendency to regularize Vitozzi's buildings produces a wonderfully coherent architectural frame for the great crowds. The multitude surrounds the pavilion—centrally placed in front of the Castello—upon which the Shroud is exhibited; the balconies of Vitozzi's uniform residences are overflowing with more privileged spectators. Tempesta must have pleased the duke's self-image and confirmed the ducal vision of Turin; his works were abundantly represented in the royal collections.[20] Just as Tempesta the artist managed to join the beautiful to the useful, so Carlo Emanuele's talent, Tesauro declared, was equally displayed in military strategy and *festa* design, since the same *ingegno* was required for both.[21]

The theme of the equestrian joust represented in Tempesta's view is amply discussed by Tesauro, who was himself one of the principal *feste* organizers for the House of Savoy in the seventeenth century. At the wedding festivities of 1620, each jouster fought for his belief that the flower—the lady—loved by

19. Borsi quotes from Paleotti's *Discorso sopra le immagini sacre e profane* (Bologna, 1582), a significant text for the imagery and iconography of Counter-Reformation Italian art (*Roma di Sisto V*, 22–23).

20. See the 1631 inventory of the ducal art collection in Giuseppe Campori, *Raccolta di cataloghi ed inventarii inediti* (Modena, 1870); among Tempesta's works were the map of Rome (79), battle scenes (87, 89, 90, 93), and a hunt scene (88). According to Ada Peyrot, *Torino nei secoli* (Turin, 1965), 1:11–13, Tempesta's view of Piazza Castello of 1613 (fig. 29) was altered between the first and third state in order to replace the form of address in the dedicatory part of the text (Serenissimo Signore, Serenissima Casa, Serenissima Persona) with royal titles (Altezza Reale, Real Casa, etc.).

21. *Cannocchiale*, 56: "essendo opera degna del medesimo ingegno, il sapere ordinare una battaglia, et una festa." See also Jean Vanuxem, "Le baroque en Piémont: Fêtes, emblèmes, devises au XVIIe siècle," in *Renaissance Maniérisme Baroque: Actes du XIe stage international de Tours* (Paris, 1972), 289–99, for an analysis of the moral doctrine and high concepts dissimulated in princely festivities.

him was the most beautiful; thus the great garden, the scene for this contest, was appropriate for the theme, metaphorically representing a Piedmont in which spring battled with winter. The hills forming the background were the representation of the alpine peaks that surround Piedmont, with Turin's rivers (Po, Dora, and Stura) pouring down their slopes.[22] After the joust the entire setting was torn down and torched ("ogni cosa ne andò in fiamme di gioia"), the rivers of water exhaled fire ("i Fiumi versanti acqua, esalarono fuoco"), and Vulcan seemed to have snatched away the entire garden ("tutto il Giardino parve da Vulcano à gran volo rapito in Cielo"). This entire *festa* was conceived by Carlo Emanuele, who had chosen as his conceit the *pensiero*, which means both "pansy" and "thought." As Tesauro explains, this signifies that even in witty amusements the duke was always meditating upon the art of *imprese*, emblematic devices that succinctly express the essence of a thought or event; the word is also used in the edicts for the "enterprise" of expanding Turin. In fact, Carlo Emanuele composed many of the *imprese* connected with this *festa* as well as beginning an ambitious expansion program for Turin, as if to refute Botero's sardonic advice that "he who embraces many important *imprese* at once accomplishes few." On the contrary, the *festa equestre*—as well as the expansion of Turin—was used by Carlo Emanuele to further his dynastic messages, "silently alluding to some heroic and noble thought" and visually referring to Piedmont's ancient definition as the Garden of Italy and its link to Rhodes, the bedrock of Savoy kingship. By stimulating the spectators to decode his allegory, Tesauro concludes, Carlo Emanuele's conceits "ad un tempo ricreano, et ammaestrano li veditori"; they simultaneously please and instruct, thus controlling the viewers.[23]

The mental dexterity required in transforming the city into a garden representative of the entire nation was part of the cultivation of erudite wit, of the *argutezza* lauded by Tesauro and assiduously pursued at the Savoy court. Although his father had scorned the historian and epigraphist Paolo Giovio, we know that Carlo Emanuele was so taken with emblems, and so pleased with Ripa's *Iconologia*, that he presented the author with the order of San Maurizio e San Lazzaro, after which Ripa was always known as "Cavagliere."[24] Carlo

---

22. Tesauro, *Cannocchiale*, 57: "La chiusura figurava le Alpi, con le imagini di tutti i Fiumi, che da que' bianchi gioghi in questa verde falda serpeggiano."

23. Ibid., 56–57: "tacitamente alludenti à qualche heroico et honorato pensiero . . . potendo ciascuno degli Spettatori, compresa la radice, penetrar tutta l'Allegoria et goderne"; Botero, *Ragione di stato*, 63 (cited as the epigraph to this chapter).

24. Edward Maser, ed., *Cesare Ripa: Baroque and Rococo Pictorial Images* (New York, 1971), ix: "The first edition of the *Iconologia* [Rome, 1593] ... was received with great enthusiasm;

Emanuele, who had started a treatise (*De Regnorum Exordiis*) proposing to trace the history of monarchy "a Proto-parente Adamo," commissioned Tesauro to compose a series of elegies of the patriarchs and popes, a work eventually completed in 1643.[25] Carlo Emanuele's taste for refined entertainments woven through with breathtaking surprises had been manifested at his own wedding in 1585 to the Spanish infanta, Caterina. Based on concepts of change, inconstance, and delusory appearance, as well as a thorough immersion in metamorphic ostentation, the wedding arrangements were filled with images and objects that revealed themselves to be illusions. The bride boarded a boat on the Po near Turin that took her to an island; there the trompe l'oeil rocks unexpectedly became sailors who set sail to the island, now also a boat. Another rock on the island opened, revealing a great buffet laden with mouth-watering fruit, preserves and liquors—which, alas, were of silk and feathers, but then a gust of wind blew them away revealing the real fruit beneath. The goddess of Love was meanwhile singing in Italian, and Echo was replying in Spanish. These court festivities were political metaphors and *imprese* that had come to life, spectacles intended to edify the participants, and were considered as "allegories de l'estat."[26] Even in his early years, then, Carlo Emanuele was keenly interested in theatrical effects. He joined this absorption to his vested

---

it apparently filled a long-standing need. Duke Charles Emanuel of Savoy was so taken with it that he presented the author with the Order of the Sts. Mauritius and Lazarus, after which Ripa was always referred to as 'Cavagliere'." See also Giovanni Botero, *Detti memorabili di personaggi illustri* (Turin, 1608), 12–13: "Emanuel Filiberto . . . veggendo le guerre, e l'imprese de'suoi tempi, scritte molto diversamente de quel, ch'egli medesimo haveva visto, chiamava l'historie favole, e ne faceva pocchisimo conto, e non si degnò di dar à Paolo Giovio qualche somma di denari, il che fù cagione, che egli non ne facesse nelle sue historie mentione." Despite this snub, Giovio, bishop of Nocera, was the author of several widely read works, most notably *Dialogo dell'imprese militare et amorose* (Rome, 1555). The copious Renaissance literature on *imprese* is given a compelling reading by Robert Klein; see "The Theory of Figurative Expression in Italian Treatises on the *Impresa*," in his collection of essays *Form and Meaning* (Princeton, 1979), 3–24.

25. John Sparrow, *Visible Words: A Study of Inscriptions in and as Books and Works of Art* (Cambridge, 1969), 119–20; Tesauro published his elegies, to patriarchs only, in his *Inscriptiones* (Turin, 1666).

26. The term is from Menestrier, *Traité des tournois*, quoted in *Feste Reali*, 11; Jean Rousset discusses the 1585 wedding in *La littérature de l'âge baroque en France: Circé et le paon* (Paris, 1953), 19–30, drawing on Menestrier's *Des Représentations en musique anciennes et modernes* (Paris, 1681), which lists Savoy festivities mounted between 1608 and 1657. Rousset considers in detail representations of intermittence, mobility, metamorphosis, and ostentation in Baroque theater and literature.

interest in urban design and architecture, and among the results was the conception of urban architecture as an instrument of popular persuasion. Although not itself a novel concept—Nicholas V's "Renovatio Urbis" in Rome was conceived as a *Biblia pauperum*[27]—it was to be realized through the dynastic drive of the Savoy and their highly evolved fascination with the meanings that could be attached to all aspects of human activity and production.

The reception provided by the court and the city was elaborate and well attended, although dubious means were adopted in order to increase the multitudes. Two weeks later an *avviso* announced maliciously in Rome that "from Turin we hear of the solemn entry there of Her Highness the bride, who was met by great numbers of foot soldiers and cavalry; and for this prisoners had been freed, and bandits allowed to return, and suchlike," proving that no means were considered unusable when a large crowd was needed.[28] Although the Porta Nuova was not actually finished until January 1621—the payment for its builders was contested by the city council, as we have seen—the presence of these large crowds and the prestige of the arrival of a new princess of Piedmont must have acted, nonetheless, as pressure on the city council, and on all involved in the construction. The events also prompted faster completion of buildings around the Piazza Castello and along the Contrada Nuova.

The ceremonial entry of 15 March 1620 established the location of Porta Nova (fig. 46), and thus the edge of Turin's expansion to the south. On 7 December 1620, Carlo Emanuele rather blithely summoned the city council to participate, on the very same day, in the formal laying of the foundation stone and the benediction of the expansion.[29] The procession consisted of the councilors, the clergy of the cathedral, and courtiers, and was preceded by six flagbearers carrying the images of the six saints after whom the bastions of the Città Nuova were to be named.[30] The elegance and the excitement of this

27. Florence Vuilleumier, "La Rhétorique du monument, l'inscription dans l'architecture en Europe au XVIIe siècle," *XVIIe Siècle*, 39 (1987): 304.

28. BAV, MS Barberini Latini 1088, 28 March 1620, fol. 195: "Si ha da Turino la solenne entrata fatta ivi dalla Ser[enissi]ma Prencipessa sposa incontrata da grand[issi]mo n[umer]o di soldati a piedi, et a cavallo, et erano percio stati liberati prigioni, rimessi banditi, e simili."

29. ASCT, Ordinati, 7 December 1620: "S[ua] A[ltezza] con facie allegra e segno di amore ha detto le formali parole: Io vorrei che la città honorasse questa mia attione qual intendo di far oggi et venisse in corpo come osserva nelle processioni trovarsi ad accompagnar et assister alla benedittione della città nova et veder metter la prima pietra per fondamenta della muraglia di d[ett]a città."

30. Ibid.: "Et inanti detta processione et clero precedevano sei gentilhuomini con una bandiera per caduno ove erano depinti San Mauritio, San Carlo, Beato Amedeo, San Tom-

festive event, joining the civic and the religious duties of the city's administration, are paralleled perhaps by the cavalcade in figure 47, where behind Carlo Emanuele's equestrian portrait we see the 1572 view of Turin and a long procession that sinuously approaches the city. Since the same document informs us that the excavation for the foundation of the new fortifications has already begun, the ceremony for the laying of the foundation stone ought to be seen as further publicity for the expansion project and as a way of involving those religious interests that Botero had identified as essential to the well-founded state.[31]

THE WEDDING *possesso* and the ceremonial laying of the foundation stone thus made public the intention of Carlo Emanuele I to enlarge Turin. His planning study and those of his military architects and engineers established the form of the expansion, and thus of the future Turin. In keeping with the suggestions of Botero, he also sought to realize the desired expansion through two parallel series of edicts. The intention of one set of these was to regulate the building industry by controlling construction materials and the labor force. Through the second series of edicts the crown wanted to attract settlers to Città Nuova, thus providing both builders and inhabitants for the expansion area.

In an edict of 10 March 1621, Carlo Emanuele I established the *Magistrato delle Fabriche*, and appointed its first councilors; their high social status and architectural expertise reflected the importance he attached to this agency.[32]

---

maso, Santa Cristina et Catherina quali bandiera S[ua] A[ltezza] ha commandato si mettano sopra li luoghi ove si devono fabricar le bastioni."

31. Ibid.: "Volendo S[ua] A[ltezza] R[eale] che detta nova città si vadi fabricando et renderla popolata mostrando di questo gran desiderio habbi gia fatto far il cavo per dar principio alli bastioni et muraglie di d[ett]a città et havendo sempre dette Altezze cominciate le loro imprese et attioni in nome di sua divina maèsta acio col suo agiuto sia città prospera felice et sempre diffesa et proteggiata dal Sig[no]re et dalli santi protettori di questa città doppo aver risolto si dia principio alla muraglia di essa città et bastioni per insigniarla del nome del Sig[no] re et con le benedittioni di Santa Chiesa." For Botero's theories of religion, see note 59 below.

32. AST, Sez. Riunite, Editti, 1621, also in Duboin, 913–15. The Magistrato consisted of Count Ercole Negro di Sanfront, (already mentioned as a military engineer and planner), the general of artillery; Count Valdengo, the state councilor; three ducal notaries; two engineers (the architect Count Carlo di Castellamonte and Carlo Vanelli); the auditor, Gabetti;

The *Magistrato*'s mandate was to supervise the construction of ducal buildings as well as to control the quality and appearance of private development. Its authority—"la politica delle fabriche"—allowed it to impose the ducal "regulation and design" on streets and houses in Turin, accepting bids and making contracts for buildings and fortifications subsidized by the crown and watching over the price of building materials. Previously, supervision and accounting had been performed by a number of individual site intendents, dispersed throughout the duchy; the edict complains of their inexperience, lack of interest in the work, and financial negligence. The duke intended to rectify this condition by installing a central supervisory authority that would manage the finances of the official interventions and survey private ones from a distance. This central authority would ensure "the greatest possible beauty, ornament and commodity of the city and of its citizens," as befitted "our metropolis and princely residence."[33]

The jurisdiction of this building agency can be compared to that of the Procurators of San Marco in Venice. Unlike Venice, however, which was divided into three separate, but overlapping, areas of public interest (political

the treasurer of the ducal household, Isoardi; the military engineer, de' Marchi; and the superintendent of ducal buildings, Vugliengo. With the secretary, selected from among the ducal staff, there were twelve members in the first council, which met weekly in the ducal palace.

33. Duboin, 913–14: "Esse fabriche e provisioni non solo, non riescano o si fanno conforme agli ordini, e disegni dati, ma di più si rendono dispendiose con non poco interesse nostro, oltre alla dilatione che ne patisce il servitio; per il dovendo noi per buona economia rimediarvi, et non giodicandovi miglior modo, che di ridurre le sudette fabriche, esercitij, indifferentemente sotto l'autorità et distributiva d'ordini d'un solo capo formato de'soggetti intendenti in simile imprese, e menaggi, et il quale mediante ancora, si regolino particolarmente le fabriche delle case, e strade della detta città per renderla alla più bellezza, ornamento, et comodità d'essa, et degli habitanti, che sia possibile, come metropoli et residenza nostra, et de'nostri magistrati: a questo effetto con le presenti . . . erigiamo, e formiamo un magistrato, che d'hor avanti si nominarà delle nostre fabriche, e sederà in una delle stanze del nostro palazzo, o di quello del prencipe ogni settimana. . . . Per dover il detto magistrato far fare d'hor avanti tutti li mandati al thesoriere delle suddette fabriche, et imprese per li pagamenti delli prezzi degl'effetti, materie, condutte loro, cavi, vacationi delle maestranze, et operanti, e simili spese dependenti da esse fabriche et servitij. . . . Più si stabiliranno nel conseglio tutti li prezzi de' mattoni, calcine, pietre, boscami, et altri simili materie, et si delibereranno anco all'incanto avanti esso tutte le fabriche, navili, cavi, fatture, condotte, et altri simili imprese dependenti da fabriche, et artiglieria; et quanto alla politica delle fabriche, delle case et strade di questa città, ne doniamo la soprintendenza al medesimo magistrato, con l'autorità di farle redurre al regolamento, et dissegno, che da noi sarà dato."

arena at San Marco, commercial interests at Rialto, military focus at the Arsenal),[34] Turin had only two foci of power. Carlo Emanuele I's attempt to garner absolute control of the city gained an incomparably strong arm in the *Magistrato*, which was to rule over public (ducal) as well as private enterprises, those of the city council included. This made it significantly different from the comparable agency in France, the *Corps du Génie*, founded by Sully at the beginning of the seventeenth century; this body supervised the construction and fortification projects of the French crown, but had no jurisdiction over private enterprise.[35]

While the design of buildings and regulations concerning their construction were to emanate from the crown, the Magistrato delle Fabriche was to see to their faithful execution. If difficulties occurred in the implementation, the final decisions were made by the president of the Magistrato, even though the agency remained financially accountable to the Camera de' Conti. Its jurisdiction was clearly defined by the ducal Senate as pertaining only to the embellishment of the city, that is, the form, structure, and realization of buildings. The Senate reserved ultimate decision over the questions of ownership, leases, and donations. To guarantee that these would not impede construction was to prove a great task for the Senate, since the privileges granted by Carlo Emanuele to new settlers and builders in Città Nuova were under the jurisdiction of both the Senate and the Magistrato delle Fabriche.

The foundation of this agency was among the first attempts of the dukes of Savoy to centralize and to homogenize the building industry. Through it the system of contracts and payments was standardized and immediate responsibility removed from the duke. It unified urban design, centralized administration, and formalized record-keeping, as well as regulating the quality of building materials. The minutes, correspondence, and reports of the Magistrato form a uniquely rich segment of the well-preserved ducal archive, and allow us to follow closely the implementation of city planning, architectural, and fortification projects. This archive is significant in itself, moreover, since it documents the intentions and motivations behind Carlo Emanuele's numerous projects, many of which were not actually realized. The Magistrato delle Fabriche thus played an important public role by rendering visible and official the ducal building program, giving institutional and bureaucratic form to the

34. On the Rialto see Donatella Calabi, *Rialto: Le fabriche e il ponte, 1514–1591* (Turin, 1987); on the Arsenal see Ennio Concina, *L'arsenale della Repubblica di Venezia* (Milan, 1984).

35. See David Buisseret, "Les ingénieurs du roi au temps de Henri IV," *Bulletin de la section de géographie*, 77 (1964): 18–20.

construction projects and the planning ideals for Turin nurtured by the Savoy dynasty.

There was constant communication between the duke and the Magistrato. The duke passed down his decisions through Sanfront or more often through Carlo di Castellamonte, since Sanfront was also governor in Savigliano between 1619 and 1622. Agency officials also maintained relations with the city council, whose meetings they occasionally attended. Often, the city sent representatives directly to court to complain about the sums requested from them for building projects. Carlo di Castellamonte was a tireless and much appreciated intermediary in these negotiations between the city council and the Magistrato delle Fabriche.[36]

The fledgling building agency needed the support of the ruler in its first years, as several ducal letters demonstrate. Although it had been empowered to set the price of construction materials—its original mandate had asked it to "stabilize all prices of bricks, lime, stones, wood and other such"—the agency had policing and executive powers but lacked the necessary legislative mandate. Thus there are two separate orders on 30 September 1621 determining the size and price of various bricks and tiles described in minute detail, the size of sand carts, and the price of various grades of lime and plaster. These two orders are an invaluable source of information about the form, quality, origin of manufacture, and transport of construction materials, and the way in which they were made available. The opening words of the orders—"since we have had to acknowledge the numerous abuses. . . despite our many orders regarding the established price of lime and plaster they are changing and rising daily, delaying our construction work and that of the city, as well as the private sector"—indicate the extent of the black market in construction materials.[37] The rising prices were eroding the traditional quality and dimensions of building materials. The ducal legislation threatened to punish illicit speculation and the sale of altered materials. Further, by stating the size, quality, and origin of various kinds of bricks and tiles, prescribing the volume of the horse-drawn

36. ASCT, Ordinati, 29 September 1635: "Il Conte Castellamonte ha fatto molti favori alla città e mai e stato riconosciuto . . . di farlo per la qualità della persona et utilità che ne riceva la città vista percio che si deliberi. Il Conseglio ordina li s[igno]ri sindici . . . di riconoscer d[ett]o Conte come le parra esped[ien]te."

37. Duboin, 919–21: "dovendo noi provedere a molti abusi . . . non ostante parecchi ordini nostri sopra li prezzi stabiliti alle calcine e giesso, essi si vanno alla giornata alternando, et augumentando, in ritardimento delle fabriche nostre et della Città, et de' particolari ancora."

carts used for the transportation of stone and sand, and limiting the price of lime and plaster, it established a minimum standard of quality and checked speculation in building materials.[38] It is this first attempt at standardization, following the creation of the central supervisory agency, that shows the innovative aspect of Carlo Emanuele I's expansion program.

His order of 4 July 1624 repeated the injunction about the official price of lime and plaster, which had been obviously violated despite the built-in profits: "even though—because of extensive sale and use of construction materials—the manufacturers and distributors can make a reasonable profit while observing our price-stabilizing order of 30 September 1621, yet there are continuous complaints that due to the greed of these distributors the established prices have not been maintained, causing harm to the public and delays for the building program." The new order adapted nonetheless to prevailing conditions. Forbidding theft from the fortifications, and the excavation of stone and sand from empty lots (except private property), Carlo Emanuele invited builders to take sand and stone from the areas designated for the moats of Città Nuova by Carlo di Castellamonte.[39] This was, of course, a rather transparent

38. Ibid., 919: "Proibiamo ad ogn'uno di qualsivoglia stato, grado, et conditione, che sia, il fabricar, o far fabricar, o cuocer d'hor avanti nelli sudetti et altri luoghi et nelle regioni loro, mattoni, nè altra sorte di lavori, o materie infrascritte, per volerle vendere, et condurre quà in servitio di dette fabriche, salvo alla lunghezza, larghezza, et altezza, et alla ragione di prezzo per migliaio, et come a caduna sorte di dette materie è distinto et notato. Et . . . intendiamo anco che portano circa la condotta delle sabbie, pietre, terra, et altri simili materie con carrette da cavallo, prohibiamo parimente d'hor avanti ad ogn'uno come sopra, l'uso in questa città, suoi borghi et finaggio, d'altra sorte, o forma di carrette da cavallo, che della descritta, et notata al piè di queste." Ibid., 921: "prohibiamo a tutti li patroni, o mercanti de' sudette calcine, e giesso il venderli, ed alli accompratori di pagarli d'hor avanti a maggiori prezzi delli sopra stabiliti."

39. Ibid., 923: "Se ben per il gran traffico et smaltimento delle materie da fabricare, possino li fabricanti, et venditori di esse con ragionevole guadagno attendere et osservare il soprascritto ordine nostro dell'ultimo settembre mille seicento ventiuno con li prezzi in quello stabiliti; tuttavia essendovi di continuo doglianze, che per l'ingordigia di essi venditori si eccedono li prezzi stabiliti, in danno del pubblico et ritardo delle fabriche." Ibid., 924: "Di più inibiamo ad ogn'uno di cavar pietre, o sabbia, nè far cave nel circuito, e vacui pubblici della città nuova, sotto pena di scudi venticinque d'oro per caduno, et ogni volta, nella qualle incorreranno anco coloro ch'esporteranno, o faranno esportare pietre, o sabbia delle controscarpe, o baluardi della detta città, sarà però lecito ad ognuno di cavar pietre, e sabbia nel sito dove s'hanno da cavar li fossi di detta città nuova, cioè dove saranno designati dal vassallo et ingegnero nostro Carlo Castellamonte. Mandando in oltre et commandando sotto detta pena ad ognuno qual averà fatto cavi in detti vacui pubblici, et in particolare dalli fossi

ploy to save on labor, but it does hint that four years after construction had started the fortification of the expansion was not far advanced. Customarily, the digging of the moats was simultaneous with the construction of the walls, using the excavated material from the former for the raising of the latter. The duke's dependence upon the collaboration of the inhabitants is unveiled in the last paragraph of the order, requiring those who had made illegal excavations to fill them within one month. (The punishments threatened throughout these orders were all calculated in local currency, and grow increasingly draconian with each infraction; fines are replaced by public whipping at the third one.)[40] The shortage of materials that provoked speculation was in large part the consequence of the construction of the new fortifications. The large-scale institutionalized supply of building materials was directed towards fulfilling this need. Thus, the crown was forced to intervene and officially fix prices and measurements in order to defend its own interests.

Two letters patent, of 5 April and 12 May 1621, show how the duke proposed to pay, at least in part, for the onerous expense of the fortifications, streets, and royal buildings (specifically the construction of the chapel for the Holy Shroud). In order to speed up the construction process he proposed to tax all of his own extraordinary income. In effect he was taking away from other parts of his government to give funds to the Magistrato delle Fabriche. That the treasurer of the building agency encountered difficulty in collecting this substantial tax can be gathered from the repetition of the order within one month, and from a subsequent document, an order of 15 June 1621 signed by Prince Vittorio Amedeo, urging the communal administrators to comply promptly with his father's letters patent.[41]

WHILE THE REGULATION of the building industry was to be enforced through the Magistrato delle Fabriche, and by fixing the price of materials used in construction, the settlement of the Città Nuova was facilitated by the

---

della città vecchia sino alle fabriche della città nuova, di doverli riempire fra un mese prossimo dopo la publicatione di questa."

40. Ibid., 924.

41. Duboin reproduces both of Carlo Emanuele's letters patent for the historical record, although they are substantially the same (917–19): "Volendo noi, che si continui . . . s'affretti l'ampliatione, et abbellimento della città nostra di Torino, principale, e metropoli del nostro Stato . . . assigniamo per l'effetto sudetto fiorini due per cadun ducatone, ragionato a fiorini tredici di qual si voglia danaro, et effetto straordinario a noi dovuto. . . . Dichiarando

"naturalization act" of 12 August 1621. The edict acknowledges current conditions ("since we have, after the last wars, started the enlargement of Turin, and seeing now the notable progress of this project") and proclaims the duke's aim to attract new inhabitants to the expansion areas of Turin, which, eight months after the formal laying of the foundation stone, extended east as well as south. The duke hoped to accomplish this by granting privileges and immunities to newcomers: "we have thought it not only convenient, but necessary, to favor and warm this undertaking (*impresa*) by enriching it and providing it with special offers and privileges, so that through this invitation our design will be more perfectly realized. . . . We concede the following privileges and exemptions to those who will come to build within the new walls and fortifications commissioned and begun by us, both towards Porta Nuova and towards the Po."[42] Through this legislation, Carlo Emanuele hoped to build upon Botero's tenet—that the stimulation of population growth, under the control of state authority, is the chief factor in "la grandezza e la magnificenza delle città."

The ten-point edict outlined these privileges. A foreigner, whatever his status, would be granted full citizenship if he built in the Città Nuova "within (*dentro*) the specified design" (the aesthetic plan is conceived as an enclosure or containment).[43] Foreigners and native citizens who built new houses in the Città Nuova would be exempt from service in the militia for three genera-

---

danaro straordinario quello, che proverà dalli donativi, che ci venesse a far lo stato di qual si sia cosa, dalle compositioni, accordi, e cottizzi, che si faranno con communità, o privati, dalle condanne, confiscationi siano di qual si voglia sorte, dalle finanze, o prestanze per causa uffici o per qual si sia altra, da vendite de'beni, e ragioni nostre, da laudemii, introgii, e da infeudationi di qual si vogli qualità . . . e generalmente d'ogni sorta d'obventione estraordinaria a noi spettante e dovuta."

42. Borelli, 927–29: "Havendo noi dopo le ultime guerre dato principio all'aggrandimento della Città di Torino . . . vedendo hora il notabile progresso di quest'opera . . . habbiamo stimato non solo conveniente, ma necessario di favorir e riscaldar quest'impresa col'arrichirla e dotarla di particolari gratie e privilegi acciache con questo invito si dia maggior perfettione a questo nostro dissegno . . . concediamo gl'infrascritti privilegi, et esentioni à quelli, che verrano à fabricare nel termine delle nuove mura, e fortificationi già da Noi fatte disegnare, e principiare tanto verso la Porta nuova, quanto verso il Pò." Note the equal weight given, in the official phrasing, to the southern and eastern expansions.

43. Ibid., 927: "Dichiariamo, che tutti li forastieri di qualunque stato, grado, e conditione che siano, li quali faranno fabricare edifici nuovi dentro il sudetto dissegno s'intendino esser, e i loro discendenti, quali habitaranno nelli Stati nostri fatti Suddeti nostri naturali, e per consequenza gioiscano *ipso iure*, et *facto* del privilegio di naturalità."

tions.[44] No one could be seized for debts while building or inhabiting a newly built house "within the limits of the new design."[45] Anyone could open a shop or practice a craft in the Città Nuova, without ducal license, as long as they conformed to the guild laws.[46] A marketplace was opened in the Contrada di San Carlo, while the old one near San Tommaso in the Città Vecchia was suppressed—a change energetically contested by the city council.[47] The houses in the Città Nuova could not be made part of Turin's tax base for twenty-five years.[48] Those holding land in lease were ordered to build while being assured that their investment would be protected.[49] Fines up to one thousand *scudi d'oro*

44. Ibid., 927–28: "Liberiamo, et esimiamo dal carico, et obligo della nuova militia instituita, tutti quelli, tanto sudditi, che forastieri, qualli haveranno edificato, ò all'avvenire faranno fabricare case nuove nel sudetto luogo. Inibendo ad essi, et alli loro descendenti fino alla terza generatione . . . ogni molestia personale."

45. Ibid., 928: "Concediamo à tutti coloro, quali hanno gia edificato, o fabricheranno case frà i limiti del nuova dissegno, et alli loro figliuoli l'inibitione di molestia personale per li debiti da essi fatti, ò da farsi, sì per il tempo, che le faranno fabricar, che dopo, mentre in quelle continueranno la habitatione loro."

46. Ibid.: "Permettiamo anco à tutti li mercanti et artigiani di qualsivogli servitio, et a'rivenderoli di poter tener botteghe, e far banchi in esse nuove fabriche, et ivi esercire loro arti, e rivendere senza obligo di prendere la matricola, ne altra licenza, mentre però siano ammessi per habili dalli Sindici, ò consoli di cadun arte conforme alli loro privilegi."

47. Ibid.: "Ordiniamo che si faccia il mercato sudetto nella piazza della contrada di San Carlo; inibendo ad ogn'uno di tener mercato in altro luogo di questa città, sotto pena della perdita delle vittovaglie, e di scudi cento d'oro." ASCT, Ordinati, 11 September 1621: "Per raccorrer contro li privilleggi concessi alla Città nova . . . essersi publicato li privilleggi da S[ua] A[ltezza] concessi alli habitanti e fabricanti case nella Città nova fra li altri . . . che da San Michele prossime passato in poi si debba ivi et sopra la piazza di San Carlo far il mercato del grano con inhibitione di piu comprar ne vender grano in questa città vechia sopra il luoro mercato sotto la pena della perdita d'esse vittovaglie et di scudi 100 d'oro et per esser questa contra il publico servicio della città et habitanti per la distanza et incommodita delli habitanti in Torino et maggior spesa del porto e non haver stanze ivi li mercanti di habitar et tener luoro grani sicuri. . . . Hanno ordinato si raccorra da S[ua] A[ltezza] et di p[re]g[ar]la per rimedio contro detto ordine massime attese le doglianze di mercanti di grani."

48. Borelli, 928: "non possino, ne debbano esser registrate, ò collettatte le case della Città Nuova, ma s'intendino immuni per anni vinticinque."

49. Ibid.: "Saranno tenuti tutti i padroni delli terreni posti nelli limiti di detta Città Nuova di fabricarvi, o rimetterli ad altri à giusto prezzo, e quanto alli possessori de' terreni sottoposti ad emfiteusi, censi, ò livelli perpetui, ò temporali, li permettiamo, anzi li comandiamo di fabricarvi sopra, e pretendendo il signor diretto ragione di devolutione . . . in tal case sia tenuto di restituire il valore della casa fabricata."

held against those building in the Città Nuova would be annulled on the day on which they started construction.[50] Runaways and those expelled from other countries were offered safe-conduct while inhabiting a house they built or bought in the Città Nuova, but heretics and traitors were excluded from these "banditi de' stati forestieri" acceptable in Turin.[51] The tenth point of the edict clarified the beneficiaries of the previous nine points by defining the houses to be inhabited; these were to be those built *ex novo* within the previous three years, or those rebuilt according to the official ducal design.[52] An additional privilege granted was the permission for public butchering of animals to take place in the Città Nuova. This grant and the change in the site of the market-place were vociferously challenged by the city, as can be seen in ducal orders of 21 December 1628, which hint that sabotage and intimidation had taken place.[53]

Additional adjustments to these concessions were made in the edict of 25 October 1621, signed for the duke by his son Cardinal Maurizio. Some of these overturned the previous orders, or at least weighed them with such heavy requirements that the privileges granted earlier in August became much less attractive. They included the right to produce one's own bricks and tiles, and the right (but also the obligation) to sell one's land if not building upon it. More important, the entire system of privileges was rendered more onerous for builders, and of incalculable ideological advantage for the crown, by the

50. Ibid.: "Faciamo anche gratia, et abolitione a tutti coloro, quali fabricherano edificij nuovi dentro i sudetti limiti di tutte le pene nelle quale potessero esser incorsi per contravention alli ordini nostri . . . purche non ecceda la somma di mille scudi d'oro."

51. Ibid.: "Concediamo alli banditi de' stati forestieri salvocondotto perpetuo, et irrevocabile, venendo a fabricare, overo acquistando, et habitando le dette case nuovamente edificate dentro al circuito; mentre però non siano convitti di crime di lesa Maestà Divina, ò humana."

52. Ibid.: "E per levar ogni dubbio, dichiariamo restar comprese nel presente ordine, e dover gioire delli privilegi, immunità, e franchisie in esso sopradescritte quelle case solamente, che di anni trè in quà saranno state edificate da pianta overo quelle, che conforme al dissegno da Noi ordinato saranno state riformate."

53. Ibid.: "Concediamo, che in detta Città nuova si possi far, e tener macello publico per vendere à chi si sia carni di ogni sorte, mediamente che si osservino gli Ordini Politici e si paghino li dritti soliti, come si fà nelli macelli della Città vecchia." Duboin, 925: "Havendoci i particolari habitanti, ch'hanno fabbricato nella città nuova di Torino esposto per l'alligata supplica, che contra la forma di privilegi loro concessi in virtù d'editto nostro vengono dalli sindici della presente città vecchia e dagli accensatori delle carni e macelli di essa, *turbati e molestati*" (emphasis mine).

76

introduction of a clause that stated each building had to follow the design made by Carlo di Castellamonte.[54]

Eventually the entire legislative machinery intended to populate the Città Nuova was subsumed by the desire to control the physical result of the expansion process. This achievement of absolutist rule was accomplished by adopting ideas that Carlo Emanuele culled from Botero's writings on the city and the state. Thus Botero had stated that the power of the prince resides in a large population, which becomes the true source of his strength, his fundamental resource, together with money, provisions, and arms.[55] He saw two ways of increasing the population, propagation and immigration.[56] The way to attract settlers was through the concession of immunities and privileges, including freedom from taxes: Rome, whose strength was based on its large population, was said to have grown also by giving franchise and asylum to bandits and exiles; it provided a contrasting model to the Greek ideal city whose population was artificially kept below a certain limit.[57] Clearly, Carlo Emanuele favored the Roman method of expansion. He granted privileges to settlers and surrounded himself with a growing number of institutions that represented and increased his power. He knew that all great cities were the residence of a prince, and that a capital is by definition a great city, as defined by Botero. Therefore Turin would become a great city since it was his residence and Piedmont's capital. By placing emphasis on the design of the Città Nuova, endowing it with straight streets, uniform buildings, and mighty fortifications, Carlo Emanuele wanted to satisfy other Boteran requirements for the great city— magnificence, impressive artifice, and delight.[58]

We have seen, then, that the major aims of Carlo Emanuele I's expansionary

54. Borelli, 929: "Piu dichiariamo che chi vorra fabricare nella detta Nuova Città debba regolar la fabrica secondo il disegno di detto Castellamonte, senza quale non potra fabricare e cio non ostante ogni concesione nostra."

55. *Ragione di stato*, 208: "Veniamo hora alle vere forze, che consistono nella gente; perche à questa ogni altra forza si riduce: e chi abbonda d'huomini, di tutte quelle cose anco abbonda, alle quali l'ingegno, e l'industria dell'huomo s'estende."

56. *Ragione di stato*, 213: "La gente e le forze s'augmentano in due modi, col propagare il suo, e col tirare à se l'altrui."

57. *Grandezza delle città*, 27–28: "Il primo [modo] fù l'aprir l'Asilo, e dar franchezza: il che fece Romolo, affinche, essendo all'hora le terre vicine mal trattate da'Tiranni; e perciò il paese pieno di banditi, Roma s'appopolasse, e per il benefitio della sicurezza, che vi si manteneva."

58. Ibid., 11–12. See chap. 2, note 12.

campaign were to enlarge the city to the south and to the east towards the Po, to fortify the old and new parts of Turin, and to increase the population of the city. He also aimed to attract a large number of religious institutions to settle in the expansion areas of Turin, which would satisfy two of Botero's policy requirements—increasing settlement and forging an alliance with Church interests; "Christianity," according to Botero, is the religion "most favorable to Princes," because it "binds not only the hands, but the emotions and the thoughts of the ruler's subjects."[59] The desire for new religious institutions was strongly felt by Carlo Emanuele, who wanted to fight the heresy that was spreading through the valleys surrounding Turin. His simultaneous competition with the French and Spanish kings, the Most Christian and the Most Catholic majesties respectively, further strengthened his resolve to shine in the field of Counter-Reformation crusading. During his reign the Augustinians, Barnabites, Capuchins, Camaldolites and Minor Observants, among others, settled in the city. But Carlo Emanuele's encouragement of religious orders was socially and economically a questionable gesture, since the mendicant orders, which responded readily to his invitation, were to exacerbate the problem of beggars in Turin.[60] The duke made several donations of parcels in the southern expansion area, where the crown owned land. These new institutions would quickly populate the new areas of Turin—presumably by immigration—and by constructing churches and convents they would help to fill in the urban texture and complete the expansion, in addition to "binding the thoughts" and providing spiritual guidance for the new settlers.

CONSTRUCTION OF the Città Nuova proceeded slowly. There were shortages of builders and of construction materials. An almost continuous state of war in the 1620s resulted in lengthy absences of the duke from his capital. The more important architects and engineers, Carlo di Castellamonte, Ercole Negro di Sanfront, and Carlo Morello, were busy with the fortification

59. *Ragione di stato*, 96: "La Religione è fondamento d'ogni Prencipiato"; 97: "ma trà tutte le leggi non ve n'è alcuna più favorevole a'Prencipi, che la Christiana; perche questa sottomette loro, non solamente i corpi, e le facoltà de'sudditi, dove co[n]viene, ma gli animi ancora, e le conscienze; e lega non solamente le mani, ma gli effetti ancora, e i pensieri."

60. Giuseppe Michele Crepaldi, *La real chiesa di San Lorenzo a Torino* (Turin, 1963), 36, n. 15; ASCT, Ordinati, 6 July 1622: "Più che S[ua] A[ltezza] s'e lasciata intender voler metter una religione de Padri di San Francesco scalci nella città nuova et che altri gia giunti . . . et cosi si giongerano due tasche de mendicanti nella città acio si deliberi che si debba fare."

of Piedmontese towns. These wars of expansion fought by the duke, who had long since parted with Botero's cautious advice on foreign policy, diminished the treasury. The crown reduced the payments for the enlargement of Turin, and the city was generally impoverished.[61]

Aware of the recent commencement of Turin's expansion, the prince of Condé had remarked in 1622 that "some streets are already built and several monasteries and houses begun; two bastions seem already fairly well along, although not yet clad."[62] His description squares well with an early, and until now unexamined, view taken from the hill to the east of Turin, across the Po (fig. 48). The perimeter of the Roman city is quite clear, since its walls were still standing. Although the view was taken from a great distance, even the citadel is recognizably suggested. In the southern expansion area there are buildings flanking the road that leads to the inner city gate. The settlement is irregular, and its streets are not well marked. The expansion could be mistaken for an unplanned suburban development, like the one next to the Po bridge, since the fortification belt is not complete and buildings are standing only along the entry road. Their height seems to vary between one and three floors, and their functions are difficult to differentiate. But the bastions are designed according to the latest innovations; they are low and dug-in, wide, and separated from the fortification's curtain wall. There is a great gate between the full bastions, evidently the one built for the ceremonial wedding entry of 1620. However, since the walls are not completed, the expansion area is undefended and thus vulnerable and difficult to populate. Besides the open space in the defined blocks, there is a conspicuously large open space between the citadel and the Città Nuova. This area is not as large or as defined as the open space between the citadel and the Città Vecchia; nonetheless, while the new expansion could be defended with the help of the citadel, the citadel could also menace Città Nuova through its control of this sizable no-man's-land.

Given Carlo Emanuele I's military agenda in the 1620s, and the noticeable drop-off in payments for walls and moats after 1622, the construction accomplished—although not far advanced, as seen in this anonymous view—seems quite respectable. What is conspicuous, however, is the scarcity of develop-

61. Regular payments for the excavation of the moats and the building of walls are documented between January 1621 and May 1622 in AST, Sez. Riunite, art. 180, 1358–1438, and art. 207, mazzo 4, R 18 and R 20; there are few entries for payments made between 1624 and 1633, although R 20 continues to 1633.

62. *Voyage*, 6: "quelques rues sont déjà basties, et plusieurs monastères et maisons comencées, et il y aparoist déjà deux bastions fort avancées, non encore revêtus."

ment between the east wall and the river. The suburb at the bridgehead pre-dated the expansion commenced in 1619. In August 1621 Carlo Emanuele had insisted that there "are new walls and fortifications, whose design has been commissioned by us, being built towards Porta Nuova and towards the Po."[63] However, both the duke's autograph plan for the expansion of Turin and the alternative proposals in the "official" plan (disputed between Sanfront and Castellamonte) have many more bastions than the six baptized in the somewhat casually arranged but nonetheless official ritual of laying the foundation stone, carried out in 1620. Rather than commencing work on the entire fortification enclosure, it would seem that the bastions were built one by one, and that their construction slowed down considerably after the initial flurry of building in the early 1620s.

That the southern expansion was not a resounding public success and was not acknowledged outside Turin as an actual urban development can be gleaned from a view of Turin published in Antoine de Ville's military treatise of 1628 (fig. 49), where Città Vecchia and the citadel form the background for one of his illustrations of fortification design. In the preface to his work, de Ville took pride in his own, and his brother's, war experiences, including service for one of the duke's heirs, which presumably would have included some first-hand acquaintance with Turin.[64] Nevertheless, he chooses to depict Turin as a Roman castrum with its sixteenth-century citadel, omitting the incomplete expansion efforts. This old-fashioned image may be seen as an accurate representation of the city as it was acknowledged and conceived—despite the celebrations, edicts, and exertions of the 1620s—towards the end of Carlo Emanuele I's reign. "He who embraces many important *imprese* at the same time accomplishes few of them."

63. See note 42, above.

64. *Les Fortifications des villes* (Lyons, 1629), Introduction: "Je t'assure pourtant, ami Lecteur, que je n'ay rien escrit, que mon frere [sergeant-major in the regiment of Carlo Emanuele's youngest son Tommaso] ou moy, n'ayons veu, ou pratiqué." De Ville's association with Carlo Emanuele is demonstrated by the collar of the Order of San Maurizio e San Lazzaro which he wears in the portrait that follows the frontispiece of his treatise.

PART TWO

1630–56

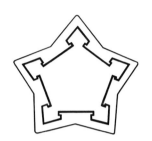

4

The Città Nuova Expansion

Fortification and Royal Claims

Enfin je veux un roi: regardez si vous l'êtes.
—Corneille, *Attila*

THE BRIEF REIGN OF Vittorio Amedeo I (1630–37), wedged in between the fifty-year rule of his father Carlo Emanuele I (1580–1630) and the twenty-five-year effective regency of Cristina (1637–63), was, despite its brevity, filled with events and difficulties. As a young man, Vittorio Amedeo had spent three years as hostage at the Spanish court, together with two of his brothers. Botero, whose concept of the *ragione di stato* paralleled closely Carlo Emanuele's notions of the national and dynastic state and whose writings about the city, as we have seen, were so influential in the planning of the capital's expansion, was his accompanying preceptor. Earlier still, when very young, Vittorio Amedeo's sensitivity to architecture and landscape was expressed in a letter sent to his father, where he described precisely the aesthetic pleasures of the ducal residence in Turin.[1]

Having inherited the title of prince of Piedmont (his elder brother died while in Madrid), Vittorio Amedeo spent the following two decades in close association with his father the duke, assisting him on all his projects. He was present while the ideals for a large, populated, beautiful, and fortified capital were evolved for Turin. The Savoy dynastic ideology—formulated through Carlo Emanuele's claims on neighboring regions, such as Saluzzo, Monferrato, and Provence, and through his relationships of alliance and competition with Henri IV and Philip III—was the foundation of Vittorio Amedeo's polit-

1. AST, Sez. Riunite, Lettere Principi Savoia, Duchi e Sovrani, Lettere di Vittorio Amedeo, mazzo 46, number 6, 1597; see chap. 2, note 22 above.

ical education.[2] Simultaneously, the bellicose engagements of the duchy during the 1610s and 1620s established the military culture that permeated his life at the court of Turin. The cultural component of the dynastic program was assiduously supported by Carlo Emanuele. Patronage of the arts and letters was the propaganda arm of the political program in dealing with foreign powers as well as the resident population. It was used to extend the ducal ruling power into every corner of Turin and Piedmont. We have seen, for example, how the temporary structures built to frame the wedding ceremonies of 1608, and Vittorio Amedeo's own nuptial feast in 1620, were important steps in claiming and displaying the growing power of the House of Savoy and its as yet unrecognized claims to royal rank. The ducal buildings and triumphal arches, the literary collections, and the commissions of painting and interior decoration were programmed to reinforce and publicize the ducal ideals. Vittorio Amedeo was heir to this military culture and dynastic ideology, and to the reputation achieved by his immediate predecessor.

But Vittorio Amedeo also inherited catastrophic problems. The plague, raging through Piedmont from 1630 to 1632, decimated the population and undermined the income and resources of the realm. The threat of war, and the continuous diplomatic negotiations intended to avoid it, monopolized the time, attention, and interest of Vittorio Amedeo and eventually plunged the duchy into the messy alliances of the Thirty Years' War. But the House of Savoy's dynastic claim to royal standing and title was forcefully and publicly stated through Vittorio Amedeo's proclamations, and through the Italian, French, and Latin publications of the theologians and historiographers employed by him. Finally, twelve years after his wedding, in 1632, the future of the dynasty was ensured by the long-awaited birth of a male heir.

These concerns about the health, security, and political future of the duchy did not, however, prevent Vittorio Amedeo from lavishing attention on Turin, which more than ever acted as the heart and stronghold of the realm. Nonetheless, practical and strategic requirements forced a thorough redimensioning of Carlo Emanuele I's grandiose and unrealized projects for the expansion of the capital. In keeping with the reduced means of the city and its diminished population, the original plan for expansion was truncated, while its military and formal ambitions were upheld. Although reduced, the expansion was accompanied by the full panoply of religious and secular commissions, both in architecture and in publications associated with the tenets of *ragione di stato* and the concept of the capital city, as proposed earlier by Botero.

2. For Carlo Emanuele's intricate foreign policy and shifting alliances, see *Monarchia piemontese*, 3:81–413, 4:2–307.

The principal architectural manifestation of Vittorio Amedeo's reign was three churches, which, although only completed later in the century, were founded in close succession: Madonna degli Angeli (1631), San Francesco di Paola (1632), and San Lorenzo (1634).[3] They were located respectively in the Città Nuova, the Borgo di Po (the suburb between the eastern gate or Porta Castello and the bridge over the Po) and the Città Vecchia. The definitive construction of San Lorenzo was delayed until the 1660s, and the church interior as it is today is largely the work of Guarino Guarini. Madonna degli Angeli was built faster, and already in 1638 its main altar had been completed using a subsidy from the regent Cristina. The church of San Francesco di Paola, built by the Minims, is the most significant of Vittorio Amedeo's religious foundations. Although the order had settled in Turin in 1621—attracted by Carlo Emanuele I, whose expansion of the city, as we have seen, envisioned an important religious revival—their church on Contrada di Po, the street that connected Porta Castello to the Po bridge, was built as the result of an ex-voto. Vittorio Amedeo and Cristina vowed to the saint, so beloved by the French, to build a church "in exchange" for a male heir.[4] The churches of both San Francesco di Paola and San Lorenzo became closely associated with the ducal house and were enriched by subsequent members of the dynasty, who made them fashionable also for the Torinese nobility. Nor were these churches the only artistic expression of Vittorio Amedeo's dynastic ambition. The striking of medals, the diffusion of prints illustrating Turin, and the publications stating his royal claims created the conditions of anticipation and the groundwork for the achievements of his own and subsequent reigns.

AT THE DEATH OF Carlo Emanuele I in 1630, Vittorio Amedeo I inherited a duchy under disastrous conditions, similar to those of his grandfather Emanuele Filiberto's inheritance: at war, held without security, ravaged and impoverished by the plague epidemic. He spent the first two years of his reign attempting to restore order and peace. Two linked imperatives marked these inauspicious opening years: the need to survive the plague, and the need to

3. Tamburini, 128–32, 140–46, 198–216.

4. For the relationship of San Francesco di Paola to the French monarchy, see Antonio Castiglione, *San Francesco di Paola* (Paola, 1982), 9–17, and Paola Hoffmann, *Rione IV: Campo Marzio,* ed. Carlo Pietrangeli, Guide rionali di Roma, 6 bis, part II (Rome, 1981), 74–102. I owe the latter reference to William McGuire.

stop the war, which could not be continued by the enfeebled population and the beleaguered courtiers.

In 1630 Turin and eventually, in a chain reaction, the smaller towns of Piedmont were subject to an intensely raging epidemic of bubonic plague. The frightened population and the terrified court were obliged to abandon Turin. As cases of plague erupted wherever it moved (Cherasco, Sanfrè, Carignano, Moncalieri), the court was forced to keep in flight for almost two years, shuttling from one Piedmontese town to another in a continuous but futile attempt to avoid contagion.[5] Thus, between 1630 and 1632 Turin served as neither the residence of the peripatetic court nor as the center of government for the duchy. Two of the fundamental requirements for the great capital city, as prescribed by Botero and legislatively constituted by Carlo Emanuele I, were unrealizable at the beginning of Vittorio Amedeo's reign.

As we have seen in chapter 3, the boosting of the population was another essential component in the dynastic program of urban expansion. By 1630 the population of the capital had risen to twenty-five thousand inhabitants. After the eruption of the epidemic, however, less than half of the population (about eleven thousand people) remained in Turin. The rest had fled to the surrounding countryside and mountain valleys, attempting to save themselves by returning to their home villages, which they thus contaminated. Of the remaining inhabitants, over eight thousand people, one-third of the population of Turin at the beginning of the epidemic, disappeared between the spring of 1630 and the late autumn of 1631. The plague definitively marked the failure of the expansionary efforts of Carlo Emanuele I; it was as a ghost town, with incomplete fortifications, abandoned houses and workshops, and an absent court, that Turin appeared to survivors in 1632.

Despite the cruel epidemic, daily activities continued as people attempted to lead normal lives. Astonished contemporaries observed the remarkable will for survival and reproduction. Despite the disastrous situation, with deaths of multiple family members occurring at brief intervals, many people continued to marry. The contemporary physician Giovanni Francesco Fiochetto, author of a treatise on the plague of 1630, wrote that no sooner was the cadaver of the husband or wife brought out in the street, than other men and women were ready to warm the bed that was barely cold.[6] This keen sense of survival has been noted by historians of the period, who have convincingly demonstrated

5. *Monarchia piemontese*, 5:4–44; Salvatore Foa, *Vittorio Amedeo I, 1587–1637* (Turin, 1930); and Michele Ruggiero, *Storia del Piemonte* (Turin, 1979), 415–23.

6. *Trattato della peste et pestifero contagio in Torino* (Turin, 1631), *passim*.

that these plague-time marriages were meant to save the financial patrimony and social strategies of families that had settled recently in Turin. In their case, these hasty marriages were contracted specifically in order to preserve previous investments in real estate. They had invested especially in Città Nuova, the southern segment of the overall expansion started in 1619 under Carlo Emanuele's reign, which became occupied by numerous craftsmen associated with the court and tied to one another by common origins in the smaller towns in the valleys surrounding Turin.[7]

The problems of health privately faced by the population of the duchy had a political counterpart. In 1630 large parts of the state were occupied by French and Spanish armies, for whom Piedmont served as a convenient battleground and buffer state. The Spanish, Carlo Emanuele I's allies at his death, were there to defend Piedmont from the French. After their invasion of Piedmont in 1630, the French attempted to dissociate the duke of Savoy from his long and customary alliance with the Spanish crown.[8] Realizing that Piedmont was a mere pawn for both Spain and France, Vittorio Amedeo sought to obtain peace for his population and to regain most of the lands lost by his father. Within the ducal family he was swayed by the two opposing parties: Duchess Cristina and her confessor, the Jesuit Pierre Monod, urged the new French alliance, while his brothers Maurizio and Tommaso and his sister Margherita inclined, and eventually turned, to the Spanish side. As we have seen, the swing of the Savoy pendulum between Spanish and French alliances had become almost traditional. The dukes married alternately French and Spanish princesses, usually in contrast with their current diplomatic policy. Vittorio Amedeo would have been the first duke of Savoy to pursue a French alliance while married to a French princess. Although supportive in principle, the Spanish were too weak, and their political situation in Lombardy was too grave, to offer actual help to the beleaguered Piedmontese.[9] This meant that Vittorio Amedeo would have to make war against his former allies, the Spanish, at the bidding of the French. On the other hand the chimerical attraction

7. Simona Cerutti, "Matrimoni del tempo di peste: Torino nel 1630," *Quaderni storici*, 55 (1984): 65–106, gives a full account with complete bibliography. I owe this reference to Carlo Ginzburg.

8. Gabriel de Mun, *Richelieu et la maison de Savoie: L'ambassade de Particelli d'Hémery en Piémont* (Paris, 1907), analyzes in detail the embassy of the cardinal's henchman Michel Particelli d'Hémery in Piedmont during the 1630s.

9. J. H. Elliott, *The Count-Duke of Olivares: The Statesman in an Age of Decline* (New Haven, 1986), 401–2.

of the dominion of North Italy (to be won from its Spanish rulers) and the assumption of the much coveted royal title were too important to resist. Both were promised in the Treaty of Cherasco, signed in 1631 by Vittorio Amedeo and Richelieu, which ended the hostilities. The French acquiesced to the transfer of the disputed territory of Monferrato to the dukes of Savoy—Carlo Emanuele I's reason for going into the war. Although this consolidated the Italian dominions of the duchy, the price paid for Monferrato—Pinerolo and a connecting corridor to the French border—laid Piedmont open to French attack from the west, a danger that remained until 1696. Furthermore, the Treaty of Cherasco brought no diplomatic respite for Vittorio Amedeo. By 1635 Richelieu had cajoled him, through the duchess and the interventions of Mazarin, into an offensive and defensive alliance with France (the Treaty of Rivoli) in exchange for Lombardy, Casale, and the recognition by the French of the Savoy dynasty's claim to royal title.[10]

In the past, the diplomatic alliances of the Savoy rulers had also been motivated by the financial subsidies offered by their allies. The alliance with France was financially disastrous for the duke of Savoy because the terms negotiated in the 1635 Treaty of Rivoli were not kept by the French, who obliged the Piedmontese to challenge and fight the Spanish army in Lombardy but did not provide the promised aid.[11] One of the ambassadors employed by Vittorio Amedeo in his dealings with Richelieu was the Jesuit Pierre Monod, whose attempts to win war compensation, make peace arrangements, and gain recognition of the royal title were fruitless.

By the time of Monod's embassy, in December 1636, both of Vittorio Amedeo's legitimate brothers had rebelled against him, changing sides; Maurizio represented Spanish interests in Rome, while Tommaso became the general of the Spanish army in Flanders. (In 1636 this army threatened the invasion of Paris, just as Tommaso's grandfather Emanuele Filiberto had done about eighty years earlier.) Simultaneously, their sister Margherita, dowager duchess of Mantua, was appointed vicereine of Portugal by the king of Spain. Earlier, Maurizio had proposed to the reigning duke a "politica dell'altalena" (a swing policy); since such ploys were not foreign to the Savoy tradition, this policy

10. Domenico Carutti, *Storia della diplomazia della corte di Savoia* (Turin, 1876), 2:357; for Mazarin's ambassadorial connections with Vittorio Amedeo, see Georges Dethan, *The Young Mazarin* (London, 1977), 122–31.

11. This, despite the notice to Richelieu from his ambassador d'Hémery that "M. de Savoye est pauvre au-delà de ce que peut croire Votre Éminence" (de Mun, *Richelieu et la maison de Savoie*, 106).

may have been practiced as a secret pact between the sons of Carlo Emanuele I.[12]

THE PLAGUE AND the war thus prevented Vittorio Amedeo from continuing Carlo Emanuele I's work on the expansion of Turin in the first two years of his reign. It was only in 1632 that Vittorio Amedeo I could consider continuing the work begun by Carlo Emanuele in 1619. Even more than before, it was essential to fortify Turin; with the French occupying the fortress of Pinerolo, the city found itself facing France, so that it was not only the capital but also a strategically crucial *piazzaforte*. As we have seen, Emanuele Filiberto, who like Vittorio Amedeo was obliged to regain his duchy from French invaders at his father's death, had set the image of the capital as an invincible fortress. Once again, Turin needed urgently to be fortified, especially in the areas left open and vulnerable to attack through the expansion project began by Carlo Emanuele I. But before continuing his father's initiative for the enlargement of Turin, Vittorio Amedeo had to consider a number of altered circumstances. These included the greatly reduced population of Turin after the plague, the diminished income that the capital produced, and the vulnerability of the duchy after the Treaty of Cherasco. The completion of Turin's fortification took place against the will of the French allies. Their barefaced protests, made openly even though they were themselves fortifying Pinerolo, underlined the subservient position of Piedmont in relation to France.[13]

Several important events, worthy of celebration, marked the return of the ducal court to Turin in 1632. These included the birth of the first male heir to Vittorio Amedeo and Cristina, and the publication of a widely advertised, criticized, and influential work by Pierre Monod, which laid out formally the evidence upon which the Savoy dynasty's claim to the royal title was based.[14]

12. Guido Quazza, "Guerre civile in Piemonte 1637–42," *Bollettino storico-bibliografico subalpino*, 57 (1959): 17: "Non incapaci daverro di simili giuochi non estranei alla tradizione sabauda."

13. *Monarchia piemontese*, 5:49.

14. *Coelum allobrogicum, hoc est, Victoris Amedei, serenissimi Cypriorum regis, atque allobrogum ducis potentissimi, corona regia panegyricus* (Lyon, 1634). The claim to royalty had been discussed under Carlo Emanuele I as well, but remained in manuscript; "Trattato delle ragioni sopra il regno di Cipro appartenente alla Sereniss[ima] Casa di Savoia," BN, Paris, MS Franc. 3662, dated 1620, is one example.

For the rest of his short reign, Vittorio Amedeo's dynastic ambition and expansionary energies were focused on this claim.

The birth of the long-awaited heir was celebrated with great splendor in September 1632. The designer of this dynastic *festa* was Emanuele Tesauro, one of the great wits of the century and one of the many Jesuits protected by the Savoy court.[15] As we have seen above, he had been associated earlier with Carlo Emanuele in a shared writing poject, and Vittorio Amedeo had asked him in July 1630 to compose the inscriptions and design the *imprese* for Carlo Emanuele's funeral ceremony. Although the funeral solemnities were not celebrated because of Vittorio Amedeo's distracted first two years in office, Tesauro's conceits and devices for the ceremony were published in his *Inscriptiones* of 1666.[16] The pageant he devised to celebrate the birth of the heir Francesco Giacinto (Hyacinth) was based on the infant's name and thus entirely floral. As one scholar describes it, "a huge triumphal arch was erected against the facade of the Cathedral, and over it, as if descending from heaven, was the figure of Celestial Genius carrying, in a golden basket, shaped like a cradle, a hyacinth of cerulean blue. . . . Tesauro's inscription on the arch, and all the decorations, elaborated this floral theme: woodland nymphs played the part of caryatids . . . while four shields adorning the capitals of the columns illustrated (with classical mottoes) those virtues of the hyacinth that were attributable to the young prince." The firework display was based on the zodiac, represented through the form of an amphitheater built in Piazza Castello. Surrounded by statues representing eleven signs of the zodiac "was the twelfth sign Taurus, eponymous symbol of the city of Turin," enthroned on silver clouds. Taurus was crowned by Jupiter, and round him were seated the Pleiades and figures representing the rivers of Turin, each pouring flames, instead of water from her urn."[17] The unification of water and fire, and the belief that opposites necessarily accompanied one another, had been absorbed into

15. John Sparrow, *Visible Words: A Study of Inscriptions in and as Books and Works of Art* (Cambridge, 1969), 109–22, defines Tesauro's standing in seventeenth-century epigraphy; see also Eugenio Garin, *Storia della filosofia italiana* (Turin, 1966), 2:789–92, and Ezio Raimondi, *La letteratura barocca* (Florence, 1961), 1–140.

16. Andreina Griseri, "Una fonte 'retorica' per il barocco a Torino," in *Essays in the History of Art Presented to Rudolf Wittkower,* ed. Douglas Fraser et al. (London, 1967), 203–38; and *Le metamorfosi del barocco* (Turin, 1967), 147–55. On the importance of inscriptions in the seventeenth century, see also Florence Vuilleumier, "La rhetorique du monument: L'inscription dans l'architecture en Europe au XVIIe siècle," *XVIIe Siècle,* 39 (1987): 291–312.

17. Sparrow, *Visible Words,* 117–18, paraphrasing the description given by Emanuele Filiberto Panealbi in his edition of Tesauro's *Inscriptiones* (1666).

seventeenth-century culture from the writings of mystics such as Teresa of Avila.[18] "At the climax of the nocturnal display," according to a contemporary description of the event, "when all the Zodiacal signs were shining brightly, a ball of fire, symbolising the royal infant, was to be precipitated from the dark sky into the bosom of Taurus, like the new star that proverbially heralded a new and happier age."[19] Unfortunately shortness of time prevented this firework from being enacted, a poor augury for the heir confirmed by his early death in 1638. In 1632, however, the emphatic dynastic statement of renewal conveyed through the lavish design of the *festa,* similarly to Vittorio Amedeo's wedding in 1620, established through its magnificence a parallel with equivalent royal events elsewhere.

There was a widespread mania for titles in early seventeenth-century Italy, as ruling dukes, princes, and princelings vied with one another for precedence at the papal court and at the royal courts of France and Spain.[20] The House of Savoy was particularly keen on these privileges, being connected with all the monarchs and ruling houses of Europe through blood and marriage relations. Emanuele Filiberto had received the title of *Altezza* or "Highness," the only one in Italy, from Emperor Charles V. This was not an empty title because he was one of the first rulers in Europe to proclaim himself freed from all legislative restraints—"Noi, come principi, siamo da ogni legge sciolti e liberi" (We, as Princes, are from all laws unbound and freed)—and thus to establish the foundations of an absolutist rule for his successors.[21] The title *Infanta* had been used for the daughters of the dukes of Savoy since 1603, when the queen of Spain had called them that.[22] The birth of a male child in 1632 assured the Savoy family's succession and momentarily distanced the French and Spanish interests in the duchy. Both the French and the Spanish ministers, Cardinal Richelieu and Count-Duke Olivares, alternated between considering Piedmont as a buffer zone to keep them apart or as a dominated region (like Lombardy for Spain or Dauphiné for France) on which they could pounce. Thus, the assured succession obliged them to treat Vittorio Amedeo with greater consideration.

The royal title was both greater and less substantial than the ducal title. It

18. For Teresa's influence see Robert T. Petersson, *The Art of Ecstacy: Teresa, Bernini and Crashaw* (London, 1970), 25–42.

19. Sparrow, *Visible Words,* 118.

20. Giulia Datta de Albertis, *Cristina di Francia, Madama Reale* (Turin, 1943), 175–78.

21. Quoted in Perry Anderson, *Lineages of the Absolutist State* (1974; rpt., London, 1979), 171.

22. *Monarchia piemontese,* 3:355.

was greatly desired by Duchess Cristina. Her mother, Maria de' Medici, had been regent of France while King Henri IV was away at war, and again after his death; her older sister Elisabeth was queen of Spain; her brother Louis XIII was king of France; and her younger sister Henrietta Maria was queen of England. It did not matter that Maria de' Medici's poor relations with her son would soon send her into exile; that Elisabeth was kept under close surveillance, which prevented any communication with her French, English, and Piedmontese relatives; or that Henrietta Maria would eventually spend her life in poverty and exile in her homeland after the execution of Charles I.[23] Cristina knew that her official standing was below that of her mother and sisters. Hence the attraction of the royal title was immeasurable. Cristina's widely known obsession with the royal title and the pressure she must have brought to bear on the duke himself remind us irresistibly of the famous line pronounced by Corneille's Honorie: "Enfin je veux un roi: regardez si vous l'êtes" (Finally, I want a king: see if you are he) (*Attila,* II, 2).

Vittorio Amedeo I was not the first duke of Savoy to claim royal status. When he entered Turin in his own wedding procession of 1620, as we saw in chapter 3, he passed through a gate loaded with royal iconography. In the same decade, the title "King of Cyprus" had been adopted by Carlo Emanuele I. This had caused irritation abroad and, in 1630, a break in diplomatic relations with Venice, which similarly claimed the royal title of Cyprus.[24] At Christmas 1632 Vittorio Amedeo declared himself *motu proprio* king of Cyprus and of Jerusalem, and closed his ducal coronet into a royal crown (fig. 50).[25] His new title was formally acknowledged neither by the Venetians nor by the French—Richelieu even mocked his pretensions—and caused considerable problems of precedence among the ambassadors. Fixed embassies were not instruments of national state; their ultimate legitimacy was given by dynastic power, not territory, since the state was seen as the patrimony of the monarch. At the same time, the mobility of titles in the seventeenth century turned foreign diplomacy, which was the institutional invention of the epoch and the absolutist state's greatest external activity apart from trade and war, into an ever-

23. For the queen mother see Deborah Marrow, *The Art Patronage of Maria de' Medici* (Ann Arbor, 1982); for problems of communication between the sisters, see Hermann Ferrero, *Lettres de Henriette-Marie de France Reine d'Angleterre à sa soeur Christine Duchesse de Savoie* (Turin, 1881), 14, 39–40; and for the suspicion in which the foreign-born queens were generally held, see Ruth Kleinman, *Anne of Austria Queen of France* (Columbus, 1985), 38–42.

24. *Monarchia piemontese,* 5:50–52.

25. Ibid., 5:52 (with sources); also Fernand Hayward, *Histoire de la maison de Savoye 1553–1796* (Paris, 1943), 2:136.

changing series of foreign relations.[26] Thus the offensive and defensive league signed in 1635 at Rivoli stipulated that Vittorio Amedeo's royal claims were to be recognized after the conquest of Milan by the joint French and Piedmontese armies. And although Vittorio Amedeo was expected to renounce Cyprus, in order to appease the Venetians, the Savoy coat of arms was to incorporate the royal emblem of France.

The official assumption of the royal title in 1632, then, after the Treaty of Cherasco had brought to an end Carlo Emanuele's wars and after the birth of the heir, can be seen as a celebratory confirmation of these two events, which were so significant for the security and future of the duchy. It was, in effect, a redefinition of the identity of the House of Savoy. This symbolic event was then provided with a physical counterpart, as Vittorio Amedeo turned to the expansion of Turin.

F O L L O W I N G   L O N G deliberation about the form of the expansion, construction began again in 1632. "After many considerations given to the design of the fortifications of this city," Vittorio Amedeo wrote to his brother Prince Tommaso on 30 June 1632, "we have established what needs to be done, and already the work has been started, and it goes on."[27] The ambitious project of Carlo Emanuele I was thoroughly redimensioned, however. Turin's enlargement was to be confined to the southern segment, the expansion area that had come to be known as Città Nuova. As we have seen in chapter 3, it was only in this area that construction work had taken place in the 1620s.

The official examination of the expansion is corroborated by a number of study drawings. The most significant of these projects is dated 1632 and signed by Montafilans, a French or Savoyard military architect, who drew his version of the expansion upon request from the crown (fig. 51).[28] Such consultation

---

26. Anderson, *Lineages,* 37–39; and Christine Trivulce de Belgiojoso, *Histoire de la maison de Savoie* (Paris, 1860), 190–208.

27. AST, Sez. Ia, Lettere Principi Savoia, Duchi e Sovrani, Vittorio Amedeo, mazzo 53: "Dopo molti consid[eratio]ni fatte sopra il dissegno delle fortiffica[ti]oni di questa città habbiamo stabilito quello che si deve fare, et gia si e meso mano all'opera la quale si va continuando."

28. Montafilans' "Maxime (Suivant lesquels desseins et calculs se fortifieront toutes autres places regulieres et irregulieres et tiendrons pour maxime que les places qui seront fortifiez comme dessus seront meilleurs que les autres)," whose text in nine paragraphs frames the planning study, provides a series of rules for the design of bastions.

was quite common, and the request for a *parere,* an opinion, did not oblige the commissioner to appoint the designer, or even to accept the proffered advice. At top right of the sheet, the military architect provided a ten-point *maxime* intended to justify the layout of the fortification enclosure, giving optimal dimensions for every part of the bastion and the curtain wall. Montafilans' plan illustrates Città Vecchia, walled, bastioned, connected to the citadel at the southwest corner, with its narrow and crooked streets separating the small city blocks from one another. To the south of Città Vecchia a dozen or so blocks, much larger than those of the old city, are illustrated. They are surrounded by five full bastions and one half-bastion, whose moat is continuous with the moat of the citadel. The easternmost bastion closest to the southeastern bastion of Città Vecchia is in turn engulfed in an eastern fortification of five bastions, separated in their turn from the Po by a moated palisade-like fortification belt without bastions. Four full and two half-bastions connect the citadel clockwise to the northeast bastion of Città Vecchia. Touching the northwest bastion of the Roman castrum, this fortification would have expanded the limits of Turin both north and west.

Montafilans thus provided Vittorio Amedeo with expansion plans for every point of the compass, but they vary greatly in their importance, quality, and applicability. The northern and western schemes, for example, are both true to the general intention to expand Turin—the expansion north towards the Dora echoes the solution proposed by Carlo di Castellamonte in his official plan of 1619, while the western extension would have enclosed the citadel more deeply into the city's fabric—but they run into one serious problem. The expense of the bastions and the wall curtain was not justified; there were almost as many bastions as suggested for the southern extension area, but they would have enclosed much less space, since the Dora provided a natural barrier to expansion towards the north and northwest. Montafilans illustrated building areas only in the southern extension, thus placing emphasis on that part of the expansion. He interpreted the expansion toward the Po as secondary, dependent upon and following the southern expansion.

Two plans of c. 1632, studies made by Carlo di Castellamonte of the immediate construction needed to accomplish the fortification of Turin, are additional evidence of the state of the work when Vittorio Amedeo decided to continue the interrupted expansion. The ink plan (fig. 52) is most likely a preparatory sketch for the watercolor plan (fig. 53). This sketch illustrates both the original connection proposed by Carlo Emanuele I in his autograph drawing (fig. 41) and the connection actually built between the citadel and the south wall (fig. 39). Variations for fortification enclosures, traced over a simplified version of Carlo Emanuele's plan, are suggested for the southern expansion area, as well as for the extension to the east. These proposals vary in the area of land enclosed and in the type of fortification, bastioned or palisaded. Distinctly different from Carlo Emanuele's drawing, the sketch shows a decision to separate the eastern and southern expansion areas. Thus the continuous fortification enclosure of the earlier planning study by the sovereign, although still visible underneath the layers of this ink sketch, would be divided into individual enclosures.

The second, colored drawing (fig. 53) illustrates constructed portions of the south wall precisely (one full, two half-bastions, two ravelins, and the south gate) and includes a minimal fortification for the area between Turin and the bridge over the Po, intended to defend the road between the city and the river. From this drawing it is evident that the expansion to the east was no longer considered simultaneously with the expansion to the south. Both drawings illustrate the road connecting the Po bridge to the Castello, testifying to the importance of this artery in the strategic defense of the city and its significance for the expansions. We have seen in chapter 3 that the eastern expansion was important both for strategic reasons (help could be expected from Lombardy in case of French attack from the west) and for dynastic-symbolic representation (since the ancient site of Turin was supposedly on the Po itself). But the citadel in the southwest corner of the city was to have long-term influence upon the development of the city. The southern expansion area could be defended by the citadel, and thus a reduced expansion policy had to develop the southern area first for strategic reasons of defense.

The new construction campaign sponsored by Vittorio Amedeo I was celebrated in a now very rare engraving by Giovenale Boetto, made c. 1632 (fig. 54). The engraving is framed by a cartouche and two putti holding a chain inscribed *RT* and *FE*—the much disputed *FERT,* motto of the House of Savoy—from which hangs the medal of the Order of the Annunziata.[29] It shows the monarch on horseback conferring with his military architect. From the hill on which they stand, the state of construction immediately after Carlo Emanuele I's death can be seen. Two and one-half bastions have been raised, but they remain incomplete. A third bastion has been begun, with a moat being dug around it. The figures in the background are carrying earth from the moat to the terrace of the bastion, suggesting that the dual activity of digging and terracing was pursued simultaneously. The citadel and Città Vecchia are clearly

29. For a detailed examination of this motto, see *I rami incisi dell'archivio di corte,* ed. Isabella Ricci (Turin, 1981), 74–93; see also chap. 3, note 8.

visible, but the center of the engraving is damaged. While the figure of the architect is assumed to represent Carlo di Castellamonte, interpretation of the identity of the equestrian figure is divided, and the figure has been considered variously as Vittorio Amedeo I and Carlo Emanuele I.

Boetto was named court architect in November 1631. Since he is assumed to have studied with Giacomo Marcucci, a Roman engraver who was in Piedmont in 1633–34, he probably began to engrave from c. 1633.[30] In 1632 Emanuele Tesauro was working on a compendium of the heroic actions of Carlo Emanuele I entitled *Dies Fasti,* having been commissioned earlier to design the funeral of the late duke and the birthday celebration of Francesco Giacinto, Vittorio Amedeo's heir, discussed above. His book, never published, was to have had illustrations by Boetto exalting the actions of Carlo Emanuele.[31] This is the best evidence we have that the equestrian figure might represent Carlo Emanuele. The engraving postdates Vittorio Amedeo's letter of June 1632, in which he informed his brother Tommaso that construction on the expansion area had begun. Thus the engraving celebrates the continuity of the military interests of the House of Savoy, whether in the person of Carlo Emanuele or in that of Vittorio Amedeo. The festive frame suggests an official commissioned view, intended to commemorate the formal beginning of the new construction campaign for the expansion project initiated in 1632—the re-inauguration of the expansion begun by Carlo Emanuele I—which reinforced the dynastic program of the succeeding dukes of Savoy. Since this engraving is representative of dynastic continuity in enlarging the capital, the actual identity of the equestrian figure, the absolute monarch, is less significant than the portrayal of the expansion itself.

An earlier engraved view of Turin (fig. 48), briefly discussed in chapter 3, corroborates the extent of construction in Città Nuova shown in the view by Boetto. Mistakenly labeled "Ville de Bude," and owned by a French collector before the end of the seventeenth century (now in the print collection of the Bibliothèque Nationale in Paris), the view is very similar to Boetto's.[32] Taken from higher up on the same hill across the Po, this unsigned illustration shows Turin seen from the southeast; the Capuchin convent is visible at right, the Villa Valentino at left. A dry moat and wall surround Turin, which is repre-

30. Nino Carboneri and Andreina Griseri, *Giovenale Boetto* (Fossano, 1966), 31–63.

31. *Schede Vesme,* 1:145.

32. Collector's mark, at top right, is "Tral," indicating that the print belonged to Nicholas de Tralage, geographer and councilor of the Parlement in Paris; at his death in 1699 he bequeathed his 32,429-piece topographical and mythological collection to the Abbey of Saint Victor.

sented as a densely built-up city, with numerous church and military towers. The east wall of Città Vecchia, the Castello, and the Galleria are clearly visible. There is a vast open area, the military parade ground, between the citadel and the Città Vecchia. Only in the southern part of the expansion is there orderly construction. Most of the buildings are concentrated along the main north-south street, which connects the two south gates to one another. There are two nearly completed bastions framing the outer south gate, and one half-bastion adjacent to the citadel. There is a seven-arch bridge over the Po, and a sizable settlement on the Turin side of the bridgehead. The viewer is placed at a greater distance from Turin than in the view signed by Boetto. This unsigned view may have been commissioned in the late 1620s in an effort to publicize the results of Carlo Emanuele's project to enlarge Turin. Thus its takeover as iconographic model by Boetto in 1632 represents the continuity claimed by Vittorio Amedeo, as well as his contributions to the embellishment of the city.

Additional corroborative evidence is provided by another engraving by Boetto (fig. 55). This is one of ten scenes illustrating a frontispiece of 1634 (fig. 56), all of which describe events in the Savoy dynasty's genealogy, with the lion's share given to Vittorio Amedeo, as reigning duke. Framed by Carlo Emanuele and Emanuele Filiberto at the top right corner of the sheet, Vittorio Amedeo is shown on horseback conferring with a figure on foot holding a sheet with the plan of the city. The new blocks in Città Nuova are shown here from a different angle, but the two figures are identical to those in Boetto's other engraving, discussed above. The more advanced construction in this view thus supports the earlier dating for the FERT view, as well as the identification of the figure with Vittorio Amedeo rather than Carlo Emanuele.

The two single views (figs. 48, 54) are the first to illustrate the expansionary efforts begun under Carlo Emanuele I. They are also among the first engraved representations of Turin. The engraved view was an important propaganda instrument since it was distributed widely and could be expected to reach a large public, even outside the city of origin. In comparison with views of other cities, such as Venice and Florence, these two engravings do not attempt to show the civic and religious command center of Turin. Instead the recent fortified expansion of the city by the dukes of Savoy is placed in the foreground at the center of the image. The other notable difference is that in comparison to views of Venice, Florence, Rome, and other great Renaissance cities, the views of Turin are late and artistically meager.

It is significant that the views of Turin are conservative in conception (although the 1572 view by Caracha enjoyed a long iconographic success) and certainly late in comparison with those of other Italian cities.[33] By contrast the military plans, studies, and complete drawings were quite plentiful, early, and innovative in their scientific abstraction and surveyed accuracy. But the autograph planning studies were kept secret due to their strategical military content. However, at a time when wars were decided through sieges, the fame of a city's fortifications would be an important factor in its ability not only to defend itself, but also to ward off enemies. Thus the engraved view produced in large numbers was a convenient way to publicize the military expansion of the capital city.

THE RESTRUCTURED AND truncated expansion campaign undertaken by Vittorio Amedeo I encountered difficulties similar to those confronted by his father. There was a shortage of both materials and laborers. Since building the walls was largely an exercise in earth moving, numerous unskilled men were needed. This work was often done by soldiers and hired hands. Vittorio Amedeo I's correspondence shows that, both as heir to the duchy and as duke, he had to search to find workmen and was not always successful. On two occasions, in 1622 and 1629, Vittorio Amedeo published an order in his father's name addressing twenty-eight towns near Turin, including Pavarolo, Moncalieri, Coconato, Rivalta, Pecetto, and Villastelone, and requiring them to supply *guastatori* (sappers) for the building of the expansion's fortifications so that there would be one thousand workers at any given time.[34] Workers were recruited from outside in 1632 as well, after the devastations of the plague. The expected arrival of two thousand *guastatori*—a huge influx of potential help—was considered newsworthy by the nuncio who reported it to the papal court at the Vatican.[35] Vittorio Amedeo's letters to his brother Tommaso—governor of Momigliano, the only fortress in Savoy that had not been taken by the French—are filled with his preoccupations about the labor force employed in the fortifications' construction. In June 1632, when seasonal ag-

33. The cartographic iconography of Italian cities has recently received detailed attention in the series *Le città nella storia d'Italia,* ed. Cesare de Seta (Bari, 1979–); twenty-three volumes have been published to date on as many Italian towns.

34. AST, Sez. Ia, Lettere Principi Savoia, Duchi e Sovrani, Vittorio Amedeo, mazzi 54, 55.

35. BAV, MS Barberini Latini 7164, 10 July 1632, fol. 35v: "S'aspettano in breve 2/m Valtesani ch'S[ua] A[ltezza] fa venir p[er] far lavorare attorno il recinto della città nuova di Torino."

ricultural tasks occupied available workers around Turin, Vittorio Amedeo asked his brother to send five hundred men from Faucigny, who, because of the different harvest times in Savoy, were then idle. These workers were to be lured by steady pay distributed daily together with their wine and bread.[36] But of the one hundred fifty men who left Savoy to come to work on the fortification of Città Nuova only thirty turned up; the others ran away or returned home.[37]

Nonetheless, at the time of his death in 1637 the fortification of Città Nuova was essentially complete. Already in 1635 the fortifications impressed visitors by their size and monumentality. Count Fulvio Testi wrote in 1635, after his third sojourn in Turin, that he had visited the fortifications of the city and that the bastions were not only designed in keeping with the shooting range of the most up-to-date firearms, but were the largest he had ever seen. Testi's criteria, moreover, were not simply strategic, but aesthetic: the fortifications were "truly most beautiful," *bellissime*.[38] The fortification was achieved at extravagant cost, which was justified, at least in part, by the menace of French troops ensconced in Pinerolo, and by the fact that Piedmont depended on Turin.

The success in fortifying the reduced expansion can be attributed to the institutionalization of the construction process and its supervision. Soon after Vittorio Amedeo reopened the construction of the expansion in 1632, he instituted the Delegazione sopra le Fabriche delle Fortificationi di Torino (19 January 1633).[39] Its mandate was to oversee, direct, and accomplish the fortification enclosure of the southern expansion. Since this council duplicated the

36. AST, Sez. Ia, Lettere Principi Savoia, Duchi e Sovrani, 30 June 1632, Vittorio Amedeo to Prince Tommaso in Momigliano: "Ma perche (come sapete) tutti li lavoratori della campagna in questi due mesi si occupano a talliar et battere gli grani non puotendolo differir in altra stagione come si fa in Savoia; per guadagnar questo tempo habbiamo pensato di far venire da 500 buoni huomoni dal Foussigni [Faucigny] li quali a quest'hora saranno dis-occupati, ne darette prontam[en]te gl'ordini necessarij facciendogl'assicurare c'haveranno oltre pane e vino la paga ogni giorno in danarj."

37. AST, Sez. Ia, Lettere Principi Savoia, Duchi e Sovrani, 17 September 1632, Vittorio Amedeo to Prince Tommaso: "Delli 150 huomini che partirono di Savoia per venir travag-liare alle ripari di Citta nuova ne sono comparsi da 30 in circa gl'altri fugirono et tornarono acasa."

38. *Il conte Fulvio Testi alla corte di Torino negli anni 1628 e 1635*, ed. D. Perrero [Milan, 1865], 126: "Andai, il giorno seguente, a vedere le fortificationi, le quali veramente sono bellissime. I baluardi sono i piu grandi che abbia mai veduti, e anco coll'orecchione le cortine sono a tiro di moschetto, a tra un baluardo e l'altro, al di fuori, sono alcune mezze lune per grandimento."

39. Duboin, 906; AST, Sez. Riunite, Lettere patenti, 19 January 1633.

responsibilities of the Magistrato delle Fabriche—instituted as we have seen by Carlo Emanuele in 1621—their respective duties were sifted apart and clarified in an edict of 17 August 1635, establishing a separate Consiglio delle Fabriche in charge of nonmilitary construction.[40] That this separation of largely overlapping functions was cumbersome and falsified the situation was proven in an edict promulgated by Vittorio Amedeo I's widow, the regent Cristina, in 1638, in which the two councils were united into one legal body, the Consiglio delle Fabriche e Fortificationi.[41] While the function of the united council was identical to that of Carlo Emanuele's Magistrato delle Fabriche, it was only in 1638 that the right name was attached to the functions of the agency.

The extensive activities of this council are closely documented in the archives of Fabriche e Fortificationi. Its members, including the first ducal engineer, Count Carlo di Castellamonte, a holdover from Carlo Emanuele's council, maintained close relations with the duke. Among others, Maurizio Valperga was employed throughout 1633 as Castellamonte's architectural assistant.[42] It is Castellamonte who on 25 April 1633 is to measure the site occupied by the fortifications, so that owners whose property has been confiscated or damaged can be reimbursed. On 4 May 1633 he is acknowledged as the designer of the bastions. He also was responsible for the simultaneous fortification of Città Vecchia, as we know from a document of 28 January 1634. Finally, in 1635 Carlo di Castellamonte was appointed architect in charge of all ducal building projects.[43]

Thanks to Vittorio Amedeo's involvement, the advanced stage of the fortification's construction and the maintenance of the continued effort needed in order to provide building supplies and the working crew are closely documented. At his order, in May 1633, contracts were announced for the construction of the half-moons, not only for Città Nuova, but also for the reinforcement of the bastion in the northwest corner of the old city, and the emergency gate of the citadel.[44] Vittorio Amedeo was thoroughly immersed

40. AST, Sez. Riunite, art. 199, 17 August 1635, fols. 281–83.

41. Duboin, 906; AST, Sez. Riunite, Lettere patenti, 30 August 1638.

42. AST, Sez. Riunite, art. 197, fol. 70, 16 June 1633, and fol. 83, 12 August 1633.

43. AST, Sez. Riunite, art. 199.1, April and May 1633, January 1634; Lettere patenti, 30 August 1635.

44. AST, Sez. Riunite, art. 199, 26 May 1643, fol. 174: "Commandando S[ua] A[ltezza] R[eale] che si dia p[rin]cipio prontam[en]te a due mezze lune che fianchino il bastione della Consolata, piu altra mezza luna alla porta del soccorso della Cittadella et le mezze lune della Città nuova, hanno detto al S[igno]r Vincendotto [a member of the council] di pratticar partiti per il cavo di esse."

in the practical aspects of the expansion, where the desired speed of construction put pressure on local manufacturing of building materials and strained the available means for their transportation to the site. To facilitate transportation a canal was opened between the Po and the Porta Nuova, along which brick made in Moncalieri and Cavoretto, small towns near Turin, could be brought to the construction site at the moat of Città Nuova. In addition, the planned output of brick manufacture in Turin was greatly expanded for the year 1635, from three and a half million pieces to five million.[45] Clearly, the construction of the fortification of Turin was the fundamental concern of the ducal government. In addition to the archive of Fabriche e Fortificationi, which bristles with information about the work in progress, the payment orders to the treasury seem to be concerned exclusively with the building of Turin's walls and the excavation of its moats. The payment orders for 1632 concern the bread, wine, and lodging for the *guastatori*—unskilled laborers recruited from the entire duchy—who are digging the moats of the southern expansion. These continue through June 1633.

On 19 January 1633 Vittorio Amedeo, having signed the Treaty of Cherasco that left Pinerolo garrisoned by the French, and having assumed the royal title, urged his council to speed up work on the fortification of Turin. One year later, 17 February 1634, the construction of the remaining bastions, San Carlo, Beato Amedeo, and Santa Cristina, was begun in earnest. A payment order of 27 December 1634 provides a summary of the construction achieved up to that date.[46] This consists of 7,177 *trabucchi* (1 *trabucco* equaled about 3 meters), of which over 4,000 had been built in 1634 alone, demonstrating the increased speed of construction. Other large payments are made in 18 December 1635

45. AST, Sez. Riunite, art. 199, 17 March 1635, fol. 241: "Faccia livelar il canale che comanda farsi da Po fin'alla Porta di Marmo [Porta Nuova], p[er]che i mattoni che si fabricheranno a Moncalieri e sotto Cavoretto [two towns across the river from Turin] se conducono in barca fin'alla riva de' fossi della Città nuova . . . che faccia cuocer quest'anno 5 milioni di mattoni non ostante che l'obligo suo sia solo di 3½."

46. AST, Sez. Riunite, art. 197, fol. 134: "Sig[nor] Gio[vanni] Fran[ces]co ricev[itor]e del danaro di d[ett]a fortificat[io]ne pagherete a capi m[urato]ri Andrea Muschio, Fran[ces]co Quattropani impressari della fabricha della muraglia della Città Nuova la somma di livre mille ottocento trent'una di argento da soldi vinti l'una e piu soldi diciotto ch'egli devono per resto a compito pagam[en]to de trabuchi sette milla cento settanta sette e mezo di detta muraglia fabricata da qui indietro negli anni 1632, 1633 e corente 1634." For the report of the surveyor Solari used in this payment order, see fol. 135: "le muraglie che si sono fatte degli anni 1632, e 1633 sonno trabucchi du'mille novecento novanta . . . piu trab[ucchi] q[uattr]o milla cento ottanta sei e piedi cinque muraglie fatte del corrente anno."

and 2 June 1637, confirming the great dispatch of construction. The contractors had agreed, on 6 September 1635, to build 200 *trabucchi* of wall each week.[47]

It is not a surprise, then, that when the council of Fabriche e Fortificationi visited Città Nuova on 28 July 1636 it found the fortification enclosure almost completed.[48] At Vittorio Amedeo's death on 5 October 1637, all walls and bastions were complete, except the bastion of San Mauritio and its connecting curtain wall to the citadel, which had been built to the height of the parapet. Other missing elements of the fortification were the half-moon between the bastion of Santa Cristina and that of Beato Amedeo, the covered ways, and the completion of the moats.[49] Despite these incomplete areas, however, Vittorio Amedeo's balance sheet is a creditable one, since the work accomplished in the five years of his effective reign in Turin was much greater than that realized in the first ten years of the expansion.

Besides the shortage of workers, an equally serious problem that had to be resolved was the production of materials and the provisioning of the construction sites. In this respect, the expansion's fortification starts on a tragicomic note: Vittorio Amedeo and his ministers had first thought to tear down the walls of Moncalieri so as to use the materials for the construction of the walls of Turin, but they were then persuasively begged by its citizens not to implement that plan.[50] Simultaneously Vittorio Amedeo encouraged legislation intended to diminish the shortages of building materials in the Città Nuova. In 1633 the means of measuring tile, brick, and masonry construction, and the responsibility of contractors were fixed by the municipality of Turin, and new estimators were appointed—at the request of the crown—in order to prevent speculation.[51] The intention of this law was similar to that of the edict promul-

47. AST, Sez. Riunite, art. 199, fol. 151.

48. AST, Sez. Riunite, art. 199, fol. 61: "trasferiti alla Città Nuova i s[igno]ri P[residen]te Furno, Conte Carlo Castellam[on]te, Aud[ito]re Vincendotto, Gio[vanni] Bat[tis]ta Tarino, et Aud[ito]re Ripis con me seg[reta]ro sotto s[critt]o dove sendosi visitata la fortifi[cation]e tutto attorno, e ritrovata tutta al cordone et in parecchi luoghi avanzatasi ne'parapeti."

49. AST, Sez. Riunite, art. 199.1, 8 October 1637. Two large payments for the moats and walls of the fortification on 5 February and 2 June 1637 (AST, Sez. Riunite, art. 197, fol. 194, fol. 203) suggest the intensified rate of construction in this year.

50. BAV, MS Barberini Latini 7174, 19 June 1632, fol. 30: "Havevano risoluti i ministri di S[ua] A[ltezza] per haver i mattoni d'incamiciar la nuova città e borghi di Torino valersi di Moncalieri, ma essendo quegl'huomini ricossi supplicando l'A[ltezza] S[ua] a non privarle delle proprie mura, il negotio resta sospeso."

51. ASCT, Biglietti Regi, 3817, 4 June 1633, Vittorio Amedeo to the syndics of Turin: "Mag[nifi]ci n[ost]ri car[issi]mi. Gli ufficiali delle n[ost]re fabriche ci hanno rappresentato

gated by Carlo Emanuele I in 1621 in that it attempted to prevent abuses such as overcharging and poor construction. The number of residences built in the Città Nuova during this five-year period was proportionately large, an increase of approximately 150 percent, as can be seen from a view of c. 1642 illustrating a relatively dense settlement (fig. 57). More materials became available for private construction, and the locally semipeaceful conditions of the period also encouraged construction. In July 1633 the municipal order established the rules for the measurement of buildings. The thickness of different types of walls had already been standardized so that materials, the number of bricks for instance, could be calculated in advance from drawings. With this important new law, payments traditionally made according to the length of wall built could be calculated in advance as well.[52] In addition, on 20 May 1633 masons were prohibited from working without a license from the first ducal engineer.[53] Thus the ducal government came to control the building industry completely.

Although the name of the supervisory agency had changed, the architect and engineers remained the same. Carlo di Castellamonte was the strongest force in the completion of the fortification and in the urban layout of the southern expansion. His supervision of the construction continued beyond the reign of Vittorio Amedeo I, as he remained politically faithful to the besieged regent and died while in her employ after the siege of Turin, probably in 1641.[54]

THE DEATH OF Vittorio Amedeo in the autumn of 1637 was quick and unexpected. Rumors spread that he had been poisoned by the maréchal de Créqui, the representative of the French crown in Piedmont as well as the

---

l'abbuso, che può correr non tanto à danno n[ost]ro, che del publico nelle misure, et stimi delle fabriche, che si fanno da'misuratori, et stimatori da noi diputati, perche sendo essi dello stato di Lugano, e muratori, po[so]nno verisimilm[ent]e avvantaggiare con qualche intelligenza l'opere de'capi m[urato]ri, che sono de medisimi paesi, et arti. E desiderando noi di porvi rimedio, vi diciamo di far nuova elettione d'altri; che siano fuori d'ogni eccettione, partecipando co' sud[etti] ufficiali; nel che crediamo non sarà da noi posta difficoltà, poiche si tratta del commune beneficio."

52. Duboin, 926–31.

53. Ibid., 929.

54. Carlo di Castellamonte is among the prisoners taken by the Spanish and listed by the nuncio Caffarelli in his *avviso* of 27–28 July 1639 (BAV, MS Barberini Latini 7174, fol. 59).

general of the French army there.[55] Vittorio Amedeo had passed the previous months fighting by his side, although much of the time was spent in issues of precedence; Vittorio Amedeo insisted on being both the general and the strategist for the armies of the allies in their joint actions against the Spanish in Lombardy. Nonetheless, he seems to have shared peaceful interests with the French marshal as well.

Créqui had acquired an important collection of paintings with lightning speed during his residence in Rome, before being posted to the court of Savoy in Turin. At Créqui's recommendation, Vittorio Amedeo engaged Antonio della Corgnia, a Roman connoisseur, to evaluate and inventory the Savoy dynasty's painting collection.[56] This stock taking not only was part of Vittorio Amedeo's systematic attempt to restore order to the duchy (the archives were also reorganized and inventoried in 1635), but also was intended to reinforce his royal claims through a bureaucratization and institutionalization of all aspects of the ducal property and administration.

Vittorio Amedeo patronized artists and promoted the arts in keeping with his means. The *feste* for which the Savoy dynasty had been famous since Carlo Emanuele I's reign were continued under Vittorio Amedeo, although credit must be given to Duchess Cristina as well. The *feste* were an important propaganda arm through which the crown conveyed public messages to its subjects in the form of pleasure, mixing the useful with the delightful according to the well-worn Horatian axiom. On the last day of the carnival in 1637 Vittorio Amedeo took part in the ballet entitled *Hercole espugnator delle Esperidi*. In it he is addressed as "Monarca del'Alpi" (monarch of the Alps), "prole di Marte" (descendant of Mars), and bridegroom of Italy, while interpreting the part of heroic Hercules. The association with Hercules had been made for him in 1620, at the *festa* designed for his wedding by Carlo Emanuele I, where, as we have seen in chapter 2, the giant hero was shown together with the mountain of virtue and the temple of righteousness. In the 1637 ballet the mountain of Atlantis, crowned with a fortress rather than a temple, also represents Piedmont, as Hercules-Vittorio is helped by the gods to a thousand victories. This *ballet de cour* format allowed for half-veiled praises to be made to Vittorio Ame-

55. *Monarchia piemontese,* 5:107.

56. For Créqui's collection see Jean-Claude Boyer and Isabelle Volf, "Rome à Paris: Les tableaux du Maréchal de Créqui (1638)," *Revue de l'Art,* 79 (1988): 22–41; Corgnia's inventory was made in 1635. For another (partial) inventory of the ducal collection made in the first year of Vittorio Amedeo's reign, see Giuseppe Campori, *Raccolta di cataloghi ed inventari inediti* (Modena, 1870), 76–104: "Inventario di quadri di pittura di S[ua] Al[tezz]a che si ritrovano in Castello fatta hoggi il primo di settembre 1631."

deo in public; the traditional panegyric permitted the *festa* writer to prescribe the monarch's virtues as well as to praise him, by suggesting qualities expected of him.[57]

The last great public event in which Vittorio Amedeo played the leading role took place in the fall of the same year, 1637, when he appeared in effigy as his departed self. His funeral was his final show and can be considered as a summary of his major actions and achievements. Representations of fame, eternal memory, dynastic continuity, and royalty abounded. The royal title coveted by Vittorio Amedeo was prominently displayed in the frontispiece of the book commemorating his demise (fig. 58) and in the arch of triumph over death placed above the cathedral's portal (fig. 59), while royal crowns were studded upon the nave walls of the cathedral itself (fig. 60). For the design of this ceremony no expense was spared by the widowed regent, and the ceremony acquired fame through the subsequent publications of memorialists.[58] The decorations for the funeral have survived through the engravings made by Giovenale Boetto for the book published in 1638 by another Jesuit employed at court, Luigi Giuglaris, documenting the funeral Giuglaris had designed for the monarch.[59]

The interior of the cathedral of Turin was transformed for the occasion into a great ancestors' gallery. A processional avenue of ancestors, crowned by illustrations of Vittorio Amedeo's diplomatic and military achievements, led to the catafalque (fig. 61), placed under the dome of the crossing. This funeral structure designed by Carlo di Castellamonte resembled an unfolded triumphal arch. It was made of four arches flanked by free-standing "funeral order" columns (the leaves of the composite order replaced by skulls); the pedestals of the columns were continuous and chamfered at corners providing bases for statues of mourning female figures. The broken pediments of the triumphal arches sheltered Savoy emblems and coats of arms, while above the parapet a

57. *Hercole espugnator delle esperidi: gran balletto di Madama Reale per l'ultimo giorno di carnevale* (Turin, 1637), *passim*.

58. These memorialists include Claude-François Menestrier, *Des Décorations funèbres* (Paris, 1684), 118; the funeral is recorded and illustrated also in Sparrow, *Visible Words*, 105 and 122, who discusses the relation between funeral ceremonies and inscriptions. The significance of the funeral as the moment of transition of sovereignty for French monarchs is the main thesis of R. E. Giesey, *The Royal Funeral Ceremony in Renaissance France* (Geneva, 1960).

59. Luigi Giuglaris, *Funerale fatto nel duomo di Torino alla gloriosa memoria [di] Vittorio Amedeo Duca di Savoia, Prencipe di Piemonte, Re di Cipro* (Turin, 1638). The following description is taken from these engravings.

pedestal of candles, diminishing in size as it rose and thus resembling a fiery pyramid, supported the equestrian effigy of Vittorio Amedeo. This statue was at the eye level of the audience of this funeral spectacle, who watched it from the gallery in the drum of the dome.

The interior of the cathedral had become a genealogical pantheon of the Savoy dynasty, with previous rulers summoned to assist at the apotheosis of Vittorio Amedeo, the crowning achievement of their collective ambition. The ancients surrounding the catafalque were the eponymous Savoy rulers, Amedeo IV, V, VI, and so on. The wall area of the nave below the clerestory windows was hung with black cloth pinned with additional family coats of arms and torches. The bays between the piers were filled in with statues of the *antenati* placed upon pedestals, flanked by their arms, *imprese,* and trophies, and surmounted by pictorial representations of events from the life of the latest duke. They included, naturally, a memorial of his greatest military victories and his hardest won diplomatic achievements, such as the Peace of Cherasco, and also an illustration of his relationship to Turin as sovereign (*duce*) in charge of its military expansion.

The decoration for the facade of the cathedral centered upon the entry door, which was flanked by coupled skeletons—raised upon bases filled with representations of river gods—acting as caryatids, supporting signs (unfortunately illegible in the engraving) on shields propped against their legs and above their heads. The top of the funeral triumphal arch consisted of the angel of glory blowing his horn between the halves of the broken pediment. The image of virtue, carried in a chariot drawn by vices and driven upon wheels of eternity, was flanked by melancholy crowned figures of Piedmont and Savoy consoling one another. But the centerpiece of this gateway composition was the inscription immediately above the door. The message was from Cristina, the widow regent, and it contained exhortations to mourn, requests for sympathy at her loss, and veiled threats to punish those who challenged her authority. In it, she urges the population to groan, shed tears, express grief. She claims to be making memorial offerings to a better Mausolus, thus positing herself as the new Artemisia, and then claims tribute to herself, now regent, as the highest authority for the inhabitants of the duchy. "Not content with her own groans, she covets the groans of others," and thus she seems to promise grief if her own sorrow at the death of Vittorio Amedeo is challenged by lack of obedience.[60]

60. Inscription on triumphal arch, figure 59:

> Pluvius vobis o cives autumnus est
> Serenitate sepulta

The funeral ceremony served two important functions. The interior decorations of the cathedral summarized the dynastic apotheosis of the ruling family, pointedly evoking the imagery connected with the genealogical gallery of ancestors and the geographical gallery of conquest. Vittorio Amedeo's accomplishments in Turin were carefully placed in the context of his national and international diplomatic and military activities. By contrast, in a more immediate, temporal vein, the exterior ornamentation of the cathedral stated the claims of the succeeding ruler, who thus sought to short-circuit the expected challenge to her own legitimacy. Such challenges, however, did not fail to materialize.

Ulciscimini fletibus
Praereritae siccitatem aestatis
Dat argvmentum Christiana
Damna vestra lugens in suis
Nova Artemisia
Meliori Mausolo parentans
Avaritia quadam doloris
Suis non contenta gemitibus
Inhiat alienis
Hoc primum pendite tributum
Regnanti
Nullum majori titulo debuistis.

For help with translation from the Latin I thank Michael Alexander.

5

The Regency of Cristina

Dynastic War and the Creation of Piazza Reale

Plus de fermeté que d'éclat.
—Motto of Cristina

La vie fut un continuel orage
à la cour et dans les affaires.
—Voltaire

CRISTINA OF FRANCE (also known as Chrétienne, Chrestienne, Christine, Christiana, and Madama Reale) was one of the three most influential seventeenth-century rulers of Piedmont and Savoy. Although her qualities and achievements were unlike those of the other two famed members of the House of Savoy, Carlo Emanuele I and Vittorio Amedeo II, she held her contemporaries equally enthralled and intrigued, and her stormy reign has been the subject of research by numerous puzzled and captivated historians.[1] Aside from her own qualities and shortcomings, her visibility was due largely to her gender. There are few critical works that deal with her reign as such; most schol-

---

1. The most extensive study is by Gaudenzio Claretta, *Storia della reggenza di Cristina di Francia* (Turin, 1868–69), 3 vols.; but see also *Monarchia piemontese,* 5:113–361, 6:3–172; Giulia Datta de Albertis, *Cristina di Francia, Madama Reale* (Turin, 1943); Amedeo Peyron, *Notizie per servire alla storia della reggenza di Cristina di Francia Duchessa di Savoia* (Turin, 1866); Augusto Bazzoni, *La reggenza di Maria Cristina Duchessa di Savoia* (Turin, 1865); Federico de Gaudenzi, "Torino e la corte sabauda al tempo di Maria Cristina di Francia," *Bollettino storico-bibliografico subalpino,* 18 (1913): 1–111; L. Franceschini, *Documenti inediti sulla storia della reggenza di Maria Cristina* (Rome, 1895); "Relation de la cour de Savoye c'est à dire des intrigues de Chrétienne de France," BN, Paris, MS Franc. 23348, fols. 272–89.

ars, following the pattern of established historical inquiry, have focused on the dynastic war that flared up at the beginning of her regency.[2] Her problems as a female regent whose authority was disputed by the male members of the ruling family were intimately connected to the development of Turin after the death of her husband Duke Vittorio Amedeo I; for this reason, they must be considered as part of this analysis of the motivations and intentions that contributed to the expansion of the capital city. As in the reigns of Carlo Emanuele I and Vittorio Amedeo I, albeit under altered circumstances, the works of art, architecture, and urban design commissioned by Cristina were treated as metaphors of power, transposing into visual images a programmatic series of political concepts and dynastic messages.

The ceremony mounted for the funeral of Vittorio Amedeo was one of these metaphors. As we have seen in chapter 4, it allowed the recently deceased duke to act one more time in his role as would-be king, with the extended cast of Savoy ancestors and emblematic representations of his military, religious, and building activities as further support for the claim to royalty. The funeral provided by his widow Cristina had been lavish, and the supportive apparatus extensive and costly. Two years later, his brother Prince Tommaso, who had not been allowed to attend the funeral because of his declared Spanish allegiance, which contradicted the Piedmontese foreign policy of Vittorio Amedeo, reproached Cristina for the garish expense that would have sufficed for the ammunition of all the fortresses in Piedmont.[3]

Tommaso was, of course, being polemical. The funereal arch at the entry into the cathedral provided not only a metaphor for Vittorio Amedeo's triumph over death, but a field for his successor's claims (fig. 59). In the inscription that dominates the triumphal arch, Cristina is named twice: as "Christiana," a Latinized version of her name used in legal documents, medals, and official portraits, and also as "Artemisia." The new ruler, the provider of the public spectacle so widely appreciated in Piedmont and generally in seventeenth-century urban life, thus established her sovereignty by proximity to the expired ruler, and, through a clever play on her own name, made further claims to the recognized Christian piety of the regent. Her legitimacy as ruler was to be reinforced by reference to Artemisia, whose story had become the accepted mythological representation of the bereaved widow ever since her

2. The war is the main focus, for example, in the works by Bazzoni, Franceschini, and Peyron cited in note 1.

3. Datta de Albertis, *Cristina di Francia,* 198–99.

imagery had been adopted by Queen Catherine de' Medici when she made her own bid for the regency of France in 1562.[4]

Like sixteenth-century pageants, seventeenth-century celebrations employed painting, architecture, and epigraphy in studied representations of power in the belief that they could help shift actual power. Self-representations of sovereigns spoke the discourses of both political and sexual power, which were indistinguishable in the dynastic strategies of the period. Even more than the Renaissance, the seventeenth century believed in the power of art to persuade, transform, and preserve.[5] During the campaign staged by Catherine de' Medici for regency she defined how she would appear in public and contrived her own official imagery. Catherine wore permanent mourning, thus forging a continuous link with her deceased royal husband. Black stood for widowhood, but it also associated her with contemporary male monarchs; also, since Henri II had worn black she seemed a stand-in for him. Finding a suitable ancient prototype for the queen's persona was not an easy matter, because such obvious female associations as Juno, Minerva, or Diana were not appropriate for the widow ruler. Artemisia, queen of Caria in Asia Minor in the fourth century B.C. and known through Boccaccio's *De claris mulieribus* as the inconsolable wife of Mausolus, was "celebrated as being something that few of the immortals were ever likely to be: a widow." Artemisia was the ideal spouse, who in addition possessed all the male virtues necessary for a competent ruler. Above all, she was a builder.

As seen in the decorations of the triumphal entries staged after Henri II's death, Artemisia entered Catherine's pantheon, and the association was incontrovertibly stated in the fifty-nine drawings of the *historiae* commissioned by her probably from Antoine Caron.[6] In these portraits, as Artemisia, the queen watches and directs all the events of her rule; actual power, such as violence, is replaced by symbolic representation of power, such as costume. Attesting to the success of Artemisia as prototype is the impact these drawings had on Maria de' Medici and Anne of Austria, who had tapestries made from them. Artemisia had been proposed as model and prototype earlier for Anne de Beaujeu by Jean Lemaire de Belges in his *Couronne Margaritique,* and taken up

4. Here and in the next two paragraphs I am quoting extensively from Sheila ffolliott, "Catherine de' Medici as Artemisia: Figuring the Powerful Widow," in *Rewriting the Renaissance: The Discourses of Sexual Difference in Early Modern Europe,* ed. Margaret W. Ferguson et al. (Chicago, 1986), 227–41.

5. Stephen Orgel, *The Illusion of Power: Political Theatre in the English Renaissance* (1975), quoted by ffolliott, "Artemisia," 229.

6. ffolliott, "Artemisia," 231.

again for the dowager duchess of Savoy in 1549. Thus the mythological widow would have been a well-established image with which Cristina could identify, and one that she could have known from both historical and familial sources.

Like Catherine, Cristina always wore widow's weeds, and like Anne of Austria, she made a great show of her Christian piety. She founded a number of religious institutions in Turin, giving expression to her piety as well as her desire to build. Her devotions were turned into public spectacles, as when she crossed Turin dressed in sackcloth, carrying a cross, and accompanied by her similarly attired ladies-in-waiting. She attempted to gain legitimacy through continuing association with her late husband and through her cultural influence upon the young duke; by controlling the latter's education, she forged the future ruler. She persevered in the three roles freely associated with female rule: those of wife, widow, and mother-educator. In this context, the pageantry of the funeral is as significant for Cristina as widowed regent and dowager duchess, as the wedding ceremony was for Cristina as would-be ruling duchess. Besides the male virtues she strove to demonstrate, Cristina also took, as modern historians have said that her mother Maria de' Medici had done, "traditionally female subjects such as marriage and made them metaphors for power, successful rule, and political legitimacy." Like her mother, she "took this female imagery out of the private sphere and introduced it into the public domain."[7] But "the image of a woman who is the virtuous equal of man is always an image of the culturally alien."[8] Thus during her reign, which in Voltaire's interpretation was an unending sequence of conflicts or "continuous tempest," Cristina worked hard to maintain a difficult balance between the twin effects of representations of power—the shift of actual power in her favor, and her endowment with overly male qualities.[9]

Her marginality ensured, of course, that her presumed and actual flaws as female and as ruler would receive ample attention from her detractors. More than any male sovereign, she was calumnied in the press, although there were also contemporaries who considered her avowed gallantry, largesse, and authority as the qualities befitting a monarch. Thus Antoine Hamilton, recalling the count of Grammont's adventures at Cristina's court, compares her favorably to her father Henri IV, appreciating that "she had inherited the virtues of her father in regard to feelings appropriate to sex; and in regard to what one calls the weakness of great hearts, her highness had not degenerated," while

7. Deborah Marrow, *The Art Patronage of Maria de' Medici* (Ann Arbor, 1982), 174.

8. Constance Jordan, "Feminism and the Humanists: The Case of Sir Thomas Elyot's Defence of Good Women," in *Rewriting the Renaissance,* ed. Ferguson, 256.

9. Voltaire, *Le Siècle de Louis le Grand,* cited in Claretta, *Reggenza,* 1:vi.

elsewhere she was reviled for her open friendship with various members of her court.[10] The same memorialist explains at length the code of gallant behavior that was adopted at the court of Savoy under Cristina.[11] This required that each lady at court have an official lover whose function was to serve the lady and to wear her colors. In military battle, the "colors" won or lost were the only tangible measure of success or failure and of recognition, since colors, or standards, were the only common collective symbol in the era before uniforms denoted a particular regiment or company.[12] Cristina's chivalric code expressed a typical seventeenth-century conceit, the parallelism of love and war; as one historian puts it, "amorous conquest in effect reproduced military conquest, with its competitions, its difficulties, and its glory."[13] The lover was required never to leave his lady in public and never to approach her in private. If Cristina herself was following this mode of behavior, her criticized closeness to Filippo d'Aglié could well have been an innocent relationship, though it may also have served as a shield for other, less honorable, connections. (As we will see later, Filippo d'Aglié held an important role at Cristina's court: considered the most enlightened judge of emblems, he became indispensable for the design and staging of the festivities through which Cristina's position and power were reiterated to a dazzled and eventually submissive citizenry.) The military metaphor employed in courtly life at Turin may reflect the military culture discussed in chapter 1, with its tendency to consider human and political relations in strategical terms. It was also an attempt to regulate the private life of courtiers through the ordering of relations at court. In this ordering tendency the spirit of the duchy in Cristina's reign followed closely the principles of absolutist monarchy in the seventeenth century, which tended to regularity in all domains of human endeavor.[14]

Initially, Cristina's claims to the title of regent were questioned both because she was female and because she was an outsider. Catherine de' Medici, Maria

10. Antoine Hamilton, *Mémoires de la vie du Comte de Grammont* (1713; rpt., Paris, 1926), 31–62, 32: "elle avait hérité des vertus de son père, à l'égard des sentiments qui conviennent au sexe; et, à l'égard de ce qu'on appelle la faiblesse des grands coeurs, son altesse n'avait pas dégénéré"; and "Relation de la cour de Savoye," BN, Paris, MS Franc. 23348, fols. 275–89.

11. Hamilton, *Grammont*, 33–34.

12. Geoffrey Parker, *The Thirty Years' War* (London, 1984), 191.

13. Paul Bénichou, *Morales du grand siècle* (Paris, 1948), 49: "La conquête amoureuse reproduisait en effet avec ses compétitions, ses difficultés et sa gloire, la conquête militaire, et pouvait exiger les mêmes vertus."

14. Ibid., 69: "Dans tous les domaines, l'esprit de la monarchie absolue tendait à la régularité."

de' Medici, and Anne of Austria all had encountered similar difficulties, with varying degrees of success.[15] All three had employed art and epigraphy in order to win support for their attempt at legitimization. Like them, Cristina attempted to demonstrate her possession of male virtues in order to overcome the results of the Salic Law. This French law—adopted also by the dukes of Savoy—successfully prevented female monarchical rule; allowing continuity only through the male line, it ensured that France and Piedmont would never have an Elizabeth on the throne.[16] Thus when Cristina's historiographer Valeriano Castiglione writes for her birthday in 1642, "You were born a Lady, yes, but still not effeminate, rather of a spirit very well suited to handle War and bargain for Peace," he is addressing the problem of female sovereignship.[17]

Beside underlining her abilities in war and diplomatic relations, Castiglione provides her with an empyrean, and by extension imperial, context that will eventually separate her from the temporal environment inhabited by men:

> Dopo fughe, ritorni, giri e strade
> Ogn'huom a terra cade:
> Tu no, Donna Reale
> Che dopo Imprese gloriose, e belle
> In un sol passo avanzerai le stelle.

Any man would fall to earth after such escapes, returns, wanderings, and crossings; but you, Royal Lady, after these glorious and beautiful undertakings, in a single move will climb to the stars.[18]

Understanding the theme of the star Astrea—with its imperial connotations—has been considered a fundamental precondition for appreciating the ethos and symbolism of the national monarchies of Europe as they developed in the late Renaissance.[19] At the beginning of the seventeenth century the concept entered the mainstream of cultural life through the writing of Honoré d'Urfé, the author of one of the most popular literary works of the century, *L'Astrée*. This

15. For the latter two see Ruth Kleinman, *Anne of Austria, Queen of France* (Columbus, 1985), 135–46.

16. For a comprehensive study of the Salic Law, see Harriet Lightman, "Sons and Mothers: Queens and Minor Kings in French Constitutional Law" (Ph.D. diss., Bryn Mawr, 1981).

17. *A Madama Reale Christiana di Francia* (Turin, 1642), 1: "esser Voi nata Donna si, ma non già effeminata, e di spirito anzi attissimo a maneggiar le Guerre, ed a trattar le Paci."

18. Ibid., 3.

19. Frances Yates, *Astrea: The Imperial Theme in the Sixteenth century* (London, 1975), 9–11, 29–38.

is a work that Cristina would certainly have known, not only because it went through numerous editions and became a highly quoted source for references to courtly and gallant love, but also because d'Urfé had lived at the court in Turin, part of the entourage in the 1620s.[20] In his birthday wishes, Castiglione may well have been referring to this work, as well as to Cristina's well-known desire for the royal title, which, as we have seen in chapter 4, had involved Vittorio Amedeo I in numerous diplomatic difficulties.

Cristina's decision to rule and to acquire the royal title may well have made her seem aggressive and ambitious. There are many contemporary references highly critical of her behavior, where she is considered the most cruel, unjust, and shameless woman living.[21] Her encounter with Christina of Sweden when the ex-queen visited Turin in 1656 came off very well, since, in one Piedmontese historian's view, they were temperamentally similar: "she enjoyed friendly conversations with our Cristina, who was of the same mind and could thus lend a sympathetic ear."[22] But since everyone agreed that the ex-queen lacked fundamental feminine virtues, that her behavior was indecorous, almost shameless, and that she went out into the world as only men were permitted to do, this favorable comparison is not actually a compliment to the regent. Cristina had gone against the grain of local customs in Piedmont from the very beginning; she wanted to keep up her French habits and "French freedom" (la libertà francese) and demanded to be served in the royal manner—alla Regina—to which she had been accustomed in Paris and which was going to be very costly for the court in Turin.[23] Her preferred mode of address, Madama, was of course only a translation of the subtle French title Madame by which the daughters of the French kings were recognized, but in Piedmont

20. L'Astrée was published in three parts between 1607 and 1619, with two posthumous parts published in 1627 and 1628. Carlo Emanuele I awarded d'Urfé the Order of the Annunziata in 1618 for his numerous ambassadorial missions on behalf of the Savoy. D'Urfé spend most of his latter years, 1619–25, in Turin. The Gallimard edition of L'Astrée, ed. Jean Lafond (Paris, 1984), contains a thorough chronology (391–6); Louis Mercier's essay of 1925 on the book's widespread fame in the seventeenth century is the preface to another edition of L'Astrée (Geneva, 1966), v–xxviii.

21. BN, Paris, MS Franc. 23348, fol. 285: "Il n'y a aujourd'hui femme sur la terre plus cruelle, plus injuste et plus impudique."

22. Claretta, Reggenza, 2:698: "Dove s'intratenne in amichevoli colloquii colla nostra Cristina, che di genio consimile essendo, poteva trovare in essa molta simpatia."

23. Archivio di Stato, Florence, Medicea 2963, 27 January 1620: "Madama sposa . . . sostiene la libertà francese vuol tenere il gabinetto, et esser servita alla Regina nella maniera del Re suo fratello, ch'importera grossa spesa."

not many could have been aware that *Madama* implied royalty. To clarify this refinement, Cristina added *Reale,* and after 1632 she was known only as *Madama Reale.* The xenophobic reception in Piedmont of French royal customs as practiced by Cristina in Turin was reiterated in the case of her two sisters, Henrietta and Elisabeth, who were considered as untrustworthy strangers at the English and Spanish courts, respectively.[24] Thus the treatment of royal wives was not a matter of rank only, but also of national identity and pride.

The rhetorical and dynastic summation of Cristina's character was made in the design of her own funeral celebration, sponsored by Carlo Emanuele II in 1664. There Cristina was framed by a circle of female regents of Savoy, whose company granted her citizenship within a native pantheon. Representations of her birth and education were surrounded by images of her achievements. These included, among others, a view of Turin enlarged and embellished: "Urbs ornata et amplificata" was the inscription below the view.[25]

But in her contemporaries' minds she did not have an undisputed place of honor despite a great deal of praise, some of it mixed, and respect, most of it grudging. According to the Venetian ambassador Catarino Berengo, writing soon after her death in 1664, Cristina made people wonder whether she deserved acclaim or malediction—having coupled many virtues with numerous defects, great prodigality with grave errors, and much lasciviousness with exemplary piety. Nonetheless, her death was universally deplored, "since she had always chained the heart [incatenate i cuori] of her people, and of strangers, with her affability, clemency, and rich offerings. She left at court and in Turin so many signs of splendor and magnificence as would be enough to decorate the memory of several princes for many centuries." He went on to praise her as a woman who many times had to fight with fate, and to face with virile breast disasters of state, and finally—to her own glory—managed to leave her heir a state free and at peace despite the aggressive armies of two powerful princes.[26] Berengo's *Relatione* is almost a panegyric, and the grudging respect

24. See, for example, Hermann Ferrero, *Lettres de Henriette-Marie de France* (Turin, 1881), 13–14, 28.

25. The funeral is described in Claude-François Menestrier, *Des Décorations funèbres* (Paris, 1684), 217–19.

26. Archivio di Stato, Florence, Carte Strozziane Serie Ia, Relationi di Diversi Principati Regni e Governi, "Relatione della corte di Turino fatta l'anno 1664 dall'ambas[ciato]re veneto Catarino Berengo," fol. 121: "lasciate alla corte et alla città di Torino tante marche di splendore, e di magnificenza che basterebbero a decorare la memoria di più Principi per molti secoli."

would no doubt have become a hymn had the "prince" in question not been a female ruler.

But the criticism is mainly focused on Cristina's royal ambitions. Despite the mobility of seventeenth-century social order, her desire for the royal title was the public political equivalent of her private family decision to fight the men in the Savoy family who followed the French Salic Law. It is on this account that even later criticism, albeit nineteenth-century nationalistic criticism, finds Cristina morally flawed. Why did she describe herself with the servile, useless title of "sister of the Most Christian King" at the top of all her decrees, edicts, and patent letters? Gaudenzio Claretta, who otherwise finds her worthy of an extremely detailed personal, political, and economic biography, wishes that the other royal references, such as *regia prole, regia casa, regia consorte* (royal children, royal house, royal spouse), had been less lavishly employed.[27] Nonetheless, even Claretta finds this terminology perhaps pardonable in the sister of two queens.

A S H A S B E E N S U G G E S T E D by Ercole Ricotti, the reign of Cristina can be divided into three parts. They are the contested regency (1637–42), the legitimate regency (1642–48), and the dissimulated regency (1648–63). Most of Cristina's achievements in the embellishment and enlargement of Turin took place in the middle period, followed by a less active caretaking period. The contested regency has received most attention from historians, since it involved numerous sieges, treaties, intrigues, and alliances, but as this battle for power influenced Cristina's subsequent activities, it must be considered here before its aftermath can be investigated.

At his death in 1637 Vittorio Amedeo left behind a duchy shackled to France by an offensive and defensive treaty that involved Piedmont in all of France's military enterprises in Italy; in the 1630s these were aimed against Spanish Milan and smaller states protected by the Spanish in the peninsula. Cristina had been instrumental in the 1630s in forging this alliance with her brother Louis XIII; its burdens were lighter to her than they had seemed to Vittorio Amedeo, whose brothers and sisters, as we have seen, harbored strong pro-Spanish tendencies. These pro-Spanish relatives spread the rumor that Cristina's regency was practically torn from the lips of the dying Vittorio Amedeo by the French ambassador Hémery. Richelieu's support of Cristina at the be-

27. Claretta, *Reggenza*, 2:601.

ginning of her regency—despite his hatred for her mother and consequent mistrust of the daughter—was based on the belief that she would be the most favorable to the French among Vittorio Amedeo's heirs.[28]

Shortly after Vittorio Amedeo's death his two brothers Prince Tommaso and Cardinal Maurizio attempted to return to Piedmont from Flanders and Rome, respectively. They were fearful of Cristina's priorities and allegiance, and doubtful of her loyalty to such Piedmontese causes as the maintenance of an independent state. They feared that under a weak rule, such as that of a foreign-born princess, the duchy risked becoming a French province, as Dauphiné, for instance, had become earlier. They were both first invited to enter, then prevented with force from entering, Piedmontese territory. Tension increased a year later at the death of the under-aged legitimate heir, Francesco Giacinto, whose birth had been celebrated so floridly in Turin six years earlier. By then Cristina had been forced to ratify the treaty that Vittorio Amedeo had previously arranged with Richelieu, and she had also begun to realize that her own interest in a peaceful and continued rule was not important for her royal brother and his minister.[29]

In this climate of tension, the fortification of Città Nuova in Turin continued. Vittorio Amedeo's reduced version of his father's expansionary ambitions was brought to completion during the first two years of the regency. The quickened pace was motivated not only by the importunate use of Piedmont by the French army, which traversed it freely during its maneuvers against the Spanish, but also by the menacing attitude of Tommaso and Maurizio. As the rift between the members of the House of Savoy widened in their individual bids for power over the policies and government of Piedmont and Savoy, the two brothers asked for the support of the Spanish government in order to overthrow the regent. Eventually, by mid-1639, the tensions, intrigues, mistrust, and misunderstanding between the regent and her brothers-in-law—fanned by Spanish and French interests in which Piedmont and its contestants became small, but crucial, pieces in a much larger conflict that involved most of Europe in the ongoing Thirty Years' War—flared up into open armed hostilities.[30]

The nature of this war has concerned a number of historians, with inconclusive results. Its dates, 1639–42, coincide with, or even slightly precede, the

28. Gabriel de Mun, *Richelieu et la maison de Savoie* (Paris, 1907), 47, 215–18.

29. Costa de Beauregard, *Mémoires historiques sur la maison royale de Savoie* (Turin, 1816), 2:191–93.

30. For a detailed analysis, see Guido Quazza, *Guerra civile in Piemonte* (Turin, 1960), *passim*.

wave of urban rebellions and political revolutions that marked the middle of the seventeenth century throughout Europe. Historians interpret the entire century through these critical middle years, which in many countries are seen as having produced a rift in continuity and a thorough shift in the locus and character of political power.[31] Although it was unlike the English revolution, the model of most revolution theories, the Piedmontese conflict was a revolution at least in a limited sense, since a change of personnel was proposed that would have replaced the female regent with the male heirs of the ruling house as coregents. The war would not have changed fundamentally the existing political system, which already tended towards absolutism, but by somewhat decentralizing the government it would have created a relative vacuum of power. Cities and the aristocracy could have more strongly reasserted their privileges, including tax-free status, under a less centralized government. This can perhaps explain the polarization of the population into *principisti* and *madamisti,* respectively supporters of the princes and the regent, turning the potential revolution into a civil war. The conflict was promoted by the marginality of Piedmont, where strong xenophobic feelings existed against both French and Spanish aggressors that were exploited by both parties in their efforts to raise support. Rather than a revolution, a label more suitable for class conflicts, this armed conflict would be best defined as a dynastic war. Through this dynastic war the national identity of the duchy was being defined in contrast to France and Spain, which opportunistically used Piedmont as a field of war, but which were in turn manipulated by the warring factions within the Savoy dynasty itself.[32]

The contest over the regency eventually culminated in 1639 in an open military conflict between French and Spanish armies in which once again Piedmont was a mere pawn. In this war Cristina was allied with, and practically the prisoner of, her brother Louis XIII of France, while her brothers-in-law Cardinal Maurizio and Prince Tommaso were manipulated by their Spanish allies. In the midst of the open war, which was led by French and Spanish generals despite the seeming deference to the Piedmontese factions, the rebel-

31. For the crisis theory of the seventeenth century, see E. J. Hobsbawm, "The General Crisis of the European Economy in the Seventeenth Century," *Past and Present,* 5–6 (1954): 33; H. R. Trevor-Roper, "The General Crisis of the Seventeenth Century," *Past and Present,* 16 (1959): 31–64; Ruggiero Romano, "Tra XVI e XVII secolo: Una crisi economica, 1619–22," *Rivista storica italiana,* 74 (1962): 480–534.

32. Perez Zagorin, *Rebels and Rulers, 1500–1660,* 2 vols. (Cambridge, 1982), defines revolutions and civil wars in vol. 1, *Society, States and Early Modern Revolution: Agrarian and Urban Rebellions,* 13–17, 236–45.

lious princes realized that no matter who won Piedmont would be held hostage.[33] Together with the regent they played instead on the stalemate between the French and Spanish ministers, who in the end preferred to have Piedmont as a buffer state, rather than as the satellite of either of them.

The siege of Turin in 1639–40 was the climax and epitome of the dynastic war, as well as a representation of French-Spanish rivalry. In this siege, the city was pitted against the citadel in a textbook example of how the citadel could be turned against the city when the two were occupied by opposing armies (fig. 57). Through the defection of the regent's officers to the *principisti*, Tommaso and an occupying Spanish force entered Turin without opposition. The regent and her supportive Piedmontese and French guard took refuge in the citadel, while Tommaso prepared Turin for the siege of its citadel by continuing its fortification and provisioning.[34] Only three months earlier the papal nuncio had sent news that the citadel was being strengthened on its city side, preparing it for just such an event in which the city was occupied by an hostile army, and preparations had been made in 1638 for the better control and defense of Turin.[35] Eventually relief was brought to the *madamisti* ensconced in the citadel, although the regent herself had left, by a French army that surrounded Turin. Thus Prince Tommaso found himself in the tragicomical situation of being besieged while he himself was laying siege to Turin's strategic nerve center. The siege of the citadel lasted from July 1639 to September 1640 (fig. 62).[36] Great damage was suffered by the citadel, whose strategic significance is evident from an alternative illustration of the siege (fig. 63), where the

33. Beauregard, *Mémoires historiques,* 193–94.

34. BAV, MS Barberini Latini 7174, 28 August 1639, fol. 71: "Si tira avanti incessantem[en]te la fortificatione di questa città, per ridurla quanto prima alla totale perfettione, et in questa non meno che nelle provisioni militari, e de viveri premendo il prencipe Tommaso con ogni ardore, si veggono entrare qua tutti i giorni quantita di munitioni si da guerra, come da bocca."

35. Ibid., fols. 40v–41: "Essendosi compiute la fortificat[io]ni aldi fuori di Torino, hora s'e cominciata una mezaluna nella Piazza della Cittadella, che riguarda l'habitato, accio quando altri si facesse P[ad]rone della citta, restasse dopo molto piu difficile l'impresa della med[esim]a Cittadella." MS Barberini Latini 7173, 12 January 1638, fol. 3v: "Havendo Madama Seren[issi]ma risoluto di far chiudere una porta di questa citta, per quale si va a Susa, hieri si diede principio a murarla." Ibid., 6 March 1638, fol. 20: "Attorno questa citta nuova si e dato principio ad alcune mezzelune tra l'uno e l'altro bastione di essa conforme il disegno."

36. For details of the siege and dynastic war, see *Monarchia piemontese,* 5:174–361; Claretta, *Reggenza,* 1:415–712; Datta de Albertis, *Cristina,* 166–209; and Quazza, *Guerra civile, passim;* for the description of the double siege, see *Le Soldat piémontois* (Paris, 1641).

forts, redoubts, and palisades are shown densely grouped against it—and against the Città Vecchia. The city's tower was seriously damaged, as were many private houses, and the residences of those loyal to the regent were looted.[37] Cannonballs, shot across the enemy, were also used to carry messages between the allies who were settled in rings around Turin. Despite the general mayhem, however, the military design of Carlo Emanuele's and Vittorio Amedeo's expansion was vindicated: the recently enlarged and completed fortifications obliged the besieging armies to set up very large circumvallation lines, reducing their chances of taking Turin.

The siege of the city demonstrated that Turin was the symbolic and strategic center of dynastic politics. As the capital of the duchy and its mightiest fortress, it was thoroughly associated with the place of power. Piedmont could not be ruled without its centrally located *piazzaforte*. The siege was stopped before the complete destruction of the city, according to the clear if implicit laws that governed most sieges in the seventeenth century. The regent and the princes had realized that Piedmont could only lose, and they decided to compromise.

A coregency was established with three separate residences: the regent in Turin, Tommaso in Ivrea, and Maurizio in Nice. The continuity of the Savoy line was ensured by the marriage of Maurizio to Cristina's oldest daughter Ludovica. In effect, the brothers were gotten out of the way, overwhelmed with French offices and pensions. Until 1645 Turin was occupied by the French, with the regent as nominal ruler. Even after that date, when Turin was returned to the regent, the French remained in the citadel and used it to control the city, as can be seen from a plan (fig. 64) of c. 1640–45, in which the gun embrasures of the three bastions aimed towards Città Vecchia and Città Nuova are carefully distinguished. They held on to the citadel until 1657, when the ducal garrison finally replaced the French occupying force (fig. 65). The siege received a great deal of attention and was commemorated in numerous engravings and paintings. It served as a great test for the form and strength of

37. BAV, MS Barberini Latini 7174, 8 November 1639, fol. 86: "Qui intanto e incessante e reciproca la batteria tra la citta e la cittadella, e dal maschio di questa aperto da piu bande s'e levato il cannone, che faceva il magg[io]r danno all'habitato. Batte la citta con diceotto pezzi di cannoni divisi in sei batterie la cittadella, la quale oltre il maschio, comincia a patire in due bastioni, e la cittadella ha all'incontro battuto giu la torre del comune, e rovinate molte case non meno col cannone che con le bourle [?] le quali tirate di notte apportano non piccolo terrore a gl'habitanti"; in the entry for 28 July 1639, fol. 61, the list of houses looted includes those of the highest court officials.

the city's fortification, and, having withstood a double siege, Turin emerged with an even greater fame as an unbreachable stronghold.

But what did all this mean for the city plan? Illustrations of the siege of Turin show the enclosure of the southern expansion fully completed, while the Roman wall still stands. As we have seen in chapter 3, construction of the fortification had been accomplished during the short reign of Vittorio Amedeo I. In a plan of c. 1637 by Carlo di Castellamonte, the achievement of Vittorio Amedeo and important subsequent additions are vividly illustrated (fig. 66). Of the four ravelins defending the southern bastions, three were built after his death in the feverish preparations to defend Turin before the threatened dynastic war. The plan shows the orthogonal grid of streets drawn over the existing moat and aligned with the square towers of the Roman wall. This extended street pattern envisioned an additional row of blocks to be laid out over the site of the ancient southern fortifications.

In itself, this planning proposal presupposes the completion of the southern fortifications that were to make demolition of the Roman wall possible. The street grid is extended over the east walls of the Città Nuova towards the Po, while a large open space is shown next to the existing northeast bastion, in turn connected through a radial street to the Po. The drawing thus echoes the original plan proposed by Carlo Emanuele I, to expand to the east as well as to the south. The plan is also the first since Montafilans' *parere* to show the Città Nuova as an expansion area separate from the eastern expansion. It can be dated decisively through the palisades that separate the citadel from both Città Vecchia and Città Nuova, which were built in 1640 during the civil war. These temporary fortifications are vivid reminders of the internal conflict that pitted the citadel against the city, and a chilling reminder and proof of the stranglehold imposed upon Turin by its *cittadella*.

ALTHOUGH CRISTINA HAD emerged strengthened from the dynastic war that legitimized her claim to sovereignty and to residence in Turin, the duchy's capital, hers was a shared victory. She entered Turin at the head of a French army, which then controlled the city for the next five years. The years after the war were focused on recovery, even though Turin and its citadel were still garrisoned by an occupying foreign force, however reticent. As we have seen in chapter 4, the expansion planned by Carlo Emanuele I had been greatly reduced according to the less ambitious designs of Vittorio Amedeo I. Although Cristina wrote to her second son Carlo Emanuele II—who became duke upon the death of his older brother Giacinto and who had spent the war period in Chambéry, the duchy's strongest fortress—in praise of her own diplomatic achievements, recounting in fulsome detail the elaborate ceremonial reception given her by the city council, it was clear to all concerned that Turin was to be French-ruled.[38] Having overcome the armed opposition of her brothers-in-law, the regent now had to persuade her subjects of the fact that she was the sovereign in Turin. To this end, following the footsteps of her immediate Savoy predecessors as well as the example of Henri IV and Maria de' Medici, she proceeded to legitimize her claim to absolute rule through an intense patronage of large-scale urban design, architecture, and art.

After the siege of Turin, since the fortification and layout of streets in Città Nuova were complete, the regent proceeded with its embellishment by encouraging private and religious construction enterprises and by rebuilding the ducal palaces. The core of this program of patronage was to be the Piazza Reale (also referred to as Piazza di Contrada Nuova, now Piazza San Carlo), a centrally located square to the south of the original southern gate, surrounded by palatial residences and wealthy churches.

The view of Turin by Boetto, illustrating the siege of 1640 but made in 1642, shows the military enclosure and the outline of ten blocks in Città Nuova (fig. 57). In this view the ancient fortifications, the moat, the wall, and an undeveloped strip of land still separate the two parts of Turin, keeping Città Nuova and Città Vecchia isolated from one another. There is, however, the germ of the future square in the opening next to the old south gate, within the ancient walls (fig. 67). This area is further examined in a study sheet by Carlo di Castellamonte that represents the first plausible study for Piazza Reale (fig. 68). This crucial drawing focuses on the square and shows its site and possible dimensions.[39] Fourteen blocks are drawn in outline, while five additional blocks were planned for the areas occupied by the moat. In this study of c. 1637–38 Piazza Reale is shown with two alternative sets of measurements. The

38. Datta de Albertis, *Cristina,* 213–17; Claretta, *Reggenza,* 3:173: "Mon cher fils. . . . Vous entendrez avec plaisir la relation de mon arrivée dans Turin où j'ai été reçue avec applaudissement de tous les peuples, et grands honneurs et respects que m'a rendu monsieur le comte d'Harcourt, tellement mon cher fils que j'ai rétabli votre autorité dans Turin, et j'espère par ma même force que j'ai servi la continuation de la protection de Sa Majesté qui nous remettra où maintenant elle n'est pas réconnue."

39. This drawing was first discussed in my "From Castrum to Capital: Autograph Plans and Planning Studies of Turin, 1615–1673," *Journal of the Society of Architectural Historians,* 47 (1988): 273.

space of the smaller square seems carved from the space of the blocks that flank it. The smaller version was approximately 24 *trabucchi* on a side (1 *trabucco* equaled about 3 meters), which would have made it about half the size of the square Carlo Emanuele I had legislated in 1620. In his edict of that year the duke had ordered the opening of a square next to the south gate that was to be used as a wine market. This was to be a *gran piazza,* about 50 *trabucchi* long.[40] Additional land was to be bought if the area owned by the ruler did not suffice. This is some of the evidence we have that Carlo Emanuele, who sponsored the initial plans for the expansion of Turin, intended a square to be built next to the old southern gate. We have seen in chapter 3 that the city council had opposed in the 1620s the market privileges granted in Città Nuova to the new settlers. The original intention was recognized, acknowledged, and pursued through a subsequent letter patent, published in 1642 by the regent Cristina, which marked the actual beginning of the construction of Piazza Reale.[41]

The smaller version of the square in figure 68 lies next to the moat, is connected to Città Vecchia through the north-south street (opened by Vitozzi in 1615, as we have seen), extends over the entry bridge, and is flanked by two parcels on each side. In contrast, the larger version proposed on the same study sheet extends over the entire moat. The dimensions of the larger version, 54 by 24 *trabucchi,* were even greater than those required by Carlo Emanuele I in his order of 1620. The proportions of its flanking blocks form Piazza Reale; thus its north-south dimension equals that of the blocks, while the width of the square is equal to the depth of the flanking blocks. (This measurement is derived from the dimensions—approximately 36 *trabucchi*—of the orthogonal blocks that separate the north-south streets.) The area of Piazza Reale and the two blocks that define it was achieved by dividing the area of two normal blocks into three strips. The outcome of this geometrical manipulation is an open and directional square that can be read as a widening of the street. Indeed, the study sheet suggests this interpretation. Piazza Reale is shown connected to Piazza Castello, at the center of Città Vecchia, through the street opened in 1615. Continuous with the street south of Piazza Reale, this axial thoroughfare bisects Città Nuova and ends at the new southern gate, while at its northern

40. ASCT, Ordinati, 1620, fol. 47: "S[ua] A[ltezza] vole la città faci accomodar alla porta nova della città vecchia un revellino piu si spiani e faci un gran piazza ivi di larghezza di 50 trabucchi et caso il sito commune ivi non basti si debba comprar tanto del terreno de vicini et in detta piazza si faci il mercato di vino."

41. Duboin, 936: "Havendo noi stabilito che per adornamento della città nova di Torino si fabrichi una piazza Reale avanti la chiesa . . . di San Carlo."

end it abuts the ducal palace. This street thus ties gate, royal square, and political command center into one linear movement.

The proposed date for this study, c. 1637–38, is reached in the following way. The siege view by Boetto illustrates the temporary fortification that separated the citadel from both Città Vecchia and Città Nuova in 1640 (fig. 67). These ramparts were studied in a plan that was probably made as part of the preparation for the siege and would thus be close in date to the siege itself (fig. 66). There the ramparts cover three of the twenty blocks south of the moat and adjacent to the citadel. In a signed and dated drawing of 1632, already discussed in chapter 4, fourteen blocks were outlined in Città Nuova (fig. 51). The same fourteen blocks are visible in this study of c. 1637–38, although only twelve blocks are shown in the illustrations of the siege (figs. 62, 63). In addition to the layout of blocks, the study plan of c. 1637–38 illustrates the fortification done around the Città Nuova, where the *mezzelune* in the southeast corner are especially visible. They suggest a strategic measure taken to defend the road between Porta Castello, the eastern gate, and the bridge over the Po, which was of fundamental importance for Turin's communications with the eastern part of the Italian peninsula.

The parceling of the blocks that frame Piazza Reale, shown already under way in figure 68, hints at the immediate need for building lots. Just as in figure 42, it is the parceling of the flanking blocks that imparts immediacy to the study; but whereas in the earlier plan the parcels were of various sizes, reflecting existing patterns of ownership, here their equal dimensions imply a development study. This parceling as development study is further confirmed and clarified by a series of letters patent issued by the regent Cristina from 1638 onwards.[42] Through these she granted lots along the square to several of her most trusted officials, bourgeois as well as aristocratic members of her court, and to religious institutions. Included were the brothers Turinetti, one of whom later became the minister of finance, and the Marchese Giulio Villa, general of the Piedmontese infantry and a frequent ambassador of the crown. The larger version of the square may have been influenced by the need to accommodate as many highly placed residents as possible. Assuming that the design of the square and the parceling of the blocks preceded construction, the date of the regent's initial parcel donation serves as the *terminus ante quem* for the first study plan of Piazza Reale. Although 1638 was not a good moment to commence construction, given the precarious state of the regency, it was the right time to grant lots to favored courtiers. This gesture of favor was also

42. Ibid., 932–36.

intended to hold and to garner the support of the officials at the court for the cause of the regent at a time when her authority was contested by Cardinal Maurizio and Prince Tommaso, her brothers-in-law. The studies for the layout of Piazza Reale continued simultaneously with the preparation for the dynastic war, which, as we have seen above, broke out in 1639.

Thus the opening of Piazza Reale in 1642 closely followed the peace treaty that ended the dynastic war. Construction in the new part of Turin continued for the next quarter-century. Between 1637 and 1652 the regent granted approximately twenty-five lots, most in the area surrounding and in the vicinity of Piazza Reale, to various religious groups and court officials. The first to receive a lot along the edge of Piazza Reale, on 23 October 1638, was the banker Giovanni Antonio Turinetti. The site was adjacent to the monastery and church of San Carlo, founded by Carlo Emanuele I in 1619. Turinetti's only obligation was to construct the facade of his palace according to the design made by Count Carlo di Castellamonte, who continued as first military architect and engineer under the regency; he would thereby "beautify" and "populate" Città Nuova.[43] On the same date the Camera de' Conti, which legalized the letters patent and edicts of the crown, confirmed the award of a site formerly occupied by the moat of the fortification, at the corner between Piazza Reale and Contrada Nuova (the main street connecting it to the Città Vecchia), to Gaspare Graneri, another important official at court.[44]

Even more significant is the letter patent of 7 July 1642 through which Cristina granted to Marchese Villa, among her closest advisers and supporters in the dynastic war and head of an outstanding aristocratic family, one of the six building sites around the Piazza Reale. It suggests that, despite previous

43. Duboin, 932–33: "Sapendo noi quanto siano affettionati al servitio di questa Corona li fratelli Turinetti banchieri in questa Città . . . hora che il maggior d'essi Giovanni Antonio si offre pronto di far fabricar un palazzo in Città nova, per abbelirla, e popolarla . . . rimettiamo al detto banchiere Gio[vanni] Antonio Turinetti il sito e luogo in detta Città nova e nella piazza Reale che si deve fare vicino il convento e chiesa de' P[adri] di San Carlo, per far fabricar detto palazzo conforme al dissegno e stabilimento fattone dal Conte Carlo Castellamonte."

44. Ibid., 934–36: "Desiderando noi che li siti dentro le mura della città nova della presente città di Torino siano habitati ed edificati, conforme al dissegno cominciato, con ogni maggior prontezza possibile, et havendoci il molto diletto fedel nostro Gaspare Graneri humilmente supplicato a volerli donare il sito avanti la chiesa di S[an] Carlo, per quello fabricare conforme al dissegno, che dal conte Carlo Castellamonte li verrà stabilito . . . rimettiamo al mede[si]mo Gaspare Graneri il sito dalli fossi della presente città vechia sino alla strada di qua dalla facciata della chiesa di S[an] Carlo in città nova."

plans and donations, the construction of the square was only then beginning in earnest. The public letter informed the city council and the inhabitants that the regent's decision to open a royal square in front of the church of San Carlo and the convent of Carmelite nuns, with the surrounding houses "of the same architecture" in the composition of the facade, was intended to further the embellishment of Turin. The concession to Villa, who had requested one of the parcels, was freely made since his service to the House of Savoy was gratefully acknowledged. Placed at the eastern corner of the old south walls, Villa's site was still occupied by the bastion of Santa Margherita. In addition to the building lot, Villa could also make a garden above the bastion, of which he could demolish as much as was needed to build his own palace. Beyond these already very generous donations, Villa was also granted the right to extract water from the *bialera,* (public water canal) that crossed Piazza Reale.[45] The lack of street addresses sometimes makes the location of lots problematic, but in this case the precise site of Villa's land grant can be established through the properties adjacent to it, named in Cristina's letter patent. Through it we find out that the regent had already granted a lot to the auditor Benedetto, another to her secretary Giovannini, and one to the postmaster, Gonteri. As late as 1648 there were still lots available on the Piazza Reale, according to the letter patent, signed by Cristina and coregents Maurizio and Tommaso, through which one was given to Marchese di Voghera, the general of artillery.[46]

45. Ibid., 936–37: "Havendo noi stabilito che per adornamento della citta nova di Torino si fabrichi una piazza Reale avanti la chiesa dei Padri Agostiniani et monastero delle monache Carmelitane . . . che le case intorno detta piazza siano fabricate sovra la medesima architettura, e dessegno quanto alla facciata . . . commettiamo al medesimo sig[nor] Marchese Villa uno de' sui posti sovra la detta piazza Reale, cioè tutto il bastione di S[anta] Margherita che si attacca alla muraglia che va dritto al castello, con le muraglie che restano dentro di detto sito del bastione inclusa la sudetta muraglia della Città vecchia, lasciando però le strade opportune per il passaggio delle ronde, e per il cannone. . . . Di più la facoltà di poter far un giardino sopra il bastione . . . con facoltà anche di poter estraer dalla dora o sia bialera della Città che viene a sboccar in testa della detta piazza Reale un'oncia d'acqua, che sarà necessaria per servitio del giardino . . . in questa donatione habbino da restar comprese tutte le materie del predetto bastione di S[anta] Margherita per quello però quantità che sarà necessario demolirlo per construer detta fabrica e non altrimenti."

46. Ibid., 934–35: "Siccome è sempre stato nostro particolare desiderio che si perfettionasse la piazza Reale principiata in città nuova a pubblico beneficio e decoro di questa città, cosi habbiamo procurato quei mezzi che ponno agevolare l'effetto, restando però da fabricare conforme al dissegno stabilito per compimento di detta piazza tra gli altri un sito di trabucchi ventinove di longhezza e ventrè di larghezza discorrente dalla chiesa di S[an] Carlo de' Padri Agostiniani scalzi, al lungo di detta piazza, coherente a levante la mede[si]ma piazza

Further grants of property were made between 1642 and 1648, and they were an important part of the works sponsored by Cristina throughout Città Nuova during her legitimated regency. The recipients were invariably members of the court, where their activities ranged from preceptor of the young duke, to magistrates, officers, suppliers, senators, and aristocrats whose allegiance had to be gained or rewarded. Few of the lots were granted unconditionally. Although some were intended to be cultivated as gardens, in all instances the perimeter of the lot had to be defined with rows of shops and apartments. Thus close control of land ownership and buildings constructed in Città Nuova was exercised by the crown, which attempted to stimulate development through parcel donations but neither encouraged nor practiced speculative building.

The six recipients of sites facing into Piazza Reale were granted their parcels with clearly stated and tight conditions, together with moral imperatives. They were obliged to build according to Carlo di Castellamonte's design (fig. 69), and to do so quickly for the greater ornament of the city. Other donations were more or less restrictive, depending entirely on the topographical location within Città Nuova. Thus Benedetti, an auditor and adviser in the ducal administration, Vallone, superintendent and supplier for the ducal buildings, and Crosa, officer in the duke's guard, were obliged to follow a prescribed design prepared for the street that connected Piazza Reale to the square in front of the citadel.[47] Although the design has not survived, the written document states clearly enough that their houses had to be tall and painted and had to define continuously the edge of the street. Pietro Catocchio, supplier and superintendent of ducal buildings, and the count of Colegno, a mayor of Turin, as well as Count Gio[v]anni Francesco di Caselette, were asked specifically to build at the public edge of their property in order to ensure the continuity of their street, placed upon the trace of the demolished southern wall.[48] However, they were not provided with a definitive design (no model or architect are mentioned), and they were allowed to build lower structures—shops and *camere* (rooms)—clearly intended for rent. The officer Carresana, receiving a site near Porta Nova, was asked not to impede traffic near the gate, and to this end the

---

. . . essendosi offerto pronto di fabricare tal sito, conforme a detto dissegno l'illustre cancelliere gran Croce nostro carissimo il Marchese di Voghera D[on] Francesco Delpozzo generale dell'Artiglieria di S[ua] A[ltezza] R[eale]."

47. Ibid., 932–33; the grants were made on 23 December 1637, 20 April 1644, and 2 May 1644, respectively.

48. Ibid., 933–34; the grants were made on 16 July 1642, 25 November 1642, and 11 October 1647, respectively.

portico underneath his house had to be tall enough to allow the passage of carts filled with hay. Only one site was granted for a garden, to a gentleman-archer of the duke, and on only one site, a very small one, was construction prohibited. Both were very close to, actually in the shadow of, the fortifications surrounding Porta Nova.[49] A larger number of the donated sites, given away in 1647 and 1648, were related to the demolition of the ancient Roman southern wall. Recipients such as Ochetto, Bosato, and Grosso were new settlers who had recently migrated to Turin (Grosso is referred to as a Savoyard, for example); they were specifically required to build upon the sites of the demolished walls.[50] Since the land of the demolished fortifications was ducal property, the regent could freely dispose of it. Since they were gifts, these donations permitted the crown to demand submission to certain preestablished building requirements.

The grantees of lots in Piazza Reale, and to a lesser extent in peripheral areas, agreed to build substantial residences of prescribed height, width, and surface decoration. The facade of the individual residence was to be subsumed behind the uniform design, which was continuous along both sides of the square. This design for the facade was by Carlo di Castellamonte, whom we have encountered as a military engineer, civic architect, and artillery officer, and also as a member of the local aristocracy. As we have seen, Castellamonte had served Carlo Emanuele I by supervising the ambitious expansion of Turin begun in 1619, and he continued to serve under Vittorio Amedeo in 1632 when Città Nuova was built in reduced form. He remained faithful to the regent's cause throughout the hostilities of the dynastic war. Although Castellamonte seems to have died in 1641 (he is not mentioned in the letter patent of Marchese Villa although he was specifically named in the letters of 1638), his design was adopted when construction commenced in earnest in the 1640s. The implementation of this design was supervised by Amedeo di Castellamonte, his son and successor as principal court architect and engineer.

The elements of the repetitive facade are presented in Carlo's extant study for Piazza Reale (fig. 69). The ground-floor arcade, composed of *serliane*, supports a tall *piano nobile*. The alternating segmental and triangular pediments over the windows of the *piano nobile* and the pilasters between the window frames, realized as wall strips, are the principal decoration. There is a low attic level with square windows also separated by wall strips in the illustration and

49. Ibid., 932: Carresana's grant is dated 2 November 1637; ibid., 936: grant to Bernardo Perrucca (30 August 1649) for a garden near the square of Porta Nuova, grant to Antonio Riolla (2 January 1652) of a site "under" the platform of Porta Nuova.

50. Ibid., 934: 18 November 1647, 30 December 1647, and 4 January 1648, respectively.

in actuality. The oculi placed between the arches were replaced with military trophies, and the space between the coupled columns was filled with piers in the eighteenth century in order to prevent the collapse of the portico. For the design of the facades the architect clearly had recourse to the porticoes of Piazza Castello, designed by his mentor Vitozzi in 1608 for the wedding party of Carlo Emanuele I's daughters. The facade by Castellamonte, open at the ground level with a deep portico, is composed of an alternating *ABA* pattern of arched openings flanked by openings with horizontal lintels, the traditional *serliana*. The design of the upper levels, comprising a *piano nobile* dominating the facade with its height and a much lower attic floor, recalled similar buildings in Arezzo, Florence, and London.[51] The cornice height was continuous but lower than that of Piazza Castello, while the slender columns of the portico were in strong contrast with the heavy piers of the portico in the older square.

The design of the continuous facades, composed of repetitive bays openly derived from the porticoes of Piazza Castello, underlines the function of Piazza Reale as a formal and visual link between ancient Turin and Città Nuova. Both Piazza Reale and Piazza Castello draw on a vernacular arrangement, common in Italy and in Piedmont, of a ground-level arcade with residential floors above, but in both squares this scheme is rationalized through uniformity and repetition of bays. In Piazza Reale, though the two parallel porticoed buildings lack a crowning balustrade, the uniformity of the materials—painted stuccoed surfaces—and the scarcity of details confer a dignified monumentality upon the space. Castellamonte's design, characterized by order, economy, and discipline, is a fundamentally military contribution to the civic expansion of Turin.

Striking testimony of the importance of Piazza Reale is given by a drawing of c. 1656 (fig. 70), the earliest plan to show the new Turin as a unified entity with the Città Vecchia and the Città Nuova—now consisting of seventeen blocks—enclosed by a continuous fortification. (Since it is a finished drawing, a presentation rather than a study sheet, it carries great authority.) Piazza Reale is the only square in Città Nuova, and thus serves as its spatial focus. It was also a market, military drill and parade ground, and meeting place. Since the new streets were not entirely contiguous with the old, because of slight divergences in block dimensions, the square became the principal connection between the two parts of town, acting as pivot between the old and the new neighborhoods. But development around the square, along the Contrada Nuova—the north-south artery that connected it to Piazza Castello and the

51. For Vasari's loggia in Arezzo see Leon Satkowski, *Studies in Vasari's Architecture* (New York, 1979), 98–135.

south gate—and the east-west street that led to the citadel, was determined by draconian building requirements decreed by the crown, and the corresponding construction proceeded slowly. Although references were made as early as 1639 to the demolition of the wall separating Città Nuova from Città Vecchia, it is not before 1647 and 1649 that payment orders were made for the completed filling of the moat and tearing down of the walls.[52] The coherent aspect of Piazza Reale as completed can be seen in Carlo Morello's study for the eastern expansion made in 1656, where the ground-floor portico separates the palace entries from the square (fig. 71).

In addition to awarding sites to her favorite courtiers, who could be relied upon to build as prescribed (even if they took a long time to fulfill their commitment), Cristina established a church dedicated to her patron saint, Santa Cristina, on the south side of Piazza Reale, across the street from San Carlo.[53] This equated the patronage of Cristina with that of her father-in-law, Carlo Emanuele I. Their twin churches reinforced the symmetry and focus of the square's composition. They also strengthened the alignment between the southern gate, Contrada Nuova, and the ducal palace. Though the present identical facades of the twin churches were not added in Cristina's lifetime (Santa Cristina's was designed by Juvarra in 1715 and became the copied source for the facade of San Carlo designed in 1834 by Caronesi), her contribution was crucial in establishing the scenographic quality of the square. The regent can be given credit not only for the realization of the square originally desired by Carlo Emanuele I, but also for the transformation of that military space into thoroughly controlled civic space, with uniform private residences and religious institutions that would provide the public frame for ducal processions. The uniformity of the private palaces, which had a greater impact than the twin churches upon the perception of the square and was derived from the original military use of this area, transfigured this residential square into the civic equivalent of military regimentation.

Cristina's interest in the Città Nuova was underlined by her sponsorship of the foundation of another church close to Piazza Reale, which was also occupied by the Carmelite order. Like the nuns of Santa Cristina, the monks of Santa Teresa were given both the site of their church, just half a block west of

52. AST, Sez. Riunite, art. 199.1, 19 July 1647, fol. 16; art. 203, mazzo 1, 18 April 1649, fol. 97.

53. Francesco Agostino della Chiesa, *Corona reale di Savoia* (Cuneo, 1655), 261: "Se ne potrebbero aggionger altre due [squares], una avanti la Cittadella, e l'altra in Cittanuova; pure essendo quella fuor dell'habitato, e questa che si dice Piazza Reale non ancor totalmente compita." For Santa Cristina see Tamburini, 147–53.

the square on the street that ends at the citadel, and the site of the adjacent monastic buildings.[54] In addition both Carmelite institutions were given sites elsewhere in Città Nuova, or even outside of the enclosed area, which they could sell or rent. Furthermore, nuns of the Capuchin, Visitation, and Augustinian orders settled in Città Nuova with the help of other members of the ducal family and the regent's more pious subjects, who attempted to emulate her religious fervor. The convents and churches of the Visitazione (1638), Madonna del Sufragio (1638), and Chiesa del Crocefisso (1647) enhanced the religious life of Città Nuova and were embellished throughout the seventeenth century.[55]

Piazza Reale in Turin occupies a significant place in the history of urban design because it was the earliest such public space in Italy. Although two churches faced into the public space of the square, the residential structures that flanked it on three sides dominated it and set the character of the space. Its predecessor, the old Piazza Castello improved by Vitozzi, had already been conceived as a theatrical space flanked by residences; but the earlier square was far less homogeneous, created piecemeal and dominated by the palace and the Castello. In addition, through a uniformity that ensured a high level of architectural reticence and modesty, the residential buildings of Piazza Reale focused attention upon the space they enclosed. The square was a well-defined entity, with a well-proportioned relationship between the open space and the surrounding buildings. Piazza Reale was the first of the three key elements to be built in the development of seventeenth-century Turin. As we will see, each of these—the Piazza Reale, the rebuilt and enlarged Piazza Castello, and Contrada di Po—served as the model or structuring central element for the two successive enlargements. In this sense, Piazza Reale played a crucial role in the immediate definition of a new neighborhood in Turin and provided clues for the completion of the seventeenth-century expansions.

Piazza Reale was one of the earliest planned regular squares built in the seventeenth century. Together with Place Dauphine and Place Royale (now Place des Vosges) in Paris, begun in the first decade of the seventeenth century, and the Covent Garden Piazza in London, built at the end of the 1620s and perhaps influenced by Vitozzi's Piazza Castello, it defined a new kind of urban

54. BAV, MS Barberini Latini 7188, 13 June 1642, fol. 59v: "Martedi X del corrente Mons[igno]re Nuntio fece la cerimonia di porre la prima pietra della nuova chiesa che si vuol fabricare nella Città nova da P[ad]ri Carmelitani Scalzi sotto la invocazione di S[an]ta Teresia, coll'intervento di Mad[am]a R[eale] chi ha loro donato il sito, di tutta la corte, e gran concorso di Popolo."

55. Tamburini, 179–85, 133–35, 136–39.

space: the residential square.[56] The public space of Piazza Reale was not dominated by a monumental church, or by a palace. The public space was, and still is, the focus of the composition (fig. 72). The definition of this space was achieved through the building of uniform and continuous facades that do not attract attention to themselves; masking the individual residences behind the two parallel porticoes, the uniform facade denies individual expression, unlike the facades in the Parisian squares where the separation between properties is marked in the roof line. The effect in Turin—in Piazza Reale as well as Contrada Nuova—is that of a large, continuous palace, reminiscent of More's description of the streets in Utopia,[57] composed of interchangeable houses. This uniformity is evidence of the ducal interest in successfully controlling the physical appearance of Turin, while the qualities of uniformity and architectural austerity are characteristics borrowed from military architecture.

The two churches that defined one of the two short sides of the piazza were identical in elevation and reinforced the symmetry of the space while adding to it a scenographic quality. Although it could be argued that this detracted from the focus on the space itself—since the scenic element draws attention to itself—in reality the twin churches reinforced the role of the square as the idealized architectural frame of the ducal rituals. From the windows on the *piano nobile* of the Palazzo Reale, the sovereign would see a sequence of successively framed public spaces, the long perspective ending at Porta Nuova, the southern gate. Although the facades of the twin churches were rendered equal only in the mid-nineteenth century, they were considered as twin buildings from the foundation of Santa Cristina in 1639, and so represented from at least 1660, when a plate (fig. 72) portraying them as identical structures was made for *Theatrum Statuum Sabaudiae,* the cartographic album eventually published in 1682.

Although the conception of Piazza Reale was based upon the traditional squares adjacent to the gate of the city, which channeled traffic in various directions, the design and function of Piazza Reale were novel in the seventeenth century. As we have seen in chapter 1, in fifteenth- and sixteenth-century dis-

56. For Covent Garden see John Summerson, *Inigo Jones* (Harmondsworth, 1966); for the Parisian squares see Anthony Blunt, *Art and Architecture in France 1500–1700* (1953; rpt., Harmondsworth, 1973), 159–64. Jones visited Turin in the entourage of the earl of Arundel, in September 1614.

57. Thomas More, *Utopia* (1516; rpt., Leeds, 1966), fol. 1v: "Aedificia neutiquam sordida, quorum longa, et totum per vicum perpetua series, adversa domorum fronte conspicitus" (the buildings, far from mean, are set together in long rows, continuous throughout the block and faced by a corresponding one). I owe this rendering to James G. Turner.

cussions of the ideal city one of the principal strategic and organizational questions was whether a town's layout should be comprehensible upon entry, that is, from the square next to the gate. To a large extent the plan of the ideal city, with radial or orthogonal streets, determined the resolution of this question. In both instances the streets opening from the square next to the gate led to the principal public spaces and the center of town.

Piazza Reale was conceived initially as such a square, directly connected to the new south gate, opened by Carlo Emanuele I in 1615, and to Piazza Castello, the center of government. As we have seen above, under Cristina the square—an enlargement of the 1620s marketplace—replaced the military gate and the fortifications that had surrounded it. While the new square maintained the functions of the earlier one, as market, drill ground, and meeting place, its former strategic military function was invalidated by the expansion to the south. Nevertheless, the memory of its military content was maintained through the repetitively uniform and schematic buildings that flanked it on each side. In stripping the residences of the individuality of their inhabitants, the square achieved its impersonal and regimented character. The first square in Turin to be planned on the site of a demolished gate, Piazza Reale became the connection between the existing town and the expansion area. This transformed context translated the military site into an important civic space, while maintaining the military vocabulary. In conception, form, and function, Piazza Reale became an important model for subsequent expansions; as the city grew beyond its seventeenth-century fortifications, the demolished military gates were replaced with similar civic squares.

THE CONSTRUCTION OF Piazza Reale, reconstruction of the damaged Palazzo Reale, the education of the heir, Carlo Emanuele II, and the maintenance of peace were the main occupations of Cristina between 1642 and 1645. After the ratification of the Treaty of 1645, made between the two female regents, the French left Turin (on 25 March 1645) and gave Cristina total control of the city.[58] She felt safe to allow the return of Carlo Emanuele, who had spent the intervening years in Chambéry, Fossano, and Rivoli. Their joint ceremonial entry into the capital on 8 April 1645 showed distinctly the significance of the city in defining the dynastic identity of the House of Savoy.

The ceremony is described in great detail in a publication by Valeriano Cas-

58. Claretta, *Reggenza*, 2:122–24.

tiglione.[59] Regent and heir are compared throughout to shining stars, suns, and heroes returning home. The Savoy dynasty's claim to royalty was amply recognized and flattered. Their return to Turin was marked by an accomplished and elaborate welcome apparatus replete with triumphal arches, fireworks, cannon, and musket shots. The regent was additionally hailed as Amazon, Pallas Alpina, Minerva, Alcmene, Astrea, "Diva dell'Alpi" (Goddess of the Alps), and Christiana—thus amply acknowledging her power and authority as well as her intense piety—while the eleven-year-old Carlo Emanuele was a young Mars, but also Amor. Their entry and reception are compared to famous Roman models by Castiglione, and although he mentions these precedents in order to underline the liberality of Cristina in opening the prisons, the row of noblemen he describes—on foot preceding the open carriage of the regent and the duke—were doubtless *principisti* who had accepted the renewed order, and who, alluding to the prisoners in the Roman triumphal march, were making public penance for their previous political choice.

The southern gate, Porta Nova, built initially in honor of Cristina's wedding to Vittorio Amedeo (as we have seen in chapter 2), was decorated with a triumphal arch; Contrada Nuova and Piazza Castello were ablaze with torchlight. The latter contained a make-believe town, fortified with bastions, walls, guardhouses, and gates, representing Turin with the municipal tower at its center surmounted by the city's bull device.[60] Another triumphal arch—probably not unlike the one engraved by Baldoino in 1644 (fig. 73)—greeted the returning rulers at the opening of Doragrossa, the Roman *decumanus* of Città Vecchia, which connected Piazza Castello to the municipal square ablaze with torches, inscriptions, and statues. A *Te Deum* in the cathedral, also decorated for the occasion, completed this *possesso*-like procession through the most significant public spaces of the city. The reception was concluded with fireworks, considered as a conflagration of love ("incendio d'amore") and the funeral of past suffering ("funerali all'andate tristezze"), and with a ritual burning of the model representing Turin: "la finta città parve ch'ardendo risplendesse aguisa di cielo illuminato nella notte, il simbolo rappresentante l'acque del vicino fiume si consumasse infocato, colonne di bittumi accesi . . . facevano corteggio alla città combustibile" (the false city seemed, burning, to shine like a

59. *Le pompe torinesi nel ritorno dell'altezza reale di Carlo Emanuele II* (Turin, 1645).

60. Castiglione, *Pompe,* 15: "La piazza del Castello s'offrì à gli occhi delle R[eale] A[ltezze] abondatissimo parimente di lumi. Una Città finta munita di baloardi, cortine, sentinelle con quadratira d'angoli, ed apertura di porte, faceva un gentil spettacolo. . . . Nel mezzo della Cittàfinta di Torino, era inalzata apunto una Torre, alla quale sovrastava piramidal cimiero, e nella cui sommità eretto un Toro dorato."

brightly lit night sky; the symbol of the nearby river heatedly consumed itself; columns of burning bitumen having been set alight . . . accompanied the combustible city). The accompanying musket fire seemed to applaud the burning of this toy-scaled Troy.[61] The tower at the center of the model city representing the municipal campanile, whose bull emblem had in fact been toppled by bombing during the siege of Turin, was torched together with the rest of the model: "il toro . . . significante la città si distruggeva in giubilo" (the bull representing the city to great rejoicing self-destructed). The ritual destruction of Turin may well have been an exorcism of the fears engendered by the siege, during which the inhabitants had been caught in the cross-fire of *madamisti* and *principisti* cannon. Setting ablaze the party staging was an important feature of baroque festivities (occasionally foreshadowed in sixteenth-century royal celebrations), whose designers delighted in stupefying novelties, shocking contrasts, and breathtaking effects.

The fire and fireworks staged by the municipality had been designed by Bernardino Boetto, whose brother Giovenale Boetto had made the engraving illustrating the siege of Turin, and who was himself not only a pyrotechnicist but a captain in charge of real "war machinery."[62] This great party was part of an ongoing Savoy family tradition that continued successfully under the reign of Cristina, marking births and marriages in the family as well as carnival entertainments. Several of these *feste* have survived in specially commissioned contemporary illustrated books. The relationship between this kind of festivity, practiced from the end of the sixteenth century throughout Italy, France, England, and Flanders, and the more ancient tradition of carnival feasting is probably fundamental, especially since most of the Savoy *feste,* jousts, and *ballets de cour* took place in the period between Christmas and Lent. By the 1630s they had been formalized and enriched into three types: entry or triumph, mock-battle (*giostra,* allegorical ballet), and comedy combined with ballet. It is the association between procession, combat, and theater that perhaps explains why the festivity did not have an established site, even for regular plays.[63] Its place was the daily space of the city, the street, square, or court transformed by a stage setting. The place of the party was metamorphic and fantastic, and led to the transformation of the city with temporary or false

61. Ibid., 22: "tante fiamme sembravano disposte ad arder una Troia frà le tenebre" (the numerous flames seemed disposed to burn Troy among the shadows).

62. Ibid.: "La lode di tant'arte fù attribuita al Capitano Bernardino Boetto Fossanese sovraintendente generale delle machine da guerra, e da fuoco."

63. For the association between *feste* and the city, see André Chastel, "Le lieu de la fête," in *Les Fêtes de la Renaissance,* ed. Jean Jacquot (Paris, 1956), 1:419–23.

architecture. The theme of the party, whether entry, ballet, or comedy, embodied the message that the sponsors wanted to propagate.

In Fossano, where Carlo Emanuele II danced in the role of the sun in *Felice rinovata* (staged on 10 February 1644), the theme was renewal, appropriate after the trials of the dynastic war. In Cuneo the previous year, Cristina and Carlo Emanuele were honored with double triumphal arches. An extant print illustrates their reception and may also help to give a visual idea of what the arches in Turin, of which we have no graphic documents, may have looked like (fig. 74). The capitals and entablatures of the giant order of the triumphal arch were engraved with Cristina and Carlo's initials, the pediments of the upper level were filled with the Savoy device *noeuds d'amour,* and military triumphs were placed in the pedestal of the order. Beside the numerous symbolic statues—of Charity, Faith, Justice, and so on—that crowded the architecture, the recently adopted royal tiara crowned every available space. The frieze of the second triumphal arch was occupied with Cristina's name, surmounted by the lilies of France and Florence, and enveloped in fireworks (more *incendii d'amore*). The message of victorious royalty, strengthened by its difficulties, was inescapable. The role of public spectacle is thus fundamental for establishing ideological claims and architecturally of great interest since the temporary *festa* setting often found its way into permanent constructs.

The definitive message was provided on 10 February 1645, in another royal birthday, celebrated at Rivoli, where the festivity was designed by the regent's principal adviser and companion Filippo d'Aglié and titled *Il dono del Re dell'Alpi a Madama Reale (The Gift of the King of the Alps to Madama Reale).*[64] The comedy-ballet took place in four distinct rooms, each decorated as a province of the state (Savoy, Nice, Piedmont, Monferrato) and represented, on the backdrop, by their respective capitals (Chambéry, Nice, Turin, Casale). It was the royal box, rather than the scenery, that moved, trundling from room to room as the ballet unfolded (fig. 75). As in the view of Turin made by Righettino in 1583 (fig. 27), examined in chapter 1, the entries and pageantries sponsored by the crown used the parts of the realm as part of the decorative arrangement, thus laying public claim to them.

Invariably, the designers involved in the ephemeral staging of the *feste* were also involved in the building program sponsored by Cristina. The same Lanfranchi who designed the triumphal arch at the beginning of the old city's main street for the 1645 entry of Cristina and Carlo was also responsible for one of the two fanciful pavilions built in the Piazza Castello for the carousel of 1650,

64. Described in *Feste Reali,* 46–49.

celebrating the marriage of a royal offspring, Adelaide, to the elector of Bavaria.[65] The other pavilion was by Carlo Morello, a military architect and factotum at court. This *festa,* portrayed by Boetto and playfully titled *Herculeses* [in the plural] *Tamers of Monsters and Loves Tamers of the Herculeses* (*Gli Hercoli domatori de mostri et Amori domatori degli Hercoli*) was conceived by Filippo d'Aglié (fig. 76). The engraver Boetto was ready to represent all events at court, whether actual battles or mock combats. D'Aglié has been recognized widely as one of the earliest choreographers in the modern sense of the term.[66] Hercules was of course a popular theme (d'Aglié had provided a ballet on the same subject for the 1637 carnival, where Vittorio Amedeo danced for the last time), but the double circumvallation of the choreographical arrangement—the Hercoli attacking the monsters and then in turn besieged by the Amori—could only have been inspired by the lasting memory of the still recent double siege of Turin. Like the burning of a toy Turin, this ballet may well have served as exorcism and self-congratulation in the wake of difficulties and dangers that had been overcome. Thus one of the purposes of the *feste* was to educate the public by their interpretation as *imprese* and metaphors of political messages come to life.

These secular festivities and their pious counterpart, found in the religious exercises publicly practiced by Cristina, became a growing influence upon the appearance of the city. Following the triumphal entry in Turin on 8 April 1645, as we have seen, she made a theatrical show of piety, carrying a cross through town, dressed in sackcloth and covered with ashes, accompanied by similarly attired ladies-in-waiting. But the crowning religious event of the Savoy dynasty's return was the exhibition of the Holy Shroud on 6 May 1645.[67] The Holy Shroud was exhibited at most dynastic festivities of the dukes of Savoy, reiterating the close ties between church and state. The close spacing of these public appearances of the regent and Carlo Emanuele II were intended to

65. Ibid., 51–58.

66. Claude-François Menestrier, *Des Représentations en musique anciennes et modernes* (Paris, 1681), 319–33, lists the *feste* celebrated at the court of Savoy. Menestrier's *Art des Emblemes* (Lyon, 1662) was dedicated to d'Aglié; on Aglié see also Jean Vanuxem, "Le Baroque en Piémont: Fêtes, emblèmes, devises au XVIIe siècle," *Renaissance Maniérisme Baroque: Actes du XIe stage international de Tours* (Paris, 1972), 289–99; and Gino Tani, "Le comte d'Aglié et le ballet de cour en Italie," *Les Fêtes de la Renaissance,* ed. Jacquot, 1:221–33.

67. *Successi del mondo,* 18 April 1645 (the first year of publication of this gazette from Turin): "e M[adama] R[eale] rivestita di sacco portava la croce seguita dalla comitiva di tutte le Dame di sua corte in simil habito"; 6 May 1645, Sindone shown for the first time since 1637.

underline their ruling presence. While only the *festa* apparatus was transformed into permanent structures—the triumphal arch for Cristina and Vittorio Amedeo's wedding became the new gate, the pavilions used in the joust of 1650 in Piazza Castello inspired the design for the Sindone pavilion built by 1663—the temporary and permanent architecture was endowed with the same edifying role, educating the population and uplifting it morally. Court spectacle and urban design were both political metaphors of the absolutist government. The correspondence between the different forms of artistic expression was brought about through the patronage of a group of artists and intellectuals with reciprocal interests and talents. The *feste* design shamelessly copied previous staging ideas, which were refined and reiterated in the process and eventually became an accepted mode of expression and perception about urban space. Thus Borgonio's illustration of the 1650 *festa* in Piazza Castello (fig. 77), oriented in the opposite direction from Boetto's (fig. 76), shows the reuse of the mountains—present in many Savoy entertainments and described by Tesauro in his report of Cristina's wedding—topped by temple, triumphal arches, and model of Turin, all elements whose inspiration was borrowed from previous celebrations. The rhetoric of Tesauro, the theatrical ability of d'Aglié, and the severe taste of Castellamonte were an eloquent and ceremonial panegyric of the ruler's dignity and the magnificence of authority.

In addition to directly influencing the appearance of Turin, then, the *feste* provided a way to celebrate the city's urban and military architecture. It is Turin, and other cities of the duchy, that provided the most captivating backgrounds for the theatrical festivities. These festivities bear upon the development of the city inasmuch as its streets and squares were rebuilt and embellished for the successive ducal events. As we have seen in chapter 2, the uniform outline of Piazza Castello derives from one such ducal marriage festivity, and the continuous whitewashed facades of Contrada Nuova were ultimately realized for the ducal wedding reception of 1663.

DURING THE REMAINDER of her regency, Cristina continued to facilitate the expansion of Turin by means of legislation, architectural patronage, the education of her young successor, and the commissioning of new planning studies. The formal aspirations of the crown were clarified by the edicts that were to control the further expansion of Turin. The key elements of the formal program can be derived through a comparison of the original edicts with the zoning and building restrictions that were actually adopted, and also through the ordinances that regulated the design and materials used in construction. At the scale of urban design, the formal aspirations were characterized by large dimensions, uniformity, and economy of means in the composition of facades that defined the wide streets and squares. The attributes of the Piedmontese monarchic government, tending towards absolutism—economy, uniformity, and vastness—differed from the aspirations of most sixteenth- and seventeenth-century Italian rulers in the importance given to uniform large-scale design. The strongest and most consistent Italian example is provided by the patronage of the Farnese, who sponsored urbanistic interventions in Parma and Piacenza. They succeeded in fortifying both cities and initiating huge palaces that, had they been completed, would have rivaled the most elaborate princely dwellings. But despite the opening of new streets and squares, they altered neither city in a comprehensive manner; in striking contrast, the expansions of the seventeenth century sponsored by the dukes of Piedmont altered Turin fundamentally.

Cristina's patronage inserts itself seamlessly within the dynastic ambitions of the Savoy dukes. The edict promulgated by her on 8 April 1646, marking the triumphal return of the legitimate ruler, established her intention to continue the dynastic building and expansionary politics of her predecessors. This public message begins with taking stock and praising the ancestors. To establish city building as a royal prerogative, a parallel is made between the magnificence of patronage and the grandeur of the ruler: "Great princes have always set their minds to having their residence, in comparison with other cities, no less noteworthy [*riguardevole*] for magnificent buildings than capable of holding a large population within its ample enclosure." Aware of the Boteran concepts that moved her predecessor to attempt such lavish construction, Cristina recognizes that "among the lofty concepts nourished by Carlo Emanuele [I] this one [city building] was not excluded; he therefore began the enlargement of this ancient city with a design in keeping with the grandeur of his soul." Vittorio Amedeo continued this work with precision and diligence, so that during his reign "the bastions were quickly brought to their proper form and clad with the most beautiful walls." The enlargement and beautification of Turin is also in the interest of the regent, continues the edict, who will not only complete the enlargement started by her predecessors, guided by the *cause della grandezza delle città* proposed by Botero (great size, beauty, authority), but will add Piazza Reale—French-inspired at least in name—for the greater ornament and honor of the city.[68] Having established the lofty interests (*lodevoli massime*) of the House of Savoy and the continuity of dynastic enterprises centered in Turin that legitimize her own position, the regent slides into a very severe command. She requires that those who have been granted lots in Città Nuova fulfill their obligations to begin construction within four days after the publication of the edict, finish construction within two years, and build according to the design established previously (in 1638, one assumes) or risk being divested of their royal donation.[69]

The following two paragraphs of the edict deal with the actual aspect of the houses, and thus provide implicit evidence about the state of Città Nuova in 1646. Landowners—and leaseholders when the former were absent—were urged to paint their still "rustic" property within six months, new houses were not allowed to remain "rustic," and the houses in Piazza Reale were to be decorated according to the design established earlier. The most striking clause urged owners who had built off the street line to enclose their property at the edge of the lot, and pull their gardens and courts to the interior of their parcel in order not to deform the linearity of the street; linearity would embellish and ennoble the city through the uniformity, continuity, and order of the street facades ("accioche la Città resti più abbellita, e nobilitata per l'uniforme, e continuato corso, et ordine delle facciate delli edificij").[70] Cristina and her ar-

---

68. Borelli, 929–30: "Fu sempre particolar pensiero de'Prencipi grandi, frà le altre città, d'haver quella di loro stanza non meno riguardevole per la magnificenza delle fabriche, che capace d'habitationi con l'ampiezza del circuito . . . dalle lodevoli massime, che con tanta prudenza nutriva il fù Serenissimo Carlo Emanuel . . . non restò questa esclusa; così egli con dissegno corrispondente alla grandezza dell'animo suo . . . cominciò l'aggrandimento di questa antichissima Città. . . . Vittorio Amedeo . . . con così esatta diligenza fè l'opera proseguire, che i Bastioni alla loro forma ridotti furono di bellissime mura prontamente vestiti. . . . Noi dunque . . . habbiamo parimente questa dell'ampliatione, e abbellimento di questa città a perfettione dell'opera incominciata, non solamente in conformità di detto dissegno, mà anche con lo stabilimento di una Piazza reale da Noi stimata a proposito per maggior ornamento."

69. Ibid., 930: "Comandiamo a tutti quelli, a'quali sono stati conceduti nella sudetta Città Nuova siti da fabricarsi, che debbano metter mano a farli fabricare frà quattro giorni dopo la publicatione di queste, haverli compitamente fatti fabricare frà due anni immediatamente seguenti, osservando il dissegno in ordine alla perfettione d'essa Città stabilito, sotto pena della privatione de' medesimi siti da rimettersi subito ad altri."

70. Ibid., 930: "Essendo le facciate della maggior parte delle case di detta nuova Città per anco rustiche, ordiniamo per abbellimento maggiore, che si facciano tutte stabilire, et imbiancare fra sei messi prossimo, come anche quelle della contrada nuova, che dalla Piazza Reale va a Piazza Castello, alche over mancassero i Padroni, saranno tenuti gli Affittauoli,

chitects were attempting to alter the traditional house type, changing it in the process from a country form (free standing) to an urban form (continuous with adjacent buildings). The crown insists on uniformly stuccoed and white-washed houses, and continuous cornice heights. The edict also underlines the distinct hierarchy of squares and streets within Turin. The houses along Piazza Reale must have the *same* facade, uniform in design, plastered, and painted white. Along Contrada Nuova, the main street between Piazza Reale and Piazza Castello, houses have to be stuccoed and painted, with responsibility devolving to tenants if the owners are absent. Continuous building facades and even height, but without mention of facade composition or finish, was demanded of other significant thoroughfares, such as the street between Piazza Reale and the citadel opened on the site of Città Vecchia's demolished southern wall. This demand for conformity occurs repeatedly in the ducal edicts. Plastered masonry was not a traditional method of construction in Piedmont, and the uniformity that was thus imposed, designating them subject to an authoritative ruler, was resisted by owners who perhaps would just as soon pay the threatened fine than have houses identical to their neighbors'. But Cristina's formal aspirations, modeled largely on those of Carlo Emanuele I and on French urban designs, which she had witnessed before leaving Paris in 1619, were focused upon the uses of architecture as an instrument of power.

Cristina legitimized her contribution to the design of Turin, then, by pointing out how she had continued the projects begun by Carlo Emanuele I and Vittorio Amedeo I; indeed she extends and exalts their projects by adding a royal square. The square, although conceptually influenced by Place Royale in Paris, should be seen not as cultural homage to France but as an assertion of Savoy autonomy, yet another version of the claims to royal title promoted by both Vittorio Amedeo and Cristina. In the final paragraph of this extensive edict she turns to the future, and to the city as a whole. She intends to enlarge Turin all the way to the Po, "with a new fortification belt, according to the first design of Carlo Emanuele"; but she will do this only "when time permits." With this announcement made, Cristina warns would-be builders in the Borgo di Po area, between Porta Castello and the Po bridge, that they should

con dichiaratione, che la spesa si farà buona sopra il fitto. Comandando farsi lo stesso stabilimento, et imbianchimento alle case da fabricarsi di nuovo, subito che saranno finite, e che non si lascino per alcun modo rustiche, e cosi dovranno osservare quelli, che hanno le facciate delle case sopra la Piazza reale, facendole accomodare con gli ornamenti in conformità del dissegno d'essa Piazza. . . . Comandiamo a coloro, che tengono siti sino al livello delle medesime contrade, di dover fabricare ivi le case loro, e portare nella parte di dentro i cortili, e giardini."

build following the counsel of Amedeo di Castellamonte and the prescriptions of the engineers Morello and Valperga, in order not to disturb the sites of future streets and fortifications.[71] This implies, of course, that the members of the council of Fabriche e Fortificationi were informed and knowledgeable already in 1646 about the form that the expansion towards the Po was going to take.

Cristina's edict of 1646, regulating current construction and future expansion, was followed on 2 July 1648 by Carlo Emanuele II's first order related to the capital's physical aspects. This edict was promulgated immediately after the majority of Carlo Emanuele, who became the official ruler in 1648. However, as Louis XIV had done, Carlo Emanuele formally urged his mother to continue to rule in his name.[72] Like Cristina's, his edict was focused both on immediate material changes and on the future enlargement of the city. It ordered the immediate leveling of Contrada Nuova, the street that connected Piazza Castello and Piazza Reale in Città Nuova. Proprietors of houses along the street were required within one month to lower the street and to pave it at their expense. Further directions were to be given by Amedeo di Castellamonte, who supervised the works. Regarding the longer term, Cristina's prescriptions for building in the Po suburb were confirmed in the new edict.[73]

Beside monitoring and encouraging private construction and building fortifications and villas outside Turin, the crown sponsored several projects in the 1640s and 1650s. These included the opening and rehabilitation of Porta Nova and Porta Palazzo, gates that had been walled in during the war; the rehabilitation of the Castello; the rebuilding of Palazzo Reale; and the restructuring of

71. Ibid., 930: "Sendo nostra intentione di proseguire l'aggrandimento di questa città fino al Po, con nuovo recinto di fortificationi conforme al primo disegno fatto fare dal detto Serenissimo Carlo Emanuel quando il tempo ce lo permetta. . . . Comandiamo in questo a quelli, che fabricheranno non tanto nella sudetta città nuova, quanto al Borgo di Po, e di qua e di la da esso Borgo sovra le nuove contrade da livellarsi di non toccar in maniera alcuna la linea di dette fortificationi, ne tampocco quelle strade, ma fondar, e fabricar le case dove, e come sara loro dal Conte Amedeo Castellamonte, e dagl'ingegneri nostri Morello, e Valperga prescritto."

72. *Monarchia piemontese*, 6:60–66; Kleinman, *Anne of Austria*, 241–42.

73. Duboin, 938: "Confirmando primieramente in quanto sia bisogno l'ordine degli 8 Aprile del 1646 fatto da Madama Reale mia Sig[nora] e Madre sovra il finimento di detta Città nuova, et ampliatione sino al Po . . . commandiamo a tutti quelli, che tengono case nella detta nuova contrada . . . che fra un mese dopo la publicatione di queste debbano haverla fatto abbassare, sternire, et esportar la terra soverchia, ciascuno per quanto s'estende il sito avanti sua casa; osservandone il livello, et ordini, che ne darà il Conte Amedeo Castellamonte."

Palazzo di San Giovanni, formerly the bishop's palace but among the Savoy residences since its annexation by Emanuele Filiberto.[74] Of the five churches begun in the Città Nuova during her regency, Cristina helped to build Santa Teresa and Santa Cristina, both of which belonged to the Discalced Carmelites. Cristina used the convent of her patron saint as a retreat, especially in the last five years of her life when Carlo Emanuele II began to assume the reins of government. In this practice she resembled Anne of Austria, who frequented assiduously the convent of Val de Grâce in Paris, which she had helped to build. Like Anne, Cristina had her own apartment within the monastery, which she could use through papal dispensation.[75]

Religious fervor was quite marked during the regency of Cristina, as the war against the Waldensians made clear in the 1650s. The architectural counterpart of that bigotry, which eventually had to relent and accept the vicinity of the sectarians at least in the mountain valleys, produced some very important churches in Turin. It was during Cristina's regency that the church dedicated to San Salvario was designed by Amedeo di Castellamonte in 1646 and built south of Città Nuova.[76] Sponsored by Cristina, it marked the halfway point between Turin and her earliest suburban residence, the Villa Valentino (fig. 78). The church was Amedeo's best work. Its construction and the organization of roads around it altered the importance of Villa Valentino, which was now placed within the orbit of anyone approaching Turin from the south. Amedeo was also commissioned to redesign the chapel for the Holy Shroud (an old Savoy project, intended to provide it with a suitable permanent place, with which both Vitozzi and Carlo di Castellamonte had been involved) and began work on it in 1656.[77] The sanctuary for the supposed relic was to be placed between the cathedral and the royal palace, then still under construction, binding the two indissolubly together. The palatine chapel would thus become the main altar and dramatic focus of the city's cathedral, underscoring the spiritual dominance of the House of Savoy over Turin.

74. For Palazzo Reale and Palazzo San Giovanni, see Marziano Bernardi, "Le sedi," in *Mostra del barocco piemontese,* ed. Vittorio Viale (Turin, 1963), 1:9–18.

75. Claretta, *Reggenza,* 2:555–56; Kleinman, *Anne of Austria,* 185–87.

76. Camillo Boggio, *Gli architetti Carlo ed Amedeo di Castellamonte e lo sviluppo edilizio di Torino nel secolo XVII* (Turin, 1896), *passim;* Tamburini, 301–3.

77. *Schede Vesme,* 1:287, letter of Prince Maurizio to the duke, 4 September 1656: "Se ne va da V[ostra] A[ltezza] R[eale] il conte Amedeo Castellamonte, per mostrarle il disegno del S[anti]s[simo] Sudario con le memorie che ho fatto a questo proposito. . . . confermo che a me sodisfa molto, non perchè sia mio pensiero, ma per esser stato così bene accomodato et aggiustato dal medesimo conte Amedeo."

While the ducal building program continued full steam under Cristina, the ancient part of Turin and the expansion area were finally bound together through the removal of the fortification that had always separated them. Such a fusion only became possible after the dynastic war had been concluded and internal tensions solved. Between 1647 and 1649 the moat was filled in and the southern wall completely demolished. In 1650 the street tying the citadel and Piazza Reale together was straightened, and in 1657, after the departure of the French garrison, the walls of the citadel and its connection to Città Nuova were rebuilt.[78]

Cristina's great achievements as a patron of military, religious, and civic architecture were celebrated in the decorative program of a building designed for her by Andrea Costaguta, a Carmelite monk from the monastery of Santa Teresa who was her theologian and engineer. It was yet another villa, known as Vigna della Madama Reale, whose decoration absorbed Cristina's interest and the ducal treasury until 1659. It was sited across the Po from Turin, and being out of town its design is of less concern to us here. It is however, a significant element of her patronage of architecture and painting. Its interiors were decorated with, among other things, allegorical paintings representing events from her own life. They illustrated her participating in her wedding, taking the reins of government, being besieged in Turin's citadel by her brothers-in-law, conferring at Grenoble with her brother Louis XIII (the meeting that established Piedmont as more than just a French province), making a triumphal entry into Turin after the dynastic war, signing a treaty with her brothers-in-law, constructing Villa Valentino (a gift from Carlo Emanuele I and which she had enlarged and decorated), founding the Carmelite monastery, and attending the wedding of Carlo Emanuele II (an event through which the regent's power was both legitimized, since she had picked the bride, and relinquished).[79] The allegorical representations were obviously inspired by the canvases in which Rubens depicted the events of Maria de' Medici's turbulent life. In addition to echoing what was by then a well-known work of art to which Cristina could justly claim proximity, these paintings provided a testimony of her politically most significant activities.

Less visible than building and decorative programs, but equally important, was the attention given to the education of the heir and the emphasis placed on preserving and incrementing the royal art collections and library. An inven-

78. AST, Sez. Riunite, art. 199.1, March 1657.

79. For the Vigna see Riccardo Marini, "La Vigna di Madama Reale sul colle di San Vito presso Torino," *Bollettino della società piemontese di archeologia e belle arti,* 10 (1927): 57–127.

tory of the library's holdings made in 1659 demonstrates the extent of the regent's interest and the interest of the duke's preceptors in maintaining a collection that was up to date in a number of significant areas.[80] As we have seen in chapters 1 and 2, Emanuele Filiberto and Carlo Emanuele I had amassed an important princely library in which the greatest emphasis was placed on military and architectural subjects, an interest that mirrored their fortification and enlargement of Turin.

Although not involved in warlike activities, Carlo Emanuele II was being groomed as a worthy successor to his great-grandfather and grandfather, who were both famous military leaders. Like that of many princes, his education included a thorough grounding in military strategy as well as riding, fencing, dancing, and other courtly activities.[81] Indeed, when he was still a young child he received a personally dedicated copy of a treatise by Pagan, the celebrated author and strategist. His early agility was remarked in the accounts of the triumphal entries in Cuneo in 1643, during his stay in Fossano in 1644, and during the joust staged in Turin in 1650. Carlo Emanuele had a military preceptor from 1643 in the person of Maurizio Vanello. His preceptor from 1648 was the famous Jesuit Luigi Giuglaris, recommended to Cristina by her confessor Pierre Monod, and one of the many Jesuits (such as Botero and Tesauro, to name the most important) closely associated with the House of Savoy. As we saw in chapter 4, Giuglaris had designed the ceremony and inscriptions for the funeral of Vittorio Amedeo in 1637, which he published, with illustrations engraved by Boetto, in 1638. His other contribution to the Savoy dynastic historiography, analyzed below in chapter 6, was in the form of a treatise on princely pedagogy derived from his educational efforts on behalf of Carlo Emanuele II.

In the meantime, Cristina's diplomatic activities were successful, and in 1656 she obtained from Cardinal Mazarin and Anne of Austria the liberation of Turin's citadel, an event celebrated by the engraved view discussed above (fig. 65). The imminent departure of the French troops from Turin brought about a renewed flurry of urban planning. As Vittorio Amedeo had done in 1632 when he decided to revive his father's expansion plans for Turin, the crown requested *pareri* for the further expansion of the city from a number of architects and military engineers. The ducal intentions to expand Turin, stated, as we have seen above, in Cristina's and Carlo Emanuele's edicts of 1646 and 1648, respectively, were confirmed by this request for planning studies made

---

80. AST, Sez. Ia, Real Casa, mazzo 5 d'addizione, number 30, 10–75.
81. AST, Sez. Ia, Lettere Particolari, P, mazzo 1; see also Ch. 6 below.

in 1656. As long as the French garrison remained in the citadel, Turin was a divided city. The dynastic war had necessitated not only the completion of the fortification girdle around Città Nuova, but also the construction of defenses to separate the citadel from the old and new parts of the city. And the negotiated settlement of the dynastic war had still left the citadel in enemy hands; its warring relationship with Turin during this entire period is clearly illustrated, as we have seen, in a plan in which the gun ports oriented towards the city are carefully drawn (fig. 64). The dynastic war and the French presence had evidently prevented the Savoy monarchs from continuing the expansion project begun in 1619 and only partly realized after 1632. Thus the solicitation of the *pareri* should be interpreted as an expression of freedom from the overbearing French allies and as a confirmation of dynastic continuity.

The range of proposals received by the crown can be seen in a number of extant drawings. The proposal attributed to Amedeo di Castellamonte called for a semicircular addition, inspired by the platonic geometry of the Renaissance ideal city, oriented towards the Po (fig. 79). In his version, the new extension was to be separated from the existing parts of town by a canal that connected the Dora and the Po. The orthogonal street grid of Città Vecchia and Città Nuova was extended to form the street system of the Po expansion, but the grid was then surrounded by a curvilinear fortification wall. The resulting blocks equaled and in some cases exceeded the size of the blocks in Città Nuova. The doubling of the Piazza Castello, like a mirror image of the original square, allowed the Castello to stand at the center of the newly enlarged space; this part of Amedeo's scheme eventually was carried out. In his drawing the straight street connecting the Castello and the Po bridge was realigned with the orthogonal grid of streets, implying that the existing bridge would be moved downstream.

The proposal signed by Carlo Morello suggested an expansion with an oval perimeter but proposed two different enclosures, of seven and eight bastions respectively (fig. 71). Since it contains a 105-item legend, this drawing is particularly useful, and it is further enhanced by Morello's autograph comments.[82] The plan for the Piazza Castello, similar to the one proposed by Amedeo, is shown with surrounding porticoes that extend into the main street that connected the Castello to the Po bridge. Two tridents of streets, one emanating from the Piazza Castello and the other from the Po gate, structure the new expansion area, whose spatial focus is a trapezoidal piazza halfway between the

82. His entire album of drawings illustrating the fortresses of the dukes of Savoy is now reproduced in Giorgio Beltrutti, *Le fortezze di Savoia* (Cuneo, 1980).

Po and Città Nuova. The two streets flanking the north and south sides of this piazza lead respectively to the southeast corner of Città Vecchia and to the citadel. Several of these features recall the intentions documented in the autograph ducal drawing prepared in c. 1612–19 (fig. 41) and illustrate the original discussions about the fortification of the city near the bridge. Morello's drawing is extremely useful and detailed, especially in its careful documentation of gardens, churches, and the main ducal residences.

The third *parere*, which exists in two versions with only slight differences between them, was signed by the engineer Pietro Arduzzi, whose text, surrounding his drawing, is part of our evidence that the crown consulted several military architects about how to proceed on the enlargement of Turin (figs. 80, 81). His projected expansion and fortification trace clearly benefited from earlier studies, such as the sketch of 1632 and the study of c. 1637–38 (fig. 68) by Castellamonte, and his drawing is dedicated to the marchese di Pianezza, general of cavalry and the most important councilor at court. Arduzzi advises against expansion all the way to the river because of the expense involved, suggesting instead that the fortification be kept near the church of San Antonio, which, set on a slight rise above the river, would provide a strategic site for a bastion. The dotted lines north and east of Città Nuova indicate the walls that would have to be demolished for this relatively economical expansion, which required only five new bastions. But his proposal is interesting not only for its design but also for its spelled-out criticism of the fortifications of Città Nuova, which, according to Arduzzi, were built without the benefit of specialists' advice.[83] Both he and Morello provide us with hints and insights about the competitiveness of the architects and military engineers employed by the court. The dotted lines in the north wall of his proposed fortification enclosure suggest that he was attempting to resolve another scheme that he considered mistaken.

The *pareri* requested by the crown in 1656 suggest that preparations were being made for an imminent expansion campaign no longer hindered by the French military presence. Simultaneously with their departure from Turin the French relinquished Vercelli, leaving Cristina and Carlo Emanuele II in control

83. BRT, MS Coll. Saluzzo, Militari 177, "Piante di fortezze," fol. 1: "In tutti li tempi da tutti li quelli ch'intendono l'arte di fortificar siti furono e sarano di parere che si avanzi verso del fiume Po almeno passato la chiesa di Sant'Antonio nel posto piu rillevato per valersi del vantaggio del sitto fabricato dalla natura . . . ho fatto il mio parere in disegno et in scritto *volesse dio che prima di circonvalar la citta nuova si fosse ventilato quello che si doveva risolvere intorno di essa fortificatione per la quale si sarebbe risolto altra miglior figura della affettuata*" (emphasis mine).

of a stronger Piedmont. Their departure was followed by a great fortification effort throughout the duchy, as well as in Turin. This marked the transfer of power from the regent to Carlo Emanuele, for whom the edict of 1648 and the *pareri* of 1656 were the earliest efforts to embellish the capital city. The realization of these efforts became the framework for the larger ducal building program proposed by Carlo Emanuele; it was the continued public manifestation of the Savoy dynasty's military and aristocratic culture in the capital of the duchy.

PART THREE
1 6 5 6 – 8 o

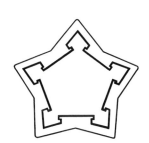

6

The Theater of State

Carlo Emanuele II's Preparations for the Borgo di Po Expansion

Il duca suol dire, che piu tosto vuol
errare da sè, che far bene col parere de gl'altri.
　　　—Venetian *Relatione,* 1664

Più che la forza un bel'inganno è in pregio.
　　　—Emanuele Tesauro, *Cannochiale aristotelico*

THE RELEASE OF THE citadel of Turin in 1657 from the French garrison that had occupied it since 1640 was Cristina's last notable achievement in her diplomatic dealings with Cardinal Mazarin and Anne of Austria, regent of France during Louis XIV's minority. During her remaining years, she attempted to arrange ambitious marriages for Carlo Emanuele II and his younger sister. Her intentions were to consolidate further the dynastic claims of the House of Savoy through a continued close alliance with France. Her hopes of marrying her daughter to Louis XIV were dashed by the terms of the Peace of the Pyrenees (1660), under which the king, like his father Louis XIII, married a Spanish princess; this same peace did, however, put an end to the Franco-Spanish conflicts for which Piedmont had served as the theater of war during the previous six decades.[1] No longer coveted by the two great European powers, the duchy of Savoy began to enjoy a period of stability and prosperity that had its most significant counterpart in the development of Turin, which under the reign of Carlo Emanuele II was greatly enlarged.

---

1. The articles of the Peace of the Pyrenees that concern the duchy of Savoy are in *Monarchia piemontese,* 6:138–41.

While his mother continued to preside, until her death in 1663, over the duchy's foreign relations and to plan for its future through dynastic marriage, Carlo Emanuele, who had been carefully groomed and educated by the preceptors Cristina had appointed for him, governed from 1657 the internal affairs of the duchy. He manifested great interest in such representations of ducal power and prerogative as building, hunting, and *feste,* occupations that Cristina had assiduously practiced before and during her own ascent to sovereign authority.[2]

In this chapter I will examine the cultural events related to the development of Turin between the years 1657 and 1673. These years marked the transition of power from Cristina, who died in 1663, to Carlo Emanuele II. The lingering influence of the regent continued to be seen and felt in the education of Carlo Emanuele and the public festivities celebrated at court, while the assertion of the new duke's rule found expression in his commissions of buildings in and near Turin, begun in the early 1660s. This earned him, in 1670, the characterization of "great lover of buildings" from the visiting English ambassador.[3] But Carlo Emanuele's most important project for Turin, considered from 1657 and officially begun in 1673, was the expansion of the city towards the Po. As we have seen in chapters 2 and 4, Carlo Emanuele I had planned in 1620 to expand the capital to the shore of the Po River, but his ambitious plans were redimensioned in 1632 by Vittorio Amedeo I, who in building Città Nuova realized only a small part of his father's expansion plans. Cristina had demonstrated her political acumen in her edict of 1646, examined in chapter 5, where she stated her intentions to realize the overall expansion promoted by Carlo Emanuele I. Thus, when Carlo Emanuele II decided to revive and implement the eastern extension of Turin, he was inserting himself within the most expressive representation of dynastic continuity adopted by several generations of Savoy sovereigns. Moreover, this loyalty to family projects had also a polemical aspect, since the methods used to implement it and the actual results differed from the original projects of the second decade of the seventeenth century in some fundamental aspects.

2. *Monarchia piemontese,* 6:328: "Prima di assumere effetivamente il governo, Carlo Emanuele II era stato profuso nelle fabbriche, caccie, feste e in ogni sorta di solazzi, a cui unicamente attendeva."

3. Thomas Belasyse, second Viscount Fauconberg, "Report to the King, upon his mission to Italy" (1670), in Historical Manuscripts Commission, *Report on Manuscripts in Various Collections* (1903), 2: 206: "The Duke of Savoy is vigorous, active, amorous, free of discourse, a great lover of buildings."

THE EFFECTS OF his royal upbringing upon Carlo Emanuele were described one year after his mother's death, in 1664, in the *Relatione* of the Venetian ambassador. Diplomatic relations between the Republic of Venice and the
duchy were reestablished in 1662 when the duke publicly if temporarily re-
voked Pierre Monod's *Coelum Allobrogicum*, published under Vittorio Amedeo, and with it the Savoy claim to Cyprus. The young duke was socially very
ambitious, and "having been nourished to believe that he was the greatest of
rulers, fit for comparison to the most powerful, passionately desired to be
recognized as such by all princes."[4] This drive earned him the love of his subjects, and he was accurate in considering himself "the only Italian prince who
kept alive among his subjects the ancient valor of the nation that, abundant in
leaders and officials, deserves to be preferred—after France—to all others."[5] A
lively and talented practitioner of dissimulation, creativity, and the art of making a good first impression ("professore nell'arte di fingere et di prima im-
pressione"), a social grace greatly admired in the late seventeenth century,
Carlo Emanuele wanted to be an absolute ruler, erring alone ("errare da sè")
rather than doing well through the counsel of others.[6] As we have seen, Carlo
Emanuele had been the subject of a disguised regency between 1648, when he
had come of age, and 1663, when Cristina died, a period when he was encouraged to declare himself only the nominal ruler. If these circumstances are
remembered, then such prideful statements of independence should not come
as a surprise, spoken one year after Carlo Emanuele became the ruler in his
own right.

The tradition of *precettistica* based on historical lessons, which Carlo Emanuele I had established through the appointment of Giovanni Botero as the tutor
of his children, was continued by the regent Cristina. A series of preceptors,
appointed by Cristina to give Carlo Emanuele II a princely and military education, closely supervised by her, provided him with the foundation for his

4. Archivio di Stato, Florence, MS Carte Strozziane, Serie Ia, Relationi di Diversi Principati, "Relatione della Corte di Savoia fatta l'anno 1664 dal'ambas [ciato] re veneto" (Catarino Berengo), fol. 132: "Essendo stato nutrito et alimentato con l'opinione d'esser piu
grande, e potersi agguagliare alle maggiori corone, si mostra apassionato per esser riconosciuto tale da ogni Prencipe."

5. Ibid., fol. 124: "Potendosi vantare il Duca di Savoia d'esser il solo Prencipe d'Italia che
tenga vivo ne suoi popoli l'antica valore della natione abbondando de Capi, et uffitiali, a
segno che doppo la Francia respetivam[en]te merita sopra ogn'altro il suo stato la prefer-
enza."

6. Ibid., fol. 132.

public and private attitudes, while enabling him to make the gestures of independence and claims to royal rank examined above. The Jesuit Pietro Paolo Orangiano served from 1640 to 1643 and was followed by the physician Emanuele Reynaud; both were erudite scholars and attempted to educate their charge through historical examples and subtle prescriptions in the guise of panegyrics.[7] From 1648, as we have seen, Luigi Giuglaris was appointed Carlo Emanuele II's spiritual educator, in addition to the several tutors in other subjects who were at his disposal, such as Maurizio Vanello, his military preceptor from 1643. As Croce has demonstrated, *precettistica* was a form of princely education peculiar to the seventeenth century, teaching rulers how to behave in various circumstances of life. The modified Machiavellian debates about *ragione di stato* to which Botero and Valeriano Castiglione (who dedicated *Lo statista regnante* to Carlo Emanuele I in 1628) had contributed ceased by the middle of the century and were replaced by nationalistic constructs of natural right that postulated absolutist rule and separated politics from morality.[8] In addition, the importance of the learned intellectual came to match that of the talented artist, who had been such an important asset to princely courts in the sixteenth century. To demonstrate the importance of learning to Carlo Emanuele, Giuglaris employed the historical example of great *and* studious generals; the young duke's grandfather Carlo Emanuele I, for example, had read for several hours even on the day in which he won the fortress of Trino. In order not to forget what he has studied in his youth, continues Giuglaris, a prince should always have a *letterato di grido,* or fashionable intellectual, beside him— thus establishing *precettistica* as a lifelong need for the ruler.[9]

Giuglaris' theories of education were laid out in a treatise dedicated to Cristina and published in 1665 (although permission to publish had been granted in September 1659, when Cristina was still alive). His *Scuola della verità aperta a' Prencipi* (*The School of Truth Opened to Princes*) was written "on the occasion of the Royal education given to the Most Serene Carlo Emanuele by Madama Reale his Mother." Giuglaris' contributions to dynastic continuity began a generation earlier, with the funeral ceremony of Vittorio Amedeo in 1637, in which, as we saw in chapter 4, he had convincingly praised the late prince's accomplishments, restated the Savoy dynasty's claims to royalty, and helped

7. Gaudenzio Claretta, *Storia della reggenza di Cristina di Francia* (Turin, 1868–69), 3 vols., 2:483–86.

8. Benedetto Croce, *Storia della età barocca in Italia* (Bari, 1929), 85, 137–38.

9. *La scuola della verità aperta a' Prencipi* (Venice, 1665), 9 ("e del gran Carlo Emanuele bastera dire, che anco nel giorno ch'espugnerò Trino, havea studiato le sue hore"), 10.

to legitimize Cristina's regency. (The efficacy of his epitaphs and the magnificence of his funereal conceits were so memorable that they were admiringly remembered by Claude-François Menestrier, who described this event in his widely read *Des Décorations funèbres*.) In his educational treatise, Giuglaris stressed the importance of intellectual endeavors in the service of the state. Thus his concept that victory is acquired through the mind, rather than with the hand ("le vittorie piu co'l capo si acquistano, che cola mano"), is a reiterative variant of a widely circulated humanist topos. The statement that the learned strategist and military architect is as crucial as the captain in winning a war had been made in print as early as 1485 by Alberti, whose treatise on architecture was present in several editions in the royal library, and by every subsequent writer on civic and military architecture who attempted to elevate the intellectual content of his subject so that it could enter the pantheon of humanistic thought.[10] Further, convinced that the prince who does not cultivate humanistic studies is unconcerned with his own glory ("poco amico delle sue glorie quel Prencipe, che ne' suoi Stati le lettere non fa fiorire"), Giuglaris implicitly reminded readers that the literary community in the seventeenth century was largely employed in writing the eulogies and praises of its absolute sovereigns. The twenty-three points of the *Scuola della verità* are a *galateo* of dissimulation, proffering the conviction that one cannot rule without suppression of one's passion, that silence is more important than talk, that the ability to hear is as important as seeing, that anger is a dangerous adviser, and that the prince should be charming. Lashing out against Erasmus, whom he calls a pedant (*pedantone*) because of the war he had waged against war, Giuglaris asserts that military art is "the most necessary of all the arts." Even though "war is the breeding ground of all ills and the destruction of all goods," a prince must have the heart to fight because otherwise "he won't have the head to rule." He concludes, however, that it is just as heroic for a prince to build sumptuous buildings, to repair old cities, and to construct new ones as to fight a war.[11]

A major vehicle for the cultivation of arts and letters in Turin was the royal

10. For the concept of victory acquired through the mind, Giuglaris, *Scuola della verità*, 513. For the cultural politics of military treatises, see John Hale, "The Argument of Some Military Title Pages of the Renaissance," *The Newberry Library Bulletin*, 6 (1964): 91–102.

11. *Scuola della verità*, 503: "l'arte militare, ch'egli non vorebbe al mondo, è nel mondo piu necessaria dell'altre tutte. . . . Essere la guerra il vivaio di tutti i mali, e la destruttione di tutti beni, . . . Prencipe, che non hà cuore per poter guerreggiare, non havrà mai buon capo per comandare."

library, newly catalogued in 1659 after the books had been transferred to the archive in the wake of a fire that had severely damaged the Galleria.[12] Giuglaris' treatise took its place in this well-stocked collection of books and manuscripts, referred to already in chapter 1. Carlo Emanuele I's military writings were among the manuscripts; he had made outlines for future compositions of aphorisms about war and rules regarding the confrontation of the enemy. The inventory provides convincing evidence of the interest of the dukes of Savoy in military matters, since their library contained the richest princely collection of military books in Italy. The list includes the major works on military planning and architecture published in the sixteenth and seventeenth centuries. It indicates that urban design in Turin may have been based upon the study and adaptation of models, both abstract and realized, that had first circulated in book form.

The collection of sixteenth- and early seventeenth-century treatises, discussed in chapters 1 and 2, had been augmented and kept rigorously up to date. We have seen that Emanuele Filiberto probably owned the works of Pietro Cataneo, Galasso Alghisi, Girolamo Cataneo, Albrecht Dürer, Philibert de l'Orme, Giacomo Lanteri, Buonaiuto Lorini, Giovan Battista Bellucci, and Girolamo Maggi. In the intervening period, the works of Jacques Perret, Giulio Savorgnan, Vincenzo Scamozzi, and Carlo Theti had been added to the ducal collections. The ancient history of military architecture and strategy was documented and commented upon in the works of Vegetius, Valturio, and "Vallo," of which French, Italian, and Latin editions were available in the royal library. Numerous other listed sixteenth-century treatises on architecture contained chapters on the design and planning of cities.

The breadth of the collection, including not only Italian but also French and Flemish writers, increases the likelihood that the dukes and the court engineers were aware of the latest theoretical and technical developments. Among the seventeenth-century books were such foreign publications as Simon Stevin's *Castrametation,* and Samuel Marolois' *Des Fortifications.* Carlo Morello, the military architect whose *parere* was requested by the crown in the consultation for the enlargement of Turin in 1656—examined in chapter 5—was also Carlo Emanuele II's military preceptor, and his own interests point to a firm theoretical foundation.

The most eminent military architect of this period, Blaise Pagan (1604–65), had himself sent a copy of his treatise to Carlo Emanuele II in 1645, soon after

12. AST, Sez. Ia, Real Casa, mazzo 5 d'addizione, number 30, 1659, "Inventario della Biblioteca Ducale fatta dal Protomedico e Bibliotecario Tonini d'ordine di S[ua] A[ltezza] R[eale]."

its publication.[13] Military historians agree that his *Fortifications* was the culmination of French research and achievement in the seventeenth-century theory of military architecture; Guarini himself, as we shall see, came to the same conclusion. Pagan had joined the French royal army in his early teens; by 1643 he was a field marshal, but lost his eyesight soon after. His research continued nonetheless, and his house became a sort of salon for military men. Pagan introduced a number of theoretical and strategic innovations. He formulated a fortification with increased depth to keep the enemy farther from the walls of the city, fashioned the face of the bastion from the exterior of the polygonal fortification, and applied new advances in geometry to the conception and execution of the fortified city, now seen as a whole from the outside; his treatise contains, in fact, an entire chapter on urban design. His elaborate two-moat system was not employed in contemporary fortifications, but found acceptance in the work of Vauban, whose first two fortification systems were derived from Pagan's. Their success in rationalizing the planning of the fortification trace had a considerable influence on the development in the seventeenth century of a scientific method of city planning.

The predominance of foreign military treatises in the palatine library, and the Savoy rulers' personal relations with French strategists in particular, shows that the Savoy dukes were acutely aware of the Italian loss of hegemony in military research. While Pagan sent Carlo Emanuele II his treatise in hopes of garnering his patronage, as Antoine de Ville had done before him, Vauban went beyond him, offering his services as military architect to the young ruler of Savoy directly. Vauban was in Louis XIV's army from 1651 to 1706, as superintendent of French fortifications, responsible for their construction and maintenance.[14] His own numerous fortification designs were based on the theories of Pagan. He expanded the already wide fortification belt with addi-

13. AST, Sez. Ia, Lettere Particolari, P, mazzo 1, 20 January 1645: "Monsieur, Les advantages que V[otre] Altesse Royalle recoit desja, de ses belles inclinations et de sa glorieuse naissance, commenceant a faire esclatter sa reputation dans le monde, me portent a la envoyer ce livre de mes fortifications, accompagné des offres de mes eternelles obeissances. Il contient Monseigneur en peu de discours beaucoup de nouvelles maximes, et s'il estoit digne des illustres occupations de vostre incomparable jeunesse les recompenses de mon travail se borneroient a cet advantage." Inexplicably Pagan's treatise was not included in the 1659 inventory. For Pagan see also Charles Perrault, *Les Hommes illustres qui ont paru en France pendant ce siècle* (Paris, 1697), 27–28.

14. Pierre Lazard, *Vauban, 1633–1707* (Paris, 1934), discusses Vauban's connections to Pagan and Antoine de Ville; see also Reginald Blomfield, *Sebastien le Prestre de Vauban, 1633–1707* (London, 1938). And for a brilliant analysis of the influence of Vauban's military dis-

tional foreworks and an intricate mine system. Vauban's oeuvre included entire fortress towns, like Longwy and Neuf-Brisach, for which he designed the street layout and official buildings as well as the fortifications. The urban environment of these seventeenth-century military settlements was dominated by their strategic function, with the gates serving as the only architectural ornaments of the city's fortification. The decorated gates were significant, however, since Vauban maintained that the strength of the fortification enclosure was often measured by the beauty of the gates. As we will see when we examine the planning and execution of the Po expansion, Vauban's theories and projects were an important influence in the design of the enlarged fortifications of Turin. Indeed, Vauban himself submitted a planning study for the expansion.

THE CONTINUED GROWTH of the palatine library, already rich in architectural and military books and manuscripts, demonstrates that Giuglaris' programmatic support of an educated prince surrounded by learned counselors was given at least its external trappings. The collection of military books, extolled by visitors to Turin, was one of the many ways in which the royalty and magnificence of the House of Savoy was publicly stated; it further proclaimed the dynastic continuity of the family. Another well-established tradition of public magnificence, that of triumphal entries and lavishly organized *feste,* was likewise continued by Carlo Emanuele II. These public events were a way both of celebrating Turin and of educating the public in the urbanistic message of the Savoy dynasty's city planning and architecture. As on previous occasions, the plans to beautify and enlarge the city received new impetus from these public celebrations, which stimulated remodeling of existing buildings, the completion of imperfect projects, and the start of new ones.

Carlo Emanuele's first wedding, to a French princess chosen by Cristina in 1663, was one of these events, thoroughly documented by the ducal historiographer Valeriano Castiglione.[15] The reception of the bride, Françoise de Bourbon, took place in Turin. For three evenings the streets were brilliantly lit. The triumphal procession's itinerary, from the Villa Valentino to Palazzo Reale, was

course on eighteenth-century French literature, see Joan DeJean, *Literary Fortifications* (Princeton, 1984), chap. 1.

15. *Le feste nuttiali delle Regie Altesse di Savoia* (Turin, 1663), reprinted in Leone Tettoni and Maurizio Marocco, *Le illustri alleanze della Real Casa di Savoia colla descrizione delle feste nuziali celebrate in Torino* (Turin, 1868), 171–89.

an elaborate display of the military, civic, and religious might of the duke of Savoy; his soldiers and officers, civil servants, priests and monks, and members of the ducal court were deployed according to a rigorous order that made manifest the role of each within the absolutist monarchical hierarchy, and was contrived to enhance the powerful and central position of the duke of Savoy. The strength and beauty of the procession lay in the great number of participants and in the brilliance and color of their attire. Bright velvets and silks, feathers, gold, silver, and precious stones, with horses, carriages, and gleaming arms, made for a sparkling cavalcade that paraded, making only one right-angled turn, on the straight road from the suburban villa to the southern entry of the city.

Two hundred paces outside Turin a triumphal arch had been built by the city's magistrates; adjacent to it was a throne, which Carlo Emanuele and his consort occupied while they listened to the welcome speeches proffered by the three major administrative agencies of Piedmont: the Council of State, the Senate, and the Camera de' Conti. At the southern gate, the Porta Nuova, the bride was offered the keys to the city, twelve pages, and a highly embroidered baldachin. Thus covered, protected, and empowered, she passed under another triumphal arch, offered by the Senate, and was treated to what locally was considered the most beautiful urban perspective: the view of the straight street that led from the gate directly to the portal of the newly erected Palazzo Reale.

Although only a written description survives, the two triumphal arch gateways may have been similar to those, painted on shutters or built on the inner stage, in the scenery of *Il falso amor bandito,* a ballet presented in Turin in 1667 (fig. 82). This stage set borrows heavily from military architecture. Not only is the background designed as a triumphal arch, but also the wings that frame the proscenium stage look like a heavily fortified city wall, an aggregate of old-fashioned medieval castle towers. With gates at the back of the stage, they enclose an area shown as outside the city, outside the juridical space that defines the city, and thus an appropriate setting for *amor bandito.*

The urban perspective that greeted the wedding party at the southern gate was not what Jean Rousset calls "cité trompeuse, ville-théâtre," not a stage setting as in the *théâtre-ville* of *amor bandito,* but rather an actual urban design modeled on theatrical precedents.[16] If reality was made of theater and decoration, then the spectators can be seen as the unreal, disguised elements of the ceremony ("l'homme est déguisement dans un monde qui est théâtre et décor") at a time and place inclined to make reality out of a metaphor and to

16. *La Littérature de l'âge baroque en France: Circé et le paon* (Paris, 1953), 23.

allow theater to invade the world beyond its boundaries, turning reality into simulation and sham ("dans le monde du trompe-l'oeil, il faut le détour de la feinte pour atteindre la réalité"; "la réalité prend la figure de la feinte").[17] It must be remembered that the Venetian ambassador, no doubt a connoisseur in matters of simulation, had praised Carlo Emanuele's art of *fingere*. The street perspective was modulated along its continuous path by three squares: Piazza Reale, only recently perfected at Cristina's orders; Piazza Castello; and Piazzetta Reale, the smaller square in front of the royal palace that formed its external court, separated from Piazza Castello by a loggia raised on porticoes.[18] Decorated for the wedding reception with inscriptions, statues, paintings, arms, and flags, the central pavilion above the porticoes acted as another triumphal arch before the entry to the palace and reiterated a design element that through its repeated use for festivities in Piazza Castello had become a leitmotif of ducal self-representation.

Passing under the colonnade between the royal palace and the palace of Princess Ludovica (the widow of Prince Maurizio and Carlo Emanuele II's oldest sister), the procession stopped at the door of the cathedral, also ornamented with a triumphal arch. After the service the royal couple and the court proceeded to Palazzo Reale, which they reached by walking through the new chapel of the Holy Shroud. The chapel, containing the Savoy family's most precious relic, was being built above the choir of the cathedral, at the height of the ducal palace's *piano nobile*. The close connection of the chapel with their newly reconstructed palace, and its role as hinge between the palace and the cathedral, had been decided in c. 1657. Amedeo di Castellamonte, the son of Carlo di Castellamonte, was responsible for the design of the palace, while Bernardo Quadri designed the chapel. Quadri's design had been accepted by Carlo Emanuele and the regent in 1657 (figs. 83, 84).[19] The continuity between

17. Ibid., 28, 54, 64. On the pervasiveness of disguise see also Rosario Villari, *Elogio della dissimulazione: La lotta politica nel Seicento* (Bari, 1987).

18. Castiglione, *Feste nuttiali,* 177–78: "Investita che fu la porta Nuova . . . si scoprì con prospettiva di essa la più vaga e più aggiustata, che non si crede nell'Europa la grand'apertura, che per linea retta, e per una larga, uniforme, e bellissima strada, va a terminare nella porta del palazzo Reale, piacevolmente interrotta solo nella continuatione, ma non nella diritura, dal mezzo di tre superbe piazze, cioè da quella che è chimata Reale ultimamente perfetionata a gran portici collonati con alti palazzi; quella che si dice del Castello, d'architettura soda a portici di pilastri con ringhiere di sopra, e l'ultima che è immediatamente avanti la porta del Regio palazzo, e serve come cortile esteriore, benchè publico al mede[si]mo palazzo, divisa dalla piazza del Castello per una loggia scoperta al di sopra, e sotto a portici."

19. *Schede Vesme,* 1:286–87, 3:880.

cathedral and royal residence is underlined in the description of the next day's festivities, when the court smoothly passed back and forth between the contiguous gallery of Palazzo Reale and the chapel of the Holy Shroud in the cathedral, in order to worship and then to participate in the exhibition of the Holy Shroud in Piazza Castello.[20]

The evening's festivities were offered by the mayors at the brand-new Palazzo di Città, which like Palazzo Reale had been rebuilt in honor of Carlo Emanuele II's wedding. Francesco Lanfranchi was the architect of the new city hall, and his extant drawing of the facade (1659) shows it as originally built, before the eighteenth-century interventions by Benedetto Alfieri (fig. 85).[21] A rusticated Doric triumphal arch formed the entry, flanked on each side by two arched bays, also rusticated and filled in with a shop and mezzanine level. The large windows on the *piano nobile,* surmounted with segmental pediments, were separated by Ionic pilasters and wall moldings, with a continuous parapet functioning as window sill and pedestal for statues placed in front of the pilasters. A shorter level topped the building, decorated with dwarf pilasters and triangular pedimented windows. Ironically, in view of the actual distribution of power, this use of the orders of architecture marks the contrast between the skeletal facade of Palazzo Reale, full of windows and with a very insecure sense of hierarchy in its composition, and that of Palazzo di Città, a confident, well-proportioned design with authoritative references to Roman architecture.

From the *piano nobile* level of the palace the guests watched the fireworks exploding over the mountain that occupied the square in front of Palazzo di Città. This mountain—topped with the bull of Mars representing both the duke and the city of Turin—was an element present in many Savoy family wedding celebrations (1620, 1650); it burst into flames at the conclusion of the display, ignited by a dove with burning wings, representing the bride, which crashed into the bull from the top of the palace.[22] The incineration of the festive display, provoking exhilaration and fear, had been previously used for dramatic effect in other *feste,* such as the burning of the model of Turin in the welcoming ceremony offered by the city council to the returning Cristina and

20. Castiglione, *Feste nuttiali,* 181: "prima galleria del palazzo Reale contigua a detta Capella del Sindone"; for the arrangements and cost of the wedding reception, see AST, Sez. Riunite, art. 199.1, March 1663.

21. Nino Carboneri, "Architettura," in *Mostra del barocco piemontese,* ed. Vittorio Viale (Turin, 1963) 1:27–28; Marziano Bernardi, *Torino* (Turin, 1965), 136–38.

22. Castiglione, *Feste nuttiali,* 182–83; the mountain bore the following inscription: "Domitore Amore- / Flammivomus colchorum taurus- / Thessalici ducis, et colchidis heroine- / Regalum coniugum, ultro ambit jugum- / Et felicioribus se flammis adolet."

Carlo Emanuele II in 1645. The conflagration of a *festa* set produced by the fall of a ball of fire—itself an unmistakable reference to cannonballs, whose hiss, blaze, and incendiary character were indelible memories for the resident population—had been adopted by Tesauro in his design of 1632, discussed in chapter 4, when the birth of the Savoy heir Francesco Giacinto had been celebrated.

The naturalistic display of mountain, dove, and bull destroyed by flames was countered by the geometrical display of sweets and out-of-season fruit (a recognized Torinese whim to this day) in the *salone* of the palace. There the royal guests enjoyed the visual bravura of the pyramids of fruit and watched with glee the "sacco di detta tavola," the sack of the table, and the "scalata alla piramide fruttata," the scaling of the pyramid.[23] The terms used to describe the shameless enjoyment of the courtiers, who destroyed the theatrically arranged refreshments, have a deadly equivalent in military operations, where scaling and sacking would spell the end of a city's liberty and prosperity. The rhetorical use of such terms here, while echoing their military significance, demonstrates not only the persuasiveness and ubiquity of the military culture but also the desire to exorcise the fears associated with war.

The following days the newlyweds spent in taking possession of the various ducal villas and castles in the vicinity of Turin, including Moncalieri, Vigna della Regina, and Venaria Reale. In each instance they were welcomed by a festive reception intended to show off the amenities of the place. All of these entries, in the capital itself and in the outlying villas, combined two kinds of ceremonial procession: the *possesso* of the acknowledged sovereign, and the triumphal welcome entry of the illustrious new resident, which were fused and extended in time and meaning. The sovereign's new consort entered the city and took possession of it; the elements possessed were military, civic, and religious. In the process, Turin itself became the best theatrical stage for the public event. Although additional decorations were erected, as was the practice elsewhere, Contrada Nuova, Piazza Reale, and Piazza Castello were themselves the most striking parts of the display, and they were unique to Turin. It is at this moment that the completion of Città Nuova can be considered accomplished. Turin had become the appropriate stage setting for the events in the life of its rulers, and it framed perfectly the requirements of royal pomp and ideology. The three buildings visited by the royal couple in the city represented the three loci of the Savoy dynasty's power: royal political might more or less dissembled in the ducal residence, the municipal independence repre-

23. Ibid., 183.

sented by the city hall, and the religious center at the cathedral. All three buildings—the chapel of the Holy Shroud, Palazzo Reale, and Palazzo di Città—had been constructed, remodeled, or begun in the five years preceding the wedding. Of the two palaces the first was built as the new residence of the soon-to-be married duke, while Carlo Emanuele demanded from the city council the reconstruction of Palazzo di Città as a gesture of respect and of compliance with his intentions to marry.

The elaborate and brilliant wedding ceremony was matched by the equivalent theatricality of the funeral ceremony provided by Carlo Emanuele II in March 1664, only six months later, when he buried both duchesses, his spouse and his mother. "Il teatro del dolore" (the theater of suffering) was staged in the cathedral, which was decorated for the occasion with a Doric facade and with numerous inscriptions—considered the soul of funeral decorations—that inspired high praise from Menestrier: "the court of Savoy which is so magnificent in its great entertainments is no less so with funeral decorations; these are given all the ornament that pain can bear." [24] In a manner reminiscent of Vittorio Amedeo's funeral decorations, in which his military feats had foretold Cristina's armed conflicts, Cristina's funeral, focusing on her achievements in construction—decorations included a view of Turin enlarged and embellished with the inscription "Urbs ornata et amplificata" [25]—seemed to forecast the dominant interest of her successor Carlo Emanuele II in making his own mark upon Turin and Piedmont. His twin tasks, to maintain the ideological and dynastic continuity of the Savoy, and to establish his own identity even if it meant *errare da sè* (making his own mistakes), were to become his distinguishing feature and the driving force in the expansion of Turin to the Po.

THE TWO CEREMONIES, wedding and funeral, thus had a close bearing upon building activity in Turin in the early 1660s. Improvements were made at the Castello and at Palazzo Reale, whose facade on Piazzetta Reale was rebuilt between 1658 and 1660, partly in reaction to the challenge of the city, which began to build Palazzo di Città in 1659, and partly to accommodate the soon-to-be-married duke. The rebuilding of the facade of Palazzo Reale in Turin was began in 1658 by Amedeo di Castellamonte. He laid out the facade

24. *Des Décorations funèbres*, 168: "la cour de Savoye qui est si magnifique dans les grandes festes, ne l'est guère moins aux décorations funèbres; elle leur donne tous les ornemens que la douleur peut souffrir."

25. Ibid., 217–19.

of the palace across the north side of the Piazzetta Reale, which was cleared in 1659 of the foundry buildings and miscellaneous houses that were still there.[26] As we have seen, a porticoed structure had been built in front of Palazzo Reale separating the Piazzetta from Piazza Castello; beside its function as urban screen, it served as a focal point for triumphal processions and as foundation for festive temporary pavilions within which the Holy Shroud was exhibited. Building was also taking place in the cathedral at the chapel of the Holy Shroud and at the site of San Lorenzo, turning the Piazzetta Reale into a construction site. The building activity in and around Turin in the late 1650s and early 1660s can be seen as a gathering of forces and experience to undertake a larger planning and construction enterprise.

The implications inherent in the design of Città Nuova were acknowledged in the composition of the facade of the ducal palace, the definition of the Piazzetta Reale, and the systematization of the display of the Holy Shroud. In the new Bernardo Quadri–Amedeo di Castellamonte design, the chapel had been moved from its initial place at the choir end of the cathedral, behind the high altar (fig. 86), to a much more prominent position, raised above the choir and set just behind the crossing between the nave and the transept arms. In its new location, the chapel dominated the space of the cathedral and compositionally acted as the main altar. We have seen that it provided a direct link between the cathedral and the ducal palace, allowing the royal family to go directly from their rooms in the palace to the cathedral through the Holy Shroud chapel. The chapel thus had the double role of main chapel of Turin and palatine chapel, and forged an indelible link with the city. The reconstructed Palazzo Reale was separated from Piazza Castello by porticoes and the pavilion used for the celebrative display of the Shroud. The square formed in front of the palace, Piazzetta Reale, was thus distinguished from the rest of the large square, named after the Castello, and it served as a *cour d'honneur* for the new palace. The facade of Palazzo Reale was redesigned to take full advantage of its axial relation with Contrada Nuova, and its portal was aligned with the southern Porta Nova in a way that made one visible from the other. This direct visual connection between city gate and the ruler's palace had been postulated earlier in treatises on the form of the ideal city; as the individual elements of Carlo Emanuele I's initial plan were slowly realized, the dukes of Savoy refashioned Turin into a three-dimensional expression of their absolutist policies.

26. Marziano Bernardi, "Le sedi," in *Mostra del barocco piemontese*, ed. Vittorio Viale (Turin, 1963), 9–18.

The crown was involved in numerous projects of fortification, urban planning, and architecture not only within the city, but also outside Turin and throughout Piedmont. Among the largest were the fortification of Vercelli and Verrua, and the creation of a city, Villafranca, as a small Piedmontese outlet on the Mediterranean, with an open city status modeled on that of Livorno, which would have increased sharply the revenues of the duchy.[27] But the largest sums were spent on the development of Venaria Reale, a hunting lodge just west of Turin, begun in 1658 and paid for in large part from the duke's personal income. The architect in charge of the Venaria was again Amedeo di Castellamonte, who was also working on the maintenance of the palaces of Moncalieri and Rivoli, both visited often by Carlo Emanuele II while the Venaria was under construction.[28]

The design and construction of the Venaria Reale might well be considered a rehearsal for the development of Turin. It was an important experiment in city planning and urban design, which drew on the precedent provided by Città Nuova and served as a laboratory for future developments. The project comprised the hunting lodge, rebuilt at palatial scale, and the layout of a semiurban settlement beside it. The plan of the settlement was orthogonal, with the main street of the town axial to the main portal of the entrance pavilion of the lodge, and surrounded by a palisade. (fig. 87). Most houses were two stories tall with interior gardens and courts. The center of town was marked by a large porticoed piazza, with exedras perpendicular to the main street within which the facades of the church and the hospital were placed (fig. 88). A semicircular piazza opened in front of the palace's main entrance. The layout of the settlement is closely similar to the town of Richelieu founded by the eponymous French minister (fig. 89); the relationship between town and palace is achieved in the same way through a connecting street and an open space between the palace and the town.[29] The plan of Venaria Reale was an

27. *Monarchia piemontese*, 6:250.

28. AST, Sez. Ia, Fondo Provincia Torino, mazzo 32, "Conto della spesa del palazzo della Venaria Reale"; about 205,000 *lire* were spent between 1660 and 1663. I owe to Elisabeth B. MacDougall the transcription of the payments related to the villa; see also *Schede Vesme*, 1:290; Nino Carboneri, "Architettura," 30–31. The English ambassador records the delight Carlo Emanuele took in Venaria Reale, not least because it was out of sight of the French-occupied Pinerolo (*Report on Manuscripts*, 206).

29. For Richelieu the town, see Maurice Dumolin, *La Construction de la ville de Richelieu* (Poitiers, 1935); Enrico Guidoni and Angela Marino Guidoni, *Storia dell'urbanistica: Il seicento* (Bari, 1979), 305–6; Pierre Lavedan et al., *L'Urbanisme a l'époque moderne* (Paris, 1982), 88–90.

improvement over that of Richelieu, however. A clear understanding of public building and civic service was manifested in the juxtaposition of hospital and church, while at Richelieu there is only a church on the main square. More important, the main street of Venaria ended at the gate of the ducal compound, making an axial connection between town and palace. The street connecting Richelieu to the chateau passed parallel to its main entry, reducing the importance of the chateau as climax. While Richelieu was merely adjacent to the chateau, Venaria became the forecourt of the palace, providing a spatial experience similar to that of crossing Città Nuova in Turin along the axial Contrada Nuova focused on the portal of the ducal palace. The great landscaped garden and park, filled with extraordinary fountains, pavilions, and a canal, began at the other side of the villa's main wing (figs. 90–93).

With the construction of Venaria Reale, the crown of villas built by the Savoy rulers around Turin was completed, and Carlo Emanuele could truly take his place among the royal ancestors he emulated.[30] At the time of its implementation, Venaria Reale was the largest ducal project to be subsidized entirely from the ducal treasury. It was referred to as a villa, but Carlo Emanuele II expected his courtiers to form a large settlement by building their own country houses there. Finding enough settlers quickly was difficult, and Venaria Reale did not achieve uniformity of facade even along its main street; while the site had been chosen for its abundant game, the foggy, marshy land did not make it auspicious for permanent residence. Nevertheless, its main urbanistic elements—the ornamental gate, the uniform axial street, the open square providing a spatial connection, and distance between town and palace—had been employed in the design of Turin's southern expansion. The axiality of the main street is significant because it dominated the urban plan; its length and uniformity gave hierarchy to the street grid. The attractions of the palace, garden, and city were fully illustrated in *La Venaria Reale,* published by its architect Amedeo di Castellamonte with engravings by Giorgio Tasniere, composed in the guise of a conversation between Amedeo and Gian Lorenzo Bernini, who had stopped in Turin on his way to Paris in 1665. The two architects discussed urban design, dynastic siting, and royal pastimes, in an attempt to define the parallel, or even equivalence, between hunting (the explicit function of Venaria), war, and patronage of architecture. The first parallel,

---

30. Amedeo di Castellamonte, *Venaria reale* (Turin, 1674), 2: "Volendo tuttavia [even though there were already several Savoy villas around Turin] ad imitatione de suoi reali antenati fabbricar ancor lui [Carlo Emanuele II] il suo palazzo, non vi restava che questa parte di mezza notte, non occupata per compiere un'intiera corona di delitie à quest'Augusta Città di Torino."

associating hunting and war as equal arts in the inscription above the entry to the hunting lodge, was provided by the indefatigable Tesauro.[31] A further equivalence is then made in the conversation of the two architects between *fortezza,* the quality of a prince required for war, and *magnificenza,* whose object is building. Since Carlo Emanuele's reign is a peaceful one, he has amused himself by embracing construction wholeheartedly.[32]

Amedeo di Castellamonte, the architect of Palazzo Reale and Venaria Reale, was of ancient Canavese origin, and belonged to the Cognengo branch of the Castellamonte counts. Like his father, Carlo di Castellamonte, the chief architect of Carlo Emanuele I, Amedeo was an artillery officer, strategist, spy, military engineer, and architect; father and son worked together in the enlargement and decoration of Villa Valentino. During his long career he served the regent Cristina, Carlo Emanuele II, and the regent Giovanna Battista (widow of Carlo Emanuele II). He had studied law, then architecture under the guidance of his father. His titles were ducal engineer (1639), ducal architect (1646), general superintendent of Fabriche e Fortificationi (1659), and state councilor (1666). In 1667 Amedeo became lieutenant-general of artillery, and with a letter patent of 1678 he was named chief engineer of the crown. Amedeo's multiple offices and appointments kept him occupied with the major fortresses of

31. Ibid., 8:

La Venaria Reale

Questo è un Genio Guerrier gradito hostello

Delle Caccie Reali

Fondò il secondo Carlo Emanuello

Per avvezzar gli strali

Della Dea delle cacie à quei di Marte

Che la caccia, e la guerra è un'istess'arte.

(This is the favored lodge of the royal hunt, founded by Carlo Emanuele the Second, the martial genius, in order to accustom the arrows of the goddess of the hunt and those of Mars to one another, since hunting and war are the same art).

32. Ibid., 85: "Possiede senza dubbio l'Alt[ezza] S[ua] R[eale] quelle due Reggie virtù Fortezza e Magnificenza, e non potendo essercitare la prima, che ha per oggetto il Valore, e questo la Guerra, mercè il continuato già per trè lustri, e general riposo dell'armi, con non picciolo suo rammarico, havendolo io più d'una volta sentito dolere, che la pace togliesse à lui quegli honori, e quelle Glorie che questa Regia Virtù ha con tanto liberalità compartito a' suoi Reali Antenati . . . che perciò abbracciando con tutto l'animo la seconda, cioè la magnificenza in questa parte, che ha per fine l'eternità, l'utilità, e il decoro, et ha per oggetto le Fabriche, quali con la mole loro rendono immortale il nome degli Edificatori con la construttione, utilità à popoli, e con la proportione, e simetrià, ornamento, e decoro alle città, si è attorno queste divertito parte del tempo del suo governo."

Piedmont and of Savoy, and his contribution was prodigious; he provided designs for the rehabilitation of Momigliano, Ceva, Zucarello, Cherasco, and Cuneo, as well as Verrua, Santhia, Villanova d'Asti, and Mondovi.[33] All were strongholds located at strategic points in the duchy.

Construction at Venaria Reale was in its final stages when Carlo Emanuele II decided to enlarge Turin. Amedeo was the most experienced planner available at court; his position at the time was that of superintendent of fortifications, and when Carlo Emanuele merged Fabriche e Fortificationi with the council of finance in 1666 he became a cabinet member in charge of ducal construction. He had a large group of assistants, principal among them being Michelangelo Garove, a military architect, and Gian Francesco Baroncelli, referred to as "giovine del conte Amedeo Castellamonte" and after 1683 as engineer.[34] Castellamonte's role in the expansion can be inferred from the recorded ceremony of the laying of the foundation stone in 1673; as director of fortifications he was directly responsible to Guglielmo Balbiano, the military governor of Piedmont. Though Amedeo's role in the design of the Borgo di Po enlargement is not directly discussed in these documents of 1673, his was certainly a major contribution to its planning, layout, and realization. Designs for the specific architectural elements—the facades of the main street and square—were provided by Amedeo separately, after the layout was established, as we learn from the edicts of the regent Giovanna Battista in the later 1670s.[35] Besides contributing to the layout of the Po expansion and the facade designs, Amedeo was also the architect of the ducal building program in the Borgo di Po enlargement. His relationship with the star architect at court, Guarino Guarini, was somewhat ambiguous. However, from Carlo Emanuele II's impatience with the aging Amedeo and the fact that Guarini was given the commission to finish the Holy Shroud chapel upon his arrival in Turin, it can be surmised that there was friction between the two architects.[36] Nonetheless, it was Amedeo who supervised the construction of the Po extension, and as the leading ducal architect he even had occasion to evaluate Guarini's design for the Po gate, as we will see in the following chapter. Although he commanded less respect and authority than his father had, Amedeo continued in the service of the crown until his death in 1683. His design of Venaria Reale,

33. *Schede Vesme*, 1:285–91.
34. Ibid., 2:515–16, 1:92.
35. Borelli, 934.
36. *Schede Vesme*, 1:290–91.

as illustrated in the eponymous book, can be considered a pilot project for the expansion of Turin to the east, which commenced in 1673.

THE REVIVAL OF the expansion project for Turin had been mentioned in edicts of 1646 and 1648, and reconsidered in the consultations with architects and engineers that took place in 1656. Finally, the expansion was once again seriously contemplated in 1668 by Duke Carlo Emanuele II, who recorded some of his motives for the enlargement of the capital in his personal diary.[37] The earliest related entry (30 May 1668) shows that the expansion was privately considered by Carlo Emanuele as a way of making money through an increase of the tax base of the city. Religious orders were to be excluded since they did not pay taxes. This attitude was in sharp contrast with that of Carlo Emanuele I, who had invited religious orders to settle in Città Nuova with various grants and privileges. While Carlo Emanuele I had tried to win the favor of the pope by permitting the foundation of several monasteries and convents, including that of the Jesuits, Carlo Emanuele II sought to prove his independence and intended to keep religious orders out.[38] This diary entry also provides a clue to the way in which the enlargement was to be financed. The duke intended to buy the available land in the area, and then resell it at its increased value (after the expansion was fortified, land values increased officially). The heightened value of property was of course due to the fact that it became part of a fortified city . In the duke's calculations, this potential profit could have covered half of the expense necessary for the construction of the fortifications. The city would be cajoled to pay the other half, needed for the bastions and the new gate, thus sparing the ducal treasury.[39] As mentioned

37. AST, Sez. Ia, Real Casa, cat. 3, mazzo 18; for convenience I have cited the text in *Memoriale*, after consulting the manuscript. On Carlo Emanuele's poor orthography and phrasing, evident in these twelve-volume memoirs written in a mixture of French, Italian, and Piedmontese dialect, see Luigi Firpo, "Immagini di un regno sognato," in *Theatrum*, ed. Firpo, 1:12.

38. *Memoriale*, 28: "In deto agrandimento non metterei frati ne monache afin di populare perche le grandi cita sono quelle che rendono molto."

39. Ibid.: "Agrandire Torino la cita li concori accomprare tutti li siti che quelli rivendendo si potra fare la meta delle fortificationi l'altra meta la cita concorendo, con poca cosa che io ci metti si farebbe senza gran costo." Early in 1669 the city council was asked to contribute 50,000 *ducatoni* for the expansion towards the Po (ASCT, Ordinati, 17 February 1669).

above, the crown was simultaneously subsidizing numerous other construction and fortification projects throughout Piedmont, and needed loans (and other, less reputable means) to finance the Po expansion.

On 1 January 1669 the duke recorded that, in order to quell the protests of property owners in the Po expansion areas, they were to be allowed to make the estimates of their own property.[40] It was a self-serving permission. The crown would profit if owners foolishly inflated the value of their land, because it would be paid a larger tax. In addition, the duke had every intention to buy out owners who were unwilling or unable to pay the tax on their property after it became part of the urban territory, and supposedly to resell it at a higher price. Thus, if owners purposely underestimated the value of their property, perhaps in hopes of owing a smaller balance to the crown, when the crown bought them out it would then gain by having to pay less for the land.

Carlo Emanuele's lengthy entry of April 1669 is divided into two parts: a note about the materials and documents needed to make final decisions about the enlargement, and an outline of the speech he had to address to the city council, the strongest impediment to his volition. The first part of the entry contained ten points, referring to fundamental issues, which demonstrated that Carlo Emanuele still had a great number of problems to solve. He first wonders about the design of the enlargement, which would have to be determined in order to know its size, and whether the old fortifications should be maintained or demolished.[41] The construction costs could not be calculated without knowing the layout of streets and squares. The crown property in the area and the site of the old fortifications, also belonging to the crown, were to be sold in order to raise money for the new fortifications.[42] The duke would determine the conditions for waiving the payment of the tax on the increased value of properties.[43] Owners were allowed to determine the value of their

40. *Memoriale*, 69: "Fra altro ordine o comprender nel primo la dimanda della deta cota lasciando alli patroni delli beni et case come ho gia detto in questo libro a lungo di farne l'estimo et rimeterlo a qui vorra, con facolta a me o di prender la detta quota o di pigliare il fondo pagandolo all'estimo che ne avera fatto il patrone in qual modo alcuno non si potra dolere dell'estimo."

41. Ibid., 68: "convenire del disegno tanto per la largeza del agrandimento che per sapere se si demolisce la vecchia fortificazione o no."

42. Ibid., 69: "disegnar le piaze et le strade quali vanno al mio costo per li calcoli sul resto. . . . In caso di demolicione espor venali li siti miei con il qui preso devono farsi li preparamenti per la nova cinta."

43. Ibid.: "Et perche e guisto che li possedenti beni stiano nel circuito della detta nova cinta si come con essa si renderanno piu preziosi cosi contribuiscono un aiuto per la spesa

property, as considered in the earlier entry of 1669. Religious institutions that owned property in Borgo di Po would be obliged to exchange it for land from the farm of the Villa Valentino.[44] Emulating the French and English kings, Carlo Emanuele insisted on demonstrating his power over the religious institutions in his domain. The construction of fortifications had to be paid from an outside source; the minister of finance, Giovanni Battista Trucchi (the "Piedmontese Colbert"), when asked to examine possible indirect taxes that could be tapped for this purpose, warned Carlo Emanuele in a letter of April 1669 that, although potentially profitable for his renown and his finances, the building enterprises he was undertaking were too numerous to be supported simultaneously by the crown treasury.[45]

The first part of the April 1669 entry, then, deals almost exclusively with the financial aspects of the enlargement; there is little mention of the military needs of Turin, or of the ideological impact of an enlarged and beautified town, even though the ambitious duke was well aware of pomp and representation. All the finer motives for enlarging Turin—strategic, ideological, aesthetic, and charitable—were saved for the speech the duke prepared for the city councilors, in the second part of the diary entry. First, he argued, the demographic increase in the population warranted an expansion. (The city councilors countered this proposal by pointing out that new land was not needed since the old parts of town were not entirely built up, and that the area chosen for the expansion was almost entirely settled by suburban inhabitants.)[46] Second, the expansion area would be "ennobled with academies, colleges, and many other public places for the exercise of virtue"; these would attract foreign *virtuosi*, merchants and bankers who would make Turin famous. Turin's good location, and the renown of its great number of wealthy citizens, devoted to their

della clausura et fortificatione, percio far un ordine col quale si obbligono tutti a consegnarli per qualita e quantita minutamente sotto gravi pene . . . determinar con il consilio di chi mi piacera la cota della contributione."

44. Ibid.: "alli ecclesiastici che averanno beni nel detto circuito darliene altri della cassina del Valentino."

45. AST, Sez. Ia, Lettere Particolari, T, mazzo 32, 23 April 1669: "con due riffletioni finisco . . . il commercio [of Villafranca] divulgato per tutto il mondo incaminato con impegno, anzi gelosia a migliori porti d'Italia e di Francia. L'aggrandimento della città non ancora slergatosi fuori delle mura con la semplice notitia, l'una e l'altra e opera gloriosa e riuscibile, ma non in tempo medesimo."

46. *Memoriale*, 69: "per far logo at popolo che gia e cresciuto in tanto numero che ora mai non capisce piu nella presenta citta." For the response of the city council, see ASCT, Ordinati, 22 Februray 1669, fol. 225.

prince, were to provide further attraction.[47] Third, the new perimeter, built according to the true rules of military architecture, would make the siege of Turin difficult. Turin should be prepared to fight, since Pinerolo—the first fortress on the Italian side of the Alps, less than forty miles away—was still in French custody at the time. The closeness of the Po, sought in the expansion, would permit the city to receive help from its allies in the Italian peninsula in case of attack from France.[48] The frightfully large dimensions of its new fortifications would elevate Turin further within the hierarchy of strongholds so that a large army would be needed to attack it successfully.[49]This was to be the most convincing reason for the enlargement presented to the city councilors.

There remained the question of whether to integrate the old eastern wall of the Roman city within the newly fortified expansion area. The duke mentioned the possibility of leaving the Roman and parts of the 1630s eastern walls in place even after the new fortifications had been built. There were precedents even in Turin for this idea since the old Roman walls, preserved despite numerous repairs and alterations, possessed great symbolic meaning. Even if the inhabitants of the new parts of town had rights equal to those enjoyed within the ancient enclosure, the Roman walls carried a special significance, helping the original citizens to define themselves and to maintain an illusory superiority. The double walls might be kept for military reasons, the center—with the city hall, the cathedral, and the ducal palace—being thus defended by two layers of fortifications. On the other hand, the duke argued, leaving a double line of walls would not really help the city's defense or make it easier to rule,

47. *Memoriale*, 69–70: "per nobilitarla con la construsione di academie, collegi di nobili et molti altri loghi publici per l'esercizio delle virtu a fine d'atirarvi artefici negozianti banchieri et altri virtuosi forestieri rendendola celebre come spero mi reuscira come posto nel principio dell'Italia alli confini et passagio della Francia piu comoda di tutti li passagi che vengono in Italia e cosi numerosa d'abitanti richi et dovitiosi che anco nelle ocasioni possino servire il suo principe."

48. Ibid., 70: "ma da non legieri ma per consderare bene Torino resta frontiera di Pinerolo, per questo considerandola tale bisogna metterla tutta nel miglior stato che sia possibile . . . essendo patrone del Po che da quel fiume posso sperare soccorsi dalla banda d'Italia et tutto batte a portar avanti un lungo assedio affine che quelli principi boni italiani et politici che non conviene che il Re di Francia si rendi piu patrone della Italia."

49. Ibid., 60–70: "per renderla magiormente forte poiche formandosi la nova cinta con le vere regole militari siccome avanzandomi verso il fiume Po obbliga li assalitori a fare delli quartieri cosi lontani li uni dalli altri che la circonvalasione si renderebbe molto dificile per la sua grandezza et per la dificulta delli fiumi che venendo grossi puol [sic] separare detti quartieri et cosi facilmente socorerla o forzare li quartieri che saranno deboli e per questo fare bisogna una armata grossisima che avanti sia insieme si provedono le cose."

and if the walls were left standing the city would be less "beautiful" and less populated; Carlo Emanuele still maintains the Boteran ideal of making Turin a populous capital. All these reasons, in their turn, "must cede to the policy of making a good *piazza di guerra*." In this painstaking attempt to think through the implications of his expansion, and to convince his audience of his honorable intentions, the duke thus weighed different sides of the Renaissance dialectic of beautiful town and excellent fortress, *magnificenza* and *fortezza*.[50]

Diary entries over the next three years continue to reveal the duke's preoccupation with the Po expansion. In 1670, at mid-year, he promulgated an indirect tax on sales of meat and wheat, the income of which was to be used for the construction of fortifications.[51] In September 1671 he asked Minister of Finance Trucchi to review the expenses of the court and of the duchy; in an effort to secure the financing of the new expansion, the duke considered outside loans and the interruption of building projects elsewhere, as well as personal sacrifices.[52] By that date he was entirely involved with the expansion project, and was neglecting Palazzo Reale and the Venaria Reale. In mid-1673 the problem of how to ensure payment to the crown for the increased value of the land enclosed by the new fortifications was still not resolved; a commission was instituted to decide on the matter. Its members were a group of high-ranking officials directly involved in the administration of Turin and the development of the Po expansion. On 14 August 1673 the commission had decided the appropriate tax. This was to be three-fifths of the increase in the value of each piece of property; meanwhile the search for additional funds continued.[53]

50. Ibid., 70: "per questo bisognar demolire la vecchia non servendo per essere patrone della citta argomento molto forte si può dire che la cittadella fa l'istesso effetto che farebbe quel secondo ordine ma lasciandolo non farebbe l'effetto che si desidera che e di populare la citta, renderla bella, et con questa facilita attirare li popoli ad abitarla considerando l'accrescimento come borgo sebene fortificato, ma tutte le suddette ragioni devono cedere alla politica di fare una bona piazza di guerra."

51. Ibid., 108: "giache avemo avuto la sentenza favorevole nella causa contro la cita per le due gabelle tre denari per livra delle carni . . . farne far l'exazione d'essa e aplicarlo il ricavato per la fortificatione di Torino."

52. Ibid., 164: "veder il fondo della spesa della mia persona, li casuali, e per rimettere le fortificazioni che sono guaste, per questo che il gieneral et il presidente Turinetti si mettino insieme per vedere quello che le finanze potranno contribuire et anco in Savoia; oltre di questo vedere che sorti d'imposti il paese può portare a far il conto sicuro durabile e non fondarsi che sopra cose ben cierte."

53. AST, Sez. Riunite, Fabriche e Fortificationi, art. 195, 18 August 1673, fol. 151: "Riferisce il sig[nor] primo Presidente Trucchi si come S[ua] A[ltezza] R[eale] ha risolto d'allar-

The diary entries of Duke Carlo Emanuele II are a fundamental source for understanding the motivations for the Po expansion. They demonstrate his pragmatic approach to city planning and his careful consideration of all aspects of Turin's enlargement. Military, aesthetic, political, and financial concerns were inextricably linked. This expansion project, a revival of plans made in the beginning of the century, was developed by him both as a source of increased crown revenue, possibly to lend support to other construction projects, and as a means of endowing the capital with a significant layer of meaning encoded within an architecture of representation. The planning for the expansion showed the diplomatic ability and the tenacity of the duke—his great talent for dissimulation was amply displayed in his double-entry diary—crowned by building achievements that exceeded by far those of his seventeenth-century predecessors.

SIMULTANEOUSLY WITH the diary entries, which provide insight into the meaning and nature of Carlo Emanuele's growing interest in the enlargement of Turin, the form and layout of the future city were deliberated through planning studies. The problems investigated through these studies included the extent of the Borgo di Po expansion area, the layout of the fortification and its connection to the existing defenses, the principal and secondary gates, and the form and dimensions of the main streets and squares. Since the most important practical motivation for the eastern expansion was military, with the specific intention to defend the Po bridge, the crossing of the river, sheltered on the east by the Cappuccini hill and garrisoned by the duke's army in time of war, was to be secured from the west side as well. In the speech made to the city councilors on the eve of the beginning of construction, the protection of the bridge was one of the duke's stated motives for the expansion. In case of

---

gare la fortificatione di Torino, e pero che vedesse il Consiglio in qual modo si potra far le spese." *Memoriale*, 322: "Avvicinandosi il tempo proprio per travalliare all'ingrandimento di Torino, percio e necessario mettere in esecuzione il mio pensiero motivato nel mio libro giornaliero dell'anno 1671, a tale effetto nomino li seguenti ministri, gran cancelliere, marchese di S[an] Germano, p[residente] Novarina, Blancardi e Truchi, commendatore Balbiano, presidente Gonteri, gieneral di finanze conte Amedeo Castellamonte, auditori Becaria, Gina e Marelli per esaminare." Ibid., 323: "Avendomi il presidente Truchi detto di farci trovare un suo amico di riscattare dalli monti di fede e altri redditi demaniali alinati a 5 a 6 per 100 e li ridurra a 4 per cento, li ho comandato di coltivarne l'effetto perche e negozio bono, intanto che pensi a trovar fondi per l'ingrandimento di Torino."

attack, the river could serve as an emergency route and as a way of receiving help from the Italian allies. Since Pinerolo was still in French possession, Turin had to be not only the capital of the duchy, but also its strongest border bastion and a bulwark for the Italian peninsula against French invasion.

The enlarged walls of Turin were to be built according to the latest military innovations. Their extent was an advantage, since a large army would be required in order to besiege Turin effectively. But the increased wall perimeter also created a problem—the need for an enlarged garrison to staff the bastions. The question of whether to maintain the existing eastern fortifications after the new ones were built, debated by the duke and his Consiglio di Finanze, was decided in the negative. The citadel already functioned as an emergency refuge, and thus the maintenance of two layers of fortifications was deemed harmful for the rapid development of the Po expansion area.[54]

Beside allowing better defense and connection to the river and the bridge, the Po extension was to rectify strategic errors made in the fortification enclosure of Città Nuova, with its accompanying need for a larger garrison and its wasteful use of urban property. The eastern wall of Città Nuova—visible in all plans from the 1630s on—had been notched in towards the preexisting southeast corner of Turin's Roman walls; from it and its northeasternmost bastion the eastern wall of Turin was to have been defended. But this strategic defense was accomplished through overfortification, and consequently the ratio between the number of bastions and the area enclosed was not economical. Since the walls of Città Nuova already jutted out towards the east, moving the eastern edge of the city would increase the number of bastions by only three while gaining a proportionately much larger area of land. Expansion at the western end of the city was also considered, but then abandoned because little territory could be attached before the citadel was rendered inefficient. The ideological value of the pentagonal fortress was too great to allow for its incorporation within the walls of Turin; expansion to the west would have had partially that effect.

Although expansion to the east was facilitated by the topography—the land east of Turin was level and defended in its peninsular location between the Dora and Po rivers—another, more meaningful, reason for the eastern expansion was dynastic continuity, which would be emphasized in following and implementing the original plans made in the 1610s by Carlo Emanuele I. As we have seen in chapter 2, Carlo Emanuele I had himself designed an expansion plan for Turin that would have extended it, after demolition of its eastern

---

54. *Memoriale*, 70; see note 50 above.

and southern walls, to the shores of the Po. His expansion scheme required ten bastions, of which two would have defended the bridge, and two half-bastions, abutting the citadel and the existing northeast corner bastion (fig. 41). By returning to his predecessor's projects, Carlo Emanuele II hoped to increase Turin dramatically, almost doubling the territory of the city, which had been expanded by 50 percent through the earlier Città Nuova extension.

The area to be enclosed was diagonally crossed by an important road, Contrada di Po or Gran Strada di Po, which connected the Castello gate to the bridge over the Po, and had an undeniable commercial function. Because the Po expansion was far from the citadel, separated from it by Città Nuova, the new Po gate would have to convey a message of military prowess, while new *piazze d'armi* were opened nearby and beside the Castello. In Carlo Emanuele I's design, the Po gate would have been connected to the citadel by one of the two streets that emanated from the piazza in front of the Po gate. This connection, shortened in Castellamonte's scheme of c. 1615–19 (fig. 42) and in a plan of Turin dating from before the dynastic war (fig. 66), was still present in Morello's *parere* of 1656 (fig. 71), and it reappeared, in even more truncated form, in a planning study made between 1657 and 1669 (fig. 94).

This recently discovered drawing, called the "hidden" plan study because the design is covered by a flap of paper, provides some new clues about the form the Po expansion would take. Illustrating a more regular and abstract proposal, with six bastions and one half-bastion, this scheme was more economical than Carlo Emanuele I's original ten-bastioned fortification (fig. 41), and the subsequent proposals by the two Castellamonte (figs. 42, 79) and Morello (fig. 71). But an even more economical enclosure had been designed by Arduzzi in his *parere* of 1656 (fig. 80, examined in chapter 5), while Vauban himself proposed a similarly economical fortification enclosure, employing only five bastions, in an autograph study of c. 1670 (fig. 95). In this proposal, the topographical conditions of the eastern expansion area were extensively examined, as can be seen in the form of the northeastern bastion closest to the northeast corner of Città Vecchia; this segment of the fortification is distinguished in Arduzzi's fortification plan as well (fig. 80). A large drop-off towards the Dora River prevented both military architects from drawing a smooth, continuous fortification wall. This topographical problem did not, however, prevent Amedeo di Castellamonte and Morello from suggesting a continuous fortification in their *pareri,* but the location is recognized as a problem in the slightly notched wall shown in the "hidden" plan.

By 1670 Vauban was a widely recognized military architect, and highly praised for his talent in making strategic fortification decisions.[55] He offered his services to Carlo Emanuele II, and tried to win the duke's interest by displaying his deep knowledge of Turin through this fortification plan for the expansion. His study illustrates a proposed extension of Turin to the west, as well as to the east, providing a relatively small enclosed territory at the cost of two half-bastions and one whole bastion. His proposed connection between the citadel and the new bastioned wall to the west echoes closely the existing connection between the citadel and the wall of Città Nuova; this tacit approval can be taken as confirmation of the continued validity of this earlier construction, but also as an attempt to flatter the duke's dynastic pride. This expansion west would have enclosed within the city's walls an additional bastion of the citadel, thus rendering it less powerful in the defense of the city from outside attack, but Vauban proposed additional layers of fortification between the citadel and Turin. As we have seen in chapter 4, one of the bastions of the citadel had already been engulfed by the Città Nuova expansion. But Vauban's limited westward expansion would still have maintained the textbook relationship between city and citadel: while three bastions guard the city from outside attack, two bastions would have defended the citadel itself from uprisings within the city—a role previously fulfilled by the Turin citadel during the dynastic war of 1640. The form of Vauban's proposed expansion to the west is very close to the one suggested by Montafilans (fig. 51)—consulted by Vittorio Amedeo in 1632—which was then taken up in the "hidden" plan study. An additional effect of the expansion west would have been a more curvilinear outline for Turin's fortification trace, since it would have replaced a straight wall with a multifaceted enclosure.

Even though Vauban was denied the commission, his drawing is important because it provides important clues about the expansion and enhances the accumulated corpus of planning studies for Turin. In his study Vauban considered only the fortifications of the city, and he illustrates only existing streets and roads, as they influenced his decisions about gates and access to bastions. While making his decisions entirely from a practical and military stance, he nonetheless suggested a near oval or almond-shaped form for Turin's fortification trace, a geometrical form that had been proposed by earlier architects still under the influence of ideal-city planning, such as the Vitozzi (fig. 38), and by Duke Carlo Emanuele I, and that continued to have formal appeal later

---

55. On the international significance of Vauban's contributions, see Christopher Duffy, *The Fortress in the Age of Vauban and Frederick the Great 1660–1789* (London, 1985), 71–97.

in the 1670s. Thus he helped an idea whose original impulse was as much an aesthetic vision as a strategic design. His fortification trace bristles with successive layers of defense, bastions and walls enclosed by moats, hornworks, half-moons, tenailles, ravelins, covered way and glacis,[56] which created a formidable obstacle course between the surrounding countryside and the city, distancing them and definitively preventing any possibility of continuity from one to the other.

In comparison to Vauban's scheme for the Po extension, where the depth of the fortification trace reduced somewhat the distance between the walls and the bridge over the Po, the "hidden" plan study (fig. 94) allowed for a noticeable distance between the river and the edge of the city. In this the plan is true to another recently discovered study (fig. 68), examined in chapter 5 for its implications for the dating of Piazza Reale. There, in contrast to most of the earlier studies, such as Carlo di Castellamonte's (fig. 42), the fortifications of Turin were distinctly separated from the actual bridge over the Po. In its proposed street layout, however, the "hidden" plan study does resemble the earlier studies, as well as Castellamonte's design of c. 1637 (fig. 66). A flap of paper, with the diagonal Contrada di Po drawn on it, obscured an orthogonal street grid laid out over the Po expansion area. In the covered part, in addition to the orthogonal street grid, a trident of streets emanates from the Po gate, while another trident opens from the enlarged Piazza Castello. The double trident can also be seen in Carlo Morello's *parere* design of 1656 (fig. 71), which acknowledges Carlo di Castellamonte's design of c. 1615–19 (fig. 42), and in the expansion study of the late 1630s (fig. 66). It is from this latter plan that the rigid orthogonality of the street system proposed in the "hidden" plan study may have been borrowed, as well as from the *parere* of 1656 attributed to Amedeo di Castellamonte (fig. 79).

It might seem that the regimented order of a rigidly orthogonal street system and the theatricality of the double tridents emanating from both Piazza Castello and Porta di Po fitted perfectly the absolutist spirit of the new expansion. In the case of these two proposals, however, these qualities were presented in an excessive and unreconcilable form. A workable synthesis was therefore sought. A "presentation" drawing (so called because it is finished, unlike the sketch studies) contains the major spatial elements of the expansion as proposed in 1673 and may be considered the official plan followed between 1673 and 1675 (fig. 96). Besides the expansion to the west following the projects of Montafilans and Vauban, the fortification to the east was to add six full

---

56. For a detailed glossary of fortification terms, see Duffy, *The Fortress*, 296–99.

and two half-bastions to the city's enclosure. The Po gate is just slightly west of the bridge, at the end of Contrada di Po, which is, with the exception of a two-block spur near the Po gate that preserved the impression of a triad, the only diagonal street of the expansion area. Otherwise, the street pattern is largely orthogonal, though since Contrada di Po cuts diagonally through the expansion area from northwest to southeast, the resulting blocks are trapezoidal rather than rectangular in outline. The main public spaces of the new expansion are the porticoed and enlarged Piazza Castello, and an octagonal and porticoed square, Piazza Carlina, located south of Contrada di Po, at the center of the expanded area. The enlargement of Piazza Castello had been suggested by Amedeo di Castellamonte and by Carlo Morello in their *pareri* of 1656 (figs. 79, 71). The opening of an additional square had been promoted by Morello, by Carlo di Castellamonte in his original expansion plan from the 1610s (fig. 42), and in the planning studies of c. 1637 and c. 1657–69 (figs. 66, 94). Thus the formal aspects of the Po expansion were clearly modeled upon earlier planning studies. Among these the outline and fortification trace suggested in Vauban's study were evidently closely followed, while the ideas of the court military architects and engineers prevailed upon the internal layout of the expansion. But the dominant model, despite the differences brought about largely by improvements in defensive urban strategies, was Carlo Emanuele I's intention, made public in the 1610s, to enlarge Turin to the shores of the Po. The decision to implement his ancestors' dream for the capital confirmed Carlo Emanuele II's dynastic conception for the expansion of Turin.

WE HAVE SEEN, then, that the idea to expand Turin towards the Po was once again actively considered from 1657, while the political and legislative details were tackled from 1668. During the period between the *pareri* of 1656 and the reactivated political efforts begun in 1668, Carlo Emanuele II decided to publish a comprehensive atlas of the towns of Piedmont and Savoy, in which Turin was to play a leading part. Thus steps were taken to celebrate and publicize the beauty and strength of the capital city, as well as of lesser towns in the duchy, long before the expansion of Turin had been completed or even fully planned. The realized atlas—published only in 1682 with the support of Carlo Emmanuele II's heir, Vittorio Amedeo II—was not a precise record of fact but an illustration of Turin enlarged, rationally ordered, and fully built-up in all its parts—that is, looking like the ideal rather than the actual capital of the duchy. For this reason it is a fascinating instance of Carlo Emanuele's

expertise at simulation. The views and plan of Turin were made by Gian Tommaso Borgonio, the same artist who illustrated the *feste* staged by Cristina and
Carlo Emanuele II. He endowed these imaginary views with the same theatricality as his illustrations of stage sets; both are based on elaborate urban and
architectural perspectives.[57]

The title of the completed work, a solemn visual panegyric of the duchy, is
*Theatrum Statuum Regiae Celsitudinis Sabaudiae Ducis Pedemontii Principis Cypri
Regis,* or *The Theater of the States of His Royal Highness the Duke of Savoy, Prince
of Piedmont, King of Cyprus* (a title he had apparently resumed). It is a rare
example of a regional iconographic corpus. It was published in Amsterdam by
the heirs of the famous cartographer Joannes Blaeu, a company that specialized
in engraving and printing maps and views of cities to be bound into atlases.
The company sent forty-five copies of the atlas by boat, and four colored sets
by land, to Turin in 1682.[58] It consists of two large folio volumes, "Part I
Showing Piedmont Including Turin and Neighboring Places" and the "Second
Part Illustrating Savoy and Other Possessions." The first volume begins with
a frontispiece representing Piedmont, a warrior surrounded with the bounties
of nature and study. There follow the title page, the portrait of Vittorio Amedeo II, the stemma of the House of Savoy (a fascinating example of the Savoy
dynasty's pretensions, since half of the coat of arms represents Saxony, West-
phalia, Cyprus, Portugal, and Jerusalem, dominions aspired to rather than
ruled by them), the portrait of Carlo Emanuele II made in 1668, the lapidary
epitaph to Carlo Emanuele II composed in 1675 by Emanuele Tesauro, the
portrait of Giovanna Battista made in 1678, the dedication to Giovanna Battista, the genealogical table of the House of Savoy, the map of Piedmont, and
twenty illustrations of Turin followed by forty-four illustrations of ducal villas, towns, and fortresses in Piedmont. The theatricality of the front material
is a vivid counterpart to the Galleria decorated at the beginning of the seventeenth century under Carlo Emanuele I. Referred to as *il teatro,* it displayed the
splendors of the House of Savoy and the cosmography of the world, as well as
the immediate views of the landscape around Turin. Thus the atlas may have
acquired its title not only from other topographical publications of the Blaeu

57. For Borgonio see *Schede Vesme,* 1:174–77; also Ada Peyrot, "Le immagini e gli artisti,"
in *Theatrum,* ed. Firpo, 1:19–60.

58. Isabella Ricci and Rosanna Roccia, "La grande impresa editoriale," in *Theatrum,* ed.
Firpo, 1:63–92; also see Fernando Rondolino, "Per la storia di un libro," *Atti della società
piemontese di archeologia e belle arti,* 7 (1905): 314–59; Maristella Casciato, "La cartografia
olandese tra cinque e seicento," *Storia della città,* 12 (1979): 5–18; Andreina Griseri, "Urbanistica, cartografia e antico regime in Piemonte," *Storia della città,* 12 (1979): 19–38.

(traditionally modeled upon Ortelius' *Theatrum*), but also as a memorial of the ducal Galleria in Turin, which had recently been destroyed by fire.

The discrepancy in the dates of portraits of the royal couple, and the dedication to Giovanna Battista rather than to Carlo Emanuele, are clarified by the publication history of the atlas.[59] The lavish publication was under preparation for almost twenty-five years, but the original project was less ample and systematic. In 1657 Carlo Emanuele and Cristina had been invited by Blaeu to contribute an illustration of Turin, and perhaps also those of other Piedmontese towns, to an atlas of the principal Italian cities that Blaeu was planning to publish. Stimulated by Carlo Emanuele, the city council commissioned Borgonio to draw a plan and a view of Turin in 1657–58. He took three years to complete them, together with two views of Villa Valentino, but the engraved version of this first set of illustrations did not please the duke. In July 1661 Carlo Emanuele extended the invitation to participate in the Italian atlas to several towns within the duchy, flattering the administrators and their pride of place in order to convince them to pay for the survey and drawings. Their response was not quick enough, and Blaeu's atlas came out in 1663 without Piedmont; the initial project had in fact been trimmed down to Rome, Naples, and Sicily.

It is possible that Carlo Emanuele had decided to enlarge this publication, in order to give life to Botero's exaggeration about Piedmont being a city with a three-hundred-mile perimeter. His own ambition, fueled by Cristina's and then liberated by her death, may have prompted the decision, taken no doubt by 1664, to sponsor the *Theatrum*—a project that represents "corografia che si trasmute in coreografia della regalità," chorography that becomes the choreography of royalty.[60] In 1664 the plates for the citadel (fig. 97), Parco Regio, and the Porta Nova (fig. 44) were finished by the military architect Michelangelo Morello, copied largely from his father's *Avvertimenti*. Payments followed to Borgonio regularly between 1665 and 1674, a period during which he seems to have been increasingly occupied in mapping Turin and its surrounding royal palaces and villas. Between 1657 and 1666 Borgonio completed about ten perspectives, including Bastion Verde (the bastion upon which the royal garden was laid out), Palazzo di Città and its adjoining square, the city tower, Villa Regina, Cristina's villa, and two views of Mirafiori, another royal villa south of Turin. In 1668 he finished four views of Venaria Reale, while in 1669 he drew the churches of Corpus Domini and of the Capuchins. In 1670 he did a

59. Peyrot, "Le immagini," 1:19–60; also the documents in *Theatrum*, ed. Firpo, 2:95–98.
60. Luigi Firpo, "Immagini di un regno sognato," in *Theatrum*, ed. Firpo, 1:11.

new version of the plan and view of Turin "con augmento della nuova fortificatione e compartimento delle strade"—presumably the new expansion
planned (but not yet built) in the east.[61] That year twenty-eight of the thirty-
five illustrations of Turin and its surroundings in the planned publication had
been completed. While Borgonio monopolized the work on Turin's mapping,
the other towns of the duchy were allowed to choose their own designers.
Thus the military architects Boetto and Arduzzi designed the views of Saluzzo
and Chivasso, respectively. Since not all views were drawn by such talented
cartographers, Carlo Emanuele severely edited the results, asking for changes
and suggesting improvements in order to show off each town from its best
point of view, and occasionally employing Borgonio—for the drawings of
Susa and Chieri, for instance—to "adjust" the views in order to make them
more beautiful.[62] The close interest manifested by the duke and the fact that
the individual artists' and architects' names were suppressed from the engraved
views and plans make it seem as though Carlo Emanuele himself had done
the lot.

Descriptive texts in Latin, *relazioni,* were to accompany each illustration in
the *Libro degli Stati di Sua Altezza Reale,* the working title of the expanded
atlas. They were written between 1661 and 1678, with Pietro Gioffredo, royal
historiographer from 1663 and court librarian after 1674, in charge of their
commission and editing. As general coordinator, Count Gian Francesco Cal-
cagni was responsible for the entire project, maintaining contact between
Turin and the Blaeu office in Amsterdam. The writing team, which eventually
included a large group of professional and amateur literati, probably used
Francesco Agostino della Chiesa's manuscript *Descrizione del Piemonte,* a five-
volume work preserved in the royal library, as well as classical and Renaissance
sources, especially the writings of Justus Lipsius, another favored writer of
Carlo Emanuele I.[63]

The publication project received a very serious blow on 3 February 1672,
when 117 engraved plates and their accompanying texts—there are 140 views
and plans in the published atlas—were heavily damaged in a fire that destroyed
Blaeu's shop. Only the portrait of Carlo Emanuele II survived, and the duke
gave order to recommence the project from the start. The work continued very
slowly. A third plan of Turin was made, again by Borgonio (it showed the new
Po expansion to the east), who also redid the illustrations of Turin he had made

61. Peyrot "Le immagini," 23.

62. Ibid., 24.

63. Maria Luisa Doglio, "Le relazioni come documento letterario," in *Theatrum,* ed.
Firpo, 2:23–36.

earlier and for which he was paid in 1674.[64] The towns of Savoy seem to have become part of the *Theatrum* only from April 1674, when Carlo Emanuele sent Borgonio to draw Chambéry, possibly because of the insecure nature of the relations between the crown and its dominion in *di la de'monti;* this had already been felt by Carlo Emanuele I, who had said to Henri IV that "della Savoia incasso quanto posso e dal Piemonte tutto quello che voglio" (From Savoy I take what I can get, from Piedmont all that I want).[65] At the time of the fire in 1672, evidently, the Blaeu shop still did not have a complete set of drawings and *relazioni*—Guarini's description of Porta di Po was refused as late as 1680 by Turin's city council—and after Carlo Emanuele's death in June 1675 the project stopped almost entirely. It was, however, completed with subsidies received in 1679 from the regent, Giovanna Battista.[66]

The ability of the ducal engineers to draw plans and views was amply demonstrated in the drawings made for the *Theatrum.* They relied upon their well-established role as surveyors and superintendents of towns in Piedmont and Savoy, which they visited regularly and drew in order to illustrate the condition of their fortification. Evidence of their efforts can be seen in the album, *Avvertimenti sopra le fortezze,* drawn by Morello and bound in 1656, and an undated preparatory set of drawings containing fifty-six views, forty-two of Piedmontese towns, and the rest of foreign (Lille, Maastricht, La Rochelle) or unidentified cities.[67] Thus, the drawings sent to Amsterdam to be engraved were based not only upon on-site visits, but also on sketched views and plans originally made for military purposes. In its display of the orderly and well-fortified towns of the duchy, edited for the atlas, the *Theatrum* was intended to make conspicuous the humanistic concerns and the military might of the House of Savoy. The publication celebrated the unity of urban design and military architecture, eagerly pursued by rulers of the House of Savoy and displayed in the atlas as an achievement. The numerous fortresses of the duchy, whose clever proportioning and composition in the engraved image made them seem even more awesome than they were in reality, demonstrated that the avant-garde position of the Savoy, acquired in the sixteenth century through the construction of the citadel of Turin, had been maintained throughout the seventeenth century.

Of the twenty plates that illustrate Turin, several are important for the history of the expansions. In Borgonio's view-plan of Turin (fig. 98), drawn be-

64. *Theatrum,* ed. Firpo, 2:98; and ASCT, Ordinati, 18 April 1674, fol. 499.
65. Firpo, "Un regno sognato," 14.
66. Ricci and Roccia, "La grande impresa," 88–92.
67. BRT, MS Coll. Saluzzo, Militari 177.

tween 1672 and 1674 after the original had been lost in the fire of 1672, instead of an accurate representation of the city, the expansions that had been considered before 1669 are shown as though completed to the south, east, and west. This is an important document nonetheless, with a sixty-four-item legend that identifies all the churches and many of the more important palaces in the city. The plan is quite accurate in its representation of the Po expansion area, closely similar to the "presentation" plan of 1673–75 (fig. 96), with one significant change: here Piazza Carlina is shown as a rectangular rather than octagonal piazza. The expansion to the west included in this plan was not a work of Borgonio's fantasy or a clairvoyant prediction of the ultimate form of Turin— as has been recently maintained—but rather a demonstration of his familiarity with the planning studies examined above.[68]

In another view by Borgonio (fig. 99) Turin is shown comprising Città Vecchia, Città Nuova, and the citadel, before the Po expansion was begun in 1673. Oriented directly west, with Piazza Reale and Piazza Castello in the foreground left and center, the view illustrates the urban and architectural achievements of the preceding generation of Savoy rulers. Complemented by a forty-four-item legend, it is the earliest view of Città Nuova as a finished and integrated part of town. Closer to existing conditions, the view of Turin is so different from the plan, in its topographical up-to-dateness, that their presence in the same work is very surprising, and their proximity can be explained only by the fact that they use different means of representation.

On a separate sheet, in a "portrait" view (fig. 100), Piazza Reale is seen from the north and shown as a marketplace and a meeting ground, its two churches endowed with imaginary facades and towers, which, as we have seen in chapter 5, they were not to possess until much later. The figures were inserted in Amsterdam, as were those in the portrait of Piazza Castello (fig. 101), and the northern architectural elements that embellish the regular and stark buildings were possibly added by the engravers in Holland.[69] In both these sheets Turin is illustrated as it was before the expansion of 1673. But in another view, of Piazza Castello in its enlarged form after 1673, we see it connected to the Po expansion area (fig. 102). Less detailed than the view of Città Nuova and Città Vecchia that described existing conditions and seems to have been more accurate, this view emphasized the eastern side of the square seen from a bird's-eye view, and it stressed the continuity and uniformity of the buildings

---

68. Peyrot, "Le immagini," 55: "cosi ferrato nell'arte delle fortificazioni da poter completare, con il solo ausilio della fantasia, la regolare forma a mandorla che la città, secondo le vigenti regole di quest'arte, avrebbe dovuto assumere ad ampliamento concluso."

69. Ibid., 56.

that were planned, but not yet implemented, in the Po expansion area. These buildings are conceived as shallow wings; they are like thick walls that define the space of the squares, but not do not seem to be themselves containers of space. The even cornice height and the uniformity of the decorative vocabulary were the principal architectural characteristics of the buildings proposed in the Po expansion of Turin. Only sparsely inhabited, in contrast with the views of Piazza Reale and of pre-1673 Piazza Castello, which are overflowing with an urban population drawn from the entire social scale, the illustration of the Po expansion creates not only a strong impression of architectural discipline and austerity, but also a palpable sense of alienation. Thus both the specificity of existing squares and streets and the attractiveness of the projected ones—the "beauty" that Carlo Emanuele I hoped would encourage settlement—were lost through the homogenized rendering of the views.

Although the *Theatrum* was not the first atlas of its kind, it was among the earliest systematic representations of all urban and rural settlements within one nation and governed by an hereditary dynasty. In its focus upon the urban environment, and specifically upon the repetitive architectural and military unity of Turin, the atlas forecast the finished urban product, and was witness to the original intentions and hopes of Duke Carlo Emanuele II. The articulately designed and soon-to-be consistently built streets, squares, and disciplined buildings were an achievement that was publicized to the rest of the world through the atlas. If the Po expansion had failed, the *Theatrum* would have served as a document of foiled ambitions. Since the enlargement was successful, the atlas can be considered a document of the perspicacity of the patron; not only was the town designed and built, but also its intended polemical attributes, the display of dynastic culture and military strength, were claimed as essential characteristics in a circulated publication.

THIS INTERNATIONAL publicity for the expansion of Turin and the wealth of Piedmont was matched locally by the ceremonial laying of the foundation stone for the Po expansion.[70] This ceremony was a pivotal moment of the planning process. While it rendered official a project that was widely known, the ceremony served to reinforce the domination of Turin by Carlo Emanuele II, promoting dynastic messages similar to the ones we have seen

70. For a detailed discussion of this event, see my "Other Face of the Medal: Turin, 1673," *Art Bulletin*, 69 (1987): 256–63.

displayed in other ducal ceremonies, such as carnival *feste,* weddings, and funerals. It marked the end of a gestation period that lasted more than five years, during which the planning studies were made and the final design developed.

On the morning of 23 October 1673 the city councilors of Turin joined the ducal family in a mass celebrated by the archbishop of Turin in the chapel of the Holy Shroud. The mass was simple, as requested by the duke, and was accompanied only by instrumental music. After the mass, a special prayer by the duke asked for a blessing on the enlargement of Turin about to take place. The ducal family, followed by all present, exited through the door of the chapel leading to Palazzo Reale, and then reappeared through the main gate of the palace, parading on foot to the place designated for the laying of the foundation stone, outside Piazza Castello, at the corner of today's Via Po and Piazza Castello. The brilliant procession was flanked by infantry and by Swiss guards and archers and included, beside all the members of the royal family, the foreign ambassadors in Turin and great numbers of splendidly attired courtiers. The representatives of the city and its councilors brought up the end, while the canons of the cathedral and the archbishop led the way singing and carrying a cross.[71]

A portable altar with a rich pallium stood under a large tent at the site of the ceremony. On the altar were the foundation stone, a metal plaque, and the gold and silver medals that had been commissioned for the occasion. Upon the arrival of the ducal family before the altar, the archbishop solemnly blessed the foundation stone and medals. Then he turned towards the countryside and blessed the sites of the six new bastions, baptizing each clockwise from the north: San Mauritio, San Carlo, Sant'Antonio Battista, Sant'Adelaide, and San Vittorio.

There followed a brief performance indicative of the importance and intricacy of social hierarchy and protocol at the Savoy court. Marchese di San Germano, governor of Turin, presented the medals and the foundation stone to the duke, who consigned them into the hands of Governor Balbiano, general superintendent of the fortifications of Piedmont. He in turn passed them to Count Amedeo di Castellamonte, who as director of the new fortification was in charge of placing the foundation stone and medals in the chosen spot.[72]

71. ASCT, Ordinati, 23 October 1673, fols. 382–92; this is the source used for my description of the ceremony.

72. Ibid., fol. 288: "Finita la bened[ition]e l'ecc[ellentissi]mo Marchese di S[an] Germano Don Ottaviano San Martino d'Agliè Cavag[lie]r dell'ord[in]e sacro come governatore della città presento la tavola di metallo con le medaglie a S[ua] A[ltezza] R[eale] la quale avendola ricevuta nelle proprie mani la consegno all'Ill[ustrissi]mo Balbiano Commend[ator]e Hiero-

The ceremonial laying of the stone and medals was accompanied by music and the call of trumpets, and followed by the discharge of fifty rounds of cannon, two hundred *mortaleti,* and the musket fire of the entire infantry. This roar of firearms, applauded and cheered by the attending crowd, was an important element of Savoy rulers' festivities; public rituals, as we have seen in the *feste* sponsored by Cristina and the triumphal entries demanded by her, depended upon the display of fire and arms as a reminder of the military foundation of the Savoy dynasty's rule.

Ever conscious of the historical record, the duke had ordered the secretary of the city council to make an accurate and detailed description of the event and to preserve it for future generations. The surviving account of the foundation ceremony in the city archive proves to be not just a record but a protocol detailing each step of the event, carefully planned to ensure a flawless performance. The ceremonial blessing, the first step in officially beginning the large-scale building effort, could have been made in a less imposing manner, as was the foundation ceremony for the expansion of 1620. The solemnity of the event, with the duke acting as the commander, underlined and reinforced his absolute power by demonstrating it. The documentation ordered by the duke went beyond the need to show Turin's populace the power of the Savoy ruler; it recorded that power for people in other cities and for future generations.[73]

Other texts and images reinforced the historical significance of this event and gave permanent form to Carlo Emanuele's aspirations: the inscription on the foundation stone and its accompanying plaque, and the medals struck for the ceremony and subsequently sealed under the stone. Both were engraved in 1673 by Giorgio Tasniere, as part of the documentation of the Po expansion (fig. 103). The inscription spells out the duke's claims to leadership and his doctrine that military security at home permits a solidly based expansionary program. The message of the first half of the text was military and expansionist. It echoed the Savoy family's device *Arcet et auget* (he fortifies and expands). Carlo Emanuele II having fortified his realm will not only defend but also

---

solomitano com'Intendente g[e]n[era]le delle fortificationi degli stati di S[ua] A[lezza] R[eale], et esso la rimesse all'Ill[ustrissi]mo Conte Amedeo San Martino di Castellamonte che come direttore di questa fortificat[ion]e hebbe l'incumbenza di far riporre nel luogo destinato la pietra augurale con le medaglie in essa inscritte, et chiuse dalla detta tavola di metallo come si e detto per prospero auspicio e memoria eterna."

73. Ibid., fol. 285: "li S[igno]ri della citta di Torino faranno rogar un atto publico di tutta questa fontione con l'ordine e il modo essatam[ent]e in essa osservato per custodirlo nell'archivio."

enlarge the territory of the duchy: "non solum munit, sed ampliat." The prince who is secure at home, having fortified his capital with strong bastions, can with greater confidence invade and oppress hostile territories.[74] The major reason given for the expansion of Turin is thus to render the Savoy dukes secure at home and then to allow them to resume their expansionist policy. Since Piedmont was insecurely possessed, with its western fortress at Pinerolo still occupied by the French, its fortification had to precede expansionary wars. The inscription insists that Carlo Emanuele has spent the years since 1663, the effective date of his access to power, in restoring the wealth and military preparedness of the duchy, which allegedly had been neglected during his mother's regency. Though he had created six permanent regiments and reformed the Piedmont militia in 1669, hitherto Carlo Emanuele's reign had provided few military victories to celebrate, and the recent disastrous defeat in his attempt to conquer Genoa was a very vivid memory.[75] The inscription thus justifies the apparent lack of concerted bellicose activities normally expected of the ruling sovereigns of the House of Savoy.

The remainder of the foundation stone's text provides a historical perspective. It asserts, correctly, that the expansion had been conceived much earlier by Carlo Emanuele I, and reiterates the old and inaccurate Savoy claim that originally Turin's walls extended to the shores of the Po. Turin had been "one of the great Roman cities," claims the inscription, but after being destroyed "in the dire age of the Goths" it was "reborn in reduced form."[76] Carlo Emanuele I is credited with the first aspiration to restore Turin "to the original greatness of its august name," and Vittorio Amedeo I is praised for partially completing the restoration, but only Carlo Emanuele II would realize the plan of his predecessors: "what was conceived by his great ancestor, and begun by his even greater father, he himself, with no lesser spirit, was to complete."[77]

74. Ibid., fol. 287, the text of the foundation stone as recorded in the official record of the foundation ceremony and the foundation plaque:

>Ipsum ditiones cor, ad sui cordis exemplum
>Non solum munit sed ampliat
>Nam qui sua securus possidet
>Hostilia securius invadet
>Et amplior quo pressior
>Infestos infestabit.

75. *Monarchia piemontese*, 6:192–212.

76. ASCT, Ordinati, 23 October 1673, fol. 287:

>Maximis Italiae urbibus equatam
>Tum diro Gothorum seculo saepe dirutam,
>Semperque angustiore specie renatam.

Carlo Emanuele glaringly omits praise, or even mention, of the contribution of Cristina to the embellishment of Turin. And yet her concern for the capital had been remarked with great flourish at her funeral ceremony, where Turin as "Urbs ornata et amplificata" was featured as a great tribute to the achievement of the regency. The ceremonial inscription is thus focused upon the praise of Carlo Emanuele II's individual accomplishments and endeavors, expressions—like his attempt to win Genoa—of his intention to *errare da sè*. While the requirements of the dynasty and its continuity of ideals are also acknowledged, the immediately preceding sovereign, from whom Carlo Emanuele has to differentiate himself in order to define his own identity, is forcibly ignored.

The inscription on the foundation stone spells out the ducal achievements quite clearly, but the nature and significance of the other commemorative device, the medal, have proved more difficult to establish. Gold and silver versions of the original foundation medal, shown in Tasniere's engraving, were buried with the stone, but until recently no other version of the medal itself was thought to have survived. I have, however, discovered a version of the foundation medal and a group of related medals that help to establish no only the form but also the significance of the buried original.[78]

In Tasniere's engraving of the foundation medal (fig. 103) both obverse and reverse are clearly illustrated. On the obverse, Carlo Emanuele II is shown in the guise of a Roman hero. His body is twisted in a dynamic position, toga held back, with his left arm uncovering his breastplate while his right shoulder and arm project forward, and he holds with his right hand the staff of the military chief. His head is turned to the right, offering us his profile, with an ample but natural-looking wig. The inscription establishes his titles—duke of Savoy, prince of Piedmont, and king of Cyprus—and the foundation date for the Po expansion. The reverse carries the motto, *Arcet et Auget,* and the Savoy coat of arms, woven into a standard flying above a circular and crenellated tower, which is in turn raised upon the platform of a low, polygonal bastion.

The representation of Carlo Emanuele on the obverse engraved by Tasniere

77. Ibid.:

> Ad pristinam augusti nominis amplitudinem restituere
> Carolus Emanuel Primus voluit
> Victor Amadeus magna ex parte potuit
> Carolus Emanuel Secundus
> Magni avi cogitatum, et maximi genitoris incoeptum
> Non degeneri animo expleturus.

78. "The Other Face of the Medal," 259.

is mirrored closely in a medal *modello* of 1673 (fig. 104) upon which the realized foundation medal was probably based (fig. 105). In a smaller silver medal,
although he is shown again as a Roman hero, we see the traditional bust (fig.
106) rather than the three-quarter-length figure of the foundation medal engraving. In other, earlier medals Carlo Emanuele was portrayed in a modern
costume of ceremonial armor, jabot, and chain of the Order of Annunziata,
and with wig, moustache, and even profile closely modeled upon Louis XIV's
official portraits (figs. 107, 108), not least because the same medalists were
involved in their making.[79] These medals, of French origin, show the duke of
Savoy, Louis' cousin, subordinated to the stylistic norms of official French
culture and historiography. Their refined and severe compositions are in subtle
contrast with the Italian Roman-hero medals, which display a freedom of
movement and dynamism lacking in the French medals from which they are
in part derived.

The reverse of the small silver and the large alloy medals is almost identical
with the illustration in Tasniere's engraving. Despite noticeable differences in
quality and in content, the central element of the composition is the same in
all three versions: a modern polygonal bastion with an old-fashioned round
tower above it (fig. 109). The representation of a fortress would come naturally
to a dynasty so proud of its military traditions and so much in need of fortifications to resist the encroachments of powerful neighbors. Indeed, the particular form of this reverse image may represent the need, cultural as well as military, to be different from the royal French model, while following it closely.
In Louis XIV's France, too, the strengthening and expanding of the national
boundaries had been celebrated by medals (fig. 110). But the nature of the
representation is different in this French example, struck in 1662 to commemorate Louis' fortification of Philipsburg. The polygonal bastion there is a
straightforward depiction of a contemporary fortification, whereas in the
Piedmontese medals the combination of elements suggests a more complex
relation to reality. The close juxtaposition of tower and bastion could represent
a *cavagliere* (a lookout point at the center of the curtain wall), but to an eye
trained in the military architecture of the later seventeenth century—and in the
military culture of the Savoy court we can be sure such scrutiny was expected—it would seem quite anachronistic. The tower is crenellated and proj-

79. The medalist Jean Baptiste Dufour was at the Paris mint between 1656 and 1673. He
was a pupil of Jean Warin; his works in the series *Histoire métallique* of Louis XIV's life are
signed *D.* or *D. F.* See Josephe Jacquiot, ed., *La médaille au temps de Louis XIV* (Paris, 1970);
Leonard Forrer, *Biographical Dictionary of Medallists* (London, 1902–30), 1:642–43; and J. J.
Giuffrey, "La Monnaie des médailles," *Revue Numismatique*, 3d series, 5 (1887): 308.

ects high above the parapet of the bastion, which is pierced with embrasures, whereas the bastion is continuous in height with the adjoining curtain wall. By the beginning of the century all the elements of the fortification enclosure had been lowered in order to avoid the enemy's cannon fire; this diminution in height of the fortification girdle, wall, bastion, and gate is visually one of the most striking developments in seventeenth-century military architecture.[80]

The reverse of these Turin medals, though alluding to prominent features of the contemporary city, should be interpreted as an *impresa* or device, in which heterogeneous elements are combined in such a way that their incongruity points to a deeper symbolic meaning.[81] Contemporary fortifications were incorporated into seventeenth-century emblem books, and one of the most widely disseminated of these, Diego Saavedra de Fajardo's *Idea de un principe politico christiano,* includes a polygonal bastion combined with a garden, symbolizing the education of the ruler, and a tower within a bastion holding back the sea, symbolizing the military policy that best guarantees the monarch's security, a judicious combination of attack and defense.[82] The combination of portrait obverse and emblematic reverse is a common feature of Renaissance medals, and was eagerly practiced as learned amusement and as carrier of subtle messages, decipherable only by the élite, at the court in Turin.

The polygonal bastion represents the new fortification of Turin that surrounds the older, medieval and Roman, enclosure. The memory of ancient Roman and medieval fortification was kept present by the Castello, a Roman gate fortified in the fourteenth century, which stood at the center of the eastern wall of Turin and, after the expansion of 1673, at the center of the enlarged city. The Castello remained an important element in the symbolic representation of Turin, where it dominated the surrounding buildings both physically and emblematically. The juxtaposition of the single round tower with the most advanced expression of military architecture—the low, polygonal bastion—thus expresses the beneficial fusion of historical continuity and progressive innovation: the round tower represents the historical might of the House of Savoy, whereas the polygonal bastion demonstrates its continued bravery and

80. See Duffy, *The Fortress,* 1–62; Cosseron de Villenoisy, *Essai historique sur la fortification* (Paris, 1869), chaps. 4 and 5.

81. Emanuele Tesauro, *Il cannocchiale aristotelico* (Turin, 1670), 624–83.

82. Diego Saavedra de Fajardo, *Idea de un principe politico christiano,* 2d ed. (Milan, 1642), *imprese* 5 and 83, discussed in James G. Turner, *The Politics of Landscape* (Oxford, 1979), 55, 70. Saavedra's emblem-book, one of the few to deal directly with political and military affairs from the monarch's point of view, was reissued many times and in many languages between 1642 and 1700.

assiduity in military matters and its commitment to education and expansion. The image on the reverse of the silver medal, borrowed for the foundation medal, reinforces the message engraved on the foundation plaque: the new expansion towards the Po, the latest stage in the definition of the absolutist capital city, is intended to be seen in the light of military aggression and defense, dynastic continuity and innovation. *Arcet et Auget.*

7

Urbs Ornata et Amplificata:
The Realization of Dynastic Turin

Non solum munit sed ampliat
—Foundation stone, 1673

CARLO EMANUELE II's maturing years and his first decade as sovereign monarch were occupied with the commencement of projects that were to magnify his renown abroad and his absolutist rule at home. Motivated by political and dynastic interests, his decision to continue the enlargement of Turin was enriched by the military ideals inherited from his male predecessors of the seventeenth century, Vittorio Amedeo I and Carlo Emanuele I, and elaborated through the French-influenced notions about representations of power inculcated by his mother Cristina. The official beginning of the Po expansion in the foundation ceremony of October 1673 marked the end of a five-year gestation period during which the financing and the final design were developed, and which underlined and publicized the ducal domination of the city. Implicitly, it also marked the end of the planning process, since the resulting urban design was to be altered only in minor aspects while the construction of the city was under way. The ideological, military, and financial motivations for enlarging Turin were clearly articulated before construction began. While the urban impact of the expansion was to be achieved through the powerful architectural definition of Contrada di Po and the masterly development of Piazza Castello into the central and unifying space for the newly enlarged Turin, the convergence upon Piazza Castello of the major street of each of the three areas of Turin—Città Vecchia, Città Nuova, and Borgo di Po—would render unmistakable the commanding centrality and hierarchical significance of the royal presence.

Carlo Emanuele then promulgated a series of edicts intended to provide the resolution of the financial arrangements and legal instruments needed to effect the extension of the city. The altered Fabriche e Fortificationi, the ducal agency in charge of building and fortification subsumed into the Consiglio di Finanze since 1666, became an even more important organization responsible for not only the layout of streets and the implementation of the construction of walls and gates, but also the realization of the extensive ducal building program.

The documents of the legislative and financial planning for the Po expansion show Carlo Emanuele's diplomatic ability and tenacity, which resulted in building achievements far superior even to those of his immediate predecessors. As we have seen in chapter 6, his personal diary is a fundamental source for understanding the crown's motivations for the Po expansion. While the diary entries show his concern about the appearance of Turin, they also demonstrate that Carlo Emanuele's interests had a pecuniary aspect. But although the expansion project was intended to enrich the treasury, and possibly to subsidize other construction projects, it eventually cost the crown much more than originally calculated. The perseverance with which the Po expansion was pursued, even when it failed as a source of state revenue, suggests that it ought to be considered primarily in light of its emblematic significance as a representation of ideology and a display of power.

HAVING PONDERED FOR several years the advantages of enlarging Turin, and having discussed the potential problems with his financial councilors, Carlo Emanuele II used the ducal edicts as legal instruments to control the form and meaning of the expansion. A great number of these ducal orders—through which the government controlled the expansion to the east—were promulgated by Carlo Emanuele before and after the foundation ceremony, and after his premature death in 1675 by his widow Giovanna Battista, regent of the heir, Vittorio Amedeo II, until 1685.

The edicts promulgated in Turin were the public instruments that shaped the Savoy dynastic policy in relation to the duchy's capital. As a way of preparing the population for the impending extension of the city towards the east, Carlo Emanuele had publicly proclaimed on 28 July 1672 his intention to continue the work begun in Città Nuova in conformity with the ideas of Carlo Emanuele I and Vittorio Amedeo I (the Regent Cristina, interestingly, was not mentioned).[1] His interest in a fully settled Città Nuova, ornamented with uni-

---

1. Borelli, 930–31. "Considerando noi di quanto avvantaggio et abbellimento della Città nuova di questa Città sia per risultare l'essere quella ripiena, et ornata di fabriche in tutti suoi

form buildings in all its corners and empty lots, was made manifest through the lifting of all prohibitions impeding construction. As we have seen, the fact that the southern expansion area was not entirely settled, implicit in this official removal of mandated obstacles, weakened one of Carlo Emanuele's arguments for the Po expansion, which was that the inhabitants of Turin were cramped within the 1620s fortification girdle of the city.

But the thorough settlement of the Città Nuova was a more complex problem. One year before the formal initiation of the Borgo di Po expansion, in a letter patent of 29 October 1672, Carlo Emanuele had demanded that the city council demolish the illegal additions constructed on top of a building on the Contrada Nuova, the main north-south artery connecting the southern gate to the royal palace.[2] Fully empowered, the council was to punish the owners, who had ignored the legislated building code, and to restore the building to its originally prescribed four-story height. The illegal fifth floor was ruining the architecture, design, and beauty of the street by deforming its prescribed uniformity, the duke said. While this illegal addition may be proof of lack of land, the July 1672 edict had shown that, on the contrary, there were still many available lots to build upon in Città Nuova. However, since the Contrada Nuova was the most important street of the southern development, property along it may have been in greater demand. Thus, while lots on side streets or adjacent to the fortified walls remained empty, important frontage along central streets and squares was overdeveloped. Nonetheless, the crown preferred homogeneous development and rigorous observance of its urban design regulations, and was unwilling to acknowledge this hierarchy brought about by economic and topographic constraints. Carlo Emanuele's decrees were an attempt to sponsor a consistent and uniform development while avoiding the

---

angoli, e vacui, habbiamo voluto ordinare . . . che per compimento delle strade di detta Città nuova si facciano, e proseguiscano le fabriche, e che per tal construttione d'edificij non vi possa essere impedimento alcuno, ne proibitione ò conditione posta, ò da porsi da chi si sia, quale possi ritardare chi esser si voglia, che in esecuzione del nostro Ordine si accinga à fabricare come sopra. E per essere tale la mente nostra, in conformità anco di quella de' Duchi Carlo Emanuel, Vittorio Amedeo di gloriosa memoria miei Avo e Padre."

2. Duboin, 939: "Molto magnifici nostri carissimi. Intendiamo che alcuni particolari habbino dato principio ad una nuova elevazione di stanze della contrada nova, et che l'alzamento si faccia sovra del cornicione per formarne il quinto piano, e sovra d'esso il solar morto, il che disdice all'architettura, dissegno, et abellimento di detta contrada. E perchè non vogliamo tollerare in avvenire simili alzamenti, v'ordiniamo dunque di continuare le vostre inhibizioni, e così far rimettere il novamente fatto nel pristino stato, sotto le pene che vi parerà imporle, conferendovi l'autorità opportuna."

earlier harshness of Cristina's edicts by delegating authority, allowing the city council to act as a policing force. Nonetheless the lack of important sites in Città Nuova made the expansion towards the Po evidently desirable.

The various orders given by Carlo Emanuele show his attempt to extend the power of the crown over the native population. On 28 December 1673, in an edict promulgated soon after the placement of the foundation stone, all owners of land in the Po expansion area were asked by the crown to present within fifteen days the documents that would authenticate their claim to their property, and to authorize within ten days a real estate estimator to represent their interests.[3] This private consultant and the one representative of the crown were to establish together the value of the respective private properties before the expansion began. The estimate would be made by the crown's official alone if a private estimator was not engaged, and it would be binding.[4] Despite the authoritative tone of this printed edict, which had been formulated in Carlo Emanuele's diary entry of April 1669, landowners did not rush to obey. They were exhorted through another edict one year later, on 10 October 1674, to send in their representative.[5] Carlo Emanuele thus encountered difficulties in implementing his plan to garner the cost of the fortifications from the in-

3. Borelli, 907: "Ordiniamo a' Padroni, et à quei c'hanno l'amministratione, o cura de' siti sudetti, che debbano frà il termine di giorni quindici presentare, et haver presentato avanti il Conseglio delle nostre Finanze, e con intervento dell'Auditore Patrimoniale generale Marelli, si proceda all'estimo, e misura di tutti, e ciascuno d'essi siti fabricati, o non fabricati, nissuno eccettuato, con la sola regola del valore, c'haverebbero à loro guidicio havuto non fosse seguito, nè stato proposto il sudetto aggrandimento; mà se le cose fossero state, et havessero dovuto continuare in quei puri termini, ne'quali si ritrovavano avanti, che se ne facesse alcuna propositione. Ordiniamo à tutti quei, c'hanno, o pretendono d'haver fidei-commissi, hypotheche, o qualch'altra ragione per qual si sia causa, benche privilegiata sopra i siti sudetti, debano comparire con le scritture, e prove opportune avanti il sudetto Conseglio frà il termine di dieci giorni."

4. Ibid., 931: "Dichiarando, che quando li sudetti [landowners] non presentino frà il tempo sopra espresso i loro Estimatori, si procederà ne più ne meno all'estimo con l'intervento de'sudetti, e d'uno che sarà eletto ex officio per gli absenti, e quest'estimo havrà la medesima forza come se fosse fatto con intervento, et approvatione degli Estimatori eletti dalle Parti."

5. Memoriale, 69; Borelli, 931–32: "E se ben alcuni [landowners] sono in qualche maniera comparsi; e'l molto tempo ch'è scorso rende meno degno di scusa il mancamento de gli altri. . . . Ordiniamo à quei, che non hanno ancora fatta fede delle ragioni loro proprie, o spettanti all'amministratione, o cura loro, che debbano in ogni modo adempire, et haver adempito nella gia prescritta conformità frà il termine di giorni dieci dopo la publicatione di quest'Ordine."

creased value of private property. Although the main impulse informing this edict was to earn income for the fortifications, Carlo Emanuele did not grant special privileges in order to attract new settlers, as his grandfather Carlo Emanuele I had done in 1620. Moreover, the formal aspiration of the crown— to promote the rapid construction of well-proportioned buildings within the new expansion area—was explicitly restated and remained firm despite the reluctant response from the real estate owners in the eastern expansion.[6]

The edict of 10 October 1674 was fundamental for the realization of the eastern Borgo di Po extension. Its purpose was both political and financial; it was intended to raise money, from the sale of land in the expansion area, for the opening of streets and the building of walls, and also to establish control over the propertied population of the Po suburb. The implications of this edict, clarified subsequently in another promulgated by Giovanna Battista on 16 December 1675, were as follows. The crown's and the private landowners' representatives were to decide upon the value of each property.[7] When the property became part of the enclosed area of Turin, after the fortifications were raised, the original value as determined by the two estimators automatically increased by an agreed-upon percentage. Since this increase in value was due to the new legal status of the area, which became urban when the ducal expansion made it part of Turin, the crown claimed for itself a full three-fifths of this increase. This payment to the crown—what would later be called the *valenza*—was a kind of value-added tax and could be paid in cash or by relinquishing parts of one's property. The edict of December 1675 was concerned entirely with a certain number of sites needed by the crown for its own buildings; since these sites had to be expropriated, for their own protection the existing owners were invited to cooperate with the government official, so that they could be justly reimbursed. Owners were also free to sell their property to the crown, and thus garner a part of the increased value of their property. Since the landowners in the Po area also drew, at least theoretically, a modest benefit from the incorporation of the Po suburb into Turin, there seem to have been few who sold their now-urban property immediately. Those who fol-

6. The crown's resolution is expressed in unusually coercive language; Borelli, 932: "Dichiarando, che la publicatione di quest'Editto da farsi ne'modi, e luoghi soliti, havrà forza in quant'a tutti di personal intimatione."

7. Borelli, 932: "Cioè dovranno i Padroni d'essi [sites] frà giorni quindeci dopo la sudetta publicatione rimetter nelle mani del Consegliere, e Secretario di Stato, e del Consiglio delle Finanze sottoscritto l'estimo de i loro respettivamenti siti, che sono stati inchiusi nella linea del predetto aggrandimento, con espressione distinta del maggior valore c'hanno acquistato per esserre stati inchiusi come sopra."

lowed the law were scarcely more numerous, however. As late as 1713 the crown was bringing suits against the heirs of the initial owners for payment of the "urbanizing" tax.[8]

Preempting possible questioning of the legitimacy of the regency as well as of the legislative order, Giovanna Battista's December edict—the first to be promulgated after Carlo Emanuele II's death in June 1675—claimed that the order had been prepared by the late duke and his councilors.[9] This edict reaffirmed fully the key elements of her husband's urban design program. The crown maintained the prerogative of expropriation: privately owned property needed for the crown's building program could be purchased by the crown following the original estimate of the property's value.[10] This power of expropriation is crucial since the crown's building program required several precise sites; the design of the expansion area included the opening of numerous streets and two squares, as well as the areas to be taken for the construction of the expanded fortifications. Besides Piazza Ducale (Carlina), there was to be a square in front of the Po gate (Piazza del Corpo di Guardia). The official ducal building program included a new *galleria*, a riding academy, a headquarters for the mint and the customs, and a structure to house the Swiss Guards. In addition, there were three sites reserved for convents; one was for the order of Santo Sudario, while the other two were endowments for two existing monasteries whose properties had been fragmented by the opening of streets or requisitioned for the construction of the fortification trace.[11] The owners of

8. Ibid., 932–33; Duboin, 954.

9. Borelli, 932: "Quei medesimi rispetti, che con fini assai considerabili di ben publico persuasero S[ua] A[ltezza] R[eale] del Serenissimo Carlo Emanuel II mio Signore, e Consorte di glo[riosa] mem[oria] all'aggrandimento della presente Città, anco la spinsero non solamente ad incominciare, e continuare l'opera con quella diligenza, e fino a quel segno ch'à tutti è palese, mà insieme à prescrivere quelle regole, e dare quelli ordini, che parvero maggiormente opportuni per ridurla a perfettione . . . ne fece minutare l'Editto con le seguenti precise parole, et hora Noi fedelmente, e pontualmente riduciamo ad effetto."

10. Ibid.: "Dichiaramo in primo luogo, che quei siti, che saranno a piè delle presenti descritti, de' quali habbiamo occasione di valerci per l'opere già da Noi stabilite, si farà l'estimo con ogni buona fede del maggior valore ch'hanno probabilmente acquistato per rispetto del nuovo aggrandimento."

11. Ibid., 933: "Li siti de'quali S[ua] A[ltezza] R[eale] si vuol valere come sopra sono li seguenti. 1.Il sito della Gran Galleria. 2.Quello dell'Accademia. 3.Quello della fabrica della Zecca, e Dugana. 4.Quella della Piazza del Corpo di Guardia alla Porta di Pò. 5.Quello per la Piazza Ducale. 6.Quello per il Quartiere de' Svizzeri. 7.Quello per il convento de' Padri del Santo Sudario. 8.Quello per due conventi."

sites needed for the ducal buildings and squares were to be reimbursed for the original value of their property, plus two-fifths of its increased value. Provision was made separately for property that was cut into several pieces by the opening of public streets: each fragment was to be evaluated separately, allowing the crown to purchase parts of an owner's now scattered sites. Owners of buildings disemboweled by the opening of streets were to be reimbursed only if the crown decided to acquire the site.[12] Evidently, owners of land and buildings were to be greatly inconvenienced by the expansion, houses and shops would be demolished, and some small owners would suffer financially. Those planning to build in the Borgo di Po expansion were still granted ten years to implement their plans, but construction had to be initiated within six years, and reach a height of 2 *trabucchi* (1 *trabucco* was about 3 meters) the sixth year.[13] This clause of the edict virtually ensured that little, though not less than 2 *trabucchi*, would be built before 1681, and even that obligation could be avoided by selling one's property and buying another site. Along the lesser streets buildings could be ornamented according to the owner's wishes, though they were to be at least three stories tall; gardens and walls less than this height could not face public streets.[14] But a uniform facade design, provided by the crown, was to be followed in the construction of buildings along Piazza Cas-

12. Ibid., 932–33: "E di quest'accrescimento di valore cagionata come sopra, vogliamo farne pagare li due quinti a i Particolari de' siti, e con essi due quinti d'accresciamento provenuto meramente da Noi, e senza alcuna fatica, ne spese de' medesimi Padroni gli sarà pagato il ver prezzo de i siti. . . . Li framezzati delle strade pubbliche s'estimeranno a corpi separati, considerando tanti corpi quante sono le divisioni fatti che saranno detti estimi, e rimessi nelle mani di cui sopra, dovrà il Patrimoniale, se elegerà di prender detti siti, pagare alli Padroni oltre il valore d'essi portato dal primo estimo fatto dall'estimatore Ferrero i due quinti del maggior valore portato dal detto secondo estimo, e quando il Patrimoniale non elegga di prender i siti, saranno obligati i Particolari Padroni d'essi pagare in mani, e con quittanza del Tesorier general Belli i trè quinti di detto maggior valore."

13. Ibid., 933: "Et per maggior commodità de' Cittadini, e altri che vorranno fabricare in detto aggrandimento concediamo loro il termine d'anni dieci, comminciando dal giorno della publicatione di questo di far fare le loro fabriche, con dichiaratione però, che in quanto a quelli, che frà cinque anni non haveranno principiate le loro fabriche saranno tenuti darle principio l'anno sesto con far le fondamente, e haver fra tutto detto anno sesto alzata la muraglia sopra terra almeno per trabucchi due."

14. Ibid.: "E come l'intentione nostra è di dar ogni comodità a quelli, che vorano fabricare in detti siti, perciò permettiamo di far le fabriche con gli ornamenti, che loro piacerà, con ciò però, che le fabriche siano in altezza almeno di tre piani, e verso le strade pubbliche non si lascino alcuni giardini, ò muraglie più basse delle sudette tre piani."

tello, Contrada di Po, and Piazza Carlina.[15] Clearly, the crown's two formal aspirations remained constant: a continuous street defined by buildings of uniform height, and in the most important areas identical facade compositions. Despite a lenient construction schedule, it seems that few rushed out to start construction under these conditions.

These coercive and costly building requirements were evidently damaging the public interest and slowing down the rate of construction in the Po expansion. Consequently, Giovanna Battista relaxed them considerably in an edict of 22 January 1678—an attempt to provide a "service" to her subjects while still promoting the "beautification" and "security" of the city.[16] She allowed the construction of two-story buildings and the placement of gardens and courts, though not wider than 5 *trabucchi*, along public streets. She still insisted, however, that the building line should be maintained at intersections, and she still refused to permit contiguous gardens, thus privileging firstcomers.[17] A proposed cross-street, running between the great diagonal Contrada di Po and the fortification at the north edge of the expansion, was eliminated in this 1678 edict, and the octagonal plan of Piazza Carlina was simplified to a rectangle in order to facilitate the survey and subdivision of the area around it.[18] But the original requirement for a building height of three stories was

15. Ibid.: "Dichiariamo però, che le fabriche, che saranno fatte, o si faranno da una parte, e l'altra della strada che va dalla Piazza Castello alla Porta di Po, e sopra detta Piazza, e la Carlina, dovranno essere tutte d'un'altezza uniforme con li portici, e ornamenti, che saranno da Noi prescritti."

16. Ibid., 933–34: "Volendo Noi contribuire per quanto sia possibile à tutte quelle cose, che sono atte à maggiormente facilitare la fabrica de'siti compresi nel nuovo ingrandimento di questa Città, ci siamo volontieri disposta ad accordare quanto segue, persuasa, che con tali mezzi sia per adempirsi in questa parte nostro desiderio, non meno indrizzato all'abbellimento di detta Città, che alla sicurezza della medesima, e servitio de' Cittadini."

17. Ibid., 933: "Permettiamo a tutti quelli, che hanno accomprati siti posti nel sudetto nuovo ingrandimento, non ancora fabricati, ò che ne accompraranno in avvenire, di poter far Cortili, e Giardini, che si estendino sino alle strade publiche di larghezza fino a trabucchi cinque purche non s'incontrino detti Giardini, o Cortili sopra le cantonate di dette strade, le quali intendiamo, che siano occupate dalle fabriche delle Case, e con dichiaratione, che volendo due vicini valersi di questo beneficio non possano fare detti Giardini, ò Cortili congionti insieme sopra la medesima linea di strada, mà che debbano esservi fraposti qualche corpi di fabriche per non deformare troppo notabilmente il corso di dette strade . . . permettiamo parimente, che quelli, i quali non havranno il modo di alzare le loro Case à tre piani, le alzino solamente a due."

18. Ibid., 934: "In oltre vedendo, che nel comparto delle strade del nuovo dissegno, una di esse che tramedià la gran strada ò sia il corso di Po, deve passare dentro la Chiesa della

reinstated for the street connecting the citadel to Piazza Carlina, which, as the longest continuous street of the city, ought to be as *riguardevole* as possible.[19] This street was not clearly defined at its eastern end, but it tied the citadel to the new eastern edge, on the way bisecting Piazza Carlina and defining the short northern side of Piazza Reale, and thus connected all three additions to the original Roman plan of Turin—the citadel, Città Nuova, and the Po expansion. Nevertheless, this street was still secondary in importance to the Contrada di Po and Contrada Nuova, since it did not lead into the governmental and spatial center of the city, Piazza Castello, and because it did not end at a gate. Giovanna Battista's attempt to treat this street as a major one conflicted with the centralizing tendency of the urban organization, and did not meet with success. Defined by the great variety of churches and palaces that flanked it, it was not to achieve the monumentality of the major streets, since the lack of uniformity of the buildings called attention to them, rather than allowing them to serve as continuous flanking wings that could channel movement and transform urban space into a theatrical perspective.

Despite passive opposition to its policy of uniform urban design, the Savoy dukes' official project for Turin remained unaltered through succeeding generations. In his edict of 1685 the next sovereign, Vittorio Amedeo II, upheld the edicts promulgated in 1675 and 1678 by his mother but adopted a harsher tone: incomplete buildings, he said, "greatly prejudice the design and decorum [*decoro*] of the city."[20] Most property owners had been in default, ignoring the

---

Santissima Annonciata, portando seco la demolitione non solo di detta chiesa, mà ancora d'alcune case de' Particolari à quella vicine, dichiariamo, che si anulla la strada sudetta, sino alli terrapieni della fortificatione verso mezza notte. . . . Di più sendoci stato rappresentato, che la forma prescritta alla sudetta piazza Carolina di figura ottangolare haverebbe cagionata molta incommodità alli Particolari, che havessero in pensiero di fabricarvi Case, atessa l'obligatione delli angoli e strade oblique di detta figura ottangolare, perciò per facilitar la vendita de' siti, e la fabrica d'essi habbiamo fatto ridurre detta Piazza à figura retta, e li siti tutti riquadrati."

19. Ibid., 933–34: "del qual privilegio [two-story houses], come pure da quello de' sudetti [continuous] Giardini, e Cortili saranno esclusi li siti posti sopra la strada che principia dalla Cittadella, e passa in testa alla Piazza reale, e tramedia la nuova Piazza Carolina, la qual strada per essere la più lunga di questa Città, intendiamo altresi, che rieschi più riguardevole, che sia possibile."

20. Duboin, 942: "Se bene siano spirati detti termini, in quali si dovevano principiare dette fabriche, e corra l'anno decimo per darle fabbricate, tuttavia vi sono ancora in dett'ingrandimento molti siti, ne'quali neanco s'è dato principio alla fabrica, il che preguidica molto al decoro della città . . . commandiamo a tutti quelli che non hanno dato principio a dette fabriche, e principiate non l'hanno finite, di dover fra tutto l'anno corrente haver fatto le

edicts and neither building nor paying their debt to the crown. In the meantime, the interests of the crown had remained staunchly the same: the ruler desired a uniform and continuous building line that would emphasize the major streets and squares. Litigation between property owners and the Senate continued as late as 1713, when confiscation of the property of owners delinquent in their payment of the *valenza* was threatened.[21] In the interval, the architectural quality of the new part of the city was set and defined by the ducal buildings framing the north and east sides of Piazza Castello, by the immense mass of the hospital of San Giovanni, and by the uniform private palaces that began to be built along the Contrada di Po.

As well as the edicts, the crown tried various other methods in its attempt to realize financial gain quickly from the expansion, including a form of speculation. Before the expansion plan was made public, the crown acquired land in the Po suburb. The sites were to be used for the construction of fortifications and ducal buildings, or sold at a profit. The crown also had the option to buy out a landowner, at the price estimated by the owner, if he would not pay the *valenza* on the increased value of the property or did not build on it within the time allotted. Initially, the crown owned little land between the east wall of Città Vecchia and the Po other than the sites of the fortifications (though the cadet branch of the ducal house, the princes of Savoia-Carignano, possessed large tracts adjacent to Porta Castello). After the intense building activity of the 1660s, the better sites in Città Nuova near the ducal palace had been built upon. The duke presumably wanted to give his cramped officials the opportunity to build a suitable residence in Turin. Since the court officials would be expected to stay as close as possible to the ducal palace, they were likely to acquire lots on the site of the demolished walls, thus buying their land from the crown rather than from private owners. This demolition took place much more rapidly than in the first expansion; Carlo Emanuele took advantage of the local peace—determined in part by wars taking place elsewhere,

---

fondamenta, et alzato la muraglia fuori di terra almeno due trabucchi, e fra tutto l'anno prossimo venturo a dare qualle finite, e non havendo il modo di farlo, di vendere li siti ad altri, che compischino a quanto viene come sopra da noi ordinato, altrimente passato quest'anno faremo noi metter all'incanto detti siti per deliberarli a chi farà miglior partito, e si sottometerà avant'il conseglio delle nostre fabriche e fortificationi di sodisfar al present'ordine nostro, et il prezzo a' padroni di detti siti; ferme rimanendo le regole prescritte da dett'ordine in ciò che riguarda la forma, et architettura nella costruttione delle fabriche in dett'ingradimento portate da dett'ordine delli 16 decembre 1675 salvo in quanto vengono variate quelle de quali nell'altro ordine delli 22 genaro 1678."

21. Ibid., 954.

such as the Franco-Flemish war—to tear down the eastern walls of Turin in 1674.[22] This also suggests that the construction of the new fortifications was well along.

Although the administrators of Turin were involved in the realization of the expansion project from the very beginning, their initial response mirrored the private behavior of the property owners, who delayed payments to the crown as well as new construction; the results, however, were very different. The eastern expansion required the cooperation of the city council for a rapid and successful conclusion. At first the councilors gained time by claiming poverty.[23] They attempted to avoid any financial obligations but were eventually charged with a loan payment of fifty thousand *ducatoni* and the construction of the Po gate, financed in part from a food tax the duke had temporarily assigned to the city to use in construction. The negotiations concluded as the city council eventually acquiesced to funding the marble gate, the most expensive single element of the expansion. The council members claimed poverty even before requests were made of them, from fear of being loaded with untraditional duties. When they knew that the gate was to be their only responsibility, they renounced their opposition as abruptly as they had begun. In the relations between the council and the duke, this pattern often emerged.

The repeated edicts of the regent Giovanna Battista and of Vittorio Ame-

22. Carlo Emanuele's diary records his plans to buy and resell enough land to pay for half the fortification (*Memoriale*, 28), to put his sites up for sale and enhance their price by charging for the demolition materials (69), and to take advantage of the peace: "fare sbalzare prontamente le fortificazioni di Torino, poiche il tempo e proprio, giacchè la Francia e si occupata come è nelle guerre" (359).

23. ASCT, Ordinati, fol. 221, 17 February 1669: "Nel qual consiglio il sig[nor] Sindaco propone come S[ua] A[ltezza] R[eale] per organo del Sig[nor] Trucchi g[e]n[er]ale delle finanze gli ha fatto sapere come intende ampliare la citta, et unire alla medesima il Borgo di Po, e perche questo ingrandimen[to] et unione riflette in abellimento et utile anche alla citta pensa anco che la citta non fara difficolta di contribuire cio puotra in questa spesa qual contributione stima non puossi esser minore di ducatoni cinquanta milla, e S[ua] A[ltezza] R[eale] dara alla citta il rimborso di detta somma sopra le gabelle alla cui propositione luoro s[ignori] Sindici risposero c'havrebbero fatto chiamar il conseglio, e fattone la propositione indi gl'havrebbero portata la risposta del sentimento del conseglio havendo indi soggionto che per hora si levara mano alla richiesta delli ducatoni cinquanta milla per l'accompra dell'imbotato. Il conseglio ordina a S[ignori] Sindici di rapresentare al Sig[no]re Generale delle Finanze come la citta si ritrova carica di debiti in queste messe tali che non puo in questo incontrar il desiderio di S[ua] A[ltezza] R[eale] perche essaminando le forze della citta si vedra non puoter sodisfar alla dimanda di detta A[ltezza] R[eale] e meglio come le sara della congregatione a parte datto il progetto per la risposta."

deo II are a testimonial of the difficulties the crown experienced in convincing property owners in the Po expansion to follow the building code. While maintaining the regulations for the major streets and squares, the regent conceded in her last edict the possibility of building two-story houses elsewhere. Many courtiers were eventually given lots as presents, while others obtained privileged sites at small cost, which gave them the impetus to build. The building of palaces began only slowly, however, taking place largely after 1685 and mostly along those north-south streets close to Città Nuova where the restrictions had been lifted to allow large gardens and courts. The building code of the major streets and squares implied tall, and consequently large, palaces whose capacity was likely to be superior to the needs of even an extensive, wealthy family. The solution was the development of the apartment house, especially along the Contrada di Po. The social arrangement vertically was the same as that of an aristocratic palace, but the inhabitants living on different floors were no longer related to one another.[24]

While the social profile of owners of building sites in the Po expansion area—merchants, artists, craftsmen, court officials, and aristocrats—was not unlike that of the inhabitants of Città Vecchia and Città Nuova, there were many disparate reasons why the Po expansion, whose walls and bastions were build very quickly, was filled with private construction relatively slowly. One reason was the necessity of adapting to this new housing type, the apartment house, which evolved in response to the monumental and palatial qualities of the official urban design promoted by the Savoy dukes: large, unadorned, repetitive.[25] Other reasons were the high cost of building materials of good quality, still in short supply, and the discrepancy between the growth of the population—which had increased by only about one-third since 1630, reaching forty thousand by 1675—and that of Turin's territory, which had doubled. This relatively small population may well have been a factor in the slow development of the Po expansion.

The patterns of land ownership can be deduced from the suits that the crown brought against landlords between 1673 and 1713 in its pursuit of the *valenza*, the differential of three-fifths owed to it on the increased value of property after the expansion. An elaborate document made in July 1698 for this purpose reflects the extent of habitation and ownership in the Po expan-

24. See Stuart J. Woolf, "Some Notes on the Cost of Palace Building in Turin in the Eighteenth Century," *Atti e rassegna tecnica della Società degli Ingegneri e degli Architetti in Torino*, 19 (1961): 299–306.

25. For the evolution of the apartment building in Turin, see Augusto Cavallari Murat, ed., *Forma urbana della Torino barocca* (Turin, 1968), 1 and 2: *passim*.

sion area, halfway through the crown's fifty-year attempt to promote construction and to collect its legislated *valenza* from land and real estate owners.[26] This document is an inventory of owners, with the measurements and location of their property in the Po area, made in the wake of a royal order of 15 March 1698 that urged owners to comply with building and tax regulations.[27] Since there were no consistent street names (the same street was often referred to by several names derived from prominent monuments along it, customarily churches or monasteries), the addresses are rudimentary, relying on adjacent neighbors as a way of situating a property. The inventory also includes the price of the site and how it had been acquired (from a private party or from the crown's central financial agency, the so-called Patrimoniale). Of about 154 entries, which vary in length according to the complexity of the site and of the transaction that preceded its acquisition, in 56 cases the Patrimoniale, empowered by Giovanna Battista to deal with land transactions in the Borgo di Po expansion, was involved as the seller of land. A few cases involved the exchange of lots, since the Patrimoniale acted as a clearinghouse for the sites needed for ducal buildings and public streets. About 40 of the 150 owners listed are members of the ducal court, ranging from aristocratic families to the ducal physician, pharmacist, and engraver. There are also some merchants, jewelers, and a large number of smaller owners whose occupation is not specifically mentioned. Despite the presence of many courtiers, then, large parts of the Po expansion were accomplished mostly without the help of the aristocracy. The entire southeast portion, between Piazza Carlina and the walls of the city, was bereft of major buildings, with the exception of the hospital of San Giovanni. This was understandable, since the area had no direct connection either to Piazza Castello or the major gates. The few aristocratic palaces were clustered near Palazzo Carignano, immediately south of Piazza Castello, though from the second decade of the eighteenth century they could be found east of Piazza Reale.

26. The entire inventory is contained in AST, Sez. Riunite, art. 552, a volume bound in marbled-paper covers (the brief history of each property in the Borgo di Po expansion area illustrates also how it had changed hands).

27. Duboin, 948–49: "ordina a tutti li possidenti siti in detto nuovo ingrandimento, quali non hanno dato principio a dette fabriche, e portici respetivamente, e principiati non li hanno terminati di dover, cioè quelli che non hanno finora dato principio a dette fabriche darli principio fra un mese prossimo, indi far construere fra tutto settembre venturo le muraglie alte da terra due trabucchi, e tanto questi, che altri, quali gia hanno dato principio alle mede[si]me darle terminate fra tutto l'anno venturo 1699 e non havendo possibilità di farlo, di vendere fra tre messi prossimi detti siti."

The construction of the Borgo di Po extension may have been slow in execution, but it was eventually realized in the spirit and largely in the form proposed by Carlo Emanuele II. Through edicts, coercive land grants, financial maneuvers, and the newly strengthened ducal building agency, successive rulers enforced the key elements of the Savoy dynasty's urban design program. Continuous building height and street definition, uniform facade design for the major streets and squares, and use of a limited range of construction materials ensured the formal integration of the Po extension. Efforts were made to facilitate private building through the adoption of an orthogonal street grid, which helped in surveying and in settling disputes over property—except where it was negated by the diagonal swath cut by Contrada di Po. Both the layout of the expansion area and the building codes followed closely the formal aspects of the original studies made in the 1610s under Carlo Emanuele I. There was, however, one significant difference in the character of the ducal building program initiated by Carlo Emanuele II and completed by his widow and heir. In the 1620s Carlo Emanuele I had founded churches and monasteries, encouraging religious orders to settle in Turin. After 1673 the crown encouraged the building enterprises of existing orders—succeeding sovereigns patronized different groups—but focused its own interests on the construction of buildings to house the ducal bureaucratic institutions and secular agencies.

Like his recent ancestors, Carlo Emanuele II was concerned with matters of rank; he took his contested royal title seriously and expected to be treated as the equal of the monarchs of Spain and France. The beautification and enlargement of Turin, first propagated in the *Theatrum* and now slowly being translated into urban reality, was meant to support these claims by aggrandizing and spreading abroad the fame of the House of Savoy. At home, too, the controlled expansion of Turin enhanced the authority of the duke, by obliging the population to conform to his planning and building restrictions and by making his presence constantly felt. Entries in Carlo Emanuele's diary claimed that the beautification of Turin was one of his main reasons for expansion, and subsequent edicts enforce a program of embellishment through conformity to a uniform and coherent design; the result was the powerful "regularity" praised by visitors to the newly completed city, a regularity that "governs" both its civic and military aspects.[28] The Borgo di Po expansion, moreover, combined

28. See, for example, Maximilien Misson, *Nouveau voyage d'Italie* (The Hague, 1691), 2:213: "Rien n'est si beau que la rue qui traverse les deux places et qui va du Chasteau a la porte neuve. L'une et l'autre de ces places sont grandes et de figure reguliére; mais la nouvelle est environnée des maisons qui font une symmetrie parfaite; et une large portique règne tout autour. . . . [Carlo Emanuele] l'environna d'une fortification regulière, et bien revestue";

aesthetic power with the authority of antiquity, essential for a hereditary monarchy. Part of the significance of Turin, as we have seen in the text of the
foundation stone, depended upon its great antiquity as a pre-Roman city; the
eastward expansion, towards the Po, was believed to reclaim the area of this
ancient settlement and thus restored the city "to the amplitude of its august
name." The antiquity of the Savoy dynasty and its claim to the royal title were
thus inextricably tied to the critical fortune of the capital city.

WHILE THE EDICTS and letters patent through which the crown made
grants of land promoted the building of institutional and private edifices, the
actual construction process was supervised by a governmental agency set up
for this purpose. As we have seen in chapters 3 and 4, Carlo Emanuele I had
founded a Magistrato delle Fabriche in charge of ducal buildings and the fortification of Piedmontese and Savoyard cities; Vittorio Amedeo I then expanded and refined the functions of the agency by sifting apart civil and military construction. These two branches of the ducal building agency were
consolidated into one, the Consiglio delle Fabriche e Fortificationi, by Cristina
in 1638. Thus, under Cristina, the mandate of the agency was to supervise the
fortification of Città Nuova and, once peace had been reestablished after the
dynastic wars of 1640, to realize the ducal building program. Through a
legislative measure taken by Carlo Emanuele II in 1666, his mother's Consiglio
delle Fabriche e Fortificationi was merged with the Consiglio di Finanze, the
ducal administrative council. The contractual, supervisory, and administrative
functions of the agency in relation to fortification, opening of roads, and construction of buildings were clearly spelled out.[29] It was this agency that began
the implementation of the Po expansion.

Like the functions of the wide-ranging agency, the roles of its constituent
members were multiple. Its directors, the ministers Turinetti and Trucchi,
were both occupied with the economic and political problems of the entire
duchy, serving respectively as secretary of state and as secretary of finance.

G. B. Pacichelli, *Memorie de' viaggi per l'Europa christiana* (Naples, 1685), 3:520: "Divides'in
Città Vechia e Città Nuova, chiuse ambedue con mura, e fortificationi ordinate. . . . Chi-
unque ci entra di Germania, di Spagna, o di Francia, riman stupefatto a vederla"; Joseph-
Jérôme de La Lande, *Voyage en Italie* (Paris, 1769), 1:46: "Les dix places qu'il y a à Turin et
toutes les rues de la ville sont d'une regularité et d'un alignement qui fait le plus beau spectacle qu'on puisse voir."

29. AST, Sez. Riunite, Fabriche e Fortificationi, art. 199.1, fol. 152, 27 October 1666.

They had risen to high office through their study of law and by their own abilities, rather than through family or clan connections; neither was born into the nobility. Turinetti and Trucchi had served Cristina and were trusted servants of the crown.[30] Even before the merger, the position of the secretary of Fabriche e Fortificationi had been occupied by a secretary of finance.

The case of Amedeo di Castellamonte, a former member of the Fabriche e Fortificationi who maintained his position in the merged agency, was more complex. His aristocratic birth implied, as a matter of course, an involvement in military affairs, strategy, and fortification; as we saw in chapter 5, he was a commissioned military officer. His contribution to the government of the duchy as a state councilor was made as a nobleman in the service of his lord. Amedeo's varied employments as the civic architect of this expansion and as a writer on architectural and urban design, activities carried out in the service of Carlo Emanuele II, demonstrate further his multiple talents. They also show that, at least at the court of Savoy, the schism between military and civic architecture postulated to have taken place in Italy by the end of the sixteenth century had not occurred, since Amedeo received and carried out commissions in both areas.[31]

A recently published inventory of Amedeo's belongings, made at the time of his death in 1683, is a very important document in establishing the architect's intellectual background.[32] His three-story house on Contrada Nuova in Turin, in the southern expansion area completed by Cristina, was filled with family artifacts, such as a small cannon bearing the arms of the Castellamonte, but also with a significant collection of paintings and books. Many of the 175 books owned by Amedeo were perhaps inherited, in part from his father Carlo and in part from the ducal physician Francesco Fiochetto, his mother's father, who had distinguished himself during the plague epidemic of 1632.[33] Two as-

30. For Trucchi's importance at court see Pietr'Antonio Arnaldo, *Il ritratto panegirico; o sia l'idea del consiglier di stato* (Turin, 1673)—dedicated to Trucchi, as is Arnaldo's *Il giardin del Piemonte* (Turin, 1673)—and *L'anfiteatro del valore; overo il Campidoglio del merito spalancato alle glorie della nobiltà torinese* (Turin, 1674), where Trucchi's titles are emphatically listed: Count, Cavaglier Gran Croce, Commendatore of the Order of Santi Mauritio e Lazaro, Minister and State Councilor, and First President of the Royal Treasury. For Turinetti see letter patent of 23 October 1638 (Duboin, 932).

31. Horst de la Croix, "Military Architecture and the Radial City Plan in Sixteenth-Century Italy," *Art Bulletin*, 42 (1960): 263–90.

32. Franco Monetti and Arabella Cifani, "Un capitolo per Vittorio Amedeo Castellamonte (1613–1683), architetto torinese," *Studi piemontesi*, 17 (1988): 75–92.

33. See chapter 4, notes 6 and 7, above.

pects of his library are of particular interest here: the section on history and the section on architecture. Amedeo owned a number of fundamental texts in the theory of military planning, including treatises by Sardi, Bar-le-Duc, Maggi, Rosetti, Guarini, and Teti, as well as the works of Alberti, Capra, and Barbaro on architecture and perspective. Among the historians and ideologues most influential at the court of Turin, Botero, Giuglaris, Tesauro, and Saavedra were represented on his shelves, as were books on the antiquities of Rome and Ripa's *Iconologia*. This inventory, paralleling closely the intellectual categories of the larger palatine library, confirms that Amedeo was fundamentally rooted in the military culture of his century and equally firmly based in the contemporary Piedmontese culture of emblems and iconography. His library points to strong links between intellectuals in Turin and underlines the spiritual cohesiveness of the Savoy court.

Amedeo di Castellamonte served under four Savoy sovereigns—Vittorio Amedeo I, Cristina, Carlo Emanuele II, and Giovanna Battista—while Turinetti and Trucchi served the last three. Besides Amedeo di Castellamonte, Turinetti, and Trucchi, the members of the ducal planning council in 1673 included the chancellor Horatio Gina and the auditor Giovanni Pietro Marelli. Gina and Marelli provided the liaison between the government and the building contractors, and may have acted as contractors themselves, while after 1678 Marelli was to play a central role in the sale of lots in the Borgo di Po expansion area.

After the Consiglio di Finanze took over in 1666, the work of the planning council did not change. For the Po expansion it accepted bids for and awarded contracts. Payments for building the walls and digging the moats were ordered through the Consiglio, which also employed the surveyors in charge of checking the quality and quantity of work accomplished. Similarly, the Consiglio di Finanze discussed the bids for the building of the ducal academy, theater, ballroom, and riding school located east of Piazza Castello, and chose the contractors. Throughout the seventeenth century, the agency's meetings seem to have been representative of the political and nepotistic business manner of the ducal government. For instance, before it even called for bids for a contract to build, the Consiglio di Finanze usually favored a contractor. When the bids were returned, it regularly tried to convince the favored contractor to accept the work at the lowest bid that had been received.[34] Consequently, throughout the documents that record the building of Turin in the seventeenth century,

34. See, for example, AST, Sez. Riunite, Fabriche e Fortificationi, art. 201, 12 October 1673.

the names of the same participating builders are met with again and again. Not only are certain construction companies entrenched, but the longevity and perseverance of several are noteworthy, paralleling the councilors themselves. Although its mandate and name changed over time, the role of Fabriche e Fortificationi—the title reinstated by the regent Giovanna Battista on 18 January 1678—remained well defined.[35] It was entirely dependent on the crown, but as one of its "incorporated" agencies, Fabriche e Fortificationi could operate freely within its restrictions.

T H I S ,   T H E N ,   W A S   the agency that would begin to implement the aesthetic and military ambitions of Carlo Emanuele II, immediately after the foundation ceremony signaled the start of actual construction. Shortly before the ceremony, in fact, the site of the fortification trace—the bastions and connecting walls, moats, and gates—had been surveyed by the project director Amedeo di Castellamonte and a team of assistants.[36] The ducal authorities would now begin supervising the three main projects that together constituted the Po expansion: the creation of an imposing new gate, the moving of earth and construction of fortification walls and bastions, and the layout and paving of the streets themselves.

While several emergency gates had been marked by Amedeo di Castella-

35. Duboin, 941: "Havendo noi con patenti nostre delli sedici decembre mille seicento settantacinque conferta la cognitione di tutte le cose concernenti la nuova fortificatione di questa Città, come anche le differenze per causa de' siti, e maggior valenza d'essi, et delle case poste nel'ingrandimento nuovo d'essa Città, al consiglio delle finanze di S[ua] A[ltezza] R[eale] mio figlio amatissimo; et essendosi dopo rimesso in piedi quello delle fabriche, e fortificationi, alla cui cura sono state commesse tutte le incumbenze, che erano appoggiate al detto consiglio di finanze riguardanti materia di fabriche e fortificationi senza far espressa mentione de' siti, e case poste nell'ingrandimento sudetto; . . . dichiariamo, che al detto consiglio delle fabriche e fortificationi nuovamente ristabilito come sovra, spetterà la cognitione di tutte le cose, che erano appoggiate al consiglio suddetto delle finanze non solo riguardanti fabriche, e fortificationi, ma nominatamente quelle che concernono li siti e la maggior valenza d'essi, e delle case poste nel suddetto nuovo recinto, attorno a che tutto co'suoi annessi, e connessi, e dependenti, mandiamo ad esso consiglio delle fabriche e fortificationi di conoscer, proveder, proceder, e far procedere come meglio li parerà per via amichevole o di ragione."

36. ASCT, Ordinati, 23 October 1673.

monte's survey, there was to be only one major new gate, placed at the eastern end of Contrada di Po, facing the bridge over the river. The gate was considered as a distinct element in the enclosure of the city; in contrast with the walls and bastions, which had to instill fear and discouragement in the hearts of enemies in order to undermine their resolve, the gate ought to impress arriving visitors by advertising the wealth and power of the ruler in its lavish decoration and haughty inscriptions. Vauban insisted that the splendor of the gate made a significant contribution to the overall military strength of the city. Such a gate would be in every sense a focal point, where court aesthetics, civic pride, and military strategy converged. In political and economic terms, too, this main gate stood at a complicated juncture, since it was the only part of the new fortified enclosure that the city of Turin was obliged to subsidize directly.

The duke took advantage of the situation and demanded an expensive marble gate. In August 1674 he was presented with three design alternatives that the city council was prepared to build.[37] At that time, the council requested the right to collect the meat tax in Turin as reimbursement for the marble decorations of the old Porta Castello (demolished earlier in 1674), which normally would have been used for the new Po gate had the duke not unjustly appropriated them.[38] In September 1674 the duke granted the city council the reimbursement and further allowed the council to choose the design of the gate, on condition that a crown auditor would be part of the awarding committee; this condition was rescinded in 1677, however, so that the work could progress more quickly. Although most of the gate was constructed between 1675 and 1676, construction slowed down while the decorations were deliberated. By July 1677, the lack of agreement between the city council and the ducal representative brought the process to a halt, prompting the regent Giovanna Battista to allow the city council to get on by itself, after reminding the city council and the ducal representative that the planning of the Po gate was far from complete.[39] Following the regent's order, the contract was

37. ASCT, Carte Sciolte, number 1540, 9 August 1674.

38. Ibid.: "havuto anche riguardo che V[ostra] A[ltezza] R[eale] si e valso delli marmi che servivano d'ornam[en]to a Porta Castello quali gia lo supp[le]nte haveva disegnato di far entrare in quello di detta Porta Nova." For the food tax see chapter 6, note 51, above.

39. ASCT, Carte Sciolte, 1540, 17 July 1677: "vedendo quanto lentamente si vadi avvanzando la construtione della nuova Porta del Po a causa che da noi stessi non puotete contrattare e stabilire i prezzi di marmi necessarij per essa salvo con intervento d'uno degli auditori . . . conforme alle patenti delli tre settembre mille seicento settanta quatro . . . percio dispensandovi dall'osservanza di dette patenti."

awarded in 1678, and the gate finally completed by 1679.[40] For their design the civic authorities had shrewdly turned to the prestigious new court architect Guarino Guarini, who as crown engineer since 1667 had taken over the design and construction of the Holy Shroud chapel. Guarini's interest in the large-scale fortification and urbanistic enterprises of the crown can be gleaned from his publication in 1676 of a treatise on fortification, in which he compared the differences in the fortification methods preferred by the three national schools of defensive and offensive strategy, coming down firmly on the side of French theorists, such as Pagan and Bitanvieu, rather than the Italians.[41] Evidently he concurred with or was mimicking court tastes, where, as we have seen in previous chapters, military studies were closely pursued by the dukes of Savoy in their attempt to emulate and surpass French achievements. Thus this treatise on fortification can be seen as an attempt on Guarini's part to integrate himself within the principal discourse of the Savoy court.

An engraving of his design for the Po gate appears in Guarini's treatise on architecture, published after his death in 1683 (fig. 111). Earlier an engraving of the elevation and the plan of the gate were published in the 1682 edition of the *Theatrum* (fig. 112), after a drawing of 1674 by Borgonio. The walls that flank the entrance were angled inward in an inverted V shape. Three statues representing Fortezza, Piedmont, and Prudenza in the engraving of 1682 alternate with three reclining *taurini*, bull-headed river gods symbolizing Turin and its three adjacent rivers, the Po, Dora, and Stura; these were replaced in Guarini's (posthumous) publication by obelisks topped with flaming orbs. The fire and the bulls, in these alternative designs, recapitulate the imagery of the civic and ducal *feste*. As seen in an engraving made after Juvarra's drawings in 1722, the gate's piers and columns were banded and rusticated in the built version, the corners reinforced with an additional pier, its attic level heightened, and the statues overpowered by the military banding of the order (fig. 113).

40. ASCT, Ordinati, 29 March 1678; see also ASCT, Carte Sciolte, number 1537 ("Ristretto della spesa di Porta di Po corr[ispondent]e in questo all'infradesign[at]e carte"). Total payments between 1674 and 1690 were 87,937 *lire*, the highest payments being made in 1675, 1676, 1680. A payment order made between February 1677 and May 1678 for the gate and guardhouse (AST, Sez. Riunite, art. 86, number 1482) suggests that the crown contributed to the project.

41. *Trattato di fortificatione che hora si usa in Fiandra, Francia et Italia* (Turin, 1676), part III; on this work see Gianni Carlo Sciolla, "Note sul *Trattato di fortificatione* del Guarini," in *Guarino Guarini e la internazionalità del barocco*, ed. Vittorio Viale (Turin, 1970), 1:513–29.

The inscription tablet, commemorating Carlo Emanuele II's achievement, was installed in 1684.[42]

After the outline of the walls and moats had been traced by Castellamonte's team of surveyors and the expansion officially inaugurated, the Consiglio di Finanze announced the competition for the construction of the fortifications. Extensive discussions followed between the councilors and the various teams that presented bids.[43] Finally, the contract to excavate the moats was awarded on 22 December 1673 to six subcontractors, two from the state of Lugano, two from the state of Milan, and two presumably from Piedmont. An advance payment, the equivalent of one week's work, was made to them; subsequent weekly payments of six thousand *lire* were to be paid by the crown, with extra payments preceded by surveyed measurements made by employees of the Consiglio di Finanze who supervised the work in progress. Excavation was begun at the northeast corner, at the Bastion Verde adjacent to the royal garden, and was to proceed clockwise east and south to the bastion of Madonna degli Angeli. The completion of the moat was projected for April 1675, and

42. *Theatrum*, ed. Firpo, 1:126:

Augustam ad Eridanum portam,

A Carolo Emanuele II

Urbe intra annum septem propugnaculis aucta,

Inchoatam,

Maria Ioanna Baptista a Sabaudia,

Ut quam mors coniugi rapuit gloriam redderet,

Undequaque absolvebat.

M DC LXXVI

(Maria Giovanna Battista of Savoy, in order to return to her spouse the glory which death had taken from him, resolved in 1676 to complete the splendid Po gate begun by Carlo Emanuele II after having enlarged the city with seven bastions in a single year.)

43. AST, Sez. Riunite, Fabriche e Fortificationi, art. 195, 1 September 1673, fol. 153: "Riferisce il Aud[ito]re Gina a questo giorno il deliberamento dell'impresa delle muraglie, cavi et esportatione di terra in ordine all'ingrandimento di questa citta da farsi conforme al disegno et instruttione del sig[nor] Conte e Primo Ingeg[ne]re di S[ua] A[ltezza] R[eale] Amedeo Castellamonte, et le deleganze straordinarie da esso fatte per invitar concorrenti com'appare dalli Biletti fatti publicare in diversi luoghi del Piemonte, Oneglia, et Valle d'Aosta, in virtu de quali dice esser venute molte squadre, che doppo d'haver fatto capo da esso, e dal detto conte Castellamonte gl'hanno rimessi li loro partiti ivi presentati, eletti com'anche detta instruttione. E perche si son trovati molto *eccessivi* tanto rispetto alli prezzi, ch'alle conditioni chiamate s'è [deciso] di sentirle in voce squadra per squadra separatamente" (emphasis mine).

although it was expected that the work would be done in two stages—the area from Bastion Verde to the bastion of San Antonio, followed by the trace between San Antonio and Madonna degli Angeli—the contract stressed that the duke would be satisfied if work was begun simultaneously along the entire fortification trace, especially since there seemed to be no scarcity of laborers.[44]

The contract for the construction of the fortification walls and bastions had been awarded to the same six contractors on 11 October 1673. The stages of construction were to be the same as for the moats; the building of the fortified walls was an exercise in earth moving since excavation of moats and raising of walls proceeded in tandem. The walls were to be completed up to the height of 1½ *trabucchi* by October 1675.[45] By December 1673, however, Carlo Emanuele began to feel a sense of urgency, and he obliged the contractors to undertake the entire construction within one year. In a new contract of 22 December 1673 they agreed to the new deadline, requesting a certain number of privileges. These included permission to use lime of an inferior quality and to manufacture brick on the grounds of Villa Valentino without paying rent to the crown; if the quality of the Valentino clay was poor and bricks had to be imported from farther away, the price per built *trabucco* of wall was to increase by five *soldi*. The price per *trabucco* of the second segment would increase by one *lira* to seventeen *lire* and ten *soldi*, and an advance of sixteen thousand *lire* would be paid out to the contractors. In addition, they wanted to stop work on the repairs of the citadel for the entire year (1674), and wanted the contract

44. Ibid., art. 201, 29 December 1673: "Cominciando dal Bastion Verde sino a Sant' Antonio per tutto il mese d'aprile prossimo, et da Sant'Antonio sino al bastione della madona delli Angeli fra detto tempo nell'anno mille seicento settanto cinque. . . . Havendo S[ua] A[ltezza] R[eale] fatto a detti impresari che sarebbe di suo gusto che anche da qui a detto mese d'aprile prossimo venturo facessero travagliar alli cavi di terra et porto d'essa conforme a detta instruttione da Sant'Antonio al Bastione della madona delli Angeli per la larghezza d'otto trabucchi almeno, e profondita che richiede la fortificatione . . . tanto piu che vi sono molti operarij quali dimandano d'andar travagliare in detti posti da Sant'Antonio alla madona delli Angeli."

45. Ibid.: "Ad ogniuno sia manifesto conciosia che per contratto fatto avanti questo consiglio sotto li ondeci ottobre pross[im]e scorso li capi m[urato]ri Pietro Laurenti, del fu Giacomo di Carabia stato di Lugano, Giacomo Mosso del fu Fran[ces]co di Muzzano, Carlo Sinale del fu Bernardo di Graglia, Michel Mossino del fu Giacomo di Loggio Valsolda stato di Milano, Fran[ces]co Bariffo di Domenico di Massagno stato di Lugano, et Giacomo Bonevo del fu Matteo di Poria pur stato di Milano . . . siansi obligati di far per tutto ottobre dell'anno venturo 1674 le muraglie della cittanova del Borgo di Po dal Bastion Verde sino alla strada grossa sotto Sant'Antonio all'altezza d'un trabucco e mezzo fuori di terra e altre tanto nell'anno 1675 da detta strada fino al bastione della Madonna delli Angeli."

for the following year and for the moats, made at the same time, to become unchangeable.[46]

The conditions of the new contract were approved by both sides, but despite this agreement a new contract, requiring the completion of the entire fortification up to the level of the *cordone* by October 1674, was sworn to by the contractors and the president of the ducal Patrimoniale on 8 June 1674. In exchange for this greatly increased speed of construction the contractors received an advance of ten thousand *lire*, and the price per *trabucco* of wall, built beyond the height of 1½ *trabucchi* agreed upon previously, was raised from seventeen to eighteen *lire*. If the work was not completed in time, the contractors would have to return the difference between the old and new rates.[47] The

46. Ibid.: "Havendogli questo consiglio fatto sapere che S[ua] A[ltezza] R[eale] desidera ch'antecipino la fattura di dette muraglie da detta parte cioe da Sant'Antonio al bastione della Madonna delli Angeli col farla anche nell'istante anno 1674 li sudetti capi m[urato]ri si siano accontentati di farlo mediante le cose seguenti . . . che nella construttione delle sudette muraglie da farsi da Sant'Antonio al bastione della Madona delli Angeli puotranno impiegare per la meta calcina di Rivarà e Giaveno, et l'altra metta forte. . . . Se li fara dar un sito o siti ne beni di Valentino e vicinato per piantarvi fornaci et fabricar mattoni senza pagam[en]to d'alcun fitto ne prezzo . . . non trovandosi terra buona et in sufficienza per fabricar buoni mattoni ne sitti in detto capo espressi [Valentino] in quel caso dovendo far condurre li mattoni da Vanchiglia e Valdoc o d'altrove sara in facolta del Patrim[onia]le di S[ua] A[ltezza] R[eale] di darli soldi cinque di piu del prezzo sudetto per ogni trabucco della muraglia da fabricarsi. . . . Se li fara un antecipata di livre sedici milla per impiegarle nelle provisioni di detta fabrica . . . per la sudetta muraglia da farsi nell'anno prossimo 1674 da Sant'Antonio sino alla Madona delli Angeli sin all'altezza d'un trabucco e mezzo fuori di terra oltre le fondamenta se li pagara una livra per cad[un]o trabucco di piu del prezzo portato dal sudetto contratto ch'in tutto sono livre diecesette e soldi dieci per trabucco. . . . si fara tralasciare la fabrica da farsi per la restaurat[io]ne della Cittadella per et durante tutto l'anno prossimo 1674. . . . E per gli travagli da farsi nell'anno 1675 e susseguente come pur in tutto il resto stara intieramente fermo il sudetto contratto etiando quanto alli prezzi e l'atto puoco avanti li presente stipulato per l'escavatione de fosso."

47. Ibid., 2 June 1674: "Ad ogn'uno sia manifesto che volendo S[ua] A[ltezza] R[eale] per degni risguardi del suo real servitio s'avanzino nel corrente anno almeno sin'al cordone le muraglie tutto intorno la fortificatione ordinata all'aggrandim[en]to della presente citta ci habbia comandato di procurarne l'effetto. . . . Piu s'accorda d[ett]i impresari nuova antici-pata di livre dieci milla arg[en]to a p[ezzi] 20 l'una per impiegarle nelle provisioni e condotte de materiali. . . . Piu si dichiara che mancando d[ett]i impresari di fare la muraglia come sopra promessa tutt'intorno la cinta della sud[ett]a fortificat[io]ne ordinata all'aggrandi-mento della p[rese]nte citta sino al cordone repartitamente per tutto il mese d'ottobre si levara loro soldi cinque delli dieci d'accrescimento di prezzo sovra fattoli oltre che dovranno essi imp[resa]ri star a tutti li danni e spese che ne puotesse patire il regio servitio."

work on the fortification girdle does seem to have progressed according to the new schedule, however. On 12 October 1674 the crown treasury paid for seven marble medallions, one for each of the bastions.[48] As we know from the foundation ceremony, the Po extension was surrounded only by six bastions, so the seventh medallion must have been intended for the bastion of Madonna degli Angeli, the easternmost bastion of Città Nuova, which had to be restructured after the eastern expansion and could thus be considered among the new bastions of the enlarged fortification.

Payment for the fortification was the crown treasury's largest expense for the expansion project, and various expedients were devised to meet it. As we have gleaned from Carlo Emanuele's diary entries, funds were obtained from the sale of lots in the Po expansion. Before the expansion began the duke had arranged for a large loan from the city, and the income from the grain and meat tax, instituted in 1670, had been earmarked for the fortification of Turin. In 1672 the duke declared his willingness to reduce by one-third his personal expenses, the pensions he awarded, and the expenses of the ducal household. In addition, an entry in his diary in 1673 mentioned the possible use of funds from the Monte di Pietà, the loan institution insured by the government.[49]

Throughout the period 1673–76 there were regular payments to the contractors in charge of building the bastioned walls from the excavated earth of the moat.[50] These earthworks required a relatively small financial investment since no additional manmade materials were needed. They were called "soldier's work," a humble form of fortification that was highly resistant to cannon shot, which remained embedded in the wall rather than shattering it. The disadvantage of this kind of construction lay in the difficulty of maintenance. The earthwork fortification had to be continually rebuilt as rain and frost wore it away. In Turin, and elsewhere, this problem was solved by cladding the walls with brick. This brick veneer was part of the so-called "architect's work," a more elaborate manner of fortification based on vaulted gun-chambers and

48. AST, Sez. Riunite, Fabriche e Fortificationi, art. 197, fol. 54: "Il tes[orie]re gen[er]ale Gio[vanni] Matteo Belli pagara alli piccap[iet]re Casella e Aprile livre cinque cento e ventidue d'arg[en]to . . . per sette medaglie di marmo ch'hanno fatto e rimesse per li sette bastioni del nuovo ingrandimento di questa citta."

49. See chapter 6, notes 51, 52, 53, above, and note 22 of this chapter.

50. AST, Sez. Riunite, Fabriche e Fortificationi, art. 201; between 12 October 1673 and 16 December 1675 the total payments were: 1673, 55,000 *lire*; 1674, 385,000 *lire*; 1675, 81,000 *lire*.

rubble masonry construction, finished with well-laid brick.[51] While masonry fortification was less resistant to cannon, and the cost of construction was greater, it weathered well and required less maintenance than earthwork fortification. Furthermore, the brick wall *seemed* stronger and may have been intended to inspire greater respect in attackers by impressing them with the wealth of the fortification's builder.[52]

Since this illusion of power and wealth was strategically an important ingredient of urban fortification, the earth walls and bastions of Turin were duly clad with a layer of brickwork. As we have seen in the contractors' stipulations above, good brick was not readily available in Turin. Not all clay was considered adequate, and permission for individuals to take clay from the Po or to build kilns was seldom granted. However, shortages of materials did not become as acute a problem as they had been in the 1620s and 1630s, when they had caused Carlo Emanuele I and Vittorio Amedeo I to regulate the price and quality of building materials. These laws were not revived.

Whereas the bastions of the citadel had been provided with casemates or rooms for cannon within their structure, at both sides of the gorge defended by extruding ears, the bastions of the Po expansion had only a cannon platform. These platforms dominated the countryside, permitted freedom of movement and aim, and thus allowed the cannon to be used in a strategically offensive manner. The close placement of the bastions and the angle of their flanks ensured the defense of the curtain walls between the bastions. In addition, half-moons protected the curtains and were in turn defended by the covered way that girdled the entire fortification on the country side of the moat. The bastions were connected by a rampart that ran along the top of the fortified walls and sloped down to the level of the city streets in front of each bastion. A wide road separated the fortification from the streets and buildings of the city. This road was used for troop movements and for the transportation of cannon and ammunition.

It is very important to understand the extent of Carlo Emanuele II's achievement in forcing the speedy construction of the fortification enclosure. In contrast with Città Nuova, which was enclosed by four and a half bastions and took Carlo Emanuele I and Vittorio Amedeo I fifteen years to complete (or at least the five years employed by Vittorio Amedeo's Consiglio di Fortifica-

51. For a comparative discussion of the two methods, see Daniela Lamberini, "Giovan Battista Belluzzi, il trattato delle fortificazioni di terra," in *Il disegno interrotto; trattati medicei d'architettura,* ed. Franco Borsi et al. (Florence, 1980), 2:124.

52. John R. Hale, *Renaissance Fortification: Art or Engineering* (London, 1977), 39–40.

tione), Carlo Emanuele II succeeded in building six and a half bastions in less than two years. (His widow, with pardonable exaggeration, declared in the gate inscription that he had build seven "within one year.") Since Piedmont was at peace with its neighbors, he was able to direct all the resources of the duchy towards the enlargement of its capital.[53] He marshaled an unprecedented amount of funds and was successful in demanding prompt service from his obedient and disciplined building agency, whose members were stimulated by the unprecedented construction then taking place in Turin.

While the construction of the fortifications progressed, the streets of the Borgo di Po expansion were being laid out in their orthogonal grid. The larger east-west streets were traced together with the fortifications, while the smaller north-south streets were opened as lots were bought and construction progressed. The paving of the streets came last, lagging behind the construction of buildings. The new grid continued the east-west streets of Città Vecchia and of Città Nuova, crossed by the new north-south streets which enclosed blocks close in size to those of Città Nuova. The Contrada di Po was, at 18 meters, the widest street of the expansion; it was paved by 1680.[54] Second widest were the five east-west streets. They connected (listing from north to south) the bastion of San Carlo to Piazza Castello; the Po gate to the citadel (skirting Città Vecchia); the bastion of San Giovanni to Piazza Carlina, Piazza Reale, and the citadel; the bastion of Sant'Adelaide to Piazza Carlina, Piazza Reale, and the citadel; and the bastion of San Vittore to Città Nuova and the citadel. In the case of the first three of these streets the requirements for the building envelope were not altered by the regent Giovanna Battista.[55] They were representative arteries of the expansion area, and the continuous building line of three stories was to be maintained. These new east-west streets continued the orthogonal grid of both Città Nuova and Città Vecchia. The three east-west streets of Città Nuova were continued in the Contrada della Madonna, the Contrada di Spedale di San Giovanni, and Contrada di San Filippo. The major street of Città Vecchia, the *decumanus*, was continued on the eastern side of Piazza Castello with the Contrada della Accademia (or Zecca, now Verdi). The

53. See Enrico Stumpo, *Finanze e stato moderno nel Piemonte del Seicento* (Rome, 1979), for a study of the development of the building industry in Turin after the middle of the seventeenth century.

54. AST, Sez. Riunite, Fabriche e Fortificationi, art. 205, 21 May 1680, 27 August 1680.

55. Borelli, 933: "Dichiaramo però, che le fabriche, che saranno fatte, o si faranno da una parte, e l'altra della strada che va dalla Piazza Castello alla Porta di Po, e sopra detta Piazza, e la Carlina, dovranno essere tutte d'un'altezza uniforme con li Portici, e ornamenti, che saranno da noi prescritti."

streets flanking Palazzo Carignano were the continuation of Contrada di San Tommaso and Doirata. Eight east-west streets had been laid out in the official 1673 "presentation" plan of the Po expansion (fig. 96), but only six of them, besides the Contrada di Po, were actually opened. Since they had to be traced while the walls between parts of town were still standing, they were not always—the seeming precision of this plan notwithstanding—in precise alignment. But proximity to the Po was a major element of the ideological program, and thus, as can be seen from the dominant east-west direction of Turin in this oval plan, the east-west streets dominated the layout of the city.

The blocks were smaller in the presentation plan than as realized after 1680. The small blocks of this earlier proposal showed the intention to return to the scale of Città Vecchia, within which the possibility of interior open space, gardens, and courts would have been greatly reduced. As realized, the Po expansion had numerous gardens. Irregularities in this grid of streets, however, resulted in blocks of uneven size and shape. South of Piazza Carlina their north-south dimensions follow the blocks of Città Nuova, and north of Piazza Carlina the dimensions of the blocks of Città Vecchia. The diagonal Contrada di Po also created several trapezoidal blocks and awkward sites. Another proposal involving an angled street, the attempt to make Piazza Carlina important by connecting it to a street that went to the gate, came to nothing; it was overtaken in importance by a secondary street opening from the Po gate and leading to the Palazzo Carignano, a more accurate representation of the actual urban hierarchy within which the palace of the cadet branch of the House of Savoy had greater importance than the marketplace of the Po extension.

In the plan of 1680 by Giovanni Abbiati (fig. 114) the continuity of the north-south streets is interrupted by the Palazzo Carignano and the block with the church of Sant' Antonio. In the later plan made in 1724 by Beltramo Antonio Re (fig. 115) one can see how the large block of the church of the Annunziata further diminished the possibility of continuous movement within the neighborhood, orienting traffic west towards Piazza Castello and Città Nuova; as we have seen in the edicts of Giovanna Battista, one of the proposed north-south streets was suppressed in order to form a larger block and to save this church, which predated the expansion.[56] Despite these enlarged blocks and the irregular trapezoidal shape of the blocks flanking Contrada di Po, the average area of blocks in the Po expansion was smaller than that of blocks in Città Nuova, which were also more uniform. Their street frontage, however, was larger, which meant greater tax revenue for the crown.

56. Ibid., 934: see note 18, above.

Military considerations continued to dominate the street layout, even though the new absolutist capital had evolved far beyond the regular garrison town prescribed in the military treatises, and even though in the new design a broad peripheral street separated the city blocks from the fortifications. This *poemerium* or ring-road may have blighted the houses that faced into it, which found themselves lacking a view, isolated from commerce, and potentially endangered; but it had the effect of separating civilian from military activity by means of a bypass system that was not possible in Città Vecchia, where houses had been built next to the fortifications. This decentralization of the military defenses reinforced the focus of the urban design on the ducal palace, without diminishing the exercise of ducal powers. The military ring-road allowed easy movement between the expansion area and the citadel, whose relation to the center had always been strategic rather than direct. After the Po expansion its strategic function diminished, since the entire city perimeter was now a vast fortress; but it remained, together with the ducal palace and the Castello, a retreat for the crown and an observation center from which the city was watched and dominated. Given the width and regularity of the streets, Turin could be crossed easily by soldiers and cannon, but there was no need for them to enter the city. The military camp layout of Turin was enough of a reminder to the population of the authoritative government whose power could be speedily enforced. Military requirements demanded wide and straight streets, and it was the military spirit that maintained the order and regularity of the layout.

Though the new streets were not precisely focused on bastions as proposed in the older military treatises, each bastion could be easily reached from a city street, and the street plan was coordinated with them, as we have seen. The proposed eight east-west streets were reduced to six, one for each of the new bastions (three of the bastions were directly connected through an east-west street to the citadel's *piazza d'armi*) . It could be argued that these connections were inherent in the grid plan, but the plan also represents a conscious decision to facilitate these military connections. Turin was easily crossed and hard to hide in. Thus the fortifications, and the military strategy determining their employment, produced the dominant formal characteristics of the plan of Turin.

The sixteenth-century military ideal of a city with radial streets connecting each bastion and gate to the centrally located palace of the prince was faintly echoed in the streets that connected the ducal compound to the main gates. These three streets, Doragrossa (the *decumanus* of the Roman settlement), Contrada Nuova (the axis of Città Nuova opened in 1615), and Contrada di

Po (the shortest connection between the Castello and bridge over the Po), were the spines of their respective neighborhoods; they were also the main streets leading into town from the entry gates. Framed by uniform houses (Dora-grossa was rendered uniform in the mid-eighteenth century), these streets provided magnificent circulation channels focused on the ducal governmental center for which they functioned as theatrical frames. To contemporaries these streets, whose form was borrowed from Vitruvian and Palladian prescriptions for the *stradone*, would have had an eloquent military character in their disciplined layout and austere linearity.[57] Combining the perspective scenography of the *feste* scenery with military display, the resultant street layout was both aesthetically pleasing and a rhetorically authoritative symbol of dynastic power. Similarly, military planning continued to haunt the form considered ideal for the perimeter of the city. This aesthetic representation of military content was reiterated in a late proposal for the expansion of Turin (fig. 116), made in 1676 by Donato Rossetti, a Jesuit and court mathematician, where the square walls of castrum-Turin have been transformed into the absolutist capital's almost perfectly oval fortification trace.

THE MAJOR PUBLIC spaces of the Po enlargement were Piazza Carignano, Piazza Carlina (Carolina or Ducale, now Carlo Emanuele II), the newly enlarged Piazza Castello, and Contrada di Po (or Corso di Po, now Via Po). The appearance of Piazza Carlina and Contrada di Po was strictly regulated by the crown through Amedeo di Castellamonte's designs, legislated by ducal edicts. While the Piazza Castello complex consisted almost entirely of crown and public buildings, the Piazza Carignano became the private enclave of Carlo Emanuele II's cousin Emanuele Filiberto, prince of Savoia-Carignano and the eldest son of Tommaso, who had been Cristina's brother-in-law and nemesis in the dynastic wars of 1640. In distinct contrast with Piazza Castello, which was the political and visual center of the city, Piazza Carignano was a smaller, subordinate square, dominated by the cadet branch of the House of Savoy.

Piazza Carignano, located close to Piazza Castello, was connected directly to the eastern, expanded section of the command center through a newly opened block-long street. The most important building on this square was Palazzo Carignano, hierarchically second only to the Palazzo Reale, but architecturally a much more significant structure. The square was defined by this

57. See chapter 1, note 26.

palace, by the theater that was built later in front of it, and by the Collegio dei Nobili—an educational institution run by the Jesuits for the offspring of the aristocracy—which faced only partially onto the square, flanking its short south side (fig. 117). The palace, an immense structure designed by Guarino Guarini, was built of exposed brick, as was the Collegio dei Nobili. Guarini refined the aesthetic of exposed brick, traditional in his hometown of Modena as well as in other towns along the Po, and reinforced its use in residential architecture in Turin. The clay used in the manufacture of bricks, which was taken from the Po, might partly explain the striking similarity in the color and texture of brick found in these towns.

The property upon which the palace was built had been given to Prince Tommaso by his father Duke Carlo Emanuele I in a deed made out on 3 August 1622; the site was then nothing but unbuilt land, still outside the fortified walls of the city.[58] This gesture had been part of Carlo Emanuele's policy to encourage the development of Turin. Although it did not become part of the city until Carlo Emanuele II undertook the expansion of Turin towards the Po, the gift made by Carlo Emanuele I shows, nonetheless, that he had indeed meant to expand Turin to the east as well as to the south, as I have demonstrated in chapter 2. The Carignano parcel was the largest private property within the Po enlargement area, and, deferring to the rank of the owner, the street that had been planned to be cut through it was deleted from the expansion plans. The palace is the most original secular structure in Turin, redolent with rhetorical and regal characteristics that distinguish it from the austerely military and uniform palaces of Vitozzi and Carlo and Amedeo di Castellamonte. Commissioned in 1679, the palace was sufficiently complete to be habitable in 1683.[59] It was finished in time for the wedding in 1684 of Emanuele Filiberto, who was obliged to marry in order to ensure the dynastic succession (between 1684 and 1699 he was the heir apparent to the duchy). Although neither Guarini nor the prince could foresee this development—or the fact that the Savoia-Carignano were eventually to become kings of Italy—the palace was built on a scale fit for a royal residence (fig. 118). Its design echoes Bernini's first and second projects for Louis XIV's Louvre palace, which Guarini

58. AST. Sez. Ia, Azienda Savoia-Carignano, cat. 3, 3 August 1622.

59. The most detailed analysis of this building and its site is by Henry A. Millon, "Guarino Guarini and the Palazzo Carignano," (Ph.D. diss., Harvard, 1964); see also Mario Passanti, *Nel mondo magico di Guarino Guarini* (Turin, 1963), 17–47; and for color illustrations, Harold Alan Meek, *Guarino Guarini and His Architecture* (New Haven, 1988), 88–111.

may have seen in Paris in 1665 (fig. 119).[60] The swell of the oval *salone* and curved stair ramps at the center of the western elevation facing Piazza Carignano, and the giant Corinthian pilasters that unify the *piano nobile* and the mezzanine levels above it, recall Bernini's first project. Its design has been praised as the summation of centuries of research by Italian architects, focused on the development of a continuous movement from facade and entry, through vestibules and staircases, to the main public reception room.[61] The path from the main entry to the main salone follows a 360-degree curve, a movement subsequently extolled as most perfect in academic as well as modernist architecture.[62] The palace is unrivaled in the originality of its architectural conception and in the eccentricity of its decorative system. The surprise provoked by the ornamental detail of the orders, the tortured brick frames of the windows, and the overwrought cornices is unmatched by any other facade in Turin (fig. 120).

The only building with a similar facade, where the walls are whittled down to mere strips between the tall, densely spaced, and heavily framed windows, is the Collegio dei Nobili built by Guarini on the south side of Piazza Carignano, diagonally across the square from the palace (fig. 121). This building was initially both religious and secular, since it housed the school of the Jesuits attended by the sons of the nobility. The site originally granted to the Jesuits in 1678 by the regent Giovanna Battista—on Piazza Carlina, the new square of the Po expansion—was exchanged by them in 1679 for a much larger and more centrally located lot extending north from Piazza Reale to Piazza Castello.[63] If the original plan for the Jesuit enclave had been realized, rather than eventually facing its own theater Palazzo Carignano would have been faced with the Jesuits' church and their Casa Professa.[64] The planned Jesuit compound would have thus stretched from Piazza Castello all the way to Piazza

60. For Bernini's trip, his influence, and comments upon Guarini's work, see Cecil Gould, *Bernini in France: An Episode in Seventeenth-Century History* (Princeton, 1982), 2, 40, and *passim*; for Guarini's stay in France see David R. Coffin, "Padre Guarino Guarini in Paris," *Journal of the Society of Architectural Historians*, 15 (1956): 3–11.

61. Henry A. Millon, *Baroque and Rococo Architecture* (New York, 1963), 22.

62. I am referring to the concept of "promenade" borrowed by modernist architects such as Le Corbusier from Beaux-Arts architectural terminology.

63. Duboin, 908, 4 April 1678 and 14 January 1679.

64. AST, Sez. Riunite, Azienda Savoia-Carignano, 27 Sept. 1680: "Tenor di conventione stabilita et accordata tra il Ser[enissi]mo Principe Emanuele Filiberto Amedeo di Savoia e li R[everendissi]mi P[adri] o sia Collegio del Gesù di q[ues]ta città per causa del sito che detti P[adri] devono allienare a S[ua] A[ltezza] Ser[enissi]ma a fine di lasciare una conveniente

Reale, encompassing the cadet branch's square as well, and would have successfully challenged the prominently located Theatines, who were ensconced
next to the royal residence.

But the Collegio, begun like the palace in 1679, was not completed as
planned, because the funds offered by Giovanna Battista did not suffice for its
construction. In 1688 a portion of the building was occupied, however. As it
stands today, it is the result of construction work completed in 1824.[65] Although the elevations are visually divided into three floors by unbroken entablatures, the height of the building is enhanced by the sustained verticality and
the great number of tall windows, whose pediments embrace the mezzanine
window above and thus stretch it out further. The wall is merely hinted at
between this proliferation of openings, orders of architecture, and additional
decorative embellishment (fig. 122).[66] As in the neighboring Palazzo Carignano, the facades of the Collegio, the walls, window frames, pilasters, and
decorations, are all made of exposed brick, which enhances the expressive
quality of the fluid decoration. In the expansion of Turin exposed brick had
been used for only two kinds of construction, the cladding of the fortification
and the buildings of the ducal family. In his only two buildings with facades—
that is, with an urbanistic expression—Guarini adopted, amplified, and raised
the language of this native vernacular to higher levels of architectural meaning.
He demonstrated that exposed brick could be convincingly tortured into
forms resembling closely the orders of classical architecture, while the use of
this unlikely and ignoble material allowed him to take flights of innovative
departure from the accepted Baroque canon in Piedmont.[67]

Piazza davanti il Palazzo di d[ett]a A[ltezza] Ser[eniss]ma. . . . Da prendersi detto sitto in
modo che la giusta metta d'esso venghi a corrispondere al centro della porta mag[ggio]re
del d[ett]o Palazzo. . . . Hanno promesso [the Jesuits] di far construere la Chiesa che dovra
servir a d[ett]o nuovo Colleggio giusto avanti la Piazza, e Palazzo sud[et]to in modo che la
Porta mag[gio]re della Chiesa corisponda a quella del Palazzo di S[ua] A[ltezza]
Ser[enissi]ma." The Savoia-Carignano family built a theater in the piazza through royal dispensation (1753) that nullified this clause in the same document of 1680: "non potra S[ua]
A[ltezza] Ser[enissi]ma suoi Heredi, e success[o]ri, nel sitto della Piazza far construer alcuna
fabrica ma restera sempre d[ett]o sitto vacuo e destinato a Piazza." I owe notice of this
document to Henry A. Millon.

65. Andreina Griseri, *Le metamorfosi del barocco* (Turin, 1967), 204–5.

66. For a convincing graphic analysis see the drawings of Passanti, *Mondo magico*, 49–51.

67. On the design of the palace and its materials see Passanti, *Mondo magico*, 18–32; and
Giuseppe Luigi Marini, *L'architettura barocca in Piemonte* (Turin, 1963), 84. See also Giulio
Carlo Argan, review of *Theatrum Novum Pedemontii* by A. E. Brinckmann, in *Zeitschrift für*

Guarini's brick architecture, innovative and inimitable, nonetheless influenced greatly the appearance of the largest building of the Po expansion, the hospital of San Giovanni designed by Amedeo di Castellamonte (fig. 123). The crown donated half of the site for this hospital originally quartered in Città Vecchia.[68] Begun by Amedeo in 1680, the building was completed by Baroncello in 1689 and jointly financed by the ducal treasury and the city.[69] The crossing of its two immensely long and high wards is marked by a chapel, and surrounding wings enclose four interior *cortili*. The four facades of exposed brick are of monumental dimensions; staggeringly long and unrelieved by surface decoration, they exude power and authority (fig. 124). Although the main elevation consists of three stories with taller central and end pavilions, the interior has only two floors. Architectural detail and ornament were reserved for the vestibule and the grand staircase connecting it to the upper levels, but its military character—the column shafts are banded and rusticated—does not belie the overall effect of the building, which is one of vastness and massive but melancholy strength.

Piazza Carignano is the smallest of the planned public squares of modern Turin, but it still plays its part in the representation of power. It differs both from the Piazza Reale and the pre-1673 Piazza Castello, in that it is dominated by one single palace, whose architectural expression is reinforced by the building of the most militant religious order. It is significant, however, that the square is dominated by Palazzo Carignano rather than the church of the Jesuits as initially intended. In maintaining the secular message of the other public spaces in Turin, this square aligns itself with the principal program of the enlargement, that of proclaiming the power of the royal dukes of Savoy, despite the novel architectural detailing of the building elevations.

The other new square of the Po expansion, Piazza Carlina, was planned as an urbanistic and architectural whole. In her edict of December 1675 Giovanna Battista had listed it among the sites that were under ducal tutelage. Houses around it had to be of uniform height and decorated as prescribed in the design made by Amedeo di Castellamonte.[70] Since the intent was to match Piazza

---

Kunstgeschichte, 1 (1932): 233–36; and Argan, "Per una storia dell'architettura piemontese," *L'arte*, 4 (1933): 391–97.

68. For the history of this institution see Silvio Solero, *Storia dell'ospedale di San Giovanni Battista e della città di Torino* (Turin, 1959).

69. Nino Carboneri, "Architettura," in *Mostra del barocco piemontese*, ed. Vittorio Viale (Turin, 1963), 1:36.

70. Borelli, 933: "Dovendo però essere tutte uniformi nel disegno esteriore le fabriche, che si faranno attorno à detta Piazza, conforme al disegno del Conte Amedeo Castellamonte

Reale, the urban masterpiece of Città Nuova, the square was one of the most important elements of the ducal planning program.

Shown as a rectangular open space in Borgonio's view of Turin (fig. 125), Piazza Carlina was to have been bisected by the east-west street that connected the citadel and Piazza Reale to the eastern end of the expanded city. But in the "presentation" plan of the Po expansion it is evident that initially Piazza Carlina was designed as an octagonal space (fig. 96). As well as this east-west street tying it to Piazza Reale and the north-south street linking to Contrada di Po, the four blocks surrounding the square were further divided into eight by four short, diagonal streets. Each irregular block—four were four-sided while the other four were irregular pentagons—was to have a colonnaded portico on its elevation along the square; this unifying architectural element would have imparted continuity to the square despite the disruption caused by the eight entering streets. A detailed study sheet of the square, previously unpublished, shows that the corners of each block on the square side were to be defined, and anchored, by tower-like structures that interrupted the continuity provided by the porticoes and would be taller than the two-story wing they enclosed (fig. 126). These towers resemble elements adopted in the design of Piazza Castello, specifically the framing towers of Piazza Reale, while the coupled columns of the portico refer to the design of the ground level of Piazza Reale made by Carlo di Castellamonte but realized by his son Amedeo. The sample palace design provided in this study—unsigned, but probably by Amedeo or his assistants—has a very old-fashioned quality, especially in the design of the corners, which turns each block into an independent unit and could not be more distant from the imaginative solutions being offered by Guarini in his palace design. The overall conception had little of the elegant sophistication of the octagonal Place Vendôme in Paris, begun in 1698 by Mansart, but it owed a great debt of influence to two different sources. One is the circular *rond-point*, transferred from French landscape design into urban planning; the other is the central square of the ideal city, or more precisely the ideal fortress, whose form mimics the layout of the fortification trace. Thus, if the trace has twelve curtain walls connecting the twelve bastions, the central square must be in turn a dodecagon, with a street separating each side of the polygon and connecting it to

---

Primo Ingegniero di S[ua] A[ltezza] R[eale]." See also note 11, above; and AST, Sez. Riunite, Controllo Finanze, 4 April 1678: "Vogliamo però che detti Padri [the Jesuits] nel fabricare detto sito [in Piazza Ducale] siano tenuti all'osservanza dell'ordine nostro delli 16 Decembre 1675 ed inquante ai portici sopra la Piazza del dissegno che ne verrà fatto dal Conte Amedeo Castellamonte P[rim]o Ingegnere di S[ua] A[ltezza] R[eale]."

the fortification trace. The octagonal plan of Piazza Carlina was a fusion of the French and the military models, tamed by the classicizing porticoes.

A revision of the presentation plan signed by Garove, and datable to c. 1678, shows discomfort with the layout and location of Piazza Carlina (fig. 127). The octagonal version has been slipped farther south, below the east-west street that it had straddled and which linked it to Piazza Reale. In this version, the square is crossed by only one of the expansion's orthogonal streets, the north-south one linking it to Contrada di Po, but it is linked to the surrounding grid through the same eight short, diagonal spurs. The octagonal space seems to be carved out of the large rectangular block, and thus disconnected from the rest of the city. It is clear from the same study sheet that a square piazza was also being considered. The configuration of streets and blocks surrounding the square piazza draws heavily on military precedents, most notably the design of squares proposed by Cataneo for ideal fortified cities (fig. 128). Evidently, the form of the square was not appreciated, and conflicts arose between would-be builders and the crown. Eager to help the construction of the square, in her edict of 1678 Giovanna Battista renounced the uneconomical design, recognizing officially that the octagonal form was causing problems in land measurement and subdivision, and approved a traditional rectangular square with two streets crossing it.[71] The regulation for the design of the individual buildings, upheld but not illustrated in the edict, was not successfully enforced.

Although in the *Theatrum* Piazza Carlina was shown entirely surrounded by uniform structures, it is evident from subsequent printed and autograph plans of the entire city, as well as from partial plans of the area, that the design of this square was not thoroughly worked out. The final layout follows closely Garove's study and sacrifices spatial unity in favor of a direct connection to Piazza Reale. The blocks were redimensioned: the resulting eight building sites are rectangular, smaller than most rectangular blocks in the Po expansion, and hugely different from one another in size and proportions. The four smaller blocks at the center of the composition were intended each for one palace; two shallow and elongated rectangular blocks form the north edge of the square, while only the two southern blocks could accommodate traditional large buildings with courts and gardens. The enlarged orthogonal blocks around Piazza Carlina resulted in increased frontage; because the residential buildings forming the square were entered from the side streets, all of this frontage was used for shops. This manner of increasing commercial frontage, and of sepa-

71. Borelli, 934; see note 18, above.

rating residential and commercial circulation, was systematically adopted in the design of subsequent squares, such as the eighteenth-century Piazza Savoia in the western expansion of Turin. Measures were taken to facilitate life in the new neighborhood; the major step involved permission granted in August 1678 by the regent to the city council to set up market structures in Piazza Carlina. This was given in response to a request by the city council, but the crown reserved the right to transfer the pavilions elsewhere if they diminished the beauty (or *prospettiva*) of the piazza.[72] After the transfer of the marketplace, having worked out a design compromise with the crown architect Castellamonte, the city built four pavilions destined to shelter the vendors within the remaining open area of Piazza Carlina (fig. 129). This reduced the open area of the square and screened the four rectangular blocks north and south of it, occupied by residential buildings, from the square.

The register of 1698 listing debtors of the crown, mentioned above, shows that by the end of the century the land around Piazza Carlina was privately owned, and that, in the attempt to maneuver around the deadlines for construction promulgated periodically by the crown, many owners had sold and then reacquired lots adjacent to the square. The range of social backgrounds was quite wide, from merchants to titled nobility, including various employees of the crown, such as Giorgio Tasniere, who had engraved the foundation

72. Duboin, 942, gives the council's petition: "E parte di buona politica di procurare di dar tutte le commodità possibili a particolari, che introducono robbe nella città, ad effetto d'invitarne molti al concorso, per il che la medesima si rende più doviziosa, e popolata; che perciò avendo veduto la città come il mercato del vino resta in un luogo troppo aperto, e sottoposto a' raggi del sole, per il di cui calore il vino si guasta, et all'ingiurie de' tempi, e li commercianti non puo[so]nno col fermarsi soffrir nella maggior parte dell'anno l'ardor delli sudetti raggi, e l'incommodità delle pioggie, nevi, ed altre ingiurie del tempo, ha pensato di introdur nella piazza Carlina, ed in essa farvi ale all'intorno, o altrove quando disconvenisse alla prospettiva di essa piazza. . . . E parimenti in detta piazza distribuir luoghi, o sian quadri de' banchi per vender le vittovaglie come si pratica nella piazza dell'erbe per maggior commodità delli cittadini, ed habitanti nel nuovo recinto, ed da essi ricavarne un moderato emolumento per sovvenir alla mede[si]ma ne' publici bisogni, il che riuscerà ancora di decoro alla città, e di vantagio al commercio, e causerà, che più presto si renderà detto nuovo recinto popolato." The regent's reply is as follows (ibid.): "M[adama] R[eale] inclinata sommamente al bene del pubblico, agli avantaggi della città, e commodità de' forastieri, accorda il contenuto nel controscritto capo: con che li luoghi nei quali si dovranno tener banchi per commodità de'venditori, et per la construzione de' narrati coperti venghino approvati dal conte Amedeo Castellamonte primo ingegnere di S[ua] A[ltezza] R[eale], e riuscendo in qualsivoglia tempo tali coperti disdicevoli alla piazza, si trasportino in altro posto che dal medesimo primo ingegnere sarà stimato più proprio."

plaque of the Po expansion and the illustrations for Amedeo di Castellamonte's book on Venaria Reale, and Giacomo Henrico La Riviera, an auditor of Fabriche e Fortificationi under the regent Giovanna Battista. Both Tasniere and La Riviera, who were strategically positioned at court, probably acquired their parcels through their close connection with the Patrimoniale. The size of lots ranged from 8 *tavole* (Tasniere's) to 74 *tavole* (owned by the heirs of a Count Gotio).[73] (One *tavola* equaled 4 square *trabucchi*, or about 38 square meters.) The other inhabitants of the square included the monastery of Santa Croce, whose church was later designed by Juvarra, and the Jewish community, whose Ghetto Nuovo or Piccolo adjacent to the Ghetto Vecchio seems to have occupied an entire block on the west side of the square, as seen in the labeled plan of Piazza Carlina. The uneven blocks, the uneven social standing of the inhabitants, and the introduction of permanent market pavilions relegated Piazza Carlina to a secondary position in the hierarchy of urban spaces. Its distant location, shunned by the Jesuits, from the city's center and from Contrada di Po had by itself induced the divorce of the square from the vital spaces of Turin associated with dynastic rituals and political hierarchy.[74]

While Piazza Carlina was planned *ex novo* as the eastern counterpart to Piazza Reale, Piazza Castello was conceived as an enlargement of the existing main square of the city. After the expansion east towards the Po, Piazza Castello's visual appearance became the spatial counterpart of its role as the literal and representational center of Turin. The new square was made of two parts: the original Piazza Castello, and its mirror image added to the eastern side of the Castello. These two parts, which eventually became one large square, were separated from one another by galleries, connecting the Castello with the Palazzo Reale to the north and with the palace of Marchese di San Germano to

---

73. AST, Sez. Riunite, art. 552 (see note 26, above). La Riviera had acquired two large parcels from the Patrimoniale, one on 7 March 1676 of 17 *tavole* at 10 *doppie* per *tavola* (inventory number 54), another on 10 April 1683 of 25 *tavole* at 5 *doppie* per *tavola* (inventory number 79); on 17 April 1683 he sold 8 *tavole* to Tasniere at 7½ *doppie* per *tavola* (inventory number 108); and then on 8 May 1683 he turned around and sold 7 *tavole* to Francesco Borello for 10 *doppie* per *tavola* (inventory number 66). Gotio bought 32 *tavole* on 28 April 1684 at 11 *doppie* per *tavola* from the artillery captain Nicolo Belgrano (inventory number 50).

74. In AST, Sez. Riunite, Controllo Finanze, 14 January 1679, the regent Giovanna Battista acknowledged the request of the Jesuits for a more central site: "ci hanno fatto conoscere essere necessario per più pronta esseguitione di questa vantaggiosa intrapresa [the Collegio dei Nobili] di destinare a luogo del sud[ett]o sito posto in un angolo molto appartato della Città et in cui non s'è ancor dato principio a fabricare un'altro sito più concentrato."

the south (fig. 114). Part of the latter gallery was demolished by the end of the seventeenth century, promoting communication between the two halves of the square centered upon the Castello (Fig. 115). However, it is unclear whether the northern gallery was penetrable from one side to the other at ground level because the views from the *Theatrum* are conflicting: in the view of the gallery there is a portico only at the east side (fig. 130), while the view of Piazza Castello (fig. 102) shows a portico on the western, earlier side. It was only from the upper level of the galleries and the Castello that the open space of both halves of Piazza Castello could be enjoyed simultaneously.

The facades of the western half of Piazza Castello, designed by Vitozzi in 1608 and composed of one repeated bay, were copied for the definition of the enlarged, but still bisected, square (fig. 131). The buildings at the north and east sides, intended for the ducal administration, were clad in exposed brick, whereas on the south and east sides below Contrada di Po buildings were plastered and whitewashed. The two domains, public and private, cohabited as two halves of the same large square, and yet could be easily distinguished. The most important palaces of the nobility, however, were not built behind these uniform facades, as they had been built behind the facades of Piazza Reale; more were located along seemingly secondary streets, as free-standing structures enjoying proximity to the fashionable Palazzo Carignano.

The most glaring illustration of the absolutist ducal government was the establishment of Piazza Castello, together with the *cour d'honneur* or Piazzetta Reale, as the command center of Turin and as the pivot connecting the three parts of town. Through the design of the new expansion Piazza Castello was endowed with centrality, and thus put into relief the dominant position of the ducal family. This requirement may partly explain why two diagonal connections proposed in Carlo Emanuele I's autograph study in the 1610s and then reiterated in subsequent projects—between the citadel and the Po gate and between Piazza Reale and the Po gate—were not implemented in the final street layout. In the new scheme, to go from one part of town to the other one had to pass through the center. Piazza Castello became the terminal focus of the three streets that structured the three parts of town, the spines of the city: the Doragrossa, the Contrada Nuova, and the Contrada di Po. The convergence of these ceremonial axial streets upon Piazza Castello gave constant visibility to the ducal center. Of these three streets, the north-south Contrada Nuova was perhaps the most important. The rebuilding of the main facade of the Palazzo Reale, begun in the 1640s, had reinforced its connection with the Contrada Nuova by placement of the portal as the focus of the axial street.[75] Representations of the city, such as the one in Tasniere's illustration for Tesauro's history of Turin, demonstrate forcefully the strength of the connection between Palazzo Reale and Porta Nuova (fig. 132). In this illustration, the plan of the city is held so as to stress the north-south axis of Contrada Nuova, which is widened in order to persuade the viewer of the spatial link from entry, to traversal of the city, and to arrival at the royal palace.

The ducal residence was surrounded on three sides by the three parts of the city, but at its northern edge it bordered on the fortifications (fig. 133). It thus maintained a double character, urban and military, a palace and a fortress. On the town side, the new expansion had made it the geographical center and removed its fortress-like position at the corner of the urban enclosure. A martial aspect was preserved in the Castello, separated from both halves of the piazza by a moat, but this is a medieval, decorative, emblematic militarism, as in the tower on the foundation medal or the stage set for *Amor bandito*. Expansion towards the north, which would have placed the Palazzo Reale at the literal center of Turin, was prevented by topographical conditions: there was a sharp change in the level of the terrain at the northeastern corner of the city, and the Dora beyond the drop-off was an unpredictable stream until its canalization in the nineteenth century. Moreover, the edge location may have helped to ensure the security of the ducal family, as well as providing it with easy access to the Bastion Verde, where Carlo Emanuele II installed his *petite maison*, and the emergency gate (fig. 134); the inscription on this view of the Bastion Verde, in fact, stresses that it provides the monarch with both delight and security.[76] In many illustrations the marginal and militant quality of the ducal residence is implied; it is often shown as a fortified castle, and its relation to the city is not unlike that of the citadel (fig. 135).

Simultaneously with the doubling in size of Piazza Castello and the expansion to the east, the western part of Piazza Castello was undergoing significant transformations. Work continued on the expansion and embellishment of

---

75. For the complete history of this reconstruction effort, see Marziano Bernardi, "Le sedi," in *Mostra del barocco piemontese*, 1:14–15.

76. The inscription is:

Propugnaculum cui viride nomen

Cum regii palatii, atque hortorum prospectu

Ad securitatem, atque delicias

Regiorum Sabaudiae Ducum

For Carlo Emanuele's libertine inclinations, see Ortensia Mancini, *I piaceri della stupidità,* ed. Daria Galateria (Palermo, 1987), 90–91, n. 62. I owe this reference to Marco F. Diani.

Palazzo Reale, which had been rebuilt for Carlo Emanuele II's wedding in 1663. In 1666 work started on the new building of San Lorenzo, the palatine chapel located on the square at the corner with the street that connects Piazza Castello to the Palazzo di Città, the city hall whose reconstruction was simultaneous with that of Palazzo Reale. This chapel had been founded in 1573 as the fulfillment of an ex-voto made by Duke Emanuele Filiberto in 1557, during the battle of Saint-Quentin.[77] A representation of this crucial event for the Savoy dynasty forms the decorative low relief front of the main altar in the rebuilt church. San Lorenzo was the headquarters of the Theatines, who had been invited to Turin by Carlo Emanuele I in 1621; Vittorio Amedeo I had granted them the use of the palatine chapel in 1634, when they promised to build an important church. They attempted to fulfill their promise quickly; the foundation stone for San Lorenzo was laid on 6 June 1634, with an inscription provided by Tesauro who was at the time a favored preacher. The connection between the Savoy and the Theatine order continued, despite the dominant presence of the Jesuits, under Carlo Emanuele II, who not only led the Easter procession of 1650 dressed in the Theatine habit,[78] but in 1666 encouraged the rebuilding of their church by employing Guarino Guarini, himself a Theatine monk, as the architect of the new San Lorenzo.

Carlo Emanuele II had appointed Guarini from 1668 as engineer of the chapel for the Holy Shroud or Santissima Sindone.[79] As we have seen, this important relic, then thought to have enveloped the dead body of Christ, had been among the Savoy dynasty's treasures since the fourteenth century and in Turin since 1575. Although Guarini's two religious structures are astonishing achievements in architectural design and statics, neither has a public facade. San Lorenzo and the chapel of the Holy Shroud are both visible in Piazza Castello, but they assert themselves through their highly original domes, which dominate the skyline of the square. The chapel, buried between the cathedral and Palazzo Reale, forges the link between the religious and secular rule of the city. This link is literal, allowing easy passage from the ducal residence into the cathedral through the chapel of the Holy Shroud, as we have seen it used during Carlo Emanuele's first wedding in 1663. San Lorenzo, actually entered from Piazza Castello, was supposed to have an elaborate facade designed by Guarini; instead the church was masked by a front composed

77. For the history of this building see Giuseppe Michele Crepaldi, *La real chiesa di San Lorenzo in Torino* (Turin, 1963), reviewed by Henry A. Millon, *Art Bulletin*, 47 (1965): 532–33.

78. Crepaldi, *San Lorenzo*, 71.

79. *Schede Vesme*, 2:551.

to mimic closely the rest of the western elevation of the square, as designed by Vitozzi at the beginning of the seventeenth century.

Guarini's two other churches in Turin, although promoted if not actually commissioned by Carlo Emanuele II, do not have a public counterpart to their astonishingly original and personal interiors.[80] It is significant that, despite the appreciation and respect manifested by Carlo Emanuele and by the regent Giovanna Battista, Guarini was not given a royal commission for a building with a public facade. This suggests that his highly expressive style, although admired by the sovereign and fully adopted by the cadet branch of the family for the Palazzo Carignano, was not suitable for the austere version of the Baroque that had become entrenched in Turin through its ideological associations with the ruling dynasty.

Work on Piazza Castello itself seems to have proceeded fairly quickly. The area between the moat of the Castello and the moat of the old eastern fortification was leveled, and the earth moved by the *cavaterra* in charge was measured by November 1674. The same team was paid in October 1675 for leveling another section of the new eastern extension of the Piazza Castello.[81] Leveling of new streets and squares was followed by paving, although documents suggest that this activity was not restricted to the expansion areas. Thus in July and August 1675 payments were made for the pavement of the cathedral square, Piazza di San Giovanni; this embellishment was probably due to the preparation of the area for Carlo Emanuele II's funeral.[82] Although payments were made for the leveling of the new part of Piazza Castello biweekly, and then monthly, between July 1678 and August 1679, the project to level the

80. For the Immacolata Concezione (della Missione), see Tamburini, 232–41; for the Consolata, see Elwin Clark Robison, "Guarino Guarini's Church of San Lorenzo in Turin" (Ph.D. diss., Cornell, 1985; rpt., Ann Arbor, 1986), 208–21.

81. This was the area between the Gran Galleria—the gallery connecting the old Galleria farther east to the wing where the royal theater was later built—and the riding school (Accademia). AST, Sez. Riunite, Fabriche e Fortificationi, art. 201, 2 November 1674: "Il tes[orie]re g[e]n[er]ale Giovanni Matteo Belli pagara al cavaterra Giacomo Baijetto livre cento venti due d'arg[en]to a p[ezzo] 20 l'una per trabucchi trenta e piedi tre di cava di terra c'ha fatto per spianamento della nuova Piazza Castello tra il fosso di Piazza Castello e quello della vecchia fortificatione di questa citta com'appare per l'alligata misura." Ibid., 15 October 1675: "Tutto il cavo di terra fatto di Giacomo Baijetto per il spianamento della piazza del Castello et nell'angolo tra la gran galleria et accademia ascende a trabucchi settanta due piedi cinque oncie sette."

82. AST, Sez. Riunite, Fabriche e Fortificationi, art. 201, 12 September 1675: "Il tes[orie]re gen[era]le Giovanni Matteo Belli pagara al sternitore Bernardo Garzena livre due-

piazza entirely was put out for bids only on 22 November 1683, and the contract awarded on 1 December, requiring the work to be finished within twelve months.[83]

The centrality of Piazza Castello, as the largest square of the city surrounded by the chief ducal residences and the principal government agencies, was further reinforced by several additional buildings sponsored by the crown. These extended the actual territory dominated by the ducal family and its retainers from the center of the enlarged city deeply into the Po expansion area. Carlo Emanuele had asked his Consiglio di Finanze as early as July 1674 to request bids for the construction of these buildings, many designed by Amedeo di Castellamonte. They were a riding school or *accademia* with a chapel, *sala delle feste*, and stables; a theater; a foundry; a *trincotto* (an enclosed space for a game resembling bowls); and a portico with shops. This important complex of buildings would thus be dedicated to the duke's favorite pursuits—money-making, theatrical display, and the formation of young cavalry officers.[84] After a series of bids and negotiations, on 20 October 1674 a contract

cento quaranta quatro soldi dieci danari due d'arg[en]to a p[ezzo] 20 l'una per supplem[en]to di lire 484.16.2 simili a che rillevano li sterniti da lui disfatti e rifatti nella contrada avanti il quartiere de Todeschi e nella piazza di San Giovanni e altri sterniti nuovi fatti ivi di pietre con esportatione di terra com'appare per alligata misura e estimo del Gaspare Ferrero."

83. AST, Sez. Riunite, Fabriche e Fortificationi, art. 201, fols. 21–22, 25–26, 29–30, 33–34, 36, 39, 41, 46, 49, 51, 71; and art. 199, fols. 70, 76, 78.

84. AST. Sez. Riunite, Fabriche e Fortificationi, art. 201, 20 October 1674: "Ad'ogn'uno sia manifesto che essendosi S[ua] A[ltezza] R[eale] risolto di far fare nel recinto del nuovo ingrandimento di questa citta fra altre fabriche gia delliberate un'accademia con sala delle feste, teatro, trincotto, capella d'essa accademia, portico con botteghe e scuderie nuove il tutto conforme al disegno e instruttione del sig[no]r conte e p[rim]o ingeg[ne]re di S[ua] A[ltezza] R[eale] Amedeo di Castellamonte ci habbia verbalmente ordinato di procurarne partiti ragionevoli e deliberarne l'impresa." The competition for the building contracts had been publicly announced on 28 July, but the bids that were received on 8 August were too high. ("In seguito al cui commando habbiamo sotto li 28 luglio prossime passato fatto affiggere nei luoghi soliti della p[rese]nte citta li biletti per invitare concorrenti all'impresa d'esse fabriche e siano comparsi avanti noi li 7 dell'hora scaduto agosto, giorno in cui ne cadeva il deliberamento alcuni capi m[urato]ri con luoro partiti quali essaminati e riconosciuti che li prezzi erano troppo eccessivi doppo sentiti separatamente detti concorrenti siano seguiti alcuni ribassi de mede[si]mi prezzi ma per essersi ancora questi considerati eccessivi, habbiamo stimato di differirne il deliberamento con nuova monitione.") The bidding process was repeated on 17 August, when the Consiglio received two low bids and convinced a third group to come even further down. The duke was then informed that three teams of con-

was signed with four builders who undertook to complete the theater, *sala delle feste*, and the chapel and public rooms of the academy facing Piazza Castello by October 1675.[85] While the contractors were threatened with a large fine if they did not meet their deadline, it was the crown treasury that had to bear the burden of payments for this extensive and swift construction schedule.

The completion of this prestigious building complex drew upon the most advanced resources of design, construction, measurement, and computation. Payments were to be based on the cost of various kinds of built masonry construction, calculated per linear *trabucco*; interestingly, the ordinary wall made of four courses of stone and one course of brick was the least costly, while walls built only of brick cost more.[86] The 1674 contract explicitly referred to the regulations concerning measurement of constructed foundations and walls that had been established in 1633 by Vittorio Amedeo I.[87] But the mensuration process had reached new levels of sophistication with the publication, in Turin and under the patronage of Carlo Emanuele himself, of two treatises by Guarini: the erudite *Euclidus adauctus* (1671) and *Il modo di misurare le fabbriche* (1674), which provided practical instructions for the measurement of surfaces and volumes of increasing complexity. Guarini's methods of measuring buildings showed the overlap of interests between his research on stereotomy and the Consiglio di Finanze's concern to measure accurately the construction work for which it was billed, as well as demonstrating that the Theatine architect and priest was able to consider both theoretical and practical architectural problems. His instructions in measurement allowed him to contribute even to those ducal projects, like these buildings on and near the Piazza Cas-

---

tractors were available and invited to choose between them; he rejected the team already engaged in the construction of the expansion's fortification, as well as the lowest bidder, choosing a team of four contractors only one of whom was employed on another ducal project.

85. Ibid.: "Patto apposto e accordato e espressamente convenuto che caso detti capi m[aest]ri manchino di dar al coperto li corpi di fabrica promesi sovra e infra esspresi fra tutto ottobre dell'anno pros[sim]o cioe la salla delle feste, il teatro, trincotto, portico con botteghe, la capella dell'accademia, e stanze risguardanti verso Piazza Castello patirrano la diminutione delle lire 2,000 ribassate dal maestro Carlo Righino."

86. AST, Sez. Riunite, Fabriche e Fortificationi, art. 201, 28 October 1674; the cost of all-brick construction was sixteen *lire* rather than fourteen *lire*.

87. Ibid.: "Le grosseze delle muraglie saranno luoro date dall'ingeg[ne]re c'havera la direttione di d[ett]e fabriche, e per quelle che li saranno ordinati tutti di mattoni se li fara rag[io]ne nella misura conforme all'ordine del duca Vittorio Amedeo di glo[riosa] mem[oria] qual dovra osservarsi in'ogni misura di d[ett]e fabriche."

tello, that he did not himself design.[88] As the construction of these buildings proceeded, it was regularly measured by employees of the crown, who processed payment orders in accordance with the original contract. That document had not included hand-carved stone finishes and the iron needed for locks, which were provided separately by the ducal treasury; [89] this may well mean that the details had not been designed yet, and that they were not as advanced as the foundation, enclosure, partitioning, and paving of the buildings. As a reflection of the importance of this work, the crown raised the social status of the four chief contractors: their contract incorporated them into the bureaucracy for the duration of the enterprise and granted them the right to carry arms, an extraordinary privilege in the hierarchical military culture of the court.[90]

Amedeo di Castellamonte, who supervised the entire construction and instructed contractors about the materials to be used as the project advanced, was the designer of this large group of surprisingly uniform buildings. Despite their varied functions and spatial requirements, the architectural expression adopted by Amedeo was ruthlessly pared down. He chose to use only shallow wings, and an austerely limited set of decorative elements, in the composition of the theater, riding-school, ballroom, and stables. The result, whose spirit if not detail is accurately captured in the view of the eastern portion of Piazza Castello from the *Theatrum* (fig. 102) is a decorated "thick wall" whose primary role is the enclosure, perhaps even the fencing in, of the public spaces of the city. In addition, the relentlessly uniform facades impress viewers with their regularity, which throws a thick veil over the varied spaces and enter-

88. Guarini's methods also helped in the preparation of estimates of quantities needed for construction from drawings. The subtitle of *Modo di misurare* ("in cui non vi è corpo e quasi non vi è superficie purche godi di qualche regolarità, che matematicamente non resti misurato riducendosi a calcoli facilissimi anche quei pieni e quei corpi di cui sin hora non è stato modo, che li misuri") fully clarifies his claim to innovative contribution. See also Meek, *Guarini*, 144–46; and Werner Muller, "Guarini e la stereotomia," in *Guarini e la internazionalità del barocco*, 1:531–56.

89. AST, Sez. Riunite, Fabriche e Fortificationi, art. 201, 28 October 1674: "Saranno a carico del sig[no]r patrimoniale le radici e ferramenti che saranno necessarie alle pred[ett]e fabriche e quello di mede[si]mi capi m[aest]ri impresari di metterle in opera. . . . Tutti gl'ornamenti delle porte, finestre, architravi, fornelli, e cornicioni si pagaranno all'estimo di due esperti."

90. Ibid.: "Si concede la reten[tio]ne e porto d'armi di misura, viaggiando, a detti im[presa]ri Ferro, Pighino, Solista e Bariffo durante il tempo d'essa luoro impresa con che non si abusino e ne diano nota all'ecc[elentissi]mo Senato e al sig[no]r seg[reta]ro sottos[critt]o."

prises within, and transforms them into stage-like frames, controlled by one master-mind, for the urban rituals enacted by and for the absolute sovereign. Amedeo's institutional buildings thus reinforced the architectural code, also supplied by him, that had been legislated for the Po expansion, effectively establishing the bureaucratic urban vocabulary of the absolutist government.

These crown buildings were also clearly distinguishable from the private residential buildings of the Po expansion because of their exposed red brick exterior, which extended the ducal settlement visually from the Piazza Castello into the Po expansion. Almost as though challenging the high cost of materials and the lack of good local craftsmen (the contractors were from Lugano and Lombardy), the buildings of the ducal program, like the fortifications of the city, were all finished in brick. There were probably several reasons for this. Turin had no marble quarries in its vicinity, and the local stone was not of good quality; granite and travertine were not readily available. It seems that even high-quality brick was difficult to produce in sufficient quantity.[91] Else-where, its occasional use may have been construed as a sign of poverty since it meant lack of stone or of the means of transporting stone. In Turin this seem-ing poverty of brick became a point of pride. Augustus was famous for having found Rome brick and left it marble, but Turin's historiographers proclaimed its pre-Augustan, indeed pre-Roman, antiquity. Brick evoked associations with other powerful dynasties: it had been used in the sixteenth century in the construction of urban palaces in Rome, Parma, and Piacenza by the Farnese, and we have seen in chapter 1 that the Savoy and the Farnese had overlapping artistic and military interests. Brick was consistently displayed and made part of the Savoy building program, a distinguishing mark in the urban fabric by the contrast it formed with privately built structures.

Except for Guarini's two palaces, and perhaps Amedeo's hospital, which dazzle with the virtuosity of their architectural massing, detail, and ornament achieved in brick, the austere, massive buildings of exposed brick made a vir-tue of their poverty—a costly one, as we have seen—and impressed viewers with their force. Part of this force came from the visual association between

91. Ibid.: "E per che d[ett]i imp[resa]ri asseriscono haver di riserva qualche quantita di mattoni per impiegare in esse fabriche nel p[ri]n[ci]pio del'anno ven[tu]ro e che venendoli divestiti o presi per altre fabriche di ord[in]e di S[ua] A[ltezza] R[eale] puotrebbe dilongarli l'avanzam[en]to delle opere a coperto come restano obligati di dare nel d[ett]o ven[tu]ro anno 1675 si dichiara che quando cio accadesse dovrano darne aviso al sig[no]r patrimoniale per saper la quantita presa, e per essa in tal caso detti imp[resa]ri saranno scarrigati solamente e non altrimenti del travaglio che con essi si sarebbe potuto fare al quale saranno tenuti supplire nell'anno seguente."

the ducal buildings and the fortifications of Turin, whose wall and bastions were clad in brick. This extensive and unabashed use of brick celebrated the victory over the initial poverty of building materials, and the resolute severity of the local architectural language. It represented the paradoxical admixture of the unbending pride and consequent lavishness of the military spirit, and the alpine frugality that imbued the character of the dukes of Savoy. Finally, the parallel promoted between the ducal palaces and the fortifications through the use of identical finishes was intended to demonstrate that ideologically the dukes of Savoy were one with the defenses of their town.

THE DUCAL BUILDINGS in Piazza Castello, continuing along the streets that opened east of the square, provided an important link between the center of Turin and its eastern extension. But the most important connection between Piazza Castello and the Po expansion area—and the most important example of a fundamental unit of Baroque city planning, the unified street— was the Contrada di Po, which stretched from the eastern edge of the square to the Po gate (fig. 98). Unlike Contrada Nuova, the major axis of Città Nuova, which had been designed *ex novo* to lead from the southern entry of the city directly to the ducal palace, the Contrada di Po followed the right-of-way of an existing road between the Castello gate and the bridge over the Po. The new version of the street began in a hemicycle in front of the Po gate, whose ornate design was probably provided by Michelangelo Garove, a close follower of Guarini and the principal ducal architect after 1683 (figs. 112, 136).[92] This hemicycle masked the oblique angle of the street, while at its other end a similar irregularity—Contrada di Po entered Piazza Castello diago- nally—was cleverly masked by a wedge-shaped building.

The unification of the Contrada di Po, remarked and praised by a number of visitors to Turin, was achieved despite the existing road, the oblique siting, and the need to incorporate a number of separate entities, either religious buildings already in place or new civic institutions planned for the Po expan- sion. Going from west to east, the university, the poorhouse (Ospedale di Carità or almshouse), and the churches of the Annunziata and of Sant' Antonio occupied parts of the five blocks of the north side of the street, while in the seven blocks of the south side there was only the church and monastery of San Francesco di Paola. Only San Francesco and the Annunziata assert themselves

92. *Schede Vesme*, 2:515–16; Carboneri, "Architettura," in *Mostra del barocco piemontese*, 1:37–38.

with an individualized facade visible from the street; the former is pulled back from the street's edge and framed by the adjacent porticoes, while the latter continued the typology of the porticoed ground level but with an architectural vocabulary distinct from the rest of the street (fig. 137). The buildings of the other institutions blend in entirely with the street and are adorned, with minor variations, by the prescribed facades of Amedeo di Castellamonte. The university building, designed by Garove and built by the city, was constructed from 1713 (fig. 138).[93] It occupied the entire second block east of Piazza Castello, across from Amedeo's riding school. The central rectangular *cortile* of the university is parallel to the street at its north (Contrada della Accademia), and so between it and Contrada di Po there is a wedge-shaped wall that masks the transition from the diagonal Contrada di Po to the rectangular street plan. In order to comply with the building code of Contrada di Po, the porticoed elevation facing that street was plastered and whitewashed, whereas the side elevations and the facade on the north side were finished in exposed, unplastered brick (fig. 139). The principal facade of the Ospedale di Carità conformed to the obligatory code of height and color, while the sides and the back, as at the university, were of exposed brick. The building was organized around several *cortili*, using a modified version of the generic hospital plan (fig. 140). The actual poorhouse was separated from Contrada di Po by a wing of individual apartments for rent.[94]

These potentially disparate materials owe their coherence to Amedeo di Castellamonte's repetitive facades and uniform buildings (fig. 141). As in Piazza Reale and the private half of Piazza Castello, the facades of the block-long buildings and the interior of the porticoes were plastered and whitewashed, forming a strong contrast with the dark brown-red color of the ducal buildings clad in brick. Amedeo borrowed heavily from his father's and Vitozzi's earlier

93. A letter patent of 10 March 1713 (Duboin, 953) bound the crown to repay the city council within ten years for the 200,000 *lire* it spent on the construction of the university.

94. The transfer of the Ospedale di Carità to its site on Contrada di Po had a long and intricate history. The institution had owned land in the Po suburb before the expansion took place, south of the main street adjacent to the convent of San Francesco di Paola (Cristina had built the church itself as an ex-voto, after her prayers for male heirs were fulfilled by the birth of Carlo Emanuele himself) and near what was to become Piazza Carlina. Parts of it had been lost as new streets and the square itself were opened, and subsequently the Ospedale received a parcel equivalent in size, which occupied the entire second block west from the Po gate, on the north side of the street. See Mario Passanti, "Ospedali del Seicento e del Settecento in Piemonte," *Atti e Rassegna Tecnica della Società degli Ingegneri e degli Architetti di Torino*, 5 (1951).

contributions to urban design in Turin (figs. 69, 101). His own innovation consists of taking the accepted form of the public square and adapting it to the overall composition of a street. Each block of the Contrada di Po was considered an entity, with rusticated corners and evenly spaced windows; nothing on the facade suggested that there might be several buildings behind the unified front. Despite the lack of originality, his design is elegantly severe, based upon an austere use of planes and lines that promote classically poised structures.[95] Amedeo's composition consists of two main floors above a portico that encompasses shops at the ground level and apartments in the mezzanine. There was a third, lower, attic floor (its balconies are of later date). The windows of the first *piano nobile* have alternating segmental and triangular pediments and strapwork frames. These pediments project into the areas between the first- and second-floor windows, creating a strong vertical continuity aided also by the visual crowding of pediments, string-courses, and sills. The windows of the second *piano nobile*, lower than the first, have horizontal lintels with a cornice above them and are framed by thin pilasters.

The adoption of two main floors for the large urban building was not uncommon in Turin. The reconstructed Palazzo Reale, also by Amedeo, had two main floors, as did the buildings defining the western edge of Piazza Castello. Vitozzi's designs for the facades of Piazza Castello and Contrada Nuova—built, as we have seen, in 1608 and 1615 respectively—exerted a particularly strong influence on Amedeo. He quotes Vitozzi's design in the placement of the pediment high above the window, which makes the entire floor look taller, but he may also have been following a precept of Guarini, who likewise recommended tall windows. (Both architects were also naturally influenced by French residential architecture.) The curvature of the ground floor porticoes, which have slightly rounded vaults, is a sophisticated version of Piedmontese vaulting and does not distract from the 1:1 ratio of the height and the width of the portico bay (fig. 142).[96] The length of each block is mitigated by the strong vertical thrust, an impression created by the closely layered strips of openings and the shallow cornice. The open areas of the windows seem to occupy more of the surface of the elevation than the wall does, and when seen from an oblique angle—the normal viewpoint of someone walking down the

95. Argan, review of Brinckmann, 235: "L'ideale architettonico dei Castellamonte e invero molto limitato; superficie ampie e distese, sobriamente decorate, con nessun slancio di arte, con nessuna originalità di stile, ma con gusto severo, spesso elegante, e con austera semplicità di piani e di linee; nei loro edifici nulla exalta, ma nulla offende, anzi in essi l'occhio si compiace e riposa."

96. See Mario Passanti, *Architettura in Piemonte* (Turin, 1945), *passim*.

street—the buildings seem to dissolve into a myriad closely spaced vertical lines, or open frameworks; the effect resembles the receding wings of a stage set. Although the fragmentation and multiplication of vertical elements are not stressed as explicitly in the design of Piazza Castello and Palazzo Reale, the adoption of the combination of two tall-windowed *piani nobili* and the ground-floor portico endowed the new great street with the architectural language of the royal square. The Contrada di Po thus combines the expressive uniformity of the square, the breadth and straightness of the military *stradone*, and the exuberance of the theater.

The main street of the Po expansion had no contemporary urban projects to rival it either in size or in consistency of design. By the mid-eighteenth century it had earned a reputation as not only "the most beautiful and broad street in Turin," but "one of the most beautiful streets in the world"; it vied for attention with the Contrada Nuova, which Bernini had (reputedly) de-clared to be "unmatched in all of Italy."[97] The actual construction of the uni-form continuous porticoed street went slowly, however, as we have gleaned from the edicts of Giovanna Battista and Vittorio Amedeo II. Many buildings had to be demolished in order to make way for the construction of this wide street, its porticoes, and the exedra near the Po gate (fig. 143), and local resi-dents embroiled the crown in continuous complaint and litigation.[98] But in 21

97. The travelers who were impressed by this sight included Abbé Jérôme Richard, *De-scription historique et critique de l'Italie* (Dijon, 1766), 1:80: "La rue du Po qui va du quartier du palais jusqu'à la porte du même nom est la plus belle et la plus large de Turin; elle est bâtie d'une manière uniforme, les maisons qui la bordent sont belles, elles ne parroissent pas élevées pour leur grandeur mais la largeur de la rue en est cause"; La Lande, *Voyage en Italie*, 1:50: "La rue du Po est une des plus belles rues qu'il y ait au monde, elle est droite, large, uniforme, garnie des deux rangs de portiques couverts"; Johann Georg Keyssler, *Neueste Reisen* (Hanover, 1751), 1:220: "Die neue Strasse ist achzehn Schritte breit, die Häuser vier Stockwerke hoch. Der beruhmte Baumeister Bernini voll gestanden haben das diese Strasse ihre Gleichen in Italien nicht habe." For a more critical view see Nicholas Cochin, *Voyage en Italie* (Paris, 1758), 1:3: "On y remarque entr'autres la rue du Po, qui est fort large. Aux deux cotés de cette rue règnent de grands portiques à arcades, dont les dessous donnent une voie très-large et fort commode aux gens de pied. Si quelque chose semble diminuer l'agré-ment de cette grande et belle rue c'est que n'étant point parallèle avec les autres rues voisines celles qui y aboutissent n'y entrant pas à angle droit et que d'ailleurs les bâtimens semblables qui règnent de part et d'autre paroissent un peu trop bas pour la largeur de la rue: mais cela peut avoir été ménagé exprès, afin de ne point ôter le jour aux boutiques pratiquées sous les portiques, et qui en effet sont fort claires."

98. For the history of these legal conflicts and an analysis of this important drawing, see my "Contrada di Po: Theater and Stradone," forthcoming.

May 1680 a contract was made to level the street in order to make it even with Piazza Carlina and Piazza Castello, and by 27 August 1680 "Gran Strada di Po" was being paved at its Piazza Castello end.[99] Even so, in 1688 the porticoes of Contrada di Po (the elements of the old Italian vernacular tradition, which here became thoroughly formalized) were far from finished.[100] Yet despite these delays, which kept it from being completed until later in the eighteenth century, Contrada di Po became the most significant of the public spaces in the Po expansion, an important symbol of Turin, and a fundamental model for the subsequent enlargements of the city in the eighteenth and nineteenth centuries. Its influence spread significantly in the nineteenth century, when the king of unified Italy—a descendant of the House of Savoy—promoted the construction of a porticoed street, modeled on Contrada di Po, in every large Italian town.[101]

THE WORK ON the Po expansion, unlike the construction of Città Nuova at the death of Carlo Emanuele I, did not stop at the death of Carlo Emanuele II. Although a regency succeeded him, his projects were faithfully pursued, as we have seen in our examination of the edicts, by his widow Giovanna Battista. In comparison with Cristina, the previous regent of the seventeenth century, Giovanna Battista encountered little opposition to her rule, while her own timely motto, *In stipite regnat* (She rules from a branch), made evident her claim to sovereignty not only as regent but also as a Savoy descendant. She staged an important funeral for Carlo Emanuele that inserted itself smoothly among Savoy celebrations, since it was permeated with the familiar dynastic declarations.

The duke's elaborate funeral procession is illustrated passing through Piazza Castello—which, shown as it eventually appeared in the *Theatrum*, is even more uniform than in reality—on its way to the cathedral (fig. 144). The facade of the cathedral was decorated for the occasion with the "funereal order": skulls filled the entablature of the lower order, while coupled pilasters of the "mourning" order (*pleureuse*-like herms below Ionic capitals) supported seg-

99. AST, Sez. Riunite, Fabriche e Fortificationi, art. 205, fol. 125.

100. AST, Sez. Riunite, Fabriche e Fortificationi, art. 199, 12 February 1688, fols. 219–21, order to finish the construction of porticoes along Contrada di Po.

101. For similar streets built in the nineteenth century, see Ennio Poleggi, *Genova* (Bari, 1981), 203–5; Giovanni Ricci, *Bologna* (Bari, 1980), 140–41; Lucio Gambi, *Milano* (Bari, 1982), 212, 282.

mental pediments (fig. 145). These pediments recall strongly those of the main altar designed by Amedeo di Castellamonte for the church of San Francesco di Paola and may well have been designed by him. In the funeral decoration, the pediments are topped by Time and Death dominated by Valor, and by Vice and Envy vanquished by Virtue. The attic area of this triumphal arch composition, surmounted by emblematic lions that guard the Savoy arms and the royal crown, held a naive image of Carlo Emanuele on horseback, visiting a building site and surrounded by architects, engineers, and workers, which summarizes his great love for building.[102] Death beckons him, showing him an emptying hourglass. This is a poignant image of the prince, surprised in action while supervising the progress of his most important legacy, the capital's expansion. The seeming injustice is remarked upon in the inscription above the cathedral's portal, which exhorts mourners to see Carlo Emanuele's death as an act of heroism, while the splendid memorial offerings made by his widow Giovanna Battista should be interpreted as a conquest of that death.[103] It is significant that in this parting image of Carlo Emanuele, where claims were made for his valorous actions, his personal involvement in the enlargement of the city and its monuments should be singled out as his paradigmatic contribution. The concepts conveyed in the funeral apparatus—the magnificence of the sovereign and the dynastic continuity of the House of Savoy—were consistent with the use of architecture and urban design by the successive seventeenth-century dukes and regents as instruments of absolute rule.

102. Claude-François Menestrier, *Des Décorations funèbres* (Paris, 1684), 84: "on avoit peint un Architecte qui luy presentoit en cette occasion le plan d'un superbe Palais et la Mort qui arrestant son cheval par la bride luy faisoit signe qu'il estoit temps de penser à d'autres choses."

103. For the price of the funeral see AST, Sez. Riunite, Fabriche e Fortificationi, art. 197, 13 August 1675, fol. 142. The instructions for the mourners were stated in the inscription:

> Adeste populi
> Spectare iussit heroice moriens
> Carolus Emanuel II
> Maximos principes subesse morti
> Agnosci iubet magnifice parentans
> Maria Ioanna Baptista a Sabaudia
> Optimo principi mortem subesse

(Be present, peoples! Carlo Emanuele II, while heroically dying, ordered [you] to see that the greatest princes are subject to death; Maria Giovanna Battista of Savoy, splendidly making memorial offerings, orders it to be recognized that death is subject to the best prince.) I owe this translation to Michael Alexander.

Index

A

C

H

I

N

O

S

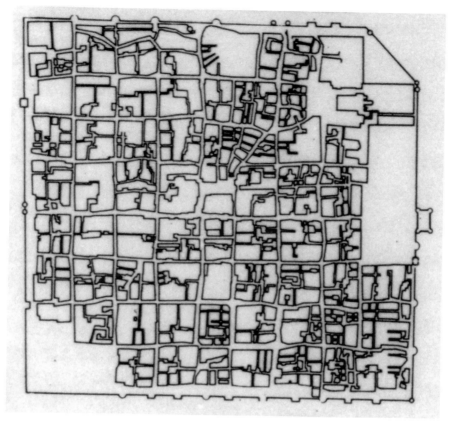

1. Castrum plan of Turin before 1564.

2. View of Castello, Turin, end of sixteenth century, brown ink and wash.

. Meo da Caprino, cathedral facade, Turin, 1491–98.

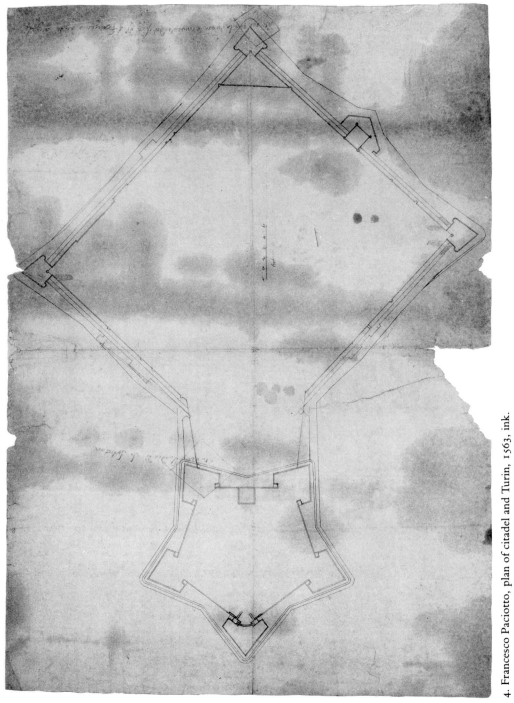

4. Francesco Paciotto, plan of citadel and Turin, 1563, ink.

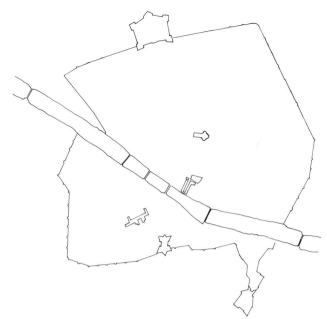

5. Plan of Florence and its Fortezza di Basso, 1540s.

6. Giacomo Barozzi da Vignola, with Antonio da Sangallo and Francesco Paciotto, Palazzo Farnese, begun 1559, Caprarola, engraving by Francesco Villamena, 1617.

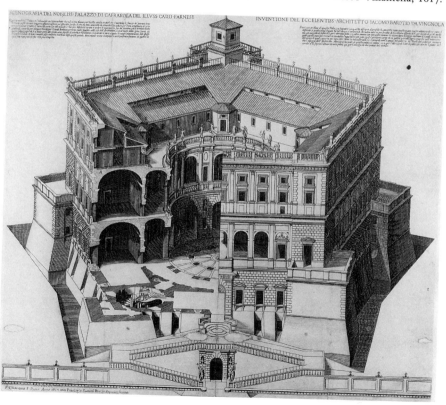

7. Francesco Paciotto, plan of citadel in Antwerp, 1567, ink and watercolor.

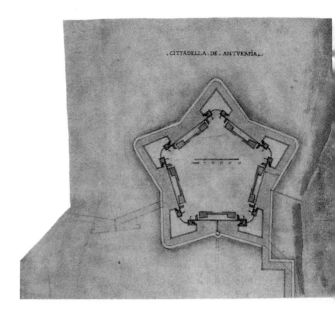

8. Francesco Paciotto, plan of Parma and its citadel, 1591, engraving by A. Sanseverini, 1804.

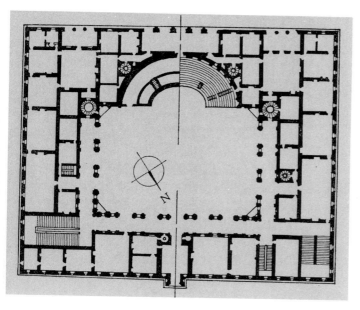

9. Giacomo Barozzi da Vignola, plan of Palazzo Farnese, Piacenza, begun 1558.

10. Antonio da Sangallo and Michelangelo, Palazzo Farnese, facade, Rome. 1541 and 1546.

11. Francesco Horologgi, plan and view of Turin from east with fortress study, ink, 1564.

12. Pietro Cataneo, design for a fortified city and citadel, engraving, from *I quattro primi libri di architettura* (Venice, 1554).

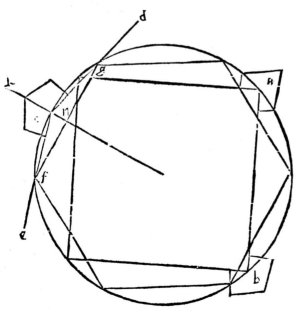

13. Giacomo Lanteri, design for fortification trace, engraving, from *Due dialoghi* (Venice, 1557).

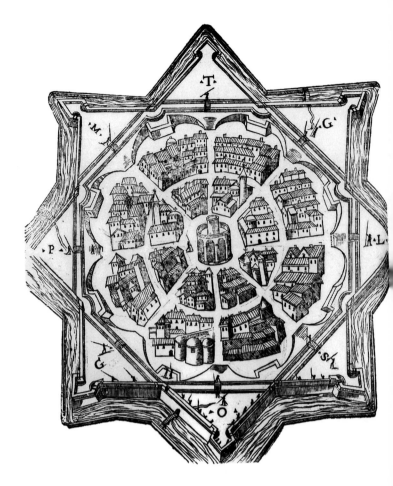

14. Girolamo Maggi, design for an eight-bastioned fortress, engraving, from *Delle fortificatione delle città* (Venice, 1564).

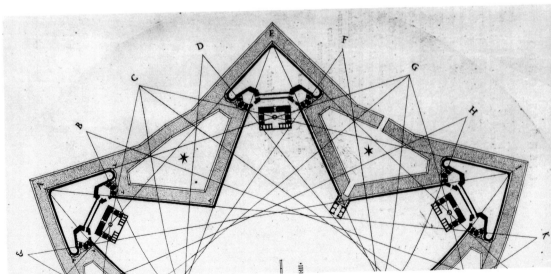

15. Galasso Alghisi, design for a bastioned fortification trace, engraving, from *Delle fortificationi* (Venice, 1570).

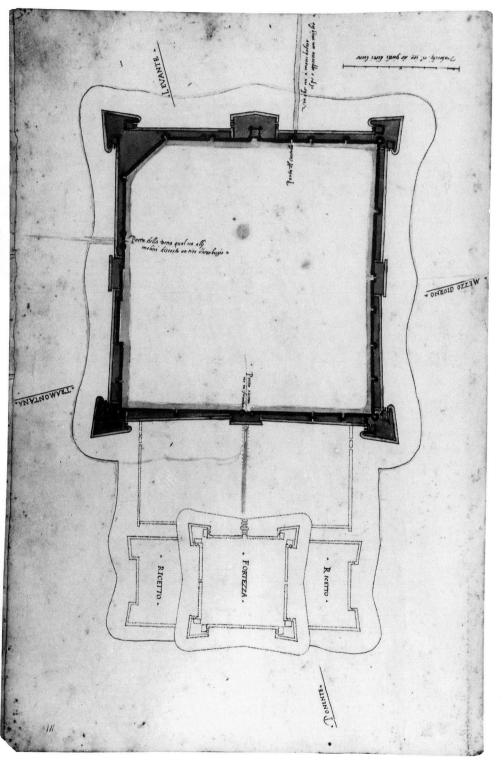

16. Francesco de' Marchi, plan of Turin with citadel next to west wall, ink, from "Atlante di piante militari," c. 1565.

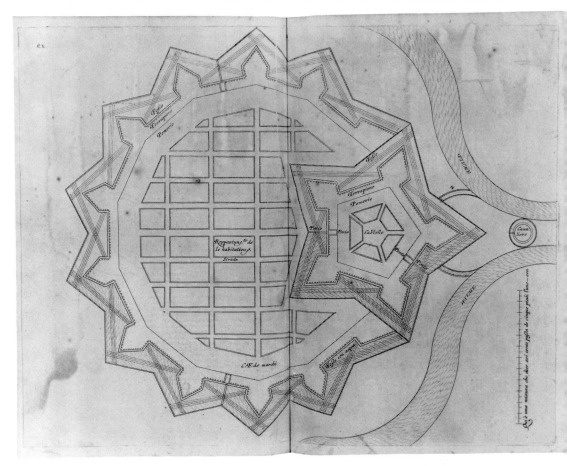

17. Francesco de' Marchi, design for fortified city with
pentagonal citadel, engraving, from *Della architettura
militare* (Brescia, 1599).

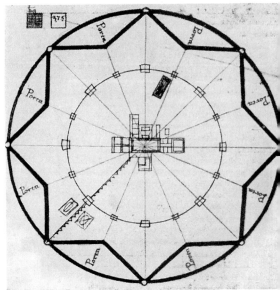

18. Antonio Averulino called "Il Filarete," plan of
Sforzinda, 1460–64, ink.

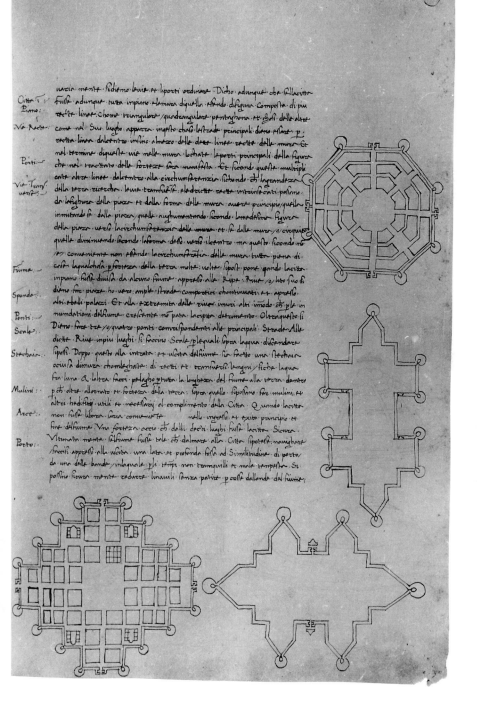

19. Francesco di Giorgio Martini, plans ideal city, 1475–92, ink.

20. Albrecht Dürer, castrum plan of fortified city, woodcut, from *Etliche Underricht zur Befestigung der Stett, Schloss, und Flecken* (Nuremberg, 1527).

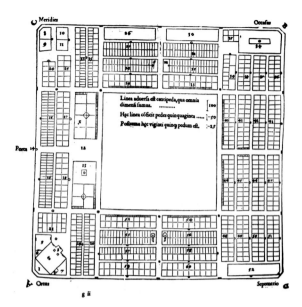

21. Plan of Palma, ink and watercolor, c. 1593.

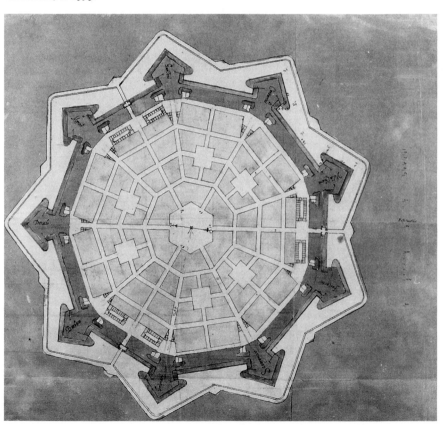

22. Plan of Granmichele, 1693.

23. Giovanni Criegher, view of Turin, 1572, wood-block by Giovanni Caracha.

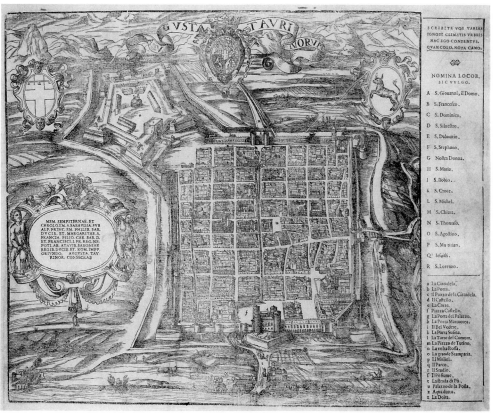

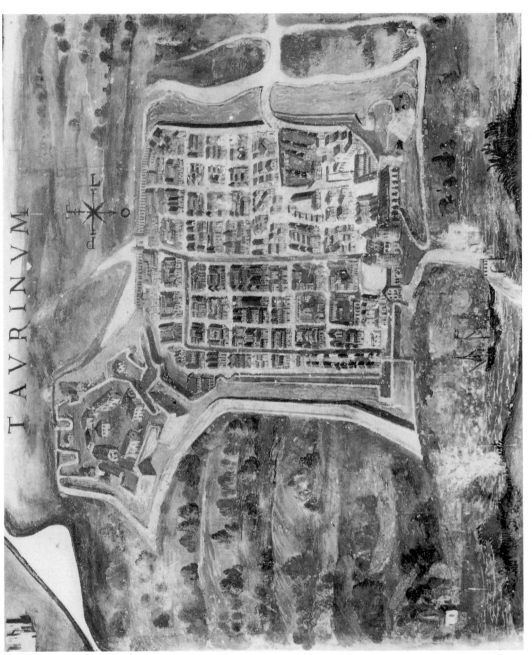

24. Girolamo and Egnazio Danti, view of Turin and its citadel, 1583, fresco, Vatican Palace, Galleria delle carte geografiche.

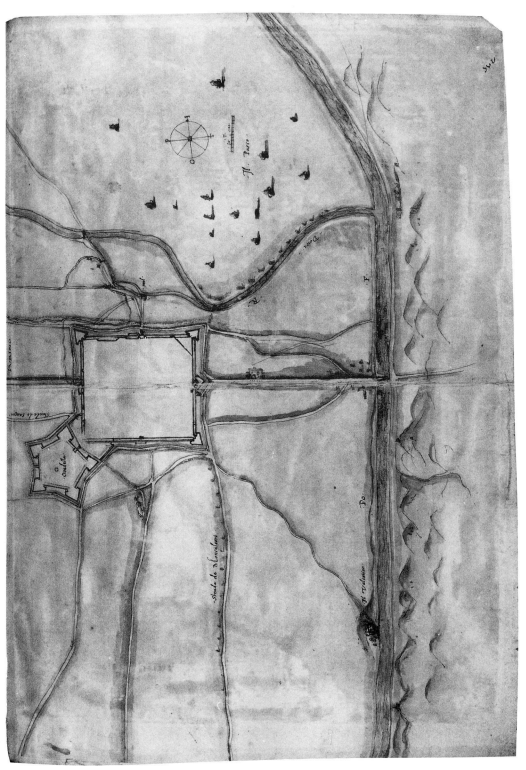

25. Plan of Turin, c. 1570, ink and watercolor.

26. Anonymous, portrait of Maria di Savoia, daughter of Emanuele Filiberto, with view of Castello, Galleria, and the ancient ducal residence, c. 1580, oil painting.

27. Girolamo Righettino, view of Turin with ornamental frames of mythological figures, views of cities, and military trophies, 1583, ink and watercolor.

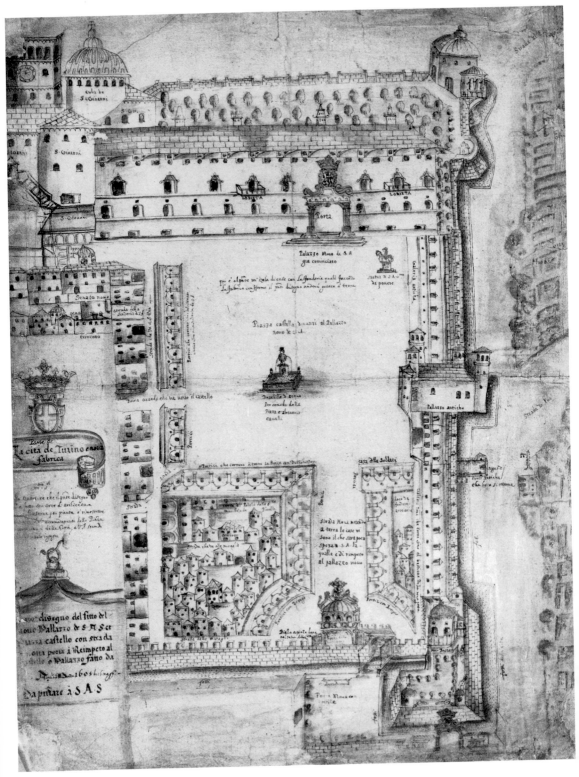

28. Monsa, design for Piazza Castello, ducal palace, and new street, 1605, ink, watercolor, and gold traces.

29. Antonio Tempesta, view of Castello and Piazza Castello during the exhibition of the Holy Shroud, 1613, engraving.

30. View of Carignano, 1682, engraving. Detail.

31. View of Carmagnola, 1682, engraving.

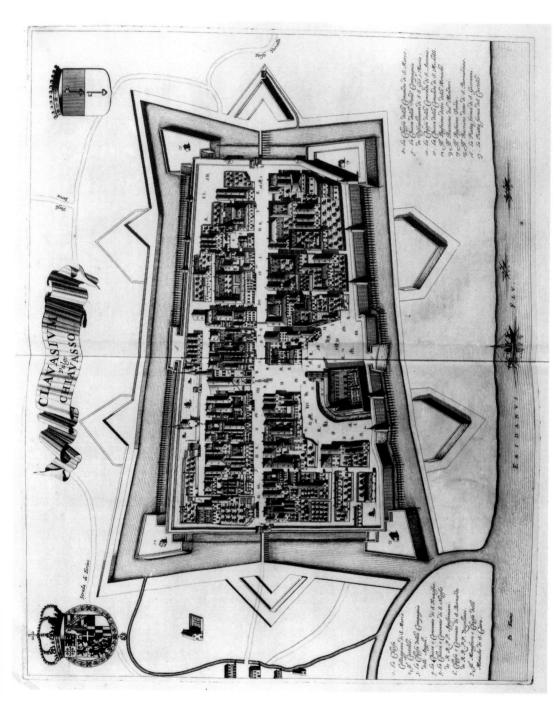

32. View of Chivasso, 1682, engraving.

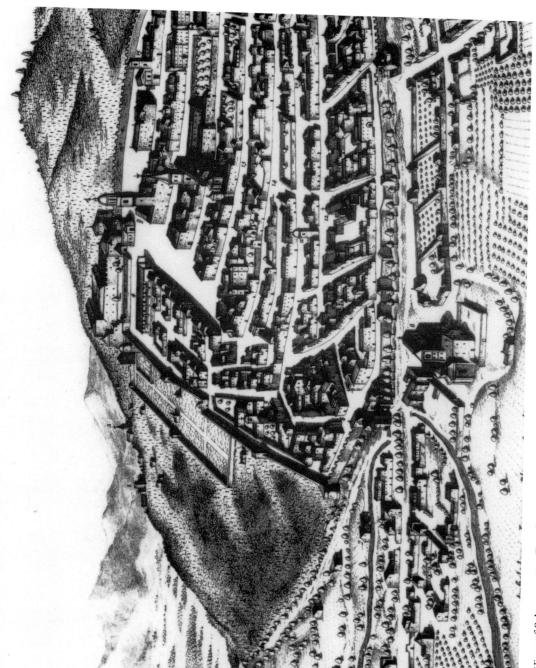

33. View of Saluzzo, 1682. Detail.

34. Ascanio Vitozzi, Contrada Nuova, Turin, 1615.

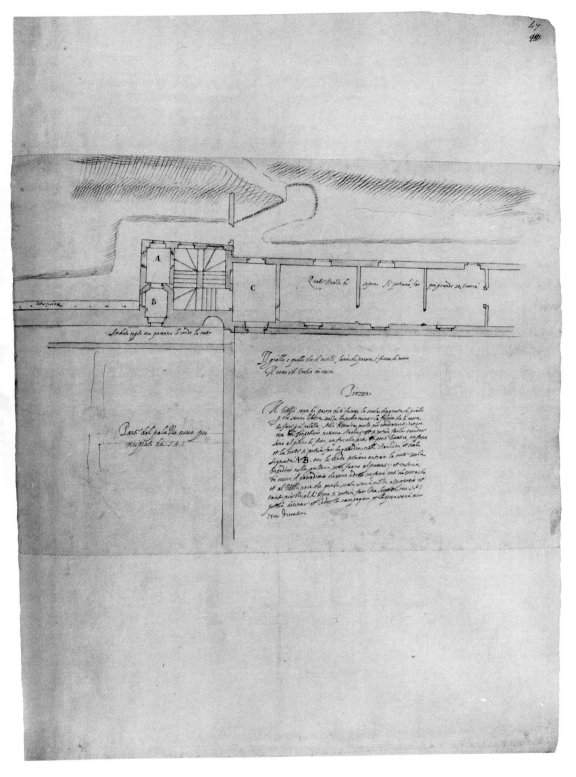

35. Ascanio Vitozzi, Palazzo Reale in Turin, design for staircase, c. 1584, ink.

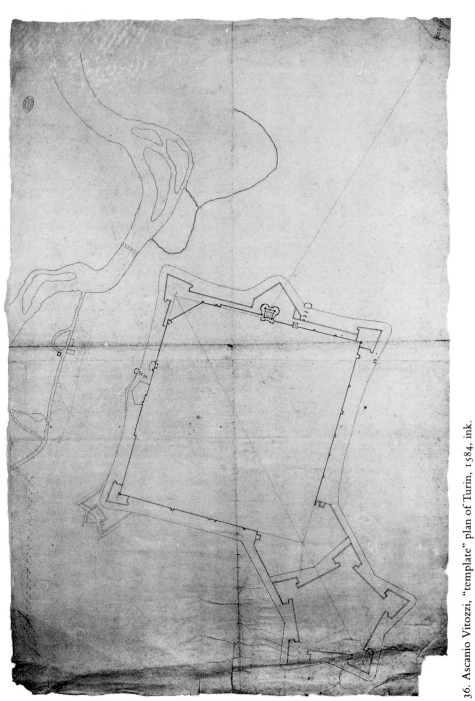

36. Ascanio Vitozzi, "template" plan of Turin, 1584, ink.

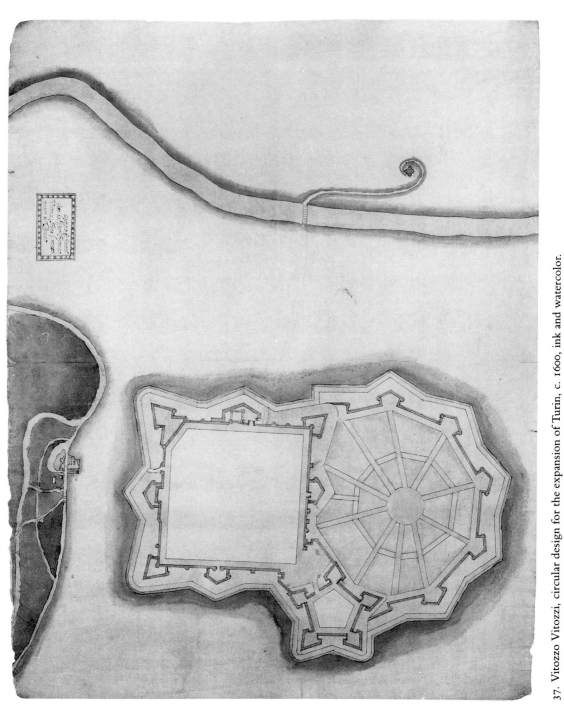

37. Vitozzo Vitozzi, circular design for the expansion of Turin, c. 1600, ink and watercolor.

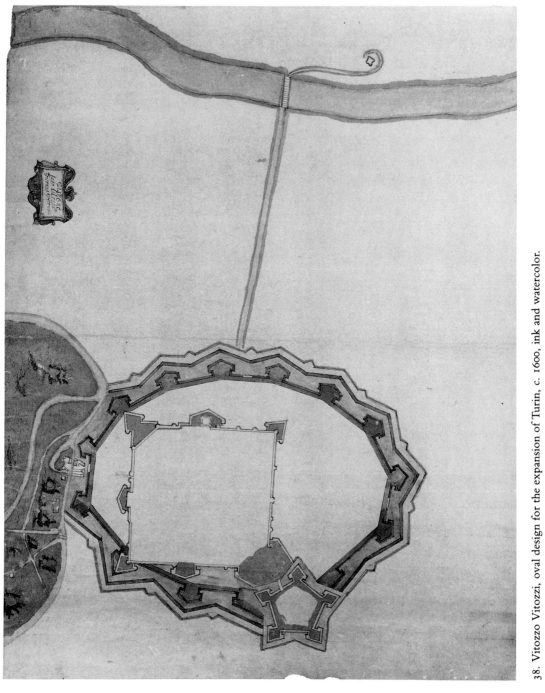

38. Vitozzo Vitozzi, oval design for the expansion of Turin, c. 1600, ink and watercolor.

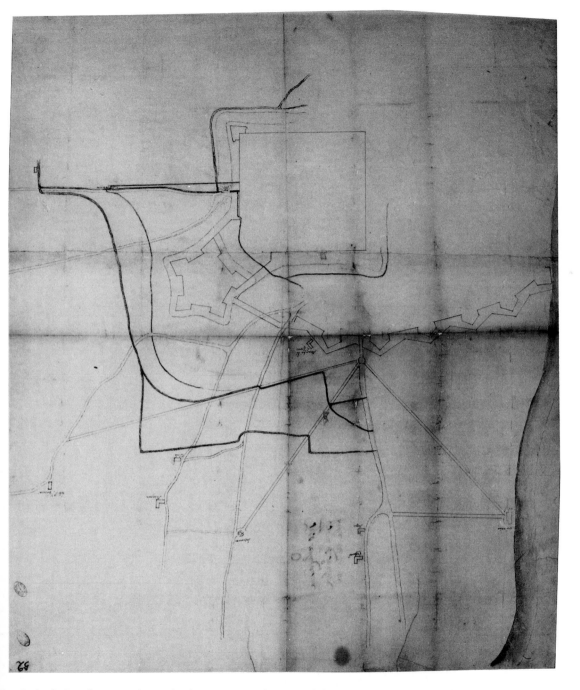

39. Carlo di Castellamonte, design for the expansion of Turin with layout of canals, c. 1619, ink.

40. Francesco de' Marchi, design for city with twelve bastions and street layout, engraving, from *Della architettura militare* (Brescia, 1599)

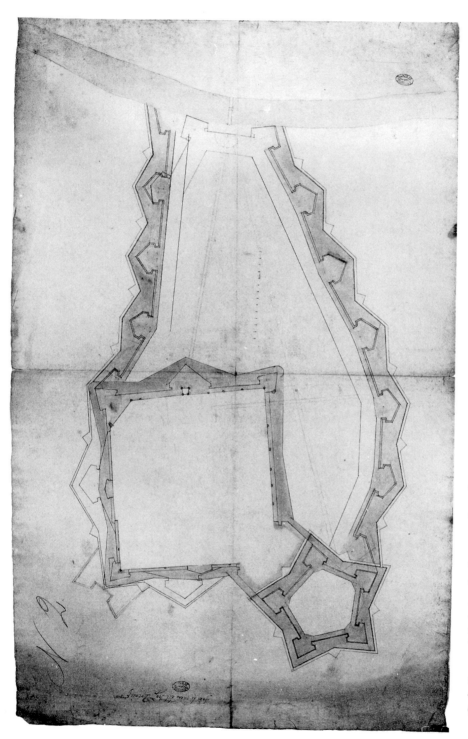

41. Carlo Emanuele I, design for the expansion of Turin, c. 1612–19, ink and watercolor.

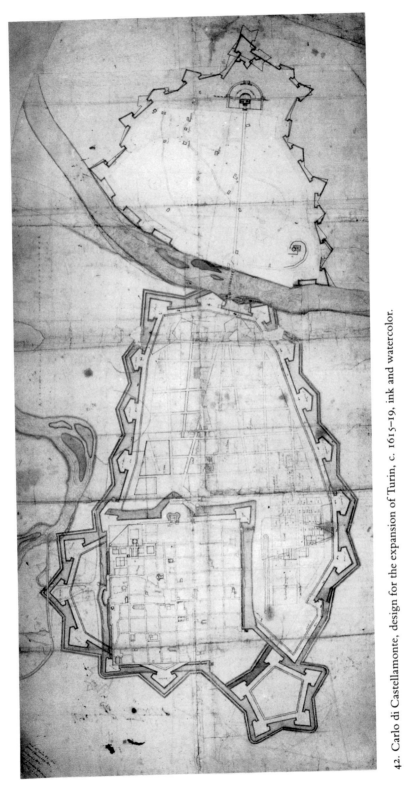

42. Carlo di Castellamonte, design for the expansion of Turin, c. 1615–19, ink and watercolor.

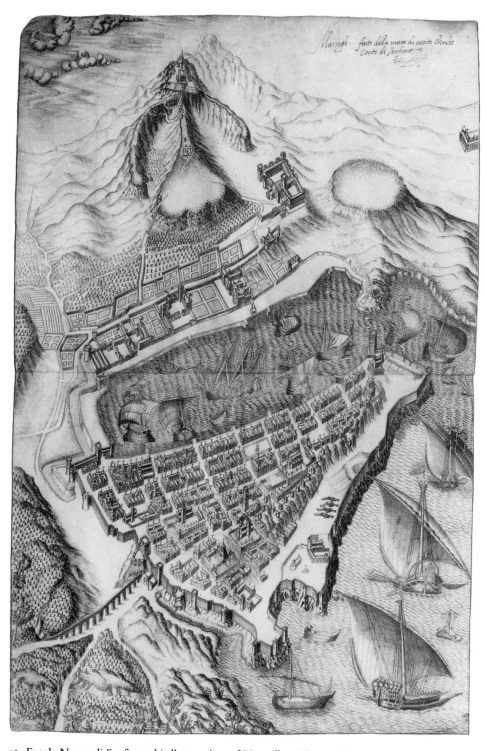

43. Ercole Negro di Sanfront, bird's-eye view of Marseilles, ink, c. 1580.

44. Carlo di Castellamonte, Porta
Nova or Victoria, 1682.

45. Antonio Tempesta, joust in
Piazza Castello, Turin, 1620, oil
painting.

46. View of Turin from east with ceremonial procession, c. 1620, ink and wash.

47. Giacomo de Fornazeris, equestrian portrait of Carlo Emanuele I, with the plan of Turin and procession behind him, c. 1612, engraving.

48. View of Turin from southeast [misnamed "la ville de Bude"], c. 1628, ink.

49. Antoine de Ville, design for the fortification of a town divided by a river with view of Turin in the background, engraving, from A. de Ville, *Les Fortifications* (Lyons 1620)

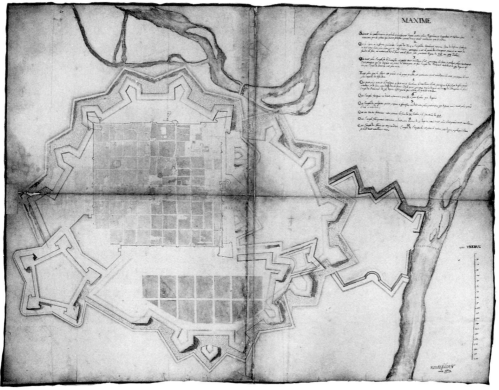

50. Frontispiece, with claim to royal title, engraving, from Pierre Monod, *Coelum Allobrogicum* (Lyons, 1634).

51. Montafilans, design for the fortification of Turin's expansion, 1632, brown ink and wash.

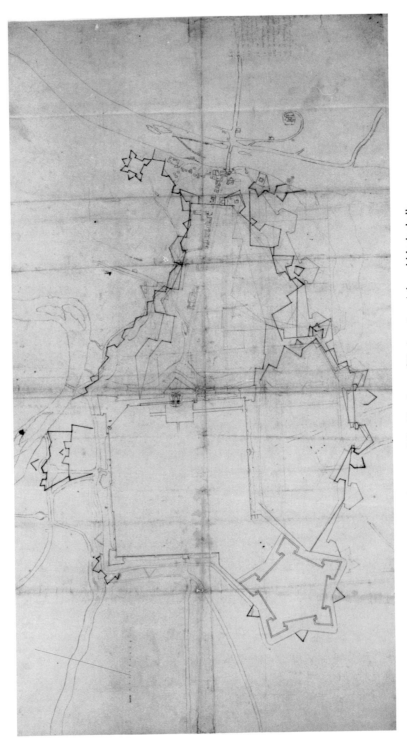

52. Carlo di Castellamonte, study of existing and proposed fortifications of Turin, 1632, ink and black chalk.

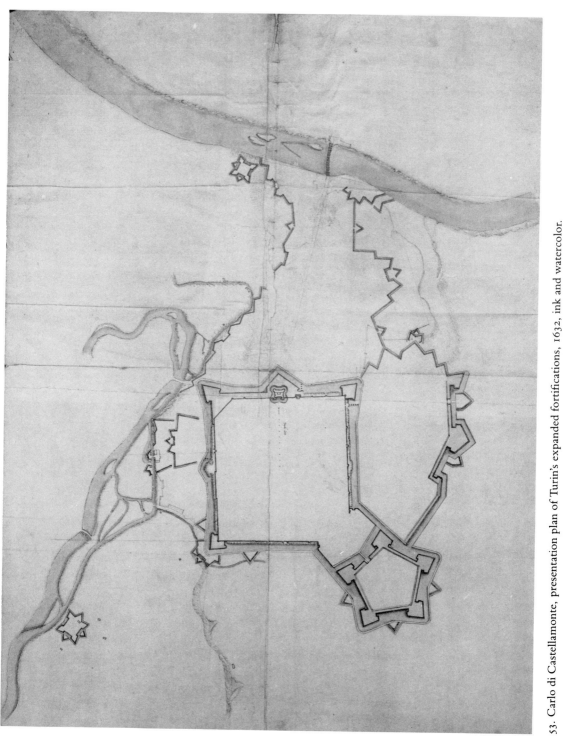

53. Carlo di Castellamonte, presentation plan of Turin's expanded fortifications, 1632, ink and watercolor.

54. Giovenale Boetto, view of Turin, c. 1632, engraving.

55. Giovenale Boetto, view of the new expansion of Turin, 1634, detail from frontispiece to the theses of Carlo Francesco di Robilant, engraving.

56. Giovenale Boetto, frontispiece to the theses of Robilant, 1634, engraving.

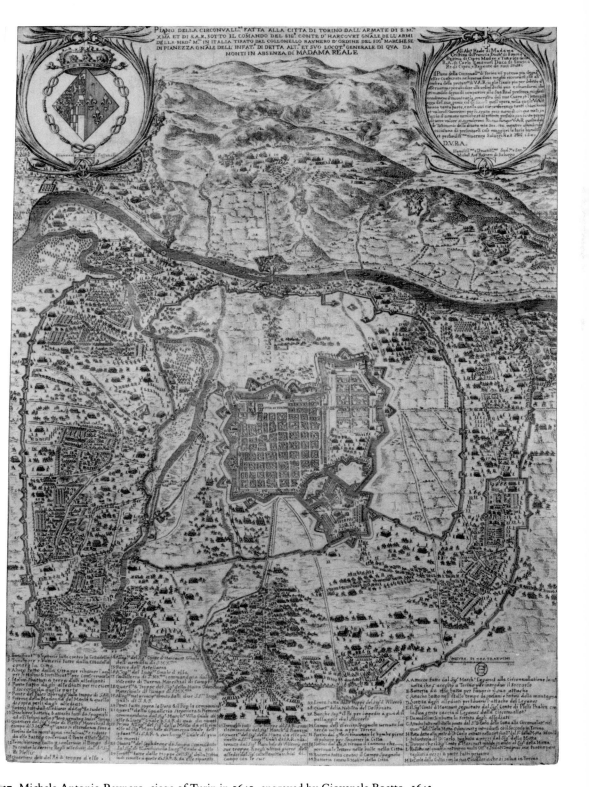

57. Michele Antonio Raynero, siege of Turin in 1640, engraved by Giovenale Boetto, 1643.

58. Giovenale Boetto, frontispiece to Luigi Giuglaris, *Funerale fatto nel duomo di Torino alla gloriosa memoria* [di] *Vittorio Amedeo Duca di Savoia, Prencipe di Piemonte, Re di Cipro* (Turin, 1638), engraving.

59. Giovenale Boetto, cathedral facade ornamented for the funeral of Vittorio Amedeo, engraving, from Giuglaris, *Funerale fatto nel duomo di Torino* (1638).

60. Giovenale Boetto, nave ornament inside cathedral of Turin, engraving, from Giuglaris, *Funerale fatto nel duomo di Torino* (1638).

61. Giovenale Boetto, catafalque of Vittorio Amedeo under cathedral dome, engraving, from Giuglaris, *Funerale fatto nel duomo di Torino* (1638).

62. Siege of Turin, c. 1642, engraving.

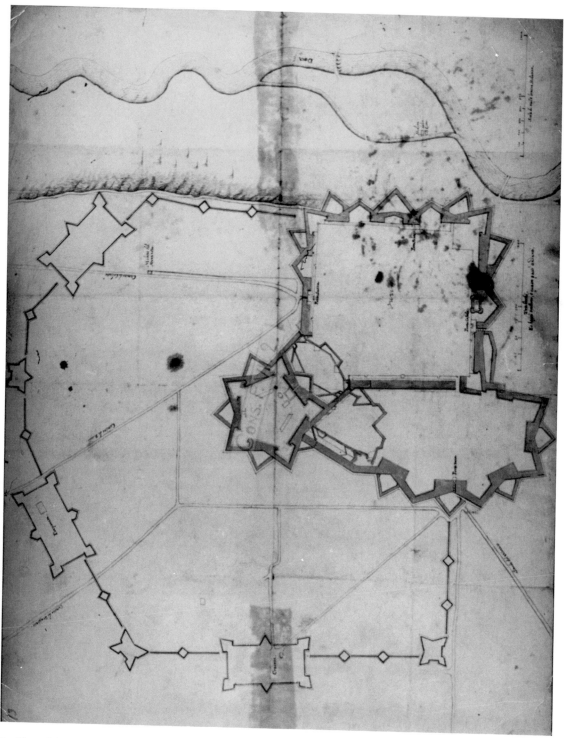

63. Plan of the siege of Turin, c. 1640, ink.

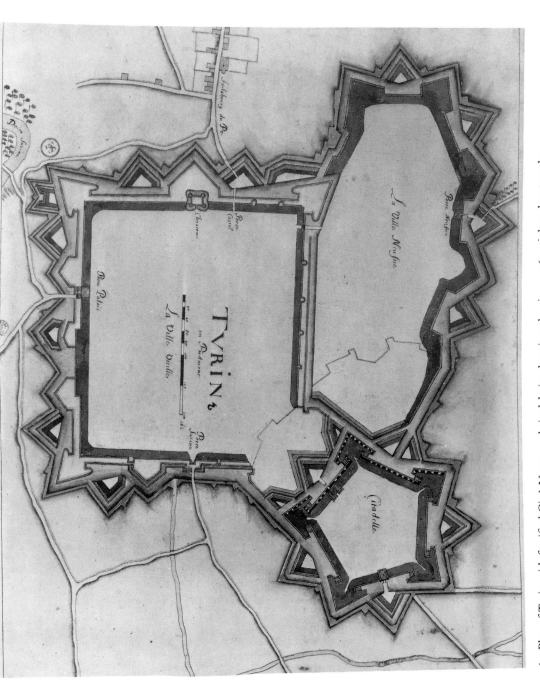

64. Plan of Turin with fortified Città Nuova and citadel pitted against the city, c. 1645, ink and watercolor.

65. Bartolomeo Fenis, the ceremony of changing the citadel's guard, with Turin in the background, c. 1657–59, engraving.

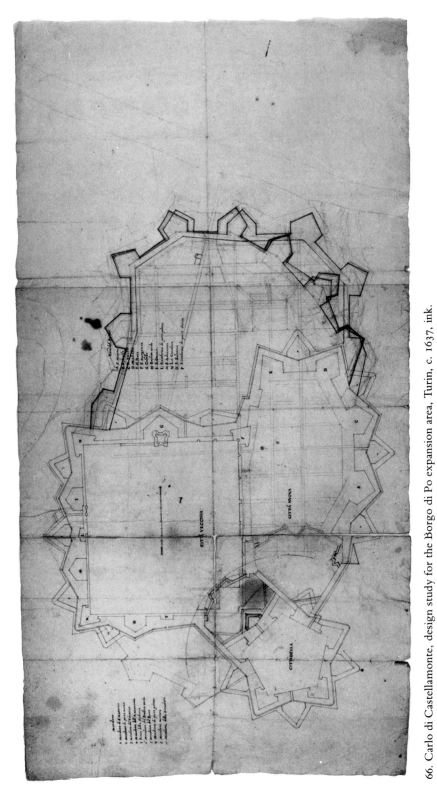

66. Carlo di Castellamonte, design study for the Borgo di Po expansion area, Turin, c. 1637, ink.

67. Michele Antonio Raynero and Giovenale Boetto, siege of Turin in 1640, detail of figure 57.

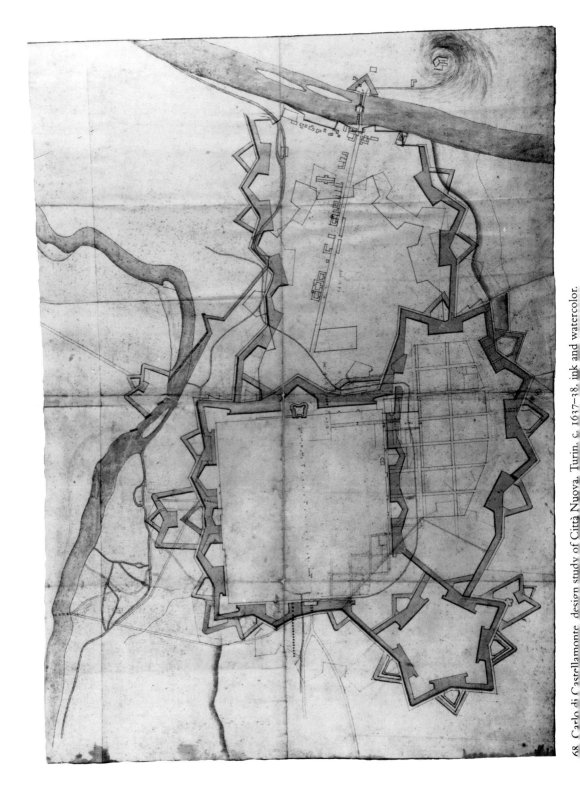

68 Carlo di Castellamonte, design study of Città Nuova, Turin, c. 1637–38, ink and watercolor.

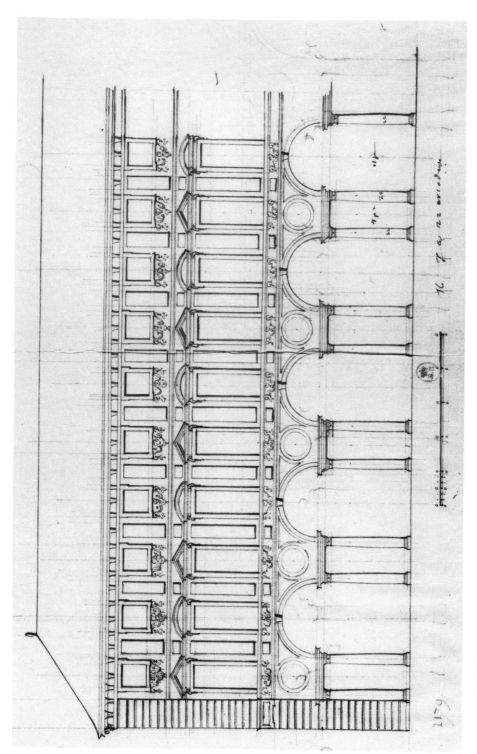

69. Design for the façade of Piazza Reale, Turin, second half of seventeenth century, ink.

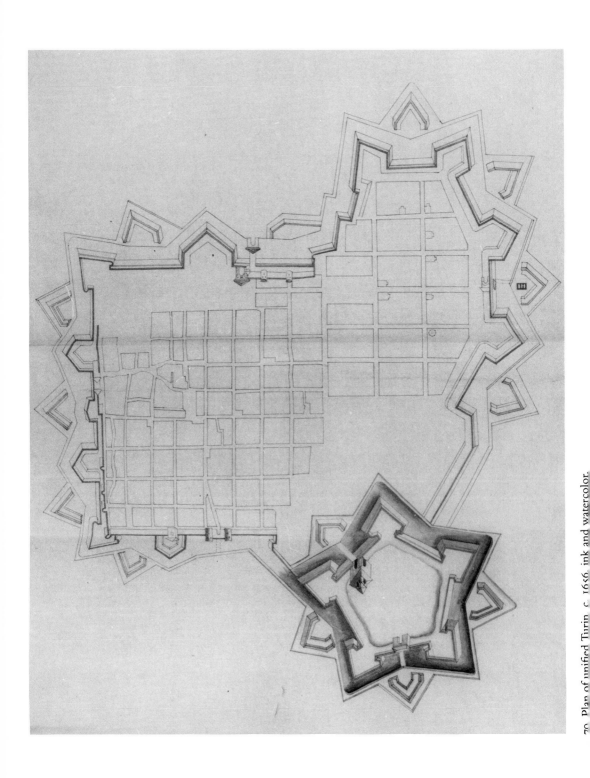

70. Plan of unified Turin, c. 1656, ink and watercolor.

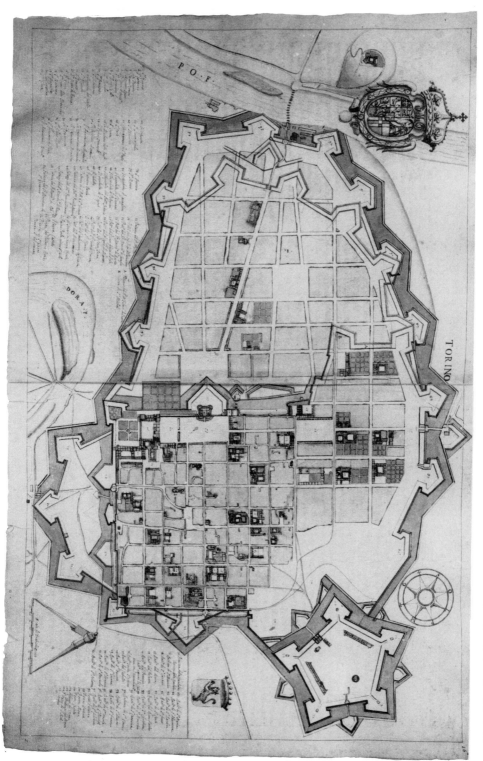

71. Carlo Morello, design for the expansion of Turin to the north, east, and south, 1656, ink and watercolor.

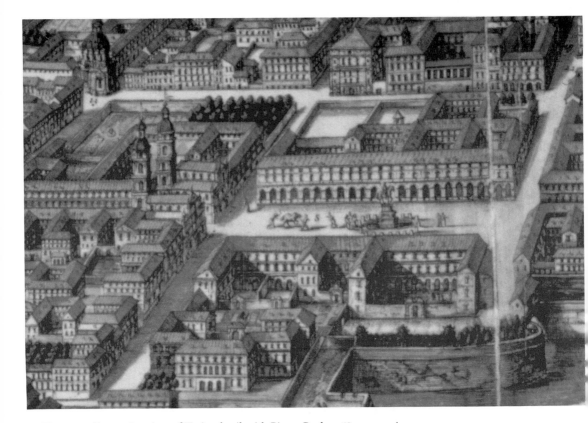

72. Tommaso Borgonio, view of Turin, detail with Piazza Reale, 1682, engraving.

73. Giovanni Gaspare Baldoino, triumphal arch with the regent Cristina, frontispiece to theses by Carlo Amedeo and Ottavio Valentino Provana, 1644, engraving.

74. Giovenale Boetto, triumphal arch in Cuneo, 1643, engraving.

75. Tommaso Borgonio, stage set for the court-ballet *Il dono del Re de l'Alpi a Madama Reale,* 1645, ink and watercolor.

76. Giovenale Boetto, joust in Piazza Castello, Turin, looking south, 1650, engraving.

77. Tommaso Borgonio, joust in Piazza Castello, Turin, looking north, 1650, watercolor.

78. Giovenale Boetto, view of San Salvario with Turin in the background, 1650, engraving.

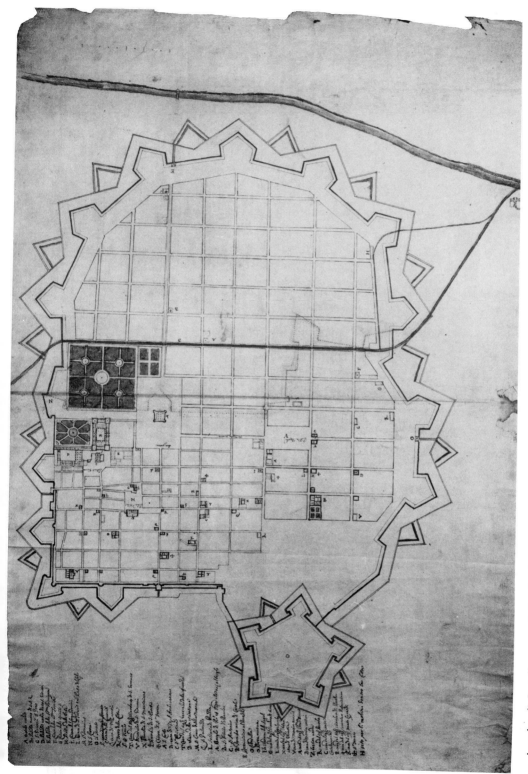

79. Amedeo di Castellamonte, design for the Borgo di Po expansion of Turin, 1656, ink and watercolor.

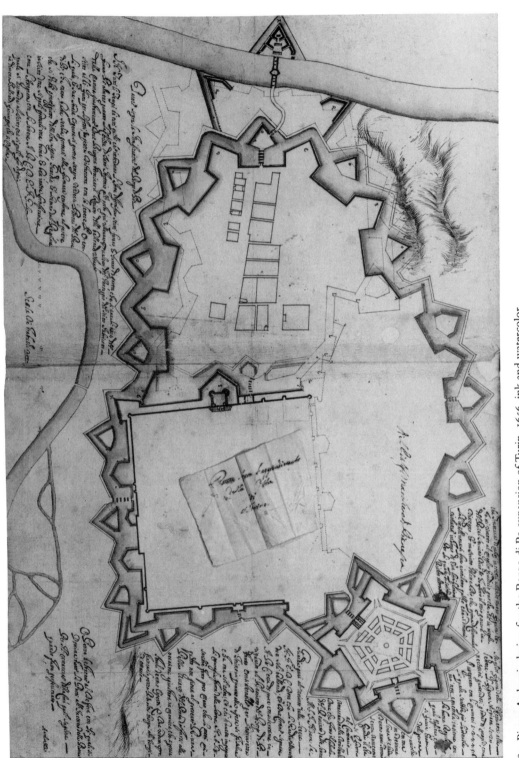

80. Pietro Arduzzi, design for the Borgo di Po expansion of Turin, 1656, ink and watercolor.

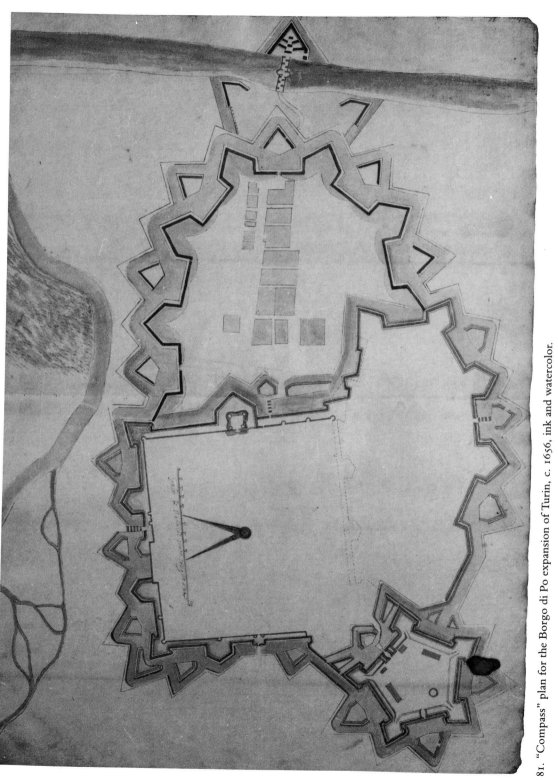

81. "Compass" plan for the Borgo di Po expansion of Turin, c. 1656, ink and watercolor.

82. Tommaso Borgonio,
stage set for *Il falso amor
bandito,* 1667, watercolor.

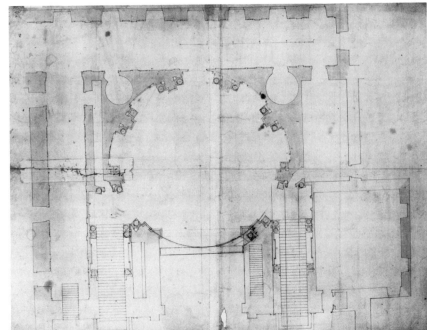

83. Bernardo Quadri, de-
sign for the Holy Shroud
chapel, Turin, 1657, ink.

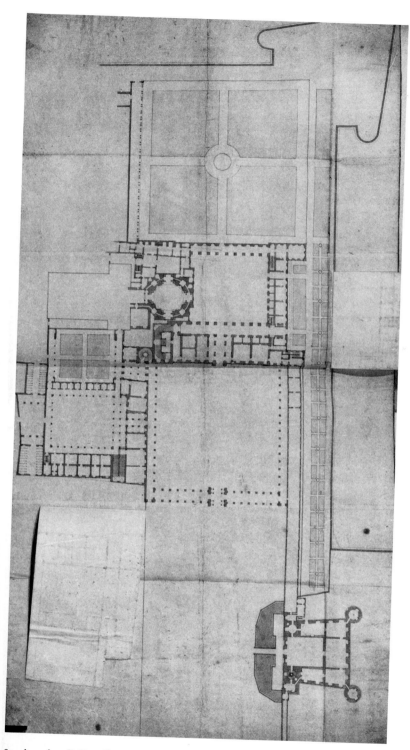

84. Amedeo di Castellamonte, design for Palazzo Reale, Turin, ground floor,
c. 1644–48, ink.

85. Francesco Lanfranchi, design for the facade
of Palazzo di Città, Turin, 1659, ink and watercolor.

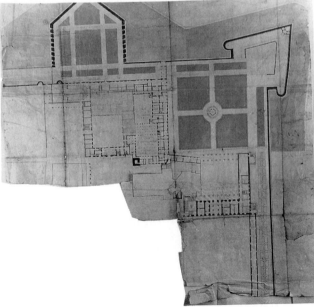

86. Carlo di Castellamonte, design for ground
floor of ducal palace, Turin, c. 1640, ink.

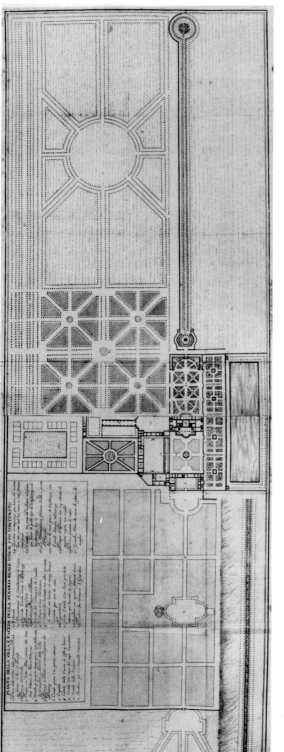

87. Amedeo di Castellamonte, plan of the town, palace, garden, and park at Venaria Reale, from his *Venaria Reale; palazzo di piacere e di caccia* (Turin, 1674), engraving by Giorgio Tasniere after Gian Francesco Baroncelli.

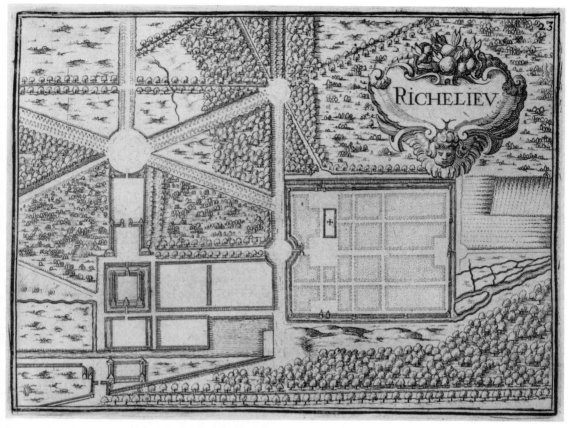

89. Nicolas Tassin, plan of Richelieu, from *Les Plans et profils de toutes les principales villes et lieux considérables de France* (Paris, 1638), engraving.

90. Hunting scene with Venaria Reale in the background, c. 1660, engraving.

FONS HERCVLEVS,

Cum suis Colosso, Piscina, Cryptoportico, Antris,
Sacellis, Scalis, Diætis, Tricliniis, Statuis, Signis,
Tabulis, cæterisque Musivis, ac marmoreis ornamentis.

92. Tommaso Borgonio, view of the temple of Diana at Venaria Reale, 1682, engraving.

Parte interiore della sala con suoi ornamenti di pitture, e scolture della Reggia di Diana

93. Amedeo di Castellamonte, *salone* of the palace at Venaria Reale, from his *Venaria Reale* (1674),
engraving by Giorgio Tasniere after Gian Francesco Baroncelli.

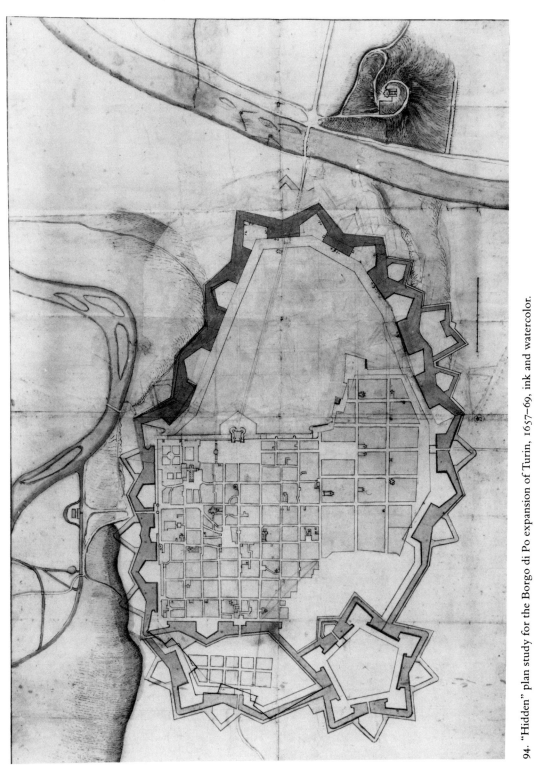

94. "Hidden" plan study for the Borgo di Po expansion of Turin, 1657–69, ink and watercolor.

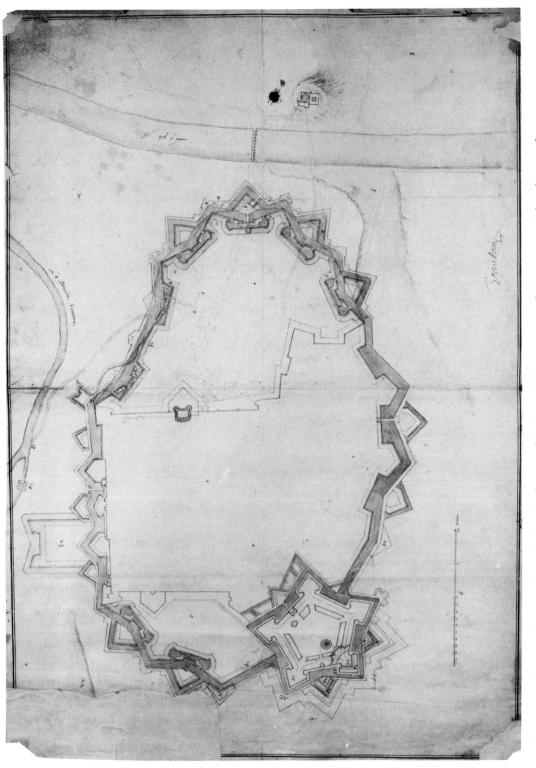

95. Sebastien Le Prestre de Vauban, design for the fortification of the Borgo di Po expansion of Turin, c. 1670, ink and watercolor.

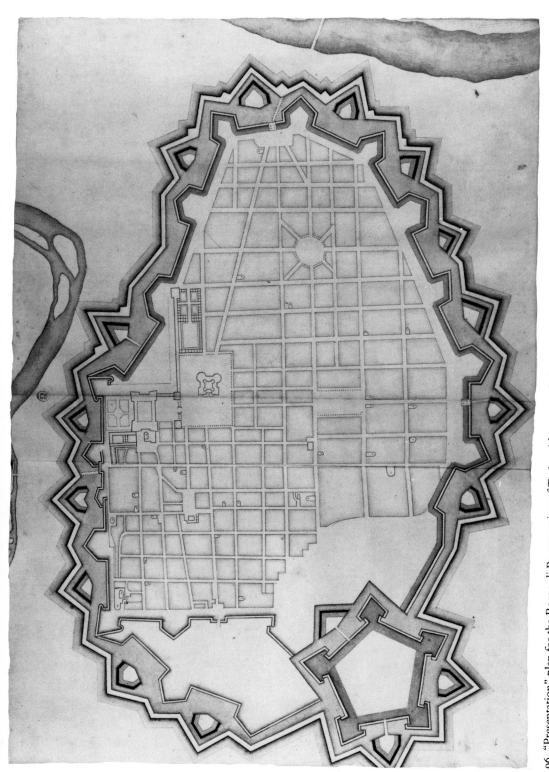

96. "Presentation" plan for the Borgo di Po expansion of Turin with octagonal piazza, 1673–75, ink and watercolor.

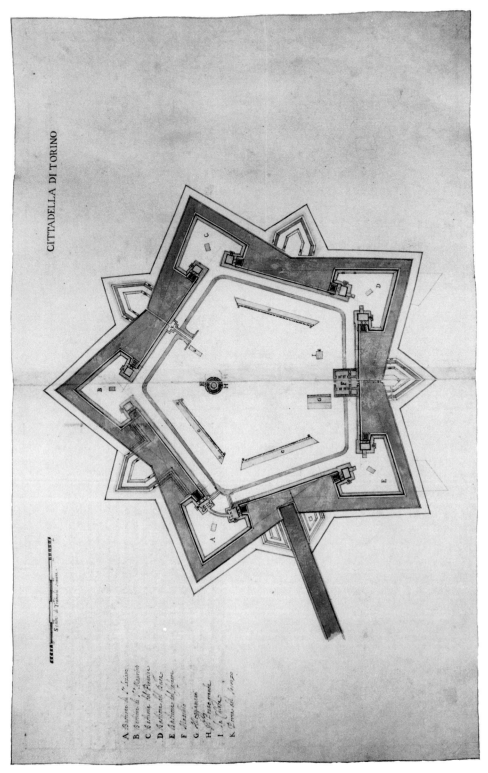

CITTADELLA DI TORINO

97. Francesco Paciotto, citadel of Turin with detail of bastion, 1664, engraving after Michelangelo Morello, 1682.

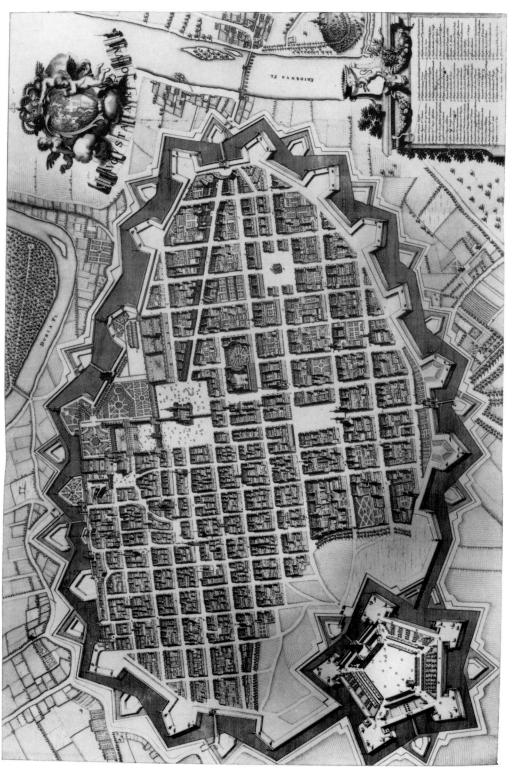

98. Tommaso Borgonio, idealized view-plan of Turin, drawing 1674, engraved 1682.

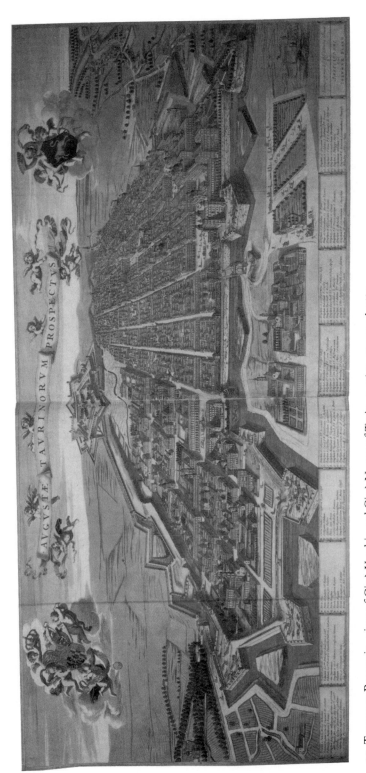

99. Tommaso Borgonio, view of Città Vecchia and Città Nuova of Turin, c. 1671, engraved 1682.

100. View of Piazza Reale in Turin, looking south, 1682, engraving.

101. Romeyn de Hoogh, view of Piazza Castello in Turin, looking north, 1682, engraving.

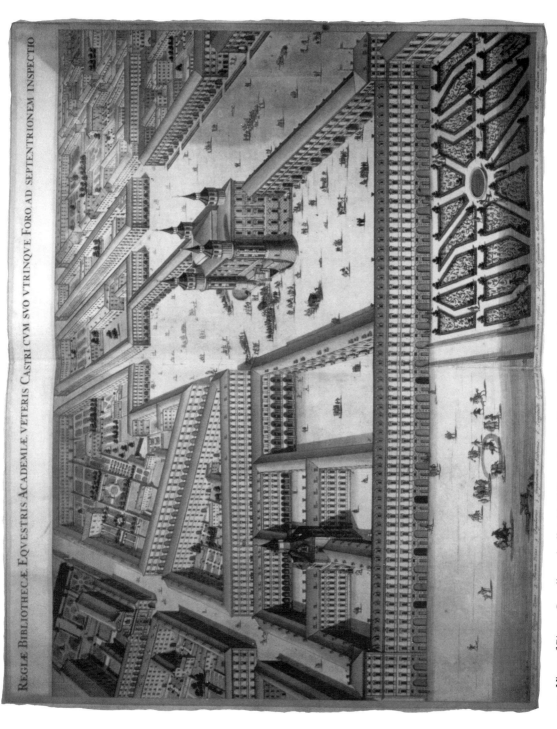

102. View of Piazza Castello and official buildings after the Borgo di Po expansion of Turin, 1682, engraving.

Primarij Lapidis Inscriptio
et
Aduersum Numisma Aureum
Cum Regiæ Celsitudinis Effigie.

CAROLVS EMANVEL II.

Allobrogum Dux, Cypri Rex.
Cæterâ Ditione fidis Arcibus communitâ,
Ipfum Ditionis Cor, ad fui Cordis Exemplum,
Non folùm mu——nit, fed ampliat.
Nam qui fua ——fecurus poffidet.
Hoftilia fecu- ——riùs inuadet.
Et amplior ——quò preffior, infeftabit.
Infeftos
Die XXIII ——Octobris
ANNO ——MDCLXXIII.

Alia Lapidis Inscriptio
Metallo Incisa
et
Auersi Numismatis Symbolum

AVGVSTÃ TAVRINORVM.

Triumphali Cæsaris Augusti Magnificentiâ
Maximis Italiæ Orbibus æquatam,
Tùm diro Gothorum feculo fepè dirutam,
Semperque angustiore fpecie renatam;
Ad pristinam Augusti No—— —minis amplitudinê restituere
Carolus Emanuel —— Primus uoluit:
Victor. Amedeus ma- —— gnâ ex parte potuit:
Carolus Ema- —— nuel Secundus
Magni Aui cogitatum et Maximi Genitoris incepti
Non degeneri Animo expleturus,
Aspirantibus Deiparæ Virginis Auspicijs,
Auguralem hunc Lapidem iacit.
Die 23. Octobris.

MDCLXXIII.

G. Tasniere fculp. Taur.

103. Giorgio Tasniere, foundation plaque and medals, 1673, engraving.

104. Foundation medal, *modello,* c. 1673, obverse, Carlo Emanuele II.

105. Foundation medal, 1673, obverse, Carlo Emanuele II.

106. Medal, c. 1669, obverse, Carlo Emanuele II.

107. Jean Baptiste Dufour, medal matrix, c. 1672, Carlo Emanuele II.

108. Louis XIV, portrait medal, 1672.

109. Foundation medal, 1673, reverse, polygonal bastion with round tower and Savoy banner above.

110. Commemorative medal, 1662, reverse, fortification of Philipsburg.

111. Guarino Guarini, Porta di Po, Turin, engraving, from *Disegni d'architettura civile e ecclesiastica* (1686).

112. Plan of Porta di Po and view of exedra, Turin, designed 1674, engraved 1682.

Perspective.   par la rue de Po

La Ville de Turin entrant

Feux de rejouïssance, au dedans et aux dehors de Turin, a l'arrivée de S. A. R. Madame la Princesse de Piedmont.

Se vendent a Turin chez Reycends et Guibert Libraires Sous les arcades de place Chateau

designe par le Ch.er Dom Filippo Juvarra 1.er Architecte de S.M.

gravé par Herisset

113. Filippo Juvarra, Porta di Po, Turin, engraving by Antoine Herisset, from *Disegni di fuochi* (1722).

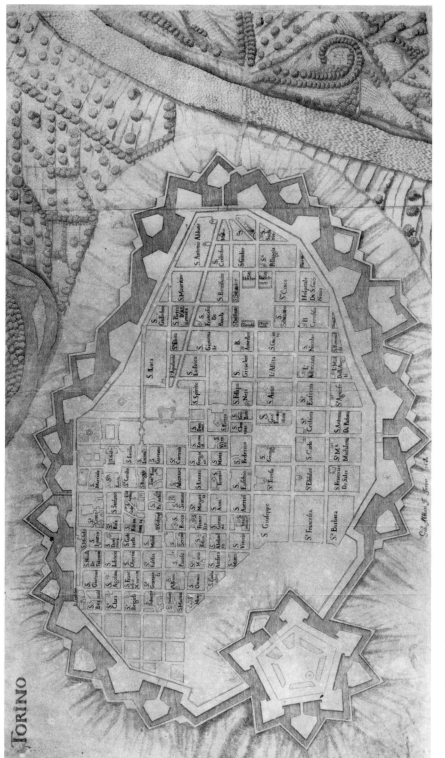

114. Giovanni Abbiati, plan of Turin, 1680, engraving.

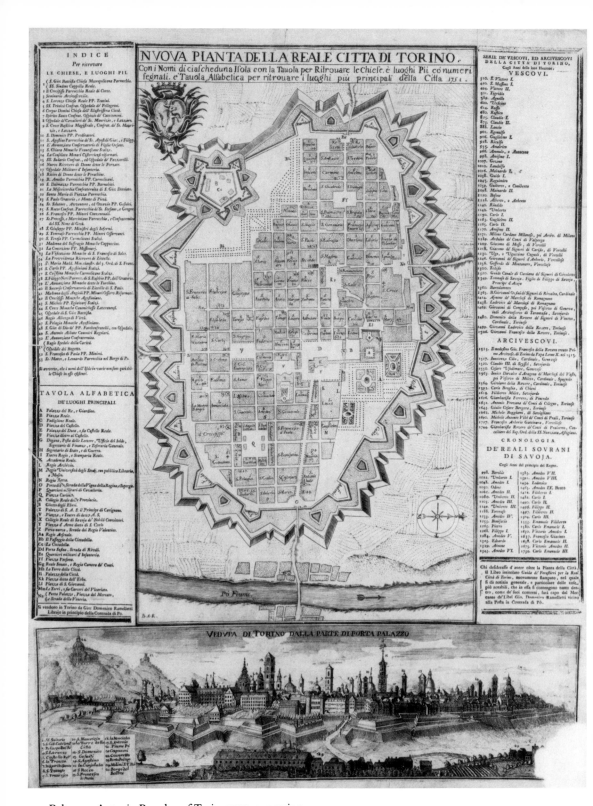

115. Beltramo Antonio Re, plan of Turin, 1751, engraving.

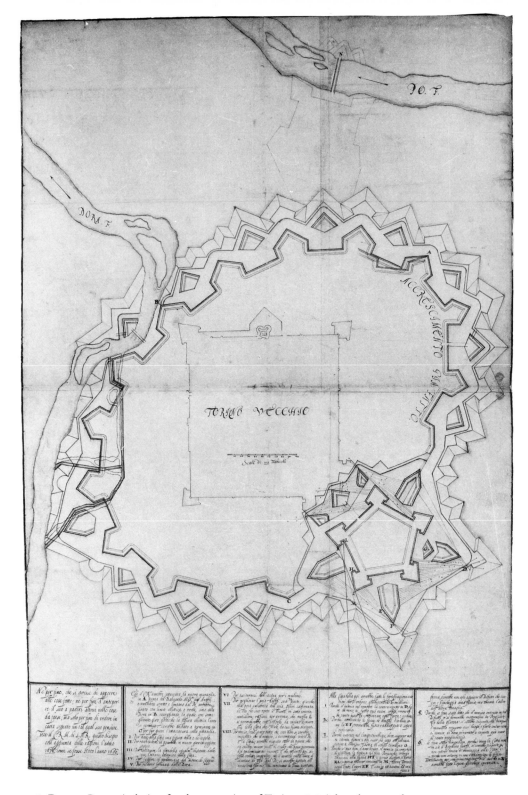

116. Donato Rossetti, design for the expansion of Turin, 1676, ink and watercolor.

PIAZZA AVANTI IL PALAZZO DI S.A.S. IL S. PR̃Ṭ.ᴱ DI CARIGNANO CON IL DISSEGNO DELLA FACCIATA DEL SUO TEATRO

117. Giovanni Battista Borra, Piazza Carignano, Turin, 1749, engraving.

118. Guarino Guarini, Palazzo Carignano, Turin, begun 1679, engraving, from *Disegni d'architettura civile e ecclesiastica* (1686).

119a. Gianlorenzo Bernini, Louvre, design for the east facade: first project, 1665, ink and wash.

119b. Gianlorenzo Bernini, Louvre, design for the east façade: second project, 1665, ink and wash.

120. Guarino Guarini, Palazzo Carignano, facade detail, Turin, 1679.

121. Guarino Guarini, Collegio dei Nobili, southeast corner, Turin, 1679.

122. Guarino Guarini,
Collegio dei Nobili,
detail of facade, Turin,
1679.

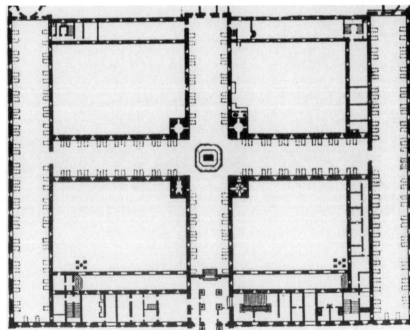

123. Amedeo di
Castellamonte, Ospedale
Maggiore di San Gio-
vanni, ground floor
plan, Turin, 1680.

124. Amedeo di Castellamonte, Ospedale Maggiore di San Giovanni, north facade, Turin, 1680.

125. Piazza Carlina, detail from figure 98, square designed by Amedeo di Castellamonte in 1674, illustration drawn by Tommaso Borgonio, 1682.

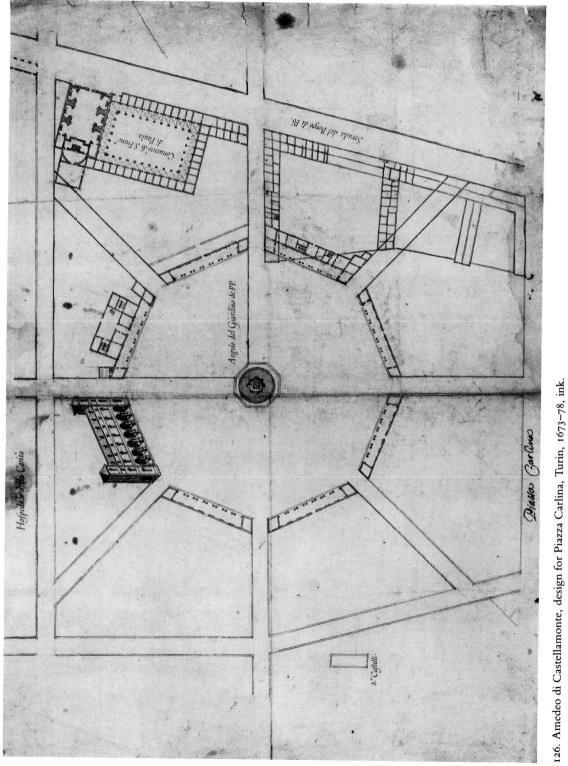

Hospedale della Caria

Angolo del Giardino de PP.

Comento di S. Franc.
di Paula

Strada del Borgo di Pò.

sᵗ Castelli.

Pianto Carlino

126. Amedeo di Castellamonte, design for Piazza Carlina, Turin, 1673–78, ink.

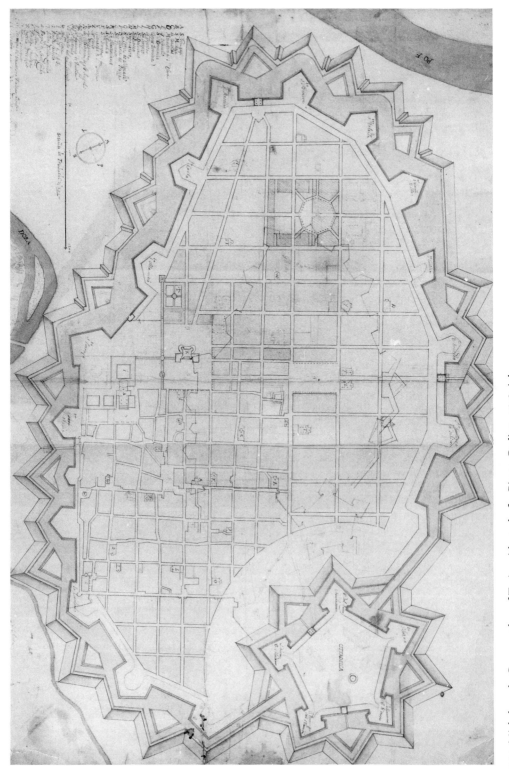

127. Michelangelo Garove, plan of Turin with study for Piazza Carlina, 1678, ink.

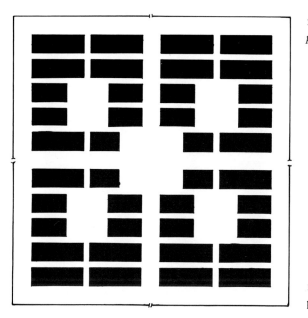

128. Pietro Cataneo, plan of ideal city, from *I quattro primi libri di architettura* (Venice, 1554).

129. Bellino, layout of Piazza Carlina with four market pavilions, 1693, ink.

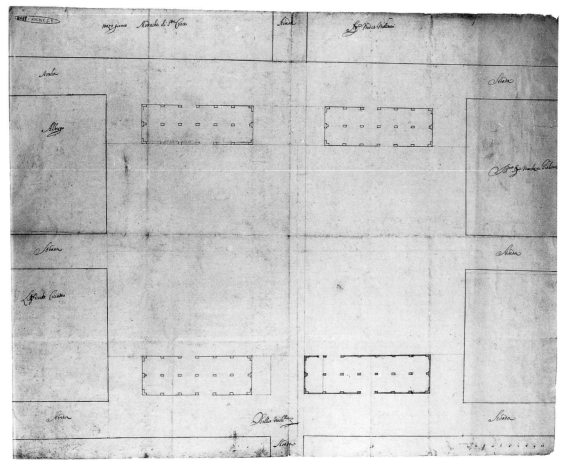

M V S Æ I,
cum Regiæ Familiæ fculptis, Geftorumque
pictis Imaginibus, Bibliotheca,
Et Statuarum veterum Ornamentis, Vulgo
LA GALLERIA.
Profpectus interior, Et exterior.

130. Piazza Castello, Turin, section through the Galleria, 1682, engraving.

131. Giovanni Battista Borra, Piazza Castello, Turin, 1749, engraving.

REGIE SEGRETERIE E TEATRO NELLA PIAZZA DIETRO IL CASTELLO

Ægyptiorum Rex Eridanus
Eridani Fluuiorum Regis in Ripâ
Urbem Ægyptio Tauro Cognominem
Inaugurat
Septē. Seculis Ante Romam conditam

D. Piola In.   G. Tasniere Sc.Taur.

132. Domenico Piola, King Eridanus holding a map of Turin, engraving by Giorgio Tasniere, from Emanuele Tesauro, *Historia della augusta città di Torino* (Turin, 1679).

133. Palazzo Reale and the Bastion Verde seen from northeast, Turin, 1682.

134. Bernardo Bellotto, view of Turin's northeast fortifications, c. 1750, oil painting.

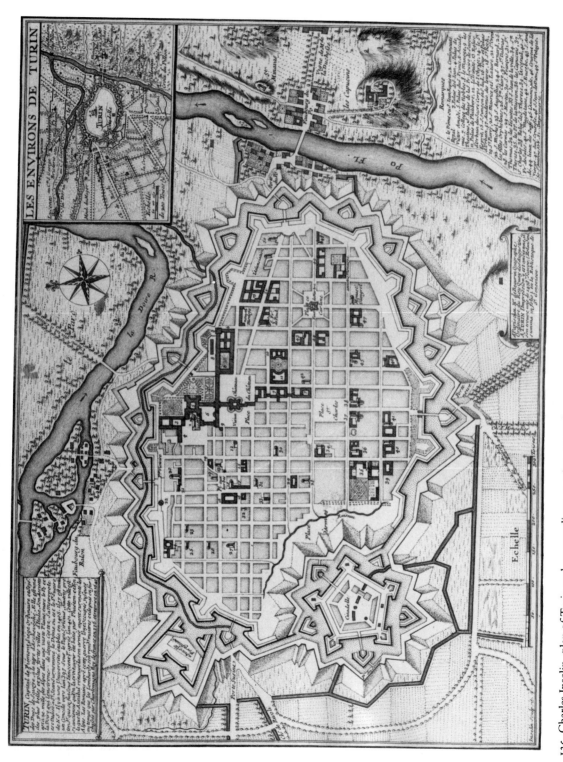

Dessein de l'illumination de La rüe de Po conduisant au Chateau de Madame pour l'entreé de S. A. R. Madame la Princesse de Piedmont.

Designé par le A. Dom, filppo Juvarra Ie Architecte de S. M.

gravé par A. Aveline a Paris.

136. Filippo Juvarra, view of Contrada di Po, Turin, engraving by Antoine Aveline, from *Disegni di fuochi* (1722).

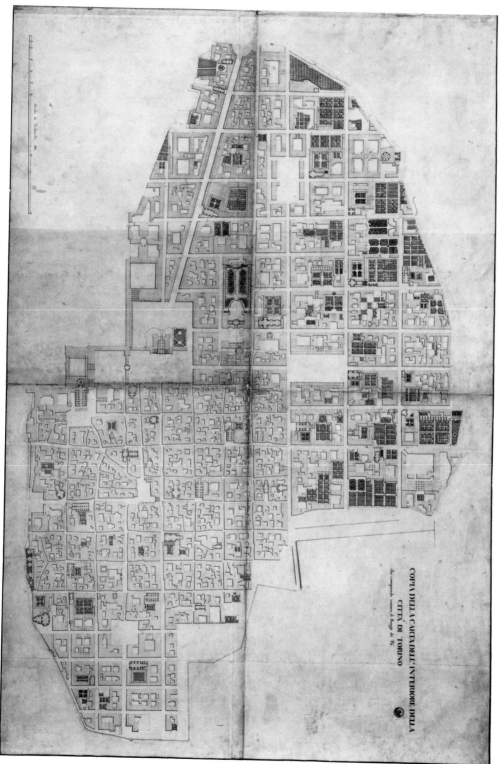

137. Plan of Turin with porticoed Contrada di Po, c. 1800, ink and watercolor.

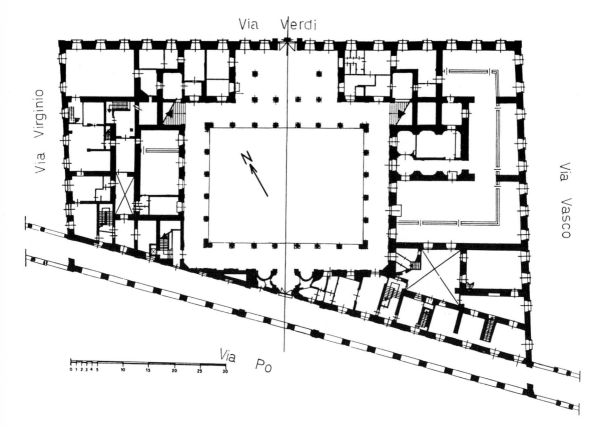

138. Michelangelo Garove, university, Turin, 1720.

139. Michelangelo Garove, university, facade on Contrada della Zecca, Turin, 1720.

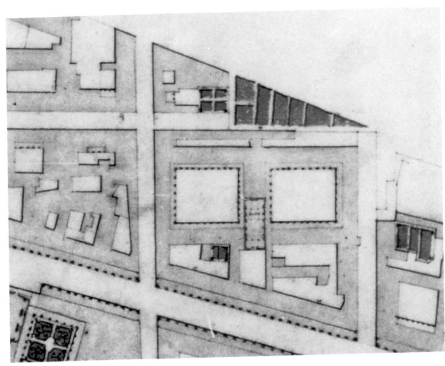

140. Plan of Ospedale della Carità, Turin, detail of figure 137.

141. Amedeo di Castellamonte, Contrada di Po, Turin, 1675.

142. Amedeo di Castellamonte, section through Contrada di Po, 1675, Turin.

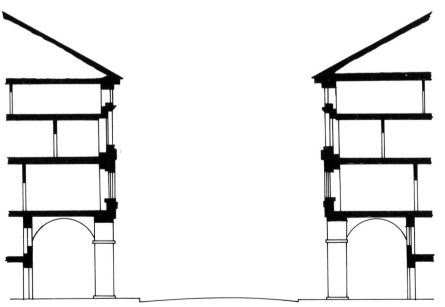

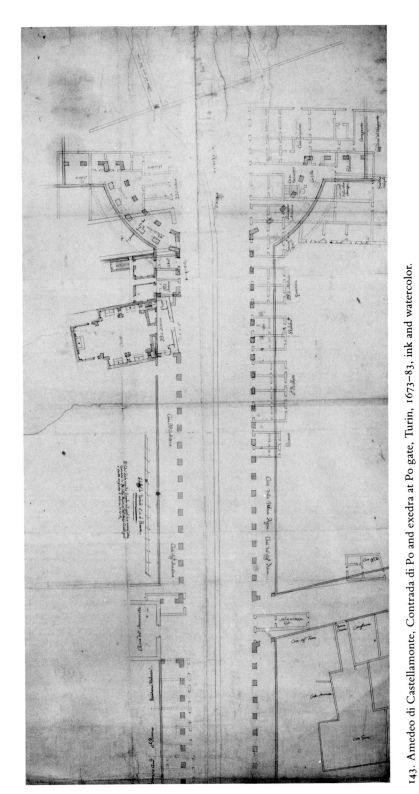

143. Amedeo di Castellamonte, Contrada di Po and exedra at Po gate, Turin, 1673–83, ink and watercolor.

144. Carlo Giuseppe Cortella and Giovanni Antonio Recchi, Piazza Castello with funeral procession of Carlo Emanuele II, Turin, 1675, engraving by Giorgio Tasniere, from Giulio Vasco, *Del funerale di Carlo Emanuele* (Turin, 1676).

145. Carlo Giuseppe Cortella and Giovanni Antonio Recchi, Turin's cathedral decorated for the funeral of Carlo Emanuele II, 1675, engraving by Giorgio Tasniere, from Vasco, *Del funerale di Carlo Emanuele* (1676).

DATE DUE